The Art of Czech Animation

The Art of Czech Animation

A History of Political Dissent and Allegory

Adam Whybray

BLOOMSBURY ACADEMIC
LONDON • NEW YORK • OXFORD • NEW DELHI • SYDNEY

BLOOMSBURY ACADEMIC
Bloomsbury Publishing Plc
50 Bedford Square, London, WC1B 3DP, UK
1385 Broadway, New York, NY 10018, USA
29 Earlsfort Terrace, Dublin 2, Ireland

BLOOMSBURY, BLOOMSBURY ACADEMIC and the Diana logo
are trademarks of Bloomsbury Publishing Plc

First published in Great Britain 2020
This paperback edition published in 2022

Copyright © Adam Whybray, 2020

Adam Whybray has asserted his right under the Copyright, Designs
and Patents Act, 1988, to be identified as Author of this work.

For legal purposes the Acknowledgements on p. xi-xii constitute
an extension of this copyright page.

Cover design: Charlotte Daniels
Cover image © Štepán Bartoš

All rights reserved. No part of this publication may be reproduced or transmitted
in any form or by any means, electronic or mechanical, including photocopying,
recording, or any information storage or retrieval system, without prior
permission in writing from the publishers.

Bloomsbury Publishing Plc does not have any control over, or responsibility for,
any third-party websites referred to or in this book. All internet addresses given
in this book were correct at the time of going to press. The author and publisher
regret any inconvenience caused if addresses have changed or sites have
ceased to exist, but can accept no responsibility for any such changes.

A catalogue record for this book is available from the British Library.

Library of Congress Control Number: 2020937419

ISBN: HB: 978-1-3501-0459-4
PB: 978-1-3501-9498-4
ePDF: 978-1-3501-0465-5
eBook: 978-1-3501-0464-8

Typeset by Integra Software Services Pvt. Ltd.

To find out more about our authors and books visit www.bloomsbury.com
and sign up for our newsletters

*This book is dedicated to my family, partner,
friends and all the other non-human actants that
have made and continue to make
this work possible.*

Thank you sincerely.

Contents

List of Figures	x
Acknowledgements	xi
Prologue	1
The self-immolation of Jan Palach	1
Introduction	3
Political encoding of objects and things	3
Objective definition	4
A distinction between objects and things	4
Methodologies	6
Thing theory	6
Actor-network-theory	8
Rhythmanalysis	10
Materialist methodologies	11
A brief history of Czech animation	14
Pre-Second World War Czech animation	14
Post-Second World War Czech animation	15
Seko, Pojar and Mergl	18
Slovak animation	19
Czech animators focused upon	19
Jiří Trnka	19
Jan Švankmajer	21
Jiří Barta	23
Other animators	24
Recovering forgotten material	24
1 'It's the simple things': Animated allegories against Nazi and Soviet oppression	27
Overcoming the poverty of object analysis	27
Introduction to allegory	31

	Ambiguity and plurality in allegories	34
	Allegory communicated through real objects	37
	Objects of resistance in *Revolution in Toyland*	38
	The springiness of the *Springman*'s springs	45
	Importance of objects to tradition in *The Czech Year*	48
	The Emperor's Nightingale as a critique of artifice	51
	Material history in *Old Czech Legends*	54
	Oppressive gestures of 'a hand of state'	61
	Reading *The Hand*	64
	Allegory's limits	68
	Visual simile in *Passion*	70
	Technological abstraction in *The Cybernetic Grandma*	73
	Simple objects and anti-political politics in Týrlová and Trnka	78
	Politically non-political objects	82
2	Jan Švankmajer and the network of things	85
	Introduction to Švankmajer	85
	Švankmajer and censorship	86
	Švankmajer's relationship with Surrealism	88
	How psychoanalysis is at once a useful tool for reading the objects of Švankmajer while also completely missing the point of the thing	91
	An alternative in ANT	94
	The Death of Stalinism in Bohemia: The most explicitly political of Švankmajer's films	96
	Death to anthropocentrism	100
	A *Picnic with Weissmann* and non-human actants	102
	A civilization of stones	104
	The political pessimism of *Dimensions of Dialogue*	107
	Let the networks be as they are – Švankmajer vs. categorization	110
	The Flat's network of dissident things	113
	Not objects but *things* ~ in defence of indeterminacy	116
	Concluding remarks: Latour ← → Švankmajer	124
3	Jiří Barta and the rhythmic difficulties of living in, or with, time and space	127
	Introduction	127
	Rational time, charismatic time and natural time	129

	Jiří Barta: An ambivalent animator	133
	The loss of *Green Wood* and the defeat of natural time	137
	Designing uniformity in *The Design*	148
	Repeating uniformity in *Disc Jockey*	152
	Twisted spirals and swollen shards: The sickened rhythms of Hameln	153
	Repeating the past in *The Club of the Laid-Off*	166
	A hopeful repetition for the future?	174
4	Animators reconstructing Prague and Czech identity after the Velvet Revolution	177
	Portrait of a city	177
	Methodological multiplicity	180
	Historicization of the objects of Prague	181
	Undermining the 'magic city' of tourism in *Faust*	182
	Networks of desire in *Conspirators of Pleasure*	186
	Consumption as a desire older than consumerism	189
	The Golem is Prague and Prague is the Golem	193
	Just orbiting bodies in abstract space	198
	Life among the dead in *One Night in One City*	200
	Desiring rhythms in *Tram*	204
	Surviving Life as an *Insect*	206
	The citizen's inner life is collective, public and dependent upon myths and stories	211
	Twenty-first-century Czech animation	212
	Political messages from past to present	218
	Communication of political messages	222
	A materialist turn	223
	A silent language	224
	Epilogue	227
	A materialist, not idealist ecocriticism	227

Notes	232
Bibliography	252
Filmography	273
Index	281

List of Figures

1.1	Objects try to revive a drowned boy in *The Day of Reckoning* (*Den odplany*)	40
1.2	A forest of crooks and branches in *Old Czech Legends* (*Staré pověsti české*)	59
1.3	Gestures of courtesy, menace, desire and threat in *The Hand* (*Ruka*)	66
1.4	A red ball helps the viewer and child to navigate space in *The Cybernetic Grandma* (*Kybernetická Babicka*)	76
1.5	An old couple treat a ball as their child in *A Little Speckle-Ball* (*Míček Flíček*)	79
2.1	Two Arcimboldoesque networks in *Dimensions of Dialogue* (*Možnosti dialogu*)	108
2.2	Indeterminate things in *A Quiet Week in the House* (*Tichý týden v dome*)	120
3.1	Koliada in *A Ballad about Green Wood* (*Balada o zeleném dřevu*)	139
3.2	The rhythm(s) of nature in *A Ballad about Green Wood*	143
3.3	The architect's tools define reality in *The Design* (*Projekt*)	149
3.4	A world of signs in *Disc Jockey* (*Diskzokej*)	153
3.5	Palatable corruption in *The Last Theft* (*Poslední lup*)	162
3.6	Architectural-ideological disease in *Rat Catcher* (*Krysař*)	164
4.1	Prague as a flattened city in *Surviving Life: Theory and Practice* (*Přežít svůj život*)	208
4.2	A disturbing erotic vision in *Dedicated to Darkness* (*Věnováno tmě*)	216
4.3	Insectoid-floral actants in *The Entangled* (*Zápletka*)	217

Acknowledgements

I wish to extend my thanks and gratitude to a wide range of people for their assistance, encouragement and advice over the last ten years, both professionally and personally, in relation to this project and otherwise.

I am very thankful to Ayla Bloom, Michela Parkin, Rachel Shohet, Ewa Mazierska, Rachele Dini, Ali Kay, Ellena Dee, Helena Bacon, Alison Frank and especially Hollie Price for their careful, sometimes critical and often insightful proofreading.

Miska Morning provided some invaluable assistance in Czech translation, as well as being a supportive friend while at Exeter. Rachael Borrill is to be thanked for accompanying me on my trip to Prague and her reflections on touring the Jewish cemetery. Peter Hames was both informative and friendly in email communication regarding a challenging part of my historical research. My brother, Leon Whybray, and my sister, Phoebe Whybray, have always lifted my spirits during any struggles of the last ten years. My parents, Andrea and Michael Whybray, have provided the material and emotional foundations without which none of this work would be possible. My partner, Antonia Howard, has intellectually and spiritually enriched and supported me during the final months of this project to a degree worthy of laudation.

Especial thanks are due to Joe Kember of the University of Exeter, who stepped in at the last moment as my primary supervisor for my PhD research, providing a greatly supportive presence, offering incisive feedback and often willing to expand his own film knowledge in his role. James Lyons, my secondary supervisor, also provided a valuable perspective on my work, contributing some key suggestions towards its development. Felicity Gee and Paul Wells offered challenging and necessary feedback in my VIVA, as did Helen Hanson in her role as my tutor. Before them, during my MA at the University of York, Geoff Hall, Judith Buchanan and Erica Sheen all gave invaluable supervision and assistance.

Suzanne Buchan, Dan North and Bill Brown should each be credited for much of the inspirational impetus for this book. Any stylistic or methodological innovations herein build upon their work in ways that I hope all three will find provocative and useful.

Finally, I gratefully acknowledge the economic support of the Arts and Humanities Research Council which has proved something of a lifeline.

Thank you all.

Prologue

The self-immolation of Jan Palach

16 January 1969, Jan Palach, in protest against the Warsaw Pact invasion and hoping to reverse the stifling despondency taking hold of his country's citizens, set himself alight in Red Army Square (Náměstí Krasnoarmějců). Self-immolation is a form of protest that dramatically bridges the personal and the political as witnesses are confronted by an abstract political statement communicated through real embodied suffering. The violent tangibility of the means of communication chosen by the self-immolating protester forces attention to the everyday material relations obscured beneath political rhetoric and ideology. It is as though the burning body screams to the oppressors, government or demagogue at whom the protest is aimed, 'This – *This* is the impact of your violence.' For Palach and the other men[1] who chose to follow in his wake, the Warsaw Pact invasion was not a matter of abstract political policy but a matter of *matter* – of tanks, soldiers and corpses.

Palach's corpse was buried in Olšany Cemetery. Hundreds of Czechs and Slovaks came to the site to lay flowers and candles.[2] The Communist Party of Czechoslovakia (Komunistická strana Československa) (KSČ), wary a figure of anti-state protest was being martyred, sought means to prevent further political pilgrimage. In July 1973 the grave's headstone was removed and, in October, Palach's parents were coerced by State Security (Státní bezpečnost) (StB) to have their son's remains exhumed and cremated. A new headstone was erected by the grave bearing the name Marie Jedlićkova.[3]

In an essay collected in a retrospective of Václav Havel's work, Timothy Garton Ash notes the StB's manoeuvre did not halt the visits from those who wished to mourn or pay tribute to the young man's sacrifice.[4] The erasing, by a state-sanctioned body, of a signifier that marked the single, official commemorative site for Palach failed to overwrite the meaning that had already accumulated there for those who had encoded the location as a site of tribute to dissent.

Palach's self-immolation and his gravesite's continued potency in spite of the absence of both body and gravestone illustrate the complex dynamics at work when objects, beings and places are invested with political meaning. Was Palach's political message contained within his act of self-immolation? Was it then transferred to his gravesite in the absence of his corpse? Can the political and emotional ideas and feelings encoded in matter continue in spite of this matter's eradication or displacement? How are political ideas materially embodied and what happens when the objects of this embodiment are transformed?

Introduction

Political encoding of objects and things

This book is concerned with acts of political encoding similar to those performed upon Jan Palach and his grave. It examines a host of politically resistant objects and dissident things taken from Czech animations (and live-action films with animation) released between 1946 and 2018.

While looking at Czech animation in all its forms, this book gives particular focus to stop-motion. This is due to a significant ontological distinction between objects in stop-motion films and objects represented by other forms of animation, such as computer-generated imagery (CGI). As with live-action cinema, objects that appear in stop-motion have a continued existence in reality outside their specific film world(s). If we consider the footage of Jan Palach's gravestone, it is subject to projection, mediation and the viewer's gaze, but the gravestone nonetheless remains a real object, situated before the camera, with an independent life transcending the limits of the cinematic frame.

To provide a less politically charged example, imagine a stop-motion director decides to animate a traditional Czech bread roll (*rohlík*). The roll has specific culinary, domestic and cultural connotations for Czech and Slovak viewers, is baked in a specific bakery, bought for a specific price and might be eaten (or thrown away) after filming. Comparatively, the drawing or CGI rendering of a roll is not possessed of the same historical nor material weight. The cultural connotations might remain, but these are liable to change depending on the appearance the object is given – the roll as drawn by Jiří Trnka would have different connotations to the same roll drawn by Hayao Miyazaki. While Jan Švankmajer might animate a roll slightly differently to Hermína Týrlová, at a material level the object remains the same.

Objective definition

This book's definition of 'object' is commonsensical. An object is any individually definable thing with a tangible existence in material reality. Man-made artefacts like knives, mugs or puppets are objects, as are those individual things like stones or tomatoes, which occur in nature.

Puppets are ontologically interesting things since they confuse a strict object/subject dichotomy. They are objects in the material sense but when on stage (or screen) perform as subjects. While watching puppets perform, we – the human audience – are aware of their object status while simultaneously able to invest in their performance of selfhood. A puppet can be the protagonist of a theatrical show even while it remains obvious its agency is not self-determined.

Many film-makers considered in this book also treat objects not intended for use as puppets as their films' principal subjects. In the work of Surrealist animator Jan Švankmajer, the natural and man-made objects on screen often seem to hold a greater degree of subjectivity than the human actors who appear alongside them. Dan Torre reflects that in stop-motion animation the audience occupies the paradoxical position of suspending disbelief that the animated objects are alive, while simultaneously recognizing them as inanimate material forms.[1] In addition to puppets as traditionally understood, *The Art of Czech Animation* stages encounters with rolling pins, toy balls, a clockwork hen, an architect's drawing tools and a wooden stump that resembles a baby, alongside a rich assembly of performing things.

A distinction between objects and things

Up to this point of writing, the word 'thing' has been used interchangeably with 'object', albeit with a sense that 'thing' is a broader and more ambiguous term. Literary theorist Bill Brown has considered the difference between objects and things, asserting that the same item can be understood as both or either an object or a thing, as follows:

The mug before me at the moment of writing is an object. It is white and made of china. The 'apperceptive constitution' of the mug 'is what we might call its objecthood'.[2] Now imagine the mug not as an object but as a *thing*. Forget, if you will, the role we have assigned it as a carrier of liquids. Forget, if you are able, its name of 'mug'. Think instead of the dull ringing sound it makes when struck unexpectedly; of its cool, smooth texture in the hand. The 'experience of the thing' is 'what we might call its thinghood'.[3] A thing is behaving as an object when it is conceptually categorized according to human schemata, dependent upon its human-given function. We can name the mug, know it is designed to carry liquids and lift it up to our mouth to drink, sure of its stable function. Brown writes elsewhere that 'we begin to confront the thingness of objects when they stop working for us … The story of objects asserting themselves as things, then, is the story of a changed relation to the human subject'.[4] We drop the mug and it smashes into pieces. Suddenly, it looks less like a mug and more like a half-shattered hollow of china that we do not know whether to repair or to consign to the trash. We are less able to categorize the thing than the object since the thing seems to exist independently upon its own terms. Brown's roots in Martin Heidegger's philosophy are apparent in such a distinction. In Heidegger's terminology the broken mug should be considered 'unhandy'[5] since its 'being-in-itself'[6] now obscures its use value within a system of human and non-human relations, previously so taken for granted as to be invisible. This is the difference between using a computer when it works as intended, interfacing via the mouse and keyboard without attending to the materiality of either object, and smashing the keyboard down upon the desk and hammering the mouse button when the cursor freezes upon the screen. To quote Heidegger: 'In its conspicuousness, obtrusiveness, and obstinacy, what is at hand loses its character of handiness.'[7]

Of course, this tricky distinction between objects and things is somewhat subjective and provisional, and my own usage differs from the distinctions made by other writers, directors and theorists who have also sought to study objects/things, as must be borne in mind when such figures are quoted.

This book's central argument is that certain Czech animations express their political ideas through objects/things (and, by extension, the temporal-spatial relations between these objects/things) rather than through dialogue, voice-over or even – in many cases – conventional narrative. *Which* objects/things are politically encoded, *what* messages they are encoded with and *how* they are encoded are questions investigated here across a selection of films produced from the end of the Second World War to the present by a number of Czech animators, including Jiří Trnka, Jan Švankmajer and Jiří Barta. This investigation works – it is hoped – towards a new method of film analysis that upholds the material underpinnings of cinematic space.

Methodologies

Across each chapter of this book a different methodological approach assists in exposing the latent political messages within each film (or, rather, within the films' objects/things, the interrelations between them and the times and spaces surrounding them). Chapter 1 uses several ideas from *thing theory*, as developed by its leading practitioner Bill Brown. Chapter 2, concerned with the short films of Jan Švankmajer, parallels the political ideas implicit in Švankmajer's work with ideas expressed by Bruno Latour that form the foundations for his *actor-network-theory*. In Chapter 3 analysis of films by Jiří Barta is illuminated by post-Marxist philosopher Henri Lefebvre's writings on *rhythmanalysis*, which are used to examine the rhythms of time and space as established through film editing. Chapter 4 employs a culmination of ideas from thing theory, ANT and rhythmanalysis to consider Prague as an ever-changing thing in itself, but also as a series of objects and actors, all interrelated in time and space.

Thing theory

Thing theory is a critical approach pioneered by the academic Bill Brown which concerns itself with the study of objects and things. Thus far thing theory has largely been confined to literary studies, but it also has some overlap with museum studies, archaeology and sociology. Thing theory asserts that there is an ontological distinction between objects and things.[8] In Brown's monograph *A Sense of Things* (2003) – one of thing theory's foundational texts – the objects in works by four American Victorian novelists (Mark Twain, Frank Norris, Sarah Orne Jewett and Henry James) are traced across a trajectory of encroaching modernism in which objects are increasingly fetishized – not just as commodities, à la Marx, but for their seductive and sometimes elusive *thingness*. While Brown focuses upon the American Victorian novel, Elaine Freedgood performs similar work for British Victorian texts in *The Ideas in Things: Fugitive Meaning in the Victorian Novel* (2006), attending to the material circumstances in which certain objects mentioned in books of the period were produced, as well as the trade economies in which they circulated.

Brown and Freedgood are concerned as much with anthropology as they are with literature and both ultimately provide a meta-commentary upon the concept that it is things that make us human, an argument taken up more straightforwardly by Daniel Miller in *The Comfort of Things* (2008). However, while Miller concerns himself with an account of the real everyday bric-a-brac within the homes of an anonymous East End London street, Brown and Freedgood might be not unfairly accused of an ontological blurring that confuses the textual thing which exists as a word-concept imaginatively given life by the reader, with those artefacts that physically exist within reality.

One of thing theory's central tenets is that current critical theory displaces objects into symbolic abstractions without first comprehending their materiality. In contrast to previous theoretical approaches, such as those informed by psychoanalysis and post-structuralism, which insist upon privileging the subject and the mediating power of the gaze, a thing theorist approach to film aims to put objects centre stage, not merely as conduits for the desires of the film viewer but as embodied presences defiant and resistant in their 'objecthood' in and of themselves. Indeed, at its core, thing theory simply bids us as readers and viewers to give a greater degree of attentiveness towards objects in literature or film, recognizing that the function of these objects isn't always to facilitate a plot or character development, or merely to 'stand in' for some higher symbolic meaning, but may hold an independent significance with meaning/s rooted in their specific materiality. The rhetoric of 'the life within things' commonly engaged in by thing theorists is given animistic, tactile immediacy through the cinematic medium of stop-motion animation.

In contrast to many of the fictional examples provided by literary thing theorists, the objects of stop-motion animation do not merely exist within the mind of an author or reader. It is the fact that the objects in the films of Jiří

Trnka examined in Chapter 1 have an independent 'real' existence outside of the films in which they appear, which ensures the applicability of thing theory to this chapter. Claims about the texture or weight of objects on screen are less hypothetical than similar claims made about objects that have never existed in 'real life'. Trnka's stop-motion works almost never involve human actors. The objects and puppets of his films are the subjects. Thing theory ensures that the focus remains upon these subjects.

Actor-network-theory

Rather than being a school or a critical framework, actor-network-theory (ANT) is more simply an approach to any given object of study that refutes the existence of external paradigms to explain a priori the material being studied. Underlying ANT and the writings of its foremost theorist Bruno Latour is the belief that there exists no given 'field' in which events unfold, such as 'nature', 'society' or a 'laboratory'. All of these are understood to be social constructs and thus never ideologically neutral. Rather, events display the workings of hugely complex networks composed of actors (called 'actants' in Latour's parlance). Conscious intent does not determine the importance or influence of any one actant. Even an actant as seemingly insignificant as a petal or a grain of rice can radically alter a network or shape an event. Jan Švankmajer's short films, in which objects and things are given the narrative weight generally afforded to human actors, provide a cinematic embodiment of this idea.

Latour's most committed introduction to ANT is *Reassembling the Social: An Introduction to Actor-Network-Theory* (2007), although sections of both *Politics of Nature: How to Bring the Sciences into Democracy* (2004) and *Pandora's Hope: An Essay on the Reality of Science Studies* (1999) work through ideas that later find more concrete expression in ANT. Graham Harman's *Prince of Networks: Bruno Latour and Metaphysics* (2009) provides a lucid and comprehensive introduction to both Latour and ANT, situating the philosopher's work within a scholarly context, giving particular weight to the influence of Heidegger upon his unique metaphysics.

To write as a thing theorist, one must simply turn one's attentions to objects/things, gathering and interrogating the material, cultural and historical information that one can, while also paying mind to the ontological and epistemological status that objects/things have been afforded in film and everyday life. This is a rigorous task but nonetheless within reach of any patient writer-thinker with recourse to a library, database and/or archive. By contrast, to write *as* an actor-network-theorist (in comparison to merely writing *about* actor-network-theory) one must accomplish a great deal of ground work observing material processes *as and when they happen*. This is why – for instance – Anita Lam gained entry to a writer's workshop for her 2013 monograph *Making Crime Television*.

Lam's text was written in response to what she refers to as the 'black-boxing'[9] of television crime drama. Lam argues that academic writers who analyse fictional portrayals of crime tend to focus upon the content of the media as though the shows discussed were always already finished. In contrast to this tendency, her work gives space to the processes by which crime dramas are produced, considering the programmes she selects as case studies in medias res as unstable, mutable and composed from myriad networked actants (computer processors, multiple script re-writes, researchers, newspaper columns, etc.) that are fundamentally irreducible. To develop this argument Lam gained access to the writers' room of Canadian television drama *The Bridge* (CBS, 2010). Inevitably, however, this approach cannot be replicated for those writing upon series or films completed prior to the point of writing.

As such, Chapter 2 necessarily differs from Chapter 1, which performs a thing theorist reading of a selection of Trnka's works, and Chapter 3, which performs rhythmanalysis upon works by Jiří Barta. In Chapter 2, Švankmajer's films are considered in terms of actors and networks, with a view to illuminating the belief system expressed by these films through considering some of the metaphysical assumptions of ANT. This chapter therefore considers Švankmajer *as* an actor-network-theorist, rather than *being* an example of actor-network-theory in itself. This might be argued to be less critically rigorous than the applied methodologies of Chapters 1 and 3, but has the significant advantage of allowing broader claims to be made *about* Švankmajer as a film-maker, rather than 'simply' providing exegeses *of* individual films.[10]

Rhythmanalysis

Rhythmanalysis is a mode of poetic-scientific investigation developed by the post-Marxist sociologist and philosopher Henri Lefebvre. For Lefebvre, it is not enough for an ideological analysis to merely consider the political meaning of things and objects in space and time, but space and time *themselves* must also be interrogated. One of Lefebvre's central arguments in *The Production of Space* (*La Production de l'espace*, 1974) is that our built environments are not simply blank, neutral spaces filled with political actors, but are politically and ideologically constructed. Certain spaces allow and, indeed, encourage certain types of political action. For Lefebvre, it would be no coincidence that Prague's Wenceslas Square (Václavské náměstí) (formerly Red Army Square) has been the historical site of so much revolutionary action – the self-immolation of Jan Palach and, later, several demonstrations of the Velvet Revolution. Rather, this will have been determined, in part, by the material construction of the square itself. Furthermore, time can be ideologically encoded, as in the example of the clock face, which spatializes time and, in doing so, estranges it from the rhythms of nature.

In Lefebvre's posthumous publication *Rhythmanalysis: Space, Time and Everyday Life* (*Éléments de rythmanalyse*, 1992), rhythmanalysis is proposed as a method for analysing the ideology encoded in the spaces and times of everyday life – a method that involves interrogating the rhythms of a given city or place. The practitioner of this work (or *rhythmanalyst*) must be able to internalize these rhythms on a bodily level, while simultaneously distancing himself/herself from the external action of these rhythms, observing them from afar like a detached sociologist. As such, the rhythmanalyst combines the rigorous objectivity of the scientist with the ecstatic subjectivity of the poet.

Immediately it should be apparent that rhythmanalysis can be applied to the study of film, since film is a temporal-spatial medium, structured according to the rhythms of editing. Film, like music, is composed of a symphony of rhythms. However, despite the clear affinities between the methodology and the medium, there is a limited amount of film studies academia that employs Lefebvre's ideas. Aga Skrodzka uses some quotations from *The*

Production of Space in *Magic Realist Cinema in East Central Europe* (2012) to illuminate the distinction between the city and nature in Piotr Trzaskalski's *Edi* (2002).[11] Mattias Frey (2006) compares Lefebvre's 'synthetic' approach to 'material culture' to that of German film-maker Oskar Roehler in a paper for *Cinema Journal*.[12] Indeed, the only paper as of 2019 that is wholly committed to applying rhythmanalysis to film is Eitan Freedenberg's currently unpublished paper 'One-Minute Boogie Woogie: Rhythmanalysis and Landscape Cinema' (2013), which unpicks the rhythms of the films of James Benning to illuminate the workings of capital within the American (often Californian) landscapes he depicts.[13]

Rhythmanalysis is ideally suited for analysing the political meaning of space and time in the filmography of the animator Jiří Barta, since his films constantly interrogate the notion that space and time are non-political. Lefebvre's identification of different forms of rhythms (linear, cyclical, arrhythmic, polyrhythmic, etc.) provides a vocabulary with which to write about rhythms in a given film scene that compliments the cinematic terminology already at one's disposal. It is essential that the rhythmanalyst of cinema remembers that the rhythms of everyday life captured on screen are transformed and augmented by the cinematic rhythms of editing. Rhythms – like objects – on screen never reach the viewer wholly unmediated.

Materialist methodologies

These three methodologies (thing theory, ANT and rhythmanalysis) share a common focus upon material reality, making them well adapted to examining how animations can, with little to no dialogue or narration, communicate political ideas. If human identity and politics are rooted in the external world of objects and things, then any academic discussion of ideology must also build its arguments from the ground-up, instead of imposing pre-existent frameworks onto the material, top-down. Thing theory, ANT and rhythmanalysis are united by the emphasis they place upon the non-human. All three methodologies are materialist, but have different conceptions of what constitutes the material world and how best to approach it.

Thing theory is materialist because it insists that the material history of objects/things is essential to understanding how they operate in a text. Thing theory refuses to treat objects/things symbolically before first interrogating their materiality. This interest in illuminating the hidden histories of power adhering within consumer goods and commodities stems from a Marxist-materialistic engagement with socio-political realities. Thing theory allows things to be read semiotically, but it also insists that things are not mere signifiers. Things may function ideologically, but their material existence is not negated by ideology.

ANT, meanwhile, is materialist due to its foundational principle that the everyday relations of things must never be ignored or distorted in order to better fit a pre-existing ideological imperative. Latour's admonition that the researcher must avoid framing concepts such as 'nature' or 'culture' to bolster his/her argumentation is materialist since it insists the actor-network-theorist must work with stuff *as is*. A theorist who subscribes to ANT's critical assumptions must resist any tendency to elevate certain 'actants'[14] above others. Like thing theory, ANT is concerned with narratives of history and labour, especially when they give rise to universal truth claims, of which ANT is sceptical. Furthermore, ANT is concerned with those non-human actors/objects that go unnoticed by other critical theories. It is fundamentally a materialist position to claim a stone is always an object worthy of analysis.

The writings of Henri Lefebvre are indebted to Marxist scientific-materialism. However, Lefebvre's work represents a departure from a dialectical methodology in favour of a mode of analysis that emphasizes the tripartite structure of melody, harmony and rhythm. As such, instead of focusing upon ideological oppositions that clash violently until a point of eventual synthesis, Lefebvre's writings tend to assume a greater sense of balance/harmony between competing impulses which – while often distorted or transfigured by political systems – are grounded in the natural or material world. For Lefebvre, discussing ideology entails discussing daily-lived life as it is experienced at ground level in the midst of things. Lefebvre's output is, therefore, more consistently materialist than many Marxist thinkers', since he is reluctant to use ideological abstractions to illustrate a point if concrete examples can be found. He tends to work from the micro upwards, rather than from the macro downwards – a tendency shared by thing theorists who analyse a single object or actor-network-theorists who interrogate a single actant.

Applying these methodologies to film studies, one must work upwards from the films themselves, attending closely to scenes and avoiding using films as case studies to fit any a priori framework or ideological assumptions. Thing theory bids the film academic to work from objects/things on screen and resist the temptation to draw symbolic readings before their materiality is considered. Both ANT and rhythmanalysis require the academic to respond moment-by-moment to ever-shifting networks of interconnected rhythms and actants, both on screen and off. If such analysis remains partial and fragmentary, this is because it seeks to describe systems neither closed nor completed. Politically this accords with an anarchist sensibility which resists authoritarian truth claims. A fragment of rhetoric from turn-of-the-century French anarchist Zo d'Axa chimes with resonance at this juncture, though d'Axa was referring to political theories, rather than academic ones:

> There is no Absolute. If the facts lead us today to specify such and such a way to see and be, every day, in the lively articles of our expressive collaborators, our determination has been clearly affirmed … Up till now nothing has revealed to us the radiant beyond. Nothing has given us a constant criterion. Life's panorama changes without ceasing, and the facts appear to us under a different light depending on the hour. We will never react against the attractions of contradictory points of view.[15]

This ground level, context-dependent, improvisatory approach to problem-solving is common to each of my chosen methodologies and allows for a partial synthesis of methods, in which the conclusions of any one theory might overlap with another or even offer a provocative contradiction.

Although this book's configuration of a tripartite methodology of thing theory, ANT and rhythmanalysis is unique, the attempt to forge a mode of film analysis that respects the materiality of the material depicted on screen, while simultaneously recognizing that an audience's ideological projections alter their reading of this material, is not unique and has its roots in both the materialist film theory of Siegfried Kracauer and the affective/phenomenological writings of academics including Laura Marks and Vivian Sobchack.

A brief history of Czech animation

Pre-Second World War Czech animation

The history of Czech animation has roots in both the formal experimentation of the interwar European avant-garde and the commercial imperatives of advertising films. While it might be assumed the two roots were ideologically divergent, they connected at the level of production in the form of Karel Dodal's and Irena Dodalová's IRE-Film studio in Prague.[16] Examining these films it quickly becomes apparent that the relationship between avant-gardism and advertising was co-dependent and reciprocal. The colourful abstraction characteristic of German *absolute film* can be seen in the Dodals's advertisement for *Telefunken* radio receivers in *The Wizard of Tones* (*Čaroděj tónů*, 1936), while non-commercial abstract films like *Erotic Fantasy* (*Fantasie érotique*, 1937) and *Ideas in Search of Light* (*Myslenka hledající svetlo*, 1938) possess the hypnotic rhythms that led advertising psychologists like Käthe Kurtzig and Hanns Kropff to admire absolute films for their affective impact upon a viewer-consumer.[17]

Across the mid-1930s IRE-Film produced over two dozen advertisements for domestic products, from footwear (*Dobyvatel srdcí*, 1934; *Tajemství lucerny*, 1938; *Od rána do noci ve skvělých botách od Papeže*, 1938) and fountain pens (*Člověče, nezlob se!*, 1934) to mouthwash (*Gibbs zubní mýdlo*, 1935) and motor oil (*Protest*, 1938).[18] Jean Ann Wright incorrectly names *The Lantern's Secret* as the first Czech animated film, which might be due to her dating its release as 1935 rather than 1938 as more commonly attributed (see above).[19] However, she is correct to situate the origins of Czech animation further back than the twentieth century within the country's tradition of puppet theatre.[20] Indeed, a number of live-action (non-animated) puppet films predate the Dodals's first graphical animations by several years. In the early 1930s Czech puppeteer Josef Skupa directed two films starring his popular marionette characters Spejbl and Hurvínek, *Spejbl's Case* (*Spejblův případ*, 1930) and *Spejbl's Fascination with Film* (*Spejblovo filmové opojení*, 1931).[21] Skupa's assistant and apprentice was Jiří Trnka, whose largely stop-motion puppet films are the principal subject of this book's first chapter. In fact, Trnka designed and carved the puppet of Hurvínek for the third Spejbl and Hurvínek film, *The Adventures of a Ubiquitous Fellow* (*Všudybylovo dobrodružství*, 1936) which was directed and written not by Skupa but by the Dodals.[22]

Post-Second World War Czech animation

Ateliér Filmových triků was a film studio in Prague, founded in 1935, which produced models, special effects and animated titles for live-action films.[23] Seized by Nazi leader Joseph Pfister in 1941 it was used during the war as the animation department for Prag-Film. Shut down in the autumn of 1944, surviving staff were rehired by Trnka at the end of the war in 1945 when he co-founded his own company, the punningly named 'Trick Brothers' (Bratři v triku) studio.

Trnka, however, is but one of the two most significant Czech animators of this period. The second was Karel Dodal's first wife, Hermína Týrlová, whose career, spanning from 1928 to 1986, far out-stripped that of her ex-husband. Like the Dodals, Týrlová tended to structure her films around everyday domestic items, but while the Dodals's largely graphical animations sought to advertise these household goods, Týrlová's stop-motion films brought these objects to life. In opposition to Trnka's studio in Prague, Týrlová operated from Tomas Bata's film studio in Zlín, where she lived until the end of her life. Týrlová's still underappreciated work is also discussed in Chapter 1.

While Týrlová had worked upon *The Lantern's Secret* with her ex-husband, she produced her first puppet film independently from Dodal in 1944, the whimsical children's short animation *Ferda the Ant* (*Ferda mravenec*) in collaboration with Ladislav Zástěra. The following year, another significant figure of Czech animation associated with the Zlín studio, Karel Zeman, directed *A Christmas Dream* (*Vánoční sen*, 1945) in collaboration with his brother Bořivoj.[24] Karel Zeman's cinema is especially notable for its technical innovations. In films like *The Fabulous World of Jules Verne* (*Vynález zkázy*, 1958) and *The Fabulous Baron Munchausen* (*Baron Prášil*, 1961) Zeman and his collaborators used matte work and other animation compositing techniques to fully integrate live actors into environments that resembled Victorian etchings. These films, like those of American stop-motion animator Ray Harryhausen, are flights of history fantasy and rarely reflect directly upon contemporary themes. As with the animator Stanislav Látal, Zeman's output was generally aimed towards a family audience, which partly explains its lack of social commentary. Indeed, a wealth of animation (puppet, stop-motion and traditional hand-drawn animation) was produced for children across the twentieth century in Czechoslovakia. The Zlín International Film Festival for Children and Youth (Mezinárodní festival filmů pro děti a mládež) – which continues to this day – was established in 1961 and screened children's films by the likes of Zeman, Látal, Týrlová, Trnka and Jindřich Polák.

Doubtlessly the most famous Czech animated character is the ubiquitous Krtek, a curious, enthusiastic and often highly resourceful and cooperative little mole, created by animator Zdeněk Miler. Riikka Palonkorpi, writing on the Krtek films, describes Miler's work as championing perceived communist virtues of selflessness and hard work.[25] She notes that these values are communicated through the films' aesthetics rather than words, thus making them accessible to children.[26] This suggests that the avoidance of dialogue and narration in more explicitly political Czech animated films aimed towards adult audiences was not simply an avoidance of censorship but also a formal technique practised by children's animators at the Bratři v triku and Zlín studios, most of whom would have also worked upon films not specifically for children.

Palonkorpi recognizes television as one of the most important distribution channels for Miler's Krtek films, noting that 'regular television broadcasting began in 1953, not long after the establishment of socialism in Czechoslovakia'.[27] Through the 1960s to the late 1990s, numerous children's animations were produced for and broadcast upon the state channels Československá televize (ČST) Praha and ČST Bratislava. Along with Krtek the Mole, there were animations featuring Jiří Šalamoun's canine character Maxipes Fik, Adolf Born's schoolchildren with a magical telephone receiver, Mach and Šebestová, and Lubomír Beneš's clumsy handymen Pat and Mat. Many of these shows were screened during the children's evening programme *Večerníček* (aka 'Little Eveninger'), which might be considered the Czech equivalent to the British children's TV series *Jackanory* (BBC, 1965–96).

The relationship between the KSČ and the Czech animation industry was rather more multifaceted and ambivalent than might at first be presumed.

Lucie Joschko and Michael Morgan point out that the nationalization of Czech animation studios was voluntarily initiated[28] by animators including Jiri Brdecka, Stanislav Latal and Josef Kluge in 1945, some three years before the coup d'état, which solidified power gained by the KSČ and Klement Gottwald in the legal elections of 1946. Indeed, some animators like Miler were card-carrying members of the Party (until the 1970s at least, when he stopped paying his fees)[29] and, for all that others like Trnka were subjected to censorship, this must be weighed against the fact that Czech animation experienced significant growth under communism, with films gaining international recognition at film festivals as exemplars of Czech cultural achievement.[30] Even the regime's censorship was less unified and homogenous than might be assumed. Palonkorpi uses the example of a KSČ censor objecting to Krtek on the grounds that his garden was infested with moles as evidence that censorship could sometimes be more personal and subjective than strictly ideological.[31] Joschko and Morgan, meanwhile, highlight that censors were ideologically, not artistically, trained and, as such, would sometimes disagree with creative decisions due, seemingly, to a lack of imagination or artistic understanding, rather than actual ideological adherence.[32]

In terms of responding to this situation, three artistic approaches distinguish themselves. The first was to produce works unlikely to fall foul of the regime's censorship bodies, whether due to ideological adherence or through being resolutely non-political – such films generally falling within the realm of children's or educational films. The second was to produce political allegories so broad and universal in their messaging and approach that it would be hard for the regime to argue that the work was counter-revolutionary or otherwise ideologically suspect. The third was to produce work subtly critical of the regime, but using deft visual allegory rather than verbal communication in the hope that censorship would be avoided. Of course, most animators fell between these three poles across their careers, sometimes switching between approaches. However, ostensibly this book is concerned with those animators who regularly took the third path. Briefly now, two animators who tended towards one of the other two approaches will be touched upon, Garik Seko and Bretislav Pojar; then finally, a third – Václav Mergl – whose filmography encompasses in micro the range of Czech animation produced under communist rule.

Seko, Pojar and Mergl

Since stop-motion animation composes the core of this project, the films of Garik Seko may seem like a curious omission. However, Seko was a formalist – his films are concerned with the pleasures of animation itself and do not tend towards political allegory. His animations that depict myths belonging to Czech culture, such as a short piece about the 'Faust House' of Prague *(Faustuv dům*, 1977), are relatively 'straight' historical works, offering little commentary on Czech national identity. Later works like *Ex libris* (1983) or *Shoe Shoe* (*Shoe show aneb botky mají pré*, 1984) are playful films for an adult audience, including mild innuendo, but little to no political content.

The remarkably prolific Bretislav Pojar produced much beautiful work, worthy of its own study. Unlike Seko, his works were often political, but universal in intent. His films cover topics including the destructiveness of war (*Bomb Mania/Bombománie*, 1960; *Balablok*, 1972; *B.O.O.O.M./Bum*, 1979; *If/Kdyby*, 1983), the means by which human perception is constructed (*Psychocratie/To See or Not to See*, 1969; *E*, 1981) and the relationship between humans and animals (*The Lion and the Song/Lev a písnička*, 1959; *Darwin Anti-Darwin/Darwin Antidarwin aneb co zízala netusila*, 1969). Like Trnka, Pojar directed several works for children (often featuring two brown bears) and later produced educational films with the financial support of the National Film Board of Canada.

Václav Mergl's graduating film was an abstract animation called *Transformations* (1964) that recalled the absolute cinema of the Dodals, which characterized the earliest days of Czech animation in the 1930s. Following *The Study of Touch* in 1966, he produced the dystopian graphical animation *Laokoon* (1970), which has stylistic affinities with the collagist works of Jan Švankmajer. *Kraby* (*The Crabs*, 1976) is an anti-war allegory of the kind Pojar tended to produce, only safe from censorship due to its universal meaning. Later, *Homunculus* (*Homunkulus*, 1984) recalls the eclectic formal experimentation of both Garik Seko and Jiří Barta, the latter of whom Mergl would collaborate with upon *The Last Theft* (*Poslední lup*, 1987). Like Barta, Mergl has also occasionally moved into making animations for children and, like Miler and Beneš, has produced work for Czech TV. As such, a reader new to Czech animation, but overwhelmed by where to start, could gain a comprehensive overview of its stylistic terrain through watching Mergl's short but impressive filmography.

Slovak animation

As may already be clear, this book restricts itself to Czech rather than Slovak animators. As such, work by Slovakian animators who lived under communist rule, such as that by Viktor Kubal or Koloman Leššo, will not be discussed. Likewise, contemporary Slovak animators, such as Ondrej Rudavsky, Noro Držiak, Ivana Zajacová and Jaroslav Baran, will be neglected. Slovak animation requires its own book-length study, which I am not currently equipped to provide.

Czech animators focused upon

Across the first three chapters of this book, thing theory, ANT and rhythmanalysis are paired with the work of three different Czech animators whose methods and ideas respectively compliment each approach. These animators are Jiří Trnka in Chapter 1, Jan Švankmajer in Chapter 2 and Jiří Barta in Chapter 3.

Jiří Trnka

Jiří Trnka was a children's book illustrator who gained prestige for his puppet films which drew from local myths and pastoral traditions, leading to his being known as the 'peasant poet'[33] of Czech cinema. During the commercial height of his career in the 1950s, Trnka's success was such that he was referred to in the English press as the 'Walt Disney of the East',[34] despite never having recourse to the kind of industrial animation processes upon which Disney built his empire.

While Ruth Fraňková reflects that it 'would be hard to meet a Czech whose childhood was not touched … by the art of Jiri Trnka',[35] the animator's work was not primarily aimed at children. Peter Hames attributes the maturity of Czech animation – of which Trnka's work was at the forefront – to Bohemia's rich history of sophisticated puppet plays,[36] remarking that during the early 1950s when Stalinist dogma within the arts was at its most severe, Czech animation was at a creative peak, maintaining a formalist tradition even as avant-gardism was purged from live-action cinema.[37]

The workshop-based production process for animation enabled films of nuance and maturity to pass through the system, sometimes unadulterated. As Liehm and Liehm observe, production scripts for animation were more specialized than their live-action counterparts, only readily understandable by those familiar with the requisite technical knowledge. So, while creators of live-action films would have to submit their scripts to the authorities before being granted approval to produce a film, animators would often submit their work already in a state of completion.[38]

While most of Trnka's films received official 'disapprobation', they were 'defended from the consequences of disapproval both by their artistic quality and by the immediate international response that they evoked'.[39] Put simply, having Trnka's gentle and artistically refined films win awards at international film festivals afforded the regime a degree of cultural legitimacy.

On the surface, Trnka only produced one political film during his career – *The Hand* (*Ruka*, 1965). However, although their politics are not overt, Trnka's earlier bucolic films are political precisely *because* they sought to be non-ideological under a regime structured around ideology. The novelist Milan Kundera reflected that the conflict Czechoslovakia faced under communist rule was not one of two competing antithetical ideologies but rather, 'conflict between the imported political system and the entire culture of a country'.[40] Following Kundera's assertion, Trnka's puppet protagonists can be considered to be those practitioners of 'small-scale work' championed by Havel in his seminal 1978 essay 'The Power of the Powerless' (*Moc bezmocných*).[41] Such work achieves its dissident status not through violent anti-state activity but through its status outside of mass collectivization. In Trnka's case, the painstaking nature of his craft – inherently resistant to the time and labour-saving methods of efficient, industrial production processes – posed, in its quiet way, a threat to the communist order. Trnka's artisanal approach to film-making is reflected in his films' celebration of rural traditions and the respect given to the traditional, everyday objects which allow these traditions to be upheld. As Trnka's small-scale, workshop-based production process increasingly became an old-fashioned and nostalgic deviation from the orthodoxy of state-funded cinema, his films became more overtly critical of the communist regime and state. This trend reached its zenith with *The Hand*, which was banned following Trnka's death.

There is little English-language writing on Trnka outside of blog articles, internet reviews and sections of Marco Bellano's recent *Václav Trojan: Music Composition in Czech Animated Films* (2019), where he also reflects upon the paucity of English-language scholarship on the film-maker.[42] Jaroslav Boček's *Jiří Trnka: Artist and Puppet Master* (1965) is the most comprehensive work on the artist to date, though its text is descriptive, rather than analytical. However, such biographical writing usefully illuminates how Trnka's relationship with the communist authorities changed over time. Adam Balz comments that while the artist's 'relationship with the Stalinist Czech government seems symbiotic' upon first inspection, the fact that his films' funding was subsidized by the government put Trnka in the ambivalent position of balancing allegiance to his art and country against the knowledge that if his films were to be made at all, they would need to be endorsed by a government with strict ideological views upon what constituted appropriate art.[43] Trnka was able to produce political animations without being persecuted because he approached political critique from a non-ideological position, as per Havel's politics without politicking. He made this critique not through characters' dialogue or narration but through the political encoding of objects.

Jan Švankmajer

Jan Švankmajer is a Surrealist globally best known for working in stop-motion, although he trained within theatrical design and, later, puppetry. He is a prolific artist, producer of collages and tactile sculptures, prop designer, animator and film-maker who has, at the point of writing, directed twenty-five short films, seven features and one music video over a career spanning five decades. Across his career he has employed a variety of animation techniques including stop-motion, pixilation, claymation and, less often, more traditional two-dimensional forms, such as cut-out animation.

Švankmajer has lived through 'six different political regimes and their attendant ideologies'[44] and defines his work in opposition to political orthodoxy, whether communist or consumer capitalist. As a result, under communist rule in Czechoslovakia, Švankmajer often came afoul of the KSČ censors and was banned from film-making across most of the 1970s.[45] Fascinatingly, for such a politically provocative artist, only one of his films explicitly refers to political figures and events.

In contrast to Trnka, Švankmajer has been the focus of a host of critical enquiries: most recently, *Jan Švankmajer – Dimensions of Dialogue: Between Film and Fine Art* (2012) by František Dryje and Bertrand Schmitt, which also doubles as a compendium of Švankmajer's non-cinematic art. There has been work published in German, including *The Cabinet of Jan Švankmajer* (*Das Kabinett Des Jan Švankmajer*, 2011) by Rebhandl, Hartel, Matt and Blicke; in Spanish, with Gregorio López's edited volume *Jan Švankmajer: The Magic of Subversion* (*Jan Švankmajer: La magia de la subversión*, 2010); in French, with Charles Jodoin-Keaton's *Jan Švankmajer, A Surrealist Animator* (*Jan Švankmajer, un surréalisme animé*, 2011); and in Italian, with Antermite's and Lanzo's *Jan Švankmajer* (2011). Švankmajer himself has published work on tactile art – *Touching and Imagining: An Introduction to Tactile Art* was released in 2014 and touches upon the artist's own tactile work, as well as that produced by other Surrealists.

Perhaps the most dedicated commentator on Švankmajer's output is Peter Hames, editor of the influential 2007 volume *The Cinema of Jan Švankmajer: Dark Alchemy*. Hames situates Švankmajer's work within a culturally specific tradition of Czech avant-garde cinema, providing historical context for the artist's films and interviewing Švankmajer on the subject of his creative practices and beliefs.

Rather than providing political readings of his work, other commentators within *Dark Alchemy* tend towards aesthetically or philosophically inclined readings sympathetic to the specific concerns of the Czech Surrealist Group. Roger Cardinal, discussing the role of puppets and animated things in Švankmajer's work, makes a brief diversion to note that 1983's *Down to the Cellar* (*Do pivnice*) contains 'political allegory'[46] but does not specify what this allegory is of. Since Cardinal identifies as a Surrealist himself, this may be his way of respecting Švankmajer's oft-repeated assertion that he regards all of his films as politically 'engaged' yet not concerned with specific political phenomena.[47] Likewise, Meg Rickards, in a paper on the uncanny in

Švankmajer's work, provides a quote from the artist from the documentary *The Animator of Prague* (James Marsh, 1990) – 'I consider all my films to be political; some more than others'[48] – in order to support her argument that Švankmajer's use of the uncanny is of 'grave socio-political import'[49] without clarifying this import's nature or the reason for its importance. Such critics and interviewers take Švankmajer at his word that his films *are* political in content, without exploring what his *specific* political agenda(s) or messages might be. It is through closely attending to the interactions of objects and things in Švankmajer's work that potential answers to these questions can be found.

Jiří Barta

Jiří Barta's critical neglect belies the fact that he has created an important body of work through the period of late communist rule known as 'Normalization' continuing up to and after the Velvet Revolution (*sametová revoluce*). Jenny Jediny, in an article from the same series as Balz's piece on Trnka, provides an overview of six of Barta's films, with a particular emphasis on *The Pied Piper of Hameln/Rat Catcher* (*Krysař*, 1986). Jediny, referring to the objects/things of Barta's work, writes: 'We recognize these objects, yet they inhabit a world of their own which often draws on the political issues of the former communist block',[50] suggesting that the recognition these objects prompt in the viewer is simultaneously undercut by the alienating and uncanny environments they are placed within.

Writing on Barta tends to appear within broader academic texts on animation, Czech cinema or fairy tale films. Providing a political reading of Barta's *Rat Catcher*, Ivana Košuličová sees the film as interrogating 'the decline of socialist society in the mid-1980s'.[51] Peter Hames in *Czech and Slovak Cinema* (2009) cites Košuličová's interpretation, but does not further it.[52] Jack Zipes in *The Enchanted Screen* (2010) provides the same reading as Košuličová, but extends its contemporary resonance with a reference to the corporate scandals and economic disasters of the twenty-first century.[53] Elsewhere, English-language references to Barta are consigned to enthusiasts on blogs, festival programmes or the broadest of accounts in stop-motion 'how to' guides and general histories of animation.

Barta's most recent films exhibit scepticism at the transition of communist Czechoslovakia to the consumer capitalist Czech Republic. For Barta, to rebuild a political system, one must also rebuild the rhythms of daily-lived life encoded in a country's built environment from the ground-up, making rhythmanalysis cogent to a discussion of his work.

Other animators

The first three chapters of the book focus on Jiří Trnka, Jan Švankmajer and Jiří Barta, respectively. Several short animations upon which Hermína Týrlová worked are also touched upon in Chapter 1, as is a film directed by Trnka's and Švankmajer's assistant animator Vlasta Pospísilová. Chapter 4, which considers the depiction of Prague in animations (and sections of animation within live-action films) produced after the Velvet Revolution, has a broader focus than the preceding chapters and includes analysis of work by not only Švankmajer and Barta but also Pavel Koutský, Jan Balej and Michaela Pavlátová. These animators produce vital and provocative work in their own right, but their inclusion is primarily due to having directed work that focuses upon the relationship between the individual citizen and his/her city – in this case, Prague.[54]

Recovering forgotten material

This book illuminates many works of Czech animation which have been previously critically neglected, whether due to certain historical realities or the comparative lack of focus upon Central-Eastern European cinema within film studies.[55] This investigation proposes some forms of materialist engagement that offer a way of talking about film quite distinct from current paradigms of critical or cognitive theory. Thing theory, ANT and rhythmanalysis (either deployed separately or in combination) will not answer every question we may ask about a film. Thing theory – due to its emphasis upon objects – is particularly suited to the discussion of stop-motion animation. Rhythmanalysis is best served as a viscerally felt, poetic augmentation to current modes of writing on film editing. ANT offers less of a methodology than it does a set of critical practices which help steer an analyst in the direction of cinematic things that would otherwise be missed – an actor always wore gloves on set, a fly entered a scene and landed on the table, the shooting script was written in cursive, etc.

The Art of Czech Animation: A History of Political Dissent and Allegory demonstrates how several Czech film-makers encoded/encode objects and things in space and time (and sometimes those times and spaces themselves) with political meaning. Some of these films were made under the rule of the KSČ, in which the threat of censorship or persecution necessitated the use of allegory. More recent films take an allegorical form in spite of purported artistic freedom. All of these films, however, have something to say about Czech identity, culture, history or politics within the twentieth century. Whether the film-makers are speaking through objects, or the objects are speaking for themselves, remains open to debate throughout.

1

'It's the simple things': Animated allegories against Nazi and Soviet oppression

Overcoming the poverty of object analysis

In Vlasta Pospíšilová's 1984 short *Lady Poverty* (*Paní Bída*), poverty is anthropomorphized as a crone in a tattered dress and headscarf. As Lady Poverty moves through the Czech countryside, she plunders households of their objects, stealing them away in a bag of cloth from which they never re-emerge. The film works as a parable, illustrating the rewards of hard work and the dangers of sloth. Characters asleep during the day are stripped of their possessions, while a hard-working, resourceful family are able to fend off Poverty. When Poverty has finished divesting a person of their property, she throws them a length of rope fashioned into a noose with which they can hang themselves. Integrally, when the resourceful family are thrown the noose, the father ties it around a wardrobe in which Lady Poverty has chosen to hide, imprisoning her inside for enough time for the wardrobe to be transported out of the house.

The family's repurposing of the noose illustrates an aspect of their collective character (their ingenuity), but how are we to interpret the object's transformation *symbolically*? If the noose represents suicide in the face of financial and material ruin, could its refashioning represent the conversion of despair into hope? If so, what does it mean that the daughter of the family later uses this same rope as a washing line? Does this indicate domestic work keeps thoughts of suicide at bay? In these moments, the allegorical meaning of the film recedes from view and the symbolic rope is replaced on screen and within the imagination by the merely physical rope, usable for binding a wardrobe shut or for hanging clothes from but not for theorizing with.

How do we, as theorists and film viewers, overcome this potential poverty of on-screen object analysis? Renira Gambarato proposes a method for paring down the sheer conflux of objects confronting the theorist to those useful for analysis. Firstly, the theorist must apply quantitative analysis to all the objects in a film, determining how many times each given item appears on screen. Those objects appearing with the greatest frequency are determined to be the most cogent for textual analysis.[1] While in their paper 'Objects of Desire' Gambarato and co-author Simone Malaguti distinguish between micro and macro objects, determining only micro objects need be analysed[2] this can only ever be a provisional distinction since the importance given to macro objects dwarfs that of micro objects in the work of some film-makers (such as in the urban landscape films of Patrick Keiller). Moreover, despite the empirical basis for Gambarato's methodology, there will always doubtless be commonsensical omissions from the theorist's quantitative analysis – objects necessarily on screen in many mid- to long-shots of household interiors, such as door handles or plug sockets; or else things that are divisible parts of actors or props, such as fingernails, screws or nose hairs. Gambarato categorizes the objects to be analysed in a chosen film via a taxonomy composed of three criteria – relevance, expressiveness and functionality[3] – which in turn include numerous sub-categories, under which objects are placed according to their given function within a scene. The noose of *Lady Poverty*, for example, does not have any 'autobiographic signification' or 'advertising' or 'ideological' function, nor relate to any particular artistic movement,[4] but might be considered to have 'scenographic'[5] value through clarifying the character and temperament of Lady Poverty and the 'semantic' function[6] of connoting suicide through metonymic association. However, if the theorist is especially interested in investigating just one of these functions (i.e. an object's ideological function) and the other functions only insomuch as they help express that one function, Gambarato's methodology fails to increase the ease or efficiency of the theorist's work, since it can only be applied ex post facto when the task of analysis has already been performed.

An implicit aspect of Gambarato's work not made explicitly part of her methodology is that, in any given paper, her analysis of objects is performed upon a series of films by the same director – a director, such as Wim Wenders or Denys Arcand, whose work has been previously determined by Gambarato to express an ideologically or aesthetically consistent approach to their use of objects on screen. Such an auteurist approach allows a director's changing or evolving relationship to objects in their work to emerge.

In this chapter, the films of Jiří Trnka are analysed chronologically to demonstrate the shifting ways in which Trnka used objects on screen across his work to embody political and philosophical ideas in response to the rule of Nazism and, later, Soviet-style communism over Czechoslovakia.

Generally, Trnka communicates the political messages of his work(s) through the encoding of aspects of the film's mise-en-scène, via cinematographic techniques that emphasize the material qualities of these aspects. In his earliest two-dimensional works, such as *Grandfather Planted a Beet* (*Zasadil dědek řepu*, 1945) or *Springman and the SS* (*Pérák a SS*, 1946), objects like a giant beet or a pair of springs are, at the level of production, not distinguished materially from the rest of the films' mise-en-scène, since they are, like everything else on screen, mere drawings. As such, these objects are made to 'stand out' from their environments through either scale or novelty. The aforementioned beet is abnormally large; the springs allow a chimney sweep to jump great heights into the air. This may be regarded as a preparatory or juvenile stage in Trnka's approach to objects, since these objects are not truly depicted in their everydayness – bestowed, as they are, with some quirk that sets them apart from the quotidian. Indeed, Hermína Týrlová's films of the same period, such as *Lullaby* (*Ukolébavka*, 1948) or *Ferda the Ant* (*Ferda Mravenec*, 1943), are more consistent in their non-miraculous depiction of objects, but rarely wedded to the political concerns that subtly characterize Trnka's work.

Trnka's approach to objects reached maturity in his first feature-length film, *The Czech Year* (*Špalíček*, 1947), which illustrates the seasonal rituals and customs of Bohemia. If the springs of *Springman and the SS* are explicitly politically resistant objects, the spiced bread rolls and folk costumes of *The Czech Year* are more benignly traditional objects, carefully rendered in accurate local detail. This traditionalist mode emphasizes the craft and care taken in the creation of the objects themselves, with parallels drawn between the labour of Czech peasants within the film and the artisanal work of Trnka himself who carved the objects and puppets of his films. If there is a political impetus to this work, it is purely descriptive and celebratory. The objects are to be appreciated and assessed in their simple objecthood. This is also the approach of the majority of Týrlová's films, even while they adopt a contemporary rather than a historical subject, as in *The Little Train* (*Vláček kolejáček*, 1959) or *Two Balls of Wool* (*Dvě klubíčka*, 1962). While Trnka develops this poetic-descriptive approach in a number of ways across his filmography, it always remains the foundation upon which later approaches are built – with the curious exception of *Passion* (*Vášeň*, 1962).

With *The Emperor's Nightingale* (*Císařův slavík*, 1949) Trnka attempted to exceed the simple, descriptive approach of his early work through the use of irony. In order to make a critique of excessive artifice in art, Trnka produced a claustrophobically artificial film filled with an excess of decorative detail. Problematically, Trnka's painstaking artisanal approach ensures the beauty of the baroque details of the film's mise-en-scène, the aspect of the film most praised by reviewers. Trnka therefore abandoned this mode, returning to a more direct historical approach for *The Prince Bayaya* (*Bajaja*, 1950) and *Old Czech Legends* (*Staré pověsti české*, 1953).

Old Czech Legends advances *The Czech Year* in technique through shifting from a strictly historical approach to a more fully allegorical, mythic mode of film-making, albeit still rooted in the everydayness of objects. This is achieved primarily through associative editing,[7] which draws metonymic connections between objects and their environments. Through using visual metonymy rather than figurative metaphor, Trnka ensures the objects of *Old Czech Legends* are never abstracted from the local environments in which they are rooted. *Old Czech Legends'* cinematic rendering of rootedness develops in two antithetical directions across the films of the following decade. Down one path, rootedness descends into earthiness, as in the coarse carnivalesque humour of *Archangel Gabriel and Miss Goose* (*Archandel Gabriel a paní Husa*, 1964). Meanwhile, the other path ascends to a kind of civilized pastoralism in which an object's rootedness is illustrative of its transcendence, as in Trnka's ornate adaptation of Shakespeare's *A Midsummer Night's Dream* (*Sen noci svatojánské*, 1959).

Finally, in the early to mid-1960s, when Týrlová was producing her most abstract and experimental work, like *A Marble* (*Kulička*, 1963) and *The Blue Apron* (*Modrá zástěrka*, 1965), Trnka achieved the most thorough-going realization of his allegorical film-making with *The Cybernetic Grandma* (*Kybernetická Babicka*, 1962) and *The Hand*, before his death in 1969. Rather than simply encode single cinematic objects with political meaning, these films allegorize an aspect of the KSČ's ideological state apparatus – technology; censorship – in microcosm, communicating this critique through the work's cinematic language rather than dialogue or voice-over narration. It is instructive to demonstrate how *Passion* of the same period (mis)uses abstract metaphor to illuminate how *The Cybernetic Grandma* and *The Hand* work more successfully within a metonymic mode, which builds its critiques from the ground-up. Within these two films political deconstruction occurs at the material level of everyday objects grounded in their everyday environments.

To insist such metonymic film-making is allegorical, it is essential to investigate the meaning of this contested term.

Introduction to allegory

Defined simply, allegory is a rhetorical or pictorial form in which surface content functions as an extended metaphor for hidden, symbolic meaning. This meaning tends to be of moral, spiritual or political import and will sometimes relate to a particular situation contemporaneous to the author/creator, but will generally also contain a more universal or generalizable message applicable to all times and places. The concept and function of allegory are debated because it can be hard to delineate precisely where a symbolic work becomes allegorical. Many authors, painters or directors seek to communicate a message to their audience, or make use of metaphors or allusions, yet not all such works are allegories. A requirement of allegory is that its symbolism is extended to the full length of a work and is internally consistent. For instance, in a novel, a rose might represent the love between two characters, but if the rose is merely a metaphor used once to illuminate the relationship between two characters who merely exist in and of themselves rather than standing in for some higher or more abstract concept, then the work is not functioning allegorically. Compounding this problem of blurred definitional boundaries is the fact that classical or early modern allegories could rely upon a common set of literary and mythic allusions known to the majority of readers or viewers, such as figures from the Bible or Greco-Roman myth. Modern writers or artists working within an allegorical mode have a far wider pool of references to draw from, yet they cannot assume common knowledge across their audience. As such, these modern allegories are likely to be open to a broader variety of readings or depend less upon prior knowledge or viewership. Such works may consequently end up being closer to moral fables or fairy tales (when simplified, relying less upon allusion) or, on the other hand, more abstract and broadly symbolic, employing a wide range of symbolism, rather than providing a coherent allegorical vision. Despite this, Theresa Kelley insists, 'allegory survives after the Renaissance, against pressures that ought to have done it in'.[8] This is because, in spite of its unfashionable status, the allegorical form has remained useful to artists working across the twentieth century and beyond.

The allegory is the ideal artistic form for artists living within a totalitarian state liable to find themselves under scrutiny from their government. This is because allegory hides its latent meaning beneath its surface. It says other than what it appears to say. The viewer of a cinematic allegory must act as an interpreter, inferring the meaning of the film and the intentions of its director through their awareness of parallels between what they see on screen and some other paradigm(s) external to the film, which, ideally, they have encountered prior to their viewing. For instance, the viewer of either of the film adaptations of George Orwell's *Animal Farm* (1954 and 1999) would need to be already acquainted with the figures of Stalin and Trotsky to recognize their doubles in the pigs Napoleon and Snowball – or, more broadly, be aware forms of totalitarian power exist within the human world – to understand the film's message. With such knowledge, the viewer can then adopt a schema taken from the world outside of the film (say, the Russian Revolution) and overlay it upon the diegetic world on screen. This is symptomatic of a key difference between the allegorical form and the morality story, fable or fairy tale, which offer self-contained stories, from which a meaning can be derived in its entirety, without reference to outside sources or specific historical, political or social knowledge. This accounts for the tendency to consider the very young as the appropriate audience for the latter and the treatment of allegory as a higher, literary form, associated less with folk culture than the literary canon of Dante and Shakespeare.

Inevitably, these are generalizations, since the definition of allegory has been historically unstable, its theorization shifting across the twentieth century.

Indeed, Jeremy Tambling even ventures, 'perhaps there is no definite thing called "allegory", only forms of writing more or less "allegorical".[9]

However, a genre or mode of expression having blurred boundaries does not mean it should be barred from use in critical analysis. Despite its contested status, allegory remains the most appropriate term to use in relation to the films studied in this book because most of the films considered herein involve the interplay between a literal meaning and a hidden symbolic meaning which is systematic, internally consistent and politically engaged.

Allegory always contains the means of its own deconstruction even while it gestures to a symbolic register outside itself. The world of the story and its objects simultaneously obscure and embody their symbolic meanings. By contrast, in a fable, the meaning of the text can be extrapolated from the dialogue and actions of the principal characters alone. Fables take place upon an empty stage. A path or road might be required for the tortoise and the hare to race upon, but it is merely a means by which the action of the story can take place; it has instrumental, but not intrinsic, value.

In a fairy tale, an enchanted object (a poisoned apple, magic bean, glass slipper, etc.) might function as catalyst for events, setting the story in motion. A fairy tale's setting often provides it with atmospheric charge which heightens and reflects the emotional journey of its protagonist – Little Red Riding Hood is as inextricable from the woods and her grandmother's cottage as the Beast is from his castle. It is not to dismiss the aesthetic power of these motifs to state they have instrumental, not intrinsic, value. However, in terms of interpretive analysis they are MacGuffins. In 'Cinderella'/'Cendrillon' the fact it is a pumpkin which transforms into a stagecoach has little bearing upon the story's moral that a godparent is essential to a young woman's advancement.

Of course, these same motifs hold the potential to be read symbolically. Angela Carter's *The Bloody Chamber* (1979) reworks fairy tales, including 'Bluebeard' and 'Little Red Riding Hood', to foreground their seemingly latent themes of sexuality, horror and maturation. However, to achieve these readings Carter must adopt a Freudian symbolic register. This suggests the fairy tale form does not contain its own coherent symbolic system which unites wolf, stones, grandmother and red cap as part of a common meaning. Rather, an a priori interpretive schema (such as psychoanalysis) must be brought to bear upon the material.

In contrast to fairy tales and fables, allegory 'is not simply produced by a storytelling process involving agents and actions, but also results from visual compositions that … establish a clear dialogue with particular iconographical traditions, ancient and modern'.[10] When studying allegorical cinema, it is therefore important one's conception of 'agents and actions' is considerably broader than just human actors, their dialogue and gestures, since allegory as a visual form is highly dependent upon visual composition and editing structures, not just characters and narrative, for the communication of its political messages. Such privileging of the visual over the semantic allows cinematic allegories to critique aspects of totalitarian regimes covertly, at a lesser risk of censorship, since avoiding language allows the artist to escape the stranglehold of literal meaning and so communicate keenly felt and experiential aspects of life under totalitarianism without outright condemnation.

Ambiguity and plurality in allegories

In the animation studies anthology *A Reader in Animation Studies*, William Moritz considers four works – Walerian Borowczyk's and Jan Lenica's *Home* (*Dom*, 1958), Trnka's *The Hand* (1965), Yuriy Norshteyn's *Tale of Tales* (*Skazka skazok*, 1971) and Priit Pärn's *Picnic on the Grass* (*Déjeuner sur l'herbe*, 1988) – to be allegorical critiques of totalitarianism. *The Hand* is a puppet film concerning an artist whose home is invaded by a sinister gloved hand that insists the artist produces clay statuettes of itself. *Tale of Tales* is a hand-drawn animation in which a wolf moves between different groups of Russian peasantry engaged in inexplicable and dream-like rituals. *Picnic on the Grass* is a Kafkaesque indictment of bureaucracy and the stolid restrictions of everyday life in 1980s Soviet Russia. *Home*, meanwhile, is an experimental short that combines cut-out animation with stop-motion and pixilation. In an apartment in what appears to be a dystopian future, a woman (Ligia Branice) has a number of visions/experiences: two men fight a taekwondo match, a wig consumes an array of objects, a man repeatedly enters a room and places his hat upon a hat-rack. After a collage-like montage of architectural buildings/forms, the woman caresses and kisses a mannequin's head, which disintegrates.

Moritz posits that through adopting non-linear narrative structures, the use of symbolic misdirection, or else their ambiguity and openness to a multiplicity of readings, these subversive animated films were able to avoid censorship while making critiques pertinent to the regimes of their respective countries.[11] If these films are allegories, they are ambiguous allegories, making Moritz's application of the term congruent with the prevalent twentieth-century understanding of allegory as 'both calling for and resisting interpretation'.[12]

Ambiguity serves a political function as it can allow an artist to produce work potentially unrecognized as politically subversive by censorship bodies potentially more receptive to counter-readings which do not incriminate the artist. So, for example, the gloved antagonist of Trnka's *The Hand* is associatively linked to the statue of liberty, Napoleon's hand-in-coat, the scales of justice and a television set, opening the work to the possibility of being read as a critique of Western imperialism. Additionally, if an artist is accused of producing politically subversive art, ensuring their work maintains a degree of ambiguity provides them with the possibility for arguing that their work has been misconstrued.

If the political message of a cinematic allegory is too unambiguous, then it becomes increasingly likely it will be banned or pulled from circulation. In an essay for *Criterion* Michael Koresky refers to Jan Němec's *A Report on the Party and Its Guests* (*O slavnosti a hostech*, 1966) as 'one of the most transparently political of all Czech New Wave films'.[13] Although its parable of a group of picnickers forced to submit to the arbitrary coercions of a group of besuited bullies could function as a universal condemnation of all forms of state power, the statement made by the National Assembly of the Czechoslovak Socialist Republic (Národní shromáždění Československé socialistické republiky) in 1967 that the film had 'nothing in common with our republic, socialism, and the ideals of Communism'[14] demonstrates the apparatchiks found the message of the film to be pointed enough to react defensively. Indeed, the lack of ambiguity in the film's political intent led to it being 'banned forever' in 1973, its reels locked away in a vault until the fall of communist rule in Central-Eastern Europe.[15]

We might imagine allegories existing somewhere upon two separate, though interrelated, axes. The first axis traces a spectrum from obfuscation at one end to clarity at the other. The second axis concerns the multiplicity of an allegory's readings: from allegories with a singular meaning to allegories with a high level of plurality. So, *The Party and Its Guests* falls at one end of the spectrum, with both a clear level of meaning and a limited number of possible readings, while *Home* is situated at the other end, with both a high level of obfuscation and a high number of potential readings. It is harder to name films with a high level of clarity, yet a multiplicity of possible readings, or a highly obscure, yet single meaning. Arguably, Věra Chytilová's eclectic New Wave masterpiece *Daisies* (*Sedmikrásky*) of 1966, which follows the hedonistic antics of two young women, is obscure in its political intent (which seems to aim for a deconstruction of patriarchal, totalitarian systems of control while simultaneously displaying scepticism towards the limits of individual freedom when solely driven by personal desires) while restricted in terms of its possible readings due to the narrow scope of the film, which limits itself to scenes in which the girls eat excessive amount of food, have absurd conversations in a bedroom and on a pier, cause trouble in a dancehall and torment various male suitors. Trnka's *Cybernetic Grandma* (1962), on the other hand, is very clear in its messages but offers multiple readings – technology alienates people from daily life, human relations are irreplaceable, children must be nurtured and so forth.

However, there must come a point at which the multiplicity of possible readings ends in ambiguity and obfuscation, cases where, to quote Ismail Xavier, 'the accumulation of data creates the risk of fragmentation'.[16] This is the case for some of the films Moritz designates as allegories. For example, Moritz writes of *Home*: 'It sets up a complex non-linear structure that the viewer must decipher, which (1) makes it hard for a censor to ban since no individual element is obviously against the rules and the overall meaning is uncertain, and (2) requires the viewer to question the norm, which is a subversive act in itself.'[17] However, 'norm' is a qualifying phrase and means little without referential terms or a context through which to grasp its meaning – which norm is Moritz talking about? If the 'overall meaning' of the film remains 'uncertain', then so does Moritz's theorizing at this juncture. How diffuse can a film's message(s) become until it ceases to function as an allegory? To return to Xavier, allegories are not only 'polymorphous', they also 'require specification'.[18]

Moritz does not specifically refer to Socialist Realism in his analysis, but this might be taken as representative of the 'norm' which *Home* seeks to question/

undermine. The fact that *Home* is difficult to read is threatening to a system that functions via prescriptive ideology imposed from above. 'Workers of the world, unite!' – or, any other party sloganeering – provides a clear message, while *Home* does not. The films which Moritz describes are not works which produce didactic lessons or laws to be followed. They are without the unity of meaning provided by works of Socialist Realism, structured around the ideological principles of 'class-mindedness' (*klassovost*), 'party-mindedness' (*partiinost*), 'idea-mindedness' (*ideinost*) and 'people-mindedness' (*narodnost*).[19]

What Moritz argues, then, is that in the face of such clear-sighted, ideological thinking, ambiguity – and the refusal to provide clear, singular meanings in one's art – is dangerous *in and of itself*.

Allegory communicated through real objects

So, ambiguity and plurality are effective allegorical strategies for film-makers working under a totalitarian regime. When such regimes collapse, artists are provided with the novel opportunity to produce allegories which are clear and singular in intent and meaning.

Two films from post-war Czechoslovakia – Trnka's and Brdečka's *Springman and the SS* (1946) and Týrlová's, Kanera's and Uzelac's *Revolution in Toyland* (*Vzpoura Hracek*, 1946) – exhibit this shift towards increased clarity and singularity of meaning following the defeat of a totalitarian government. Both films were produced to celebrate the end of the Second World War and the withdrawal of Nazi troops from Czechoslovakia.

Through closely reading these films within a framework of thing theory, we might better comprehend the myths of Czech nationhood constructed during this tumultuous point in the nation's history. Both works reinforce a national myth of the Czech nation as small but resilient – a nation of honest, simple-living craftsmen and chimney sweeps who band together to defeat larger militaristic forces from outside the nation's borders. Ladislav Holý describes this self-conception as one of 'little Czechs' who comprise a 'nation of common, ordinary and unexceptional people'.[20]

In *Springman and the SS* and *Revolution in Toyland*, Trnka and Týrlová both illustrate the homeliness of their little Czech heroes by demonstrating their familiarity and kinship with humble domestic objects. By contrast, foreign invaders – the Gestapo man who visits a toy shop in the Uzelac, Kanera and Týrlová film and the principal commanding officer of the SS in the Trnka and Brdečka work – are prone to a hallucinogenic paranoia which manifests itself as an inability to take things at face value. These Nazi officers are not at home in the small domestic interiors the films depict and display a curious antagonism towards the everyday objects which compose such spaces.

It is essential to the meaning of *Revolution* and *Springman* that the politically coded objects/things which house their allegories are not merely symbols or signs, representing through simile some political faction or persecuted group, but are themselves important as common, knowable objects – as everyday items familiar to the audience with real, physical presences. As such, one must not only ask what these two films are political allegories *of* but also question *how* the allegorical meanings of the films are delivered to the viewer in the form of politically charged objects and things.

Objects of resistance in *Revolution in Toyland*

Revolution in Toyland begins with a toy-maker (Jindra Láznička) affixing rigid wooden arms onto a block-headed Hitler toy, which he is using to stow away a secret message for the Allies. Bill Brown reminds us of the fantasy entertained by children that their toys contain some special *something*, a secret message that might illuminate the life which their toys seem to possess.[21] The toy-maker literalizes this fantasy by stuffing his toys with secret messages and, in so doing, repurposes the toys for adults, instead of children. In the original Czech version of the film, we infer the toy-maker is playing a part in the resistance from an extended sequence that finishes with his hurried stowing away of the Hitler toy when he hears knocking at the door. In the American Sterling Films release, this introductory passage is heavily cut and an English-language voice-over informs American viewers the toy-maker is 'helping our side', reminding contemporary audiences that citizens of countries occupied by the Nazis are, in a post-war milieu, America's allies and may have proved their allegiance over the preceding years in serving the resistance. The fact that the help the toy-maker provides is congruent with his peaceful, humble work as a craftsman for children helps present an image of the Czech hero as a homely figure whose moral sensibilities are inextricable from his traditional workshop-based labour.

Though *Revolution* was produced and released before the Czech communist coup of 1948, the largely positive portrayal of the artisan class present in Marxist writing is already in evidence here. Alongside this tendency is a Czechoslovak strain of nostalgia for rural, cottage-based industry, which was undermined with the industrialization of the region under Soviet rule and the accompanying deforestation of Northern Bohemia. When Václav Havel is quoted by Aviezer Tucker as imagining a medieval man encountering a factory for the first time, falling to his knees and praying to God to be saved,[22] or Havel writes during his presidency in *Summer Meditations* (1992) of renewing 'our once-picturesque countryside, woods, and fields ... the farm buildings, the churches, chapels',[23] it is this specifically Czechoslovak strain of respect for the pastoral and connection to an agricultural past[24] being drawn upon. This brief sketch does not do justice to the complex history of these dual impulses (one Marxist, one Czechoslovak) but contextualizes a narrative common to the films of both Trnka and Týrlová, in which the peasant or the artisan is the hero and the forces of modernity and technological advancement, the enemy.

The film's artisanal hero realizes he is under threat from the approach of a Gestapo agent (Eduard Linkers) who hopes to raid his studio to uncover evidence of his involvement in the resistance. Fortunately, the swift-footed toy-maker manages to escape through a window before the officer bursts his way into the room. The clearest distinction drawn between the film's two human characters is in their relationship to the space of the workshop. The toy-maker's familiarity with this space is apparent in the ease of his escape. The room provides him with no obstacles and the room's objects are pliant and receptive to his needs. The window causes him no trouble; he finds no toy underfoot. Meanwhile, the Gestapo agent struggles with the door, which raps him on the chest as he enters the room as it rebounds off the wall.

Glancing down, the agent notices something by his foot and the camera tilts to follow his gaze until it stops upon a cylindrical wooden dog. The design of this toy is far more playful than of the dull little Hitler facsimile, reducible to kitsch iconography – slicked black hair, black tie, pencil moustache, etc. By contrast, the dog has a far more contemporary appearance, with sharp protruding teeth, flexed limbs and googly eyes. Presumably disgruntled by its lack of uniformity, the agent boots the dog across the room. If we ignore the agent's hammering upon the door, this constitutes the first significant act of violence against an object within the film.

In Švankmajer's *Food* (*Jídlo*, 1992), the callous way in which a character sweeps a plate and cutlery to the floor anticipates his own later objectification at the hands of another person. It is as though Švankmajer cautions us to treat objects/things with respect, else respect might not be extended to ourselves. This is a moral which can be detected here in *Revolution in Toyland* and, more overtly, in Týrlová's later short work *The Day of Reckoning* (*Den odplany*, 1960), in which a boy who tosses crumpled paper to the floor and, cavalierly, into a fish tank finds himself transformed in a nightmare into paper himself and is all but drowned in the very same tank.

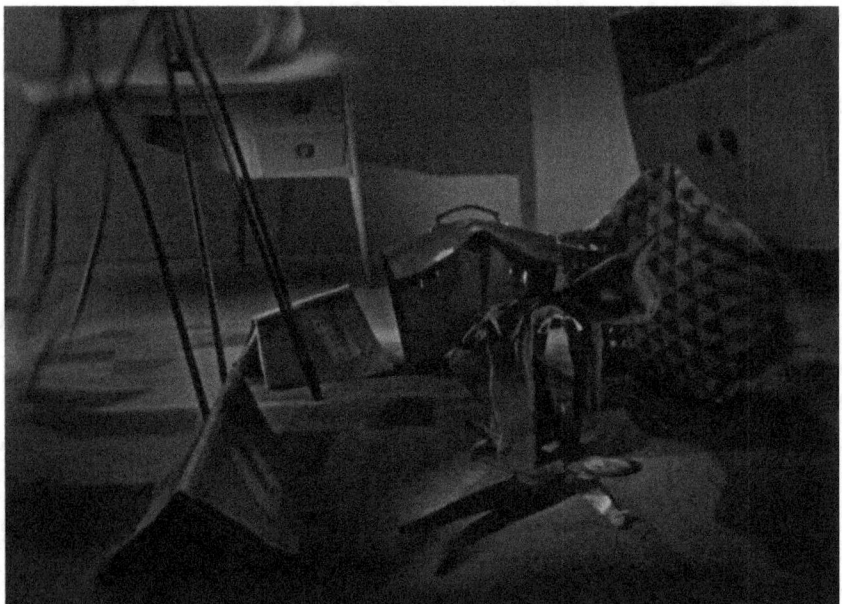

Figure 1.1 Animated objects previously treated with cavalier disrespect try to revive the half-drowned boy in *The Day of Reckoning* (*Den odplany*) (Hermína Týrlová, 1960). Image used with permission of the Czech National Film Archive (Národní filmový archive).

In the case of *Revolution*, the Gestapo agent's brutish treatment of objects acts to remind us of the Nazis' brutal treatment of human beings. However, the toy dog and the pounded upon door are not merely substitutes representing oppressed Czech citizens. Objects and subjects are linked here in a metonymic, not a metaphoric, relationship. According to the moral schema of the film, abused objects are not dissimilar but *similar to* abused subjects, which is to say the objects in the films are not stand-ins for the real victims of abuse but are victims *in and of themselves*. The mistreatment of objects in the film is positioned on an ethical continuum with the mistreatment of the toy-maker (and countless other unseen human victims of the Nazi regime). This is congruent with Daniel Miller's repeated implication in *The Comfort of Things* that moral care for objects is correlative with moral care for people.[25]

Having kicked the wooden dog, the agent begins a campaign of persecution against toys, in which a sailor, monkey, mule and miniature cannon are tossed or swept to the floor. Though narratively one could justify the man's actions as part of his search for evidence, he performs his duties with a roughness suggestive of not just simple efficiency but moral turpitude. In support of this fact, the American voice-over remarks: 'The agent of the dreaded Gestapo was wicked and destructive.' Unarguably, this is a violent sequence, even though it shows no harm extending any further than property damage.

Bill Brown, in his issue of *Critical Inquiry* on things and how they might be theorized, pauses to consider those troublesome moments in which things seem to announce their presence in the world: 'You cut your finger on a sheet of paper, you trip over some toy, you get bopped on the head by a nut ... They are occasions of contingency – the chance interruption – that disclose a physicality of things.'[26] The Gestapo agent finds himself flung into a panoply of such moments, in which 'the sense of a demonic malignancy in physical things cannot be dismissed.'[27] Having abused the toys in the room, these same objects now seem to conspire against him. The things of the room become dissidents themselves, actively resisting the fascist invasion via what Jane Bennett calls 'thing power'[28] – a thing's troublesome alterity in the face of a human subject.

Still seeking evidence, the agent searches in a heavy-looking box, which, falling closed, cracks him upon the head. After a shimmering, canted, soft-focus shot indicating the agent is either dazed or drifting into unconsciousness, a stop-motion animated cuckoo is thrust/thrusts itself through the hatch of a clock and calls the time. This marks the transition to what can be regarded either as a subjective, hallucinogenic state (aligned with the perspective of the stunned agent) or a 'real' series of events taking place within the workshop.

A cuckoo clock's cuckoo is animated, in reality, by mechanical contrivance; thus, the movement of the wooden cuckoo is not understood by the viewer as being wholly unreal. However, the means of this cuckoo's animation is not one of mechanical contrivance hidden within the body of the clock but achieved through stop-motion manipulation. It is left unclear as to whether the stop-motion animation is imitative of mechanical movement or shows the creature-thing 'come to life'.

The agent shares this confusion as he points his gun at the wooden bird and then withdraws it, suspiciously. He does not know whether to treat the thing as passive and moving according to predetermined movement or as wilful and invested with life. He points the gun above him and the cuckoo now appears through a door to the side of the clock. Though the cuckoo's pupils are not animated, their position at the bottom of the eyes suggests its gaze is falling upon the agent, hinting it's aware of his presence.

The agent shoots up, the clock gives a lurch and, with a clanging noise, part of the weighting for the clock's pendulum falls from the clock and strikes the agent on the head. This is analogous to Bill Brown's nut that falls from a tree and 'bops' the unprepared subject on their head.[29] The action may be motivated by gravity, but a vengeful force is sensed behind it. The ambiguity of this pinecone-resembling thing, its evident hardness and heaviness and the following shot of it in close-up, clearly delineated upon the floor by its darkness, announces its status as *thing*. This is matter, existing on terms disturbingly separate from humanity, violently resisting the fascistic ideology of a terrorizing subject.

At this point in the film our ontological understanding of subjects and stuff is muddled. Insensate and drooping upon the floor, the fallen Gestapo agent appears not so much a man as a leaden pile of matter. He resembles little more than a sack of potatoes. Brown quotes Merleau-Ponty when speaking of these moments where subjects are caught unawares by things: 'These are occasions outside the scene of phenomenological attention that nonetheless teach you that you're "caught up in things" and that the "body is a thing among things".'[30]

The body, so acted upon, is objectified. This is the blurring of perspective the Gestapo agent suffers. Having been a self-determined agent able to throw objects to the floor with ease, he is now the victim of a thingy fantasy, at the mercy of matter far more alive, animated and unencumbered than himself. Cropped close-up shots of the slumped man's socked feet lying alongside a discarded bottle and an over-turned metal bowl make the substances of his body seem like so much bric-a-brac.

With the agent unconscious, the toys spring to life. Their first revenge is to strip the agent of his uniform. Buttons are cut from his jacket with a pair of scissors, his boots are tugged off with a loop of rope, his jacket is winched from his torso with chains and a sock is yanked from his foot in the teeth of the toy dog. The toys' attack is waged against the clothes, rather than the body these clothes contain; however, this does not deflate the work's function as a celebration of Nazism's defeat since, as the clothes are ripped off him, the agent is stripped symbolically of his Nazi status. There is a high degree of sublimated violence during this sequence. The scissors are wielded like a sword and are brought dangerously close to the agent's chest. The rope around his feet is tied in a noose resembling a hangman's knot. The toy dog takes evident glee in its task of wrestling the sock from the agent's foot since in so doing it also gets to bite the foot the sock contains. This action rouses the slumbering agent. The toys retreat into a cupboard, which the agent douses with spirits and then mercilessly sets alight with a gunshot. The blazing cupboard filled with animate toys is a distressing image that recalls the cremations of the Nazi concentration camps. A tiny fire brigade works cooperatively to put out the flames, squirting the agent with water after he attempts to shoot one of the men. The bravery of the firemen is evident, as is their efficiency, resourcefulness and comradeship. The impression is of a fighting spirit that is determined, though not pugilistic.

Another toy snuffs out the lamplight illuminating the room. A tiny army of soldiers is summoned and they fight with toy cannon under the now chiaroscuro lighting. The cutting rate increases to a frenzy, to a point where some shots only last half-a-dozen frames. The sequence recalls the battle scenes of Eisenstein in technique if not in tone. The film cross-cuts between cannons being loaded and fired and the agent bombarded from the skies like King Kong. A cannonball is fired that strikes the agent in the rear, setting his trousers ablaze. The toys cheer while the agent is blasted out of the window into the street, where he runs off, humiliated.

If the Gestapo agent embodies the Nazi forces and the toys the persecuted Czechs, then it is through the spirited cooperation of the Czech citizens that they are able to resist the far larger force of the Nazis. The size of the antagonistic agent compared to the toys is clear as the toys clamber over his body like the Lilliputians over Gulliver, reminding us the German national body is far greater than the Czech. The narrative provides an allegory that recalls David and Goliath, with a smaller, but heroic 'body' defeating a much larger, antagonistic one, characterized as bullying and violent. Czechoslovakia is also outmatched in the size of its firepower, represented by toy cannon in comparison to the agent's 'human size' revolver. Ithiel de Sola Pool, in transcribing a series of opinion polls carried out with citizens of Czechoslovakia from 1968 to 1969 by the Czechoslovak Institute of Public Opinion (Československy ústav pro výzkum veřejného mínění), notes that in reply to the question 'What do you consider to be the most important event of the previous year?', 23 per cent of respondents answered the Israel-Palestine conflict and 19 per cent the Vietnam War. Sola Pool attributes this interest to 'concern with the problems of small nations surrounded by larger powers ... Widespread sympathy in both cases goes to what is perceived as the smaller power, namely the Israelis and the Viet Cong'.[31]

Clearly many Czechs felt they could relate to the situation of a smaller power seemingly terrorized by a larger. However, in *Revolution in Toyland* smallness does not represent insufficiency, since the tiny cannon and the little force of toy soldiers are highly effective at dispelling the Nazi threat. The film imagines a historical narrative in which Czechoslovakia was able to dispel the Nazis through collective ingenuity, determination and pluckiness. This is not a narrative of the compromises of the Beneš administration or abandonment by the British and French governments. Czechoslovakia, while staying rooted within its tradition of workshop-based labour and the national character of Hašek's 'Good Solider Švejk' (who survives within a militaristic environment through trickery rather than outright violence), is able to retain its independence and freedom in the face of belligerence from a larger outside force while preserving its essential smallness.

In terms of the two axes of allegory, *Revolution in Toyland* is a clear allegory with a single, stable message. This suits its purpose as post-war propaganda, celebrating the defeat and withdrawal of the occupying Nazi forces. It is an allegory of catharsis and of the triumph of smallness, community and ingenuity, specific to a post-war Czech context, but also generalizable to any situation where the small are persecuted by the mighty.

If *Revolution in Toyland* contains ambiguity, it comes not in the message but in the form of an ontological ambiguity which blurs the distinction between objects and subjects. If we step for a moment outside the allegorical mode and consider the film literally, it places the country's triumph within the 'hands' of objects, albeit sometimes humanoid objects playing roles such as firefighters and soldiers. As has been demonstrated, the message of the allegory is communicated through these objects, without recourse to dialogue and with minimal recourse to voice-over in the edited American release. As we now turn to Trnka's and Brdečka's *Springman and the SS*, we shall see how the humble spring is essential for the humiliation and defeat of the SS by the titular Pérák, the Springman.

The springiness of the *Springman*'s springs

Springman and the SS may seem, to those familiar with Trnka's later work such as *The Hand*, an anomaly within the animator's canon, due to its two-dimensional animated form. However, in the late 1940s and early 1950s, Trnka often worked on short, non-puppet films; indeed, it is worth noting that the paper cut-out animation *The Merry Circus* (*Cirkus Veselý*, 1951) was produced a year *after* completion of the director's third feature-length stop-motion work, *The Prince Bayaya*. At the time of *Springman*'s production in 1946, Trnka was most well established as a children's book illustrator, creating illustrations for collections of fairy and folk tales.

The Springman himself had a peculiar lineage as a recent Czech folk hero that had arisen under Nazi occupation during the Second World War. Compared to devilish Spring-heeled Jack of Victorian London,[32] Brdečka's and Trnka's Springman is merely impish and seems justified in humiliating the goose-stepping SS guards and their snivelling, hectoring leader. Indeed, in an opening English-language intertitle for the film's American release, the Springman is defined as a 'good ghost'. He saves his imprisoned countrymen, works hard at his job of cleaning chimneys and is appealingly puckish. As such, his characterization is not dissimilar to the toy-maker in *Revolution*. Neither the toy-maker nor the Springman are violent figures, but instead use objects ingeniously in order to elude capture by their violent fascistic opponents. In contrast to the thuggish and lumbering Gestapo agent in *Revolution*, the commanding officer in *Springman* crawls and snuffles his way about the frame, his voice represented by the over-dubbed yelps, sniffs and snarls of a dog. Physically he is a peculiar amalgam of sharp, stiff angles and liquid, elastic movements. This helps visually identify him from the ranks of uniform SS guards, who are rigid and robotic in their movements, exemplified by their characteristic goose-stepping.

It may be apposite here to note that many of Sergei Eisenstein's writings on the early art of Walt Disney are concerned with the idea that animation itself is a pure expression of freedom. For Eisenstein animation recalls pre-civilized ideas of 'the omnipotence of plasma, which contains in its "liquid" form all possibilities of future species and forms'.[33] Conceptualized thus, animation is understood to be life-potential *as such*. Under such a view, the rigidity of the officers is essentially *life denying*. Their uniformity runs counter to the very form of animation and, therefore, they seem not only conformist and dull-witted but unnatural, because their movement is not congruent with the form in which they exist.

What, then, can we say about the SS officer, who contorts his body so? Trnka and Brdečka perform a series of juxtapositions to ensure the viewer also experiences this character as life denying, not least in the simple contradiction between the hardness of his character design and the fluidity of his movements. Despite the potential for freedom the officer's movements suggest, the character is shown to squander this freedom by restricting his body to stereotyped and uniform gestures, such as heiling Hitler or glancing neurotically over his shoulder. For much of the short he is stooped over with his head kept close to the floor, emphasizing his 'lack of backbone'.

The Springman is, of course, the true agent of freedom within the film, embodying both 'freedom of movement' and 'freedom of transformation'.[34] Via springs, he bounds immense distances, during which his body appears to stretch and contort, before resolving itself into balletic poses. Since the Springman spends much of the film clothed in a streamlined, black body sock and mask, there are times where he resembles an inkblot, embodying through metonymy the expressive potential of animation.

Like the agent of *Revolution*, the SS officer in *Springman* has a paranoid inability to accept objects as agenda-less. Consequently, many of the victims of his persecution are common household items. A pot, boiling on the hob, tumbles to the floor and is pointed out to be seized and imprisoned. Later, on patrol, the officer spots a sign for a tool shop consisting of the silhouette of a man holding a hammer, pair of pliers and a sickle. With comic inevitability, the officer takes this to be sinister Communist Party propaganda and apprehends the sign, which is duly carted off. Trnka and Brdečka seem to be hinting that ideology obscures *the truth of things* and distorts one's true awareness of the world, breeding paranoia among the benign presence of physical objects. This defence of a rooted, phenomenological grasp of reality over ideology would become a common trope of Trnka's later work, as in *The Hand* and *The Cybernetic Grandma*.

After a montage in which various inanimate objects and innocent bystanders are arrested by the SS officer and his guards, the heroic chimney sweep, who has transformed himself into the Springman by affixing springs filched from a sofa to the bottom of his feet, *springs* into action. Pursued by the guards, he leaps across rooftops, is chased through a park and a prison yard and finally manages to trick his pursuers into falling down a series of holes. The officer, whose comeuppance receives the most detailed treatment, suffers various degradations before being kicked into the distance upon the hoof of a metal horse. All those imprisoned by the SS are set free, including, it should be noted, the objects, of which more seem to have been imprisoned than people. Clearly, in another similarity to the toy-maker, the Springman is sympathetic to objects and people alike. Objects, in the form of his two springs, are his essential allies. The springs are – typically for a Trnka animation – domestic not fantastic objects. The capacity for enhanced bounciness they bestow upon the chimney sweep is exaggerated, but it is not magical. The quality inherent in the springs (their coiled structure which allows them to retain and release energy) determines the power they provide to the wearer, rather than something from without (such as magical words or the 'Powder of Life' in Frank Baum's *Oz* books) granting some 'special quality' to the object, which is then available to the user.³⁵ The power the springs confer is *springiness itself*, which transforms the chimney sweep, rather than the other way around.

Thus, we can see an essential difference between the Springman and the officer of the SS – the officer projects his prejudices onto objects to make of them what they are not; the Springman sees things for what they are and releases the power latent within them. The villain persecutes objects while the hero lets the things determine and enhance his movements.

Despite *Springman and the SS* being a two-dimensional cellular animation, in terms of the treatment of objects/things, there is a kinship here between the Springman and a stop-motion animator like Švankmajer who, in describing his film-making, speaks of his preference for things with 'some kind of inner life'.³⁶ Švankmajer thus presents his role as an animator as being one of coaxing the already-present 'inner life' of things to their surface, as opposed to transfiguring them in such a way as would obscure their essential *thinghood*. It is this approach to animation to which Peter Hames refers when he asserts Švankmajer 'seeks to restore magic to the utilitarian'.³⁷

A subtle distinction exists between Švankmajer's approach to objects/things and Trnka's. For Švankmajer, things must be respected in their otherness from humanity, whereas for Trnka, objects are a means through which human community is facilitated. As such, an object's daily household functions should be treasured, not subverted; embraced, not overcome. The objects Trnka favours in his films – those protected and loved by his heroes – are humble objects – Pérák's springs, a child's ball in *The Cybernetic Grandma*, clay plant pots in *The Hand*. With the notable exceptions of Trnka's beautiful adaptation of *A Midsummer Night's Dream* (1595–6) and the framing narrative of *The Emperor's Nightingale* through which a boy's bedside toys become the objects of Andersen's fairy tale, his films are unconcerned with the metamorphosis of things which change or distort, but rather focus on the quiet, domestic objects from which a life is made.

Importance of objects to tradition in *The Czech Year*

In Trnka's first feature-length work *The Czech Year* (1947), such quotidian objects are historically situated within their specifically Czech context. The film is a cycle, composed of six individual shorts, which together chart the rituals and seasonal celebrations of the Bohemian peasantry.

Bendazzi, reviewing Trnka's output, writes that the animator 'brought to cinema a deep love for nature and a lyric faith in a people's traditions and their eternal spirit', making films 'rooted in the peasant traditions of people who have always turned to the land for their resources'.[38] Bendazzi does not denounce Trnka's pastoralism as nationalistic; however, his words imply the film-maker's love of nature found expression through specifically Czech traditions and rituals.

Mary Heimann in *Czechoslovakia: The State That Failed* (2009) argues it was Czech nationalism, which sought to secure hegemony over Slovak, German, Jewish, Ruthenian, Hungarian and Romanian citizens, which resulted in the country's ultimate dissolution.[39] From this standpoint one should be wary of Trnka's concern for folk tradition because of the danger such work might be susceptible to that ideological slippage by which a celebration of the *volk* becomes a demand for *Blut und Boden*. Heimann's denunciation of cultural imperialism should be commended, but the narrative she presents is selective, since it fails to recognize that the Czech National Revival and subsequent defence of specifically Czech cultural practices existed in response to the region's occupation by the Habsburg Empire and the subsequent near-eradication of the Czech language. Heimann's account makes no distinction between nationalist sentiment as expressed by the citizens of a small, occupied state, such as Czechoslovakia, and the nationalism of an empire state of great wealth and power, such as America, from where she makes her critique. Moreover, while provincialism may be regarded as narrow-minded or backwards-looking, it offers a potential challenge to nationalism, since it places value upon the specific customs of different regions at the expense of narratives of supranational unity, such as that which Soviet communism attempted to achieve for the Soviet Bloc.

Nonetheless, *The Czech Year* stays true to the focus implied by its title. In her blog of Czech/Slovak culture and heritage, Kytka Hilmar-Jezek provides a review of the film accompanied by scans of promotional postcards created to coincide with its release. In her review Hilmar-Jezek instructs readers to notice the 'little Czech details' in each picture, such as 'Czech rye bread, the pottery, details on and in the homes, the outfits, *vánočka*, mushrooms, pig slaughters (*zabijačka*), *koláče*'.⁴⁰ Indeed, in the film there is a wealth of traditional Czech details to observe as characters perform traditional Czech dances like *jihočeská kolečka* in traditional *kroje* costumes. In his biography of Trnka, Jaroslav Boček notes that the last segment of *The Czech Year*, 'Bethlehem', is essentially 'descriptive' in nature, 'an illustration in motion'.⁴¹ As such, tracing the heritage of all the objects depicted in the film would not be an inherently analytical exercise. Trnka is not, perforce, commenting upon specific Czech cultural traditions through including, say, a certain pattern upon a cup or plate; he is reflecting and preserving aspects of local culture. A simple historicization of these objects would not assist the argument that the messages of Trnka's films are encoded in their objects, save the recognition that at this early stage of his work the need to represent (and thus preserve) these objects *is the message*. However, it is worth selecting a small group of these specific objects in order to demonstrate the value they hold for Trnka and his film. In this case, like the *rohlík* given as an example in this book's introduction, the objects worth attending to are bread.

Koláčiky are heavy dough tarts baked with an indentation in their middle which holds a fruit, cheese or poppy-seed filling. The ubiquity of *koláče* to traditional Czech cuisine is suggested by the fact that Pat Martin's household guide, *Czechoslovak Culture: Recipes, History and Folk Arts* (1989), contains no less than nine individual recipes for *koláčiky* alone.⁴² Lida Dutkova-Cope, in a paper for the *Slavic and East European Journal*, emphasizes the association between the sweet tart and the Bohemian homelands for Texans of Czechoslovak descent.⁴³ While she remarks of her informants that they exhibit flexibility with regard to whether they attribute a given foodstuff to their Czech heritage, she notes the 'ever-present *koláče*' is a clear exception to this rule.⁴⁴ Indeed, the tarts can also be found upon the table in Trnka's *The Devil's Mill* (*Čertův mlýn*, 1949), while in Švankmajer's adaptation of *Alice's Adventures in Wonderland* (*Něco z Alenky*, 1987) the tarts stolen and eaten by Alice are not traditional English jam tarts but *koláčiky*.

In *The Czech Year* a peasant woman clad in a white apron (*fěrtušek*) and white head-kerchief bakes rows of *koláčiky*, dusting them with powdered sugar with a little brush. Trnka is careful to show the labour that goes into the production of these tarts, which can involve three to five risings. In an interview with Jacy Meyer, Hana Šemíková, owner of 'Simply Good' (*Karlín*) bakery in Prague, emphasizes the labour-intensive process of baking *koláčiky*. She notes that the rise of consumer capitalism following the fall of the Berlin Wall led, in her view, to a deterioration of the quality of baked goods available in the city. In doing so she draws a conflict between the economic incentives of consumerism and the time-consuming nature of traditional baking, noting that in the years following the Velvet Revolution, 'the only motivation was price ... People wanted to spend less and bakeries wanted to make more'.[45] To express this sentiment in terms of a traditional Czech folk saying quoted by Andrew Roberts: 'Without work there are no *koláč*' (*Bez práce nejsou koláč*).[46]

For Trnka, the artisan, *koláčiky* are worth recording as a cultural artefact because of the time and labour put into them both literally and symbolically (i.e. as objects they are an embodiment of artisanal labour). The peasant woman brushing her tarts is equivalent to Trnka himself in his workshop painting his puppets, a parallel which illuminates the fact that the prop tarts are, of course, a record of Trnka's own labour – as is the peasant woman herself! Time, effort and craftsmanship are afforded value in Trnka's cinema and the formal perfection of the objects in his films provides a visual embodiment of this ideology. So, the tarts are not signifiers for some higher, symbolic meaning. They are simply an everyday expression of the traditional custom of baking, which Trnka frames as taking place within a traditional, domestic space.

The Emperor's Nightingale as a critique of artifice

If in Trnka's first feature-length film he sought to extol the beauty of artisanal objects, in his following feature *The Emperor's Nightingale* (1949), he moved from a purely descriptive to an ironic mode in order to critique artistry which exceeds the realm of the artisanal to become overly decorative and baroque. In doing so, Trnka was still able to communicate his message primarily through his film's mise-en-scène in spite of making recourse to a narrator, voiced by Boris Karloff in the English-language dub. However, irony estranges literal meaning. In order for the viewer to recognize Trnka's critique, she/he must be able to recognize the sterility of what appears to be beautiful on screen, which is only clearly apparent when these objects are placed in contrast against the vitalism of those objects in *The Czech Year*.

The Emperor's Nightingale is an adaptation of Hans Christian Andersen's fairy tale of 1844. Andersen's story is of a Chinese emperor who discovers at the edge of his kingdom lives a nightingale with a beautiful voice. The Emperor orders the bird to be brought to him and upon hearing her song is moved to tears. The nightingale's song becomes a cause célèbre throughout the palace and one day the Emperor is gifted a mechanical automaton decorated to resemble the nightingale. This artificial bird replaces the original in his affections due to its musical predictability and outward finery. However, over time, the Emperor develops an illness, from which the automaton offers no respite. On his deathbed, the original nightingale, which had been banished from the kingdom, returns and with its song restores the Emperor to health.

Anna Celenza notes Andersen's tale has been 'interpreted in a variety of ways by numerous reputable scholars',[47] though Celenza favours the interpretation that the living nightingale represents the nineteenth-century Swedish soprano Jenny Lind and the mechanical nightingale, the more decorative style of Italian prima donnas. Trnka exceeds this narrow musicological reading with a broader reflection upon excessive virtuosity in art. Bendazzi notes the film's thematics do not differ from those of *The Czech Year* but, rather than offering a direct acclamation of nature, approaches the topic ironically through a sustained critique of the artificiality of the emperor's court by which the splendour of the court negatively indicates its poverty of spirit.[48]

In Andersen's story the Emperor's palace is described as being 'made of fine porcelain'.[49] Perhaps Bosley Crowther had this passage in mind when he reviewed the film for the *New York Times* in 1951 and described the film's puppets as looking 'like Chinese porcelains'.[50] While it is doubtful the film's figures were porcelain – considering the puppets of Trnka's early films were sculpted from wood and those of the later *Midsummer Night's Dream* from what the Prague Puppet Museum describes as 'a specially-made plastic'[51] – the heads of the Emperor and his courtiers are painted so as to resemble ceramic. This strengthens the metonymic relationship between the Emperor and his court since it flattens the difference between the figure and his surroundings, as though the Emperor himself is ossified by his possession of so many ornate, hand-crafted objects.

Here Trnka's strategy of having a film's objects embody its message(s) is faced with a paradox. Review after review[52] of *The Emperor's Nightingale* appraises the film's aesthetics while criticizing its slow and contemplative pace, thus denigrating the very mode of engagement which Trnka sought to encourage while celebrating the aspect of the film's world he intended to ridicule. As a contemporary reviewer, Crowther seems to have been especially seduced by the material splendour of *The Emperor's Nightingale*, rhapsodizing: 'Mr. Trnka has designed his film as a sparkling combination of colors, forms and materials. The stuffs of his settings are rich and brilliant – beautiful cloths, spun glass, tiny beads, mirrors and silvery tinkling metals, arranged in beguiling designs, and photographed in Agfa-color, which is markedly fine.'[53] Due to working in a metonymic rather than a metaphoric mode, to evoke the material over-indulgence of the Emperor and his palace, Trnka must craft his set and figures from the finest materials and thus risk exceeding his own naive artisanal style. Thus, not only is the character of the Emperor trapped within a world of artifice but also so is the film itself. The claustrophobic effect this achieves perhaps comes closest to articulating the message that unrefined, natural beauty is preferable to over-decorative mannerism, but only when juxtaposed against the sense of joy and freedom engendered by the folk rituals and practices of *The Czech Year*. The objects of the former film are situated as vital constituents of a yearly cycle and are thus imbued with the elemental life of the natural world. By contrast, in *Nightingale*, the death at the heart of mechanical objects is foregrounded. The uncanny not-quite-aliveness of the automatons – the performing nightingale and Clang, the robotic timekeeper referred to in Boris Karloff's narration as 'the ruler of routine' – only emphasizes their unbridgeable separateness from the rhythms of the natural world.

Taken together as a joint artistic statement, *The Czech Year* and *The Emperor's Nightingale* demonstrated Trnka's valuation of rural simplicity over technological modernity, yet the latter film ran the risk of imitating the very artificiality it sought to condemn; as such, it was necessary for Trnka to advance his representational system to communicate his moral vision. Writing at the end of Trnka's career in animation, his biographer Jaroslav Boček reflected that Trnka 'polarized the entire development of cinematography with his orientation towards permanent values and ideas that for years comprised both the development of national history and the essence of Czech culture.'[54] With *Old Czech Legends* of 1953 Trnka not only gave direct expression to these 'permanent values and ideas' but also changed and evolved the representational strategies used to express them.

Material history in *Old Czech Legends*

If we see Trnka's career in terms of an evolving process of how to treat objects cinematically, by 1953 his work had passed through three phases: a juvenile stage in which everyday objects were endowed with exaggerated qualities, a foundational stage in which traditional objects were depicted simply in their everydayness and, thirdly, an inversion of this natural, descriptive mode through excessive artifice. In terms of affirming the importance of being rooted in one's local culture, such an approach is a dead end. Irony cannot provide a solid foundation for affirmative culture. However, a simply descriptive mode is limited in its ability to transform the word through artistry and, while Trnka may have been a peasant, he was also a poet. With *Old Czech Legends* Trnka transcended the cinematic foundations laid down by *The Czech Year* through shifting from a historic to a mythological register. Objects could still be affirmed in their rootedness but, through associative editing and visual metonymy, they would now also be imbued with mythic significance.

Old Czech Legends is comprised of six episodes based upon stories from Alois Jirásek's eponymous 1894 collection, a key work of the Czech National Revival (*c.* 1770–1918). Holý situates the origin of the National Revival in a 'conscious effort' on the part of elites to 'revive the Czech language ... and constitute it as a literary language'.[55] While other critics, such as Robert Auty, see the institutionalization and acceptance of Czech as a literary language as symptomatic – rather than the cause – of the Revival,[56] the Czech language is unarguably closely intertwined with Czech national identity and the concomitant valorization of historic/mythic Bohemian culture.

James Underhill writes upon the ways in which language can determine the world view of a country's citizens. Using communist-era Czechoslovakia as a case study, he argues the KSČ exploited metaphor to bridge the gap between nationalistic sentiment and communism in the Czech public's imagination.

Underhill reminds us a government's ideology is primarily facilitated through language, even while it may have non-linguistic means (such as dialogue-less cinema) at its disposal for mass communication. If we accept that one's experience of the external world is not wholly contingent upon language, then a gap can be cleaved between the material realities of everyday life and the regime's ideological assertions about the same.

In relation to what Jiří Trnka achieved politically through his cinema, Underhill's most cogent observation is that 'at the heart of communist metaphysics … the forms and phenomena of reality would appear to have no bearing on the essence of the Party, the destiny of history and the unity of the two with "the people".'[57] Under communist ideology, 'the people' is an abstract construct given ontological weight that exists entirely separately from the actual people of the country who exist day-to-day with individual lives. For Underhill this does not set communist ideology at odds with Czech nationalism, quite the opposite – the Czech national self-conception as a nation of little peasants is as divorced from the (unromantic) lives of real peasants as references to 'the people' in communist rhetoric are disconnected from the lives of individual citizens.[58] The neo-romantic impulses of Czech nationalism thus leave a great abstraction at the heart of the nation's self-conception easily replaced by new ideological signifiers that refer only to abstractions. Indeed, under the KSČ, communist intellectuals and academics often 'reinterpreted' Czech history (such as the Battle of White Mountain of 1620) as evidence that the ideals of scientific socialism were intrinsic to the Czech lands and its people, thus legitimizing communist rule as the necessary and inevitable teleological outcome of the nation's development.

Trnka had already proved his aptitude for translating Czech folk history into the cinematic medium with *The Czech Year* and *Prince Bayaya*. Adapting a feature film from one of the most significant literary works of the National Revival was an escalation of this nationalistic project. What Hames appraises as 'simple, charming and naive in the best sense'[59] about Trnka's art may appear as problematically romantic, conservative and kitsch (and so open to ideological exploitation) to a less sympathetic reviewer. Certainly, the thematic concerns of almost Trnka's entire filmography are captured in Underhill's critical recounting of the Czech National Revival:

The German-speakers ... become the opposite of the Czech ideal of a wholesome community-centred people with its roots struck deep into the earth of the homeland of which the Czech people had been unfairly deprived. Hostility to progress is evident in all reactionary movements which celebrate the land, the homeland and traditional values in contrast to the perceived decadence of the city and the depravity of its dwellers.[60]

Hames reflects that the very 'fact that Trnka's work was often achieved within the folk tradition ... suggests that there must have been some accommodation with the regime or that he was, at least, working within an approved programme'.[61] He goes on to write: 'There is an inevitable tightrope walked when the state harnesses national traditions to its own ideological purposes.'[62] It is difficult for the patriotic artist to extricate national traditions from the presiding political ideology if the regime has successfully promoted a narrative that these national traditions and the political ideology stem from the same wellspring.

So, how did Trnka produce a film which is thematically and aesthetically beholden to the nationalist principles of the Czech National Revival but resistant to being read as an endorsement of communist ideology? Dutka remarks that Trnka was 'pressed to create historic myths in *The Old Czech Legends*'.[63] However, despite the film being made at the regime's behest, upon release it was neither championed by the regime nor used to endorse the KSČ as the natural heirs to a Czech historical trajectory rooted in 'revolutionary struggle', as were the films of Otakar Vávra's *Hussite Trilogy* (1954, 1955, 1956), produced under Gottwald's so-called 'Jirásek Action' to promote the writer's work.[64]

I have argued that Trnka's films were political precisely because they sought to be non-ideological under a regime structured by and defined through ideology. For the purposes of this argument, 'non-ideological' does not mean without a value system but without that strain of metaphysical abstraction – what Underhill refers to as the 'transcendental nature of the Party'[65] – which allowed the KSČ to co-opt works of the National Revival. While the neo-romanticism of the National Revival and the scientific socialism of Czech communism unfailingly translated 'the people' into an ideological abstraction, Trnka individualized his historical figures, rooting them in the material reality of their daily world through an emphasis upon pure sounds and textures, rather than an excessive use of language, which always already carries ideological associations which may be exploited in the name of political power.

In her essential survey of Central-Eastern European magic realist cinema, Aga Skrodzka identifies a modern trend of 'vernacular' film-making in the region, which in reaction to globalization turns instead to 'the earth-centred spirituality of the local, the idea of being rooted'.[66] Skrodzka's conception of rootedness is built upon that of Marxist philosopher Ernst Bloch, who argued that the German peasantry were not amenable to Nazi ideology due to their close symbiotic relationship to the land they owned and worked, binding them to the commonsensical realities of everyday life and its natural cycles.[67] If we accept Underhill's assertion that communism's apparent materialism is, in actual fact, just metaphysics by another name, then Bloch's argument should be no less true of communism than fascism. While the Central-Eastern European films of the 1990s exhibit cultural anxiety in response to the encroachment of consumer capitalism, Trnka's own concern with rootedness is alike in kind, but not in source, to this newer anti-capitalist incarnation. A turn towards vernacularism in art might be considered more broadly as a reaction to politically imposed ideology per se, whether communist or capitalist. At the point when her argument covers the greatest breadth of the political spectrum, Skrodzka reflects that the vernacular register of the films discussed in her work 'seems to arise from the deep-seated disappointment with anything grand or totalising'.[68] To return to the nineteenth-century anarchist Zo d'Axa, the contingencies of daily life as experienced by citizens – rather than theorized by politicians – require moment-by-moment localized truths and solutions, not totalizing abstractions, whether fascistic or liberal, communist or nationalist. Skrodzka's own definition of 'rootedness' is ambivalently poised between d'Axa's revolutionary pragmatism and a more backwards-looking nostalgia. She writes:

> That which is grounded implies connections, as opposed to that which is ungrounded, which can only refer to itself, and thus barely be identified as human ... The connections that allow the subject to be grounded in reality are symbolic ties that secure a sense of continuity with the place, and by extension the earth.[69]

The earth as a site of symbolic ties upon which human community is built is central to Trnka's reading of *Old Czech Legends*. In Marie Holeček's translation of Jirásek, the founding of Bohemia (*Čechy*) by Father Čech prompts a brief rhapsody upon the riches of the Czechs' native land, described as 'a beautiful country, the soil fertile and the rivers well-stocked with fish'.[70] The natural terrain of Bohemia is linked to the grains and plants which are cultivated there: 'Each tribe lived in the middle of its own land, and its members shared the meadows, fields, pastures, woods, and waters. They raised wheat, oats, barley, and rye.'[71] Trnka depicts the cultivation of the land by the settlers through a passage of remarkable brevity – it lasts no more than sixty seconds – which condenses a series of metonymic associations between soil, animal and man. An axe is thrown at a stampeding bull and embedded in its neck. The bull collapses onto its side and expires. The shot then dissolves to an extreme close-up of a field being tilled, creating a moment of superimposition in which the harrow appears to be tilling the body of the bull which, due to its similar colouration, seems to merge with the soil. Though not a match shot, there is a close visual similarity between the shape of the axe's handle and the shape of the harrow. After a few seconds of the harrow being pulled through the soil, the film cuts to a medium shot of two oxen now yoked and employed as draft animals, symbolically and literally castrated, led by the same figure who threw the axe. Man's dominion over nature is thus symbolically integrated into a natural cycle of death and rebirth, with the killing/castration of the bull transformed into a ritualistic sacrifice that feeds the soil, to which its body (and the bodies of the Czech people) eventually returns. The cultivating project is shown to be harmonious with nature.

Other visual associations within *Old Czech Legends* strengthen this theme. When, at eleven minutes into the film, Father Čech is shown driving his staff into the ground to symbolize the founding of Bohemia, all of his followers kneel in prayer and supplication. All that's left in shot are the followers' crooks, staffs, spears, pikes, axes and green-leaved branches, all rising up against the sky as trees in a forest. Tools for cultivation, weaponry and emblems of the natural world are visually undifferentiated. Likewise, a cut from the roof of a hut being thatched to stalks of wheat in a field shows the settlers are not merely stripping the natural world of its resources but are living *within* the natural world as a part among parts of the great holistic whole. By placing the actions of his characters within their contextual environment, Trnka ensures their labour is shown as being inextricable from the land.

Figure 1.2 A forest of wooden crooks, staffs, spears, pikes, axes and green-leaved branches held aloft in *Old Czech Legends* (*Staré pověsti české*) (Jiří Trnka, 1953). Image used with permission of the Czech National Film Archive (Národní filmový archive).

An often intoxicating excess of natural sounds and textures ensures sensory immersion into the pre-modern world depicted on screen: trampled sawdust, the 'twang' of spears, the sound of wood knocking upon wood, the tweeting of birds and moments when Václav Trojan's folk soundtrack merges with the diegetic world. The film's concluding depiction of a battle from the Lučan Wars becomes, at times, avant-gardist in its cinematography, editing and sound-design, with ground-level shots half-obscured by puppets photographed in extreme close-up and Trojan's score at its most dissonant and fractured, matched to a staccato and irregular editing rhythm. The sequence's most gravely expressionistic image is of a hawk with a broken wing spiralling upon the ground as two swordsmen circle each other in a battle to the death. At this point Trnka transcends the ironic mannerism of *The Emperor's Nightingale* to achieve a fully realized vision of an irrefutably material world.

Old Czech Legends and, before it, *The Czech Year* are paeans to rootedness, which in Trnka's visual articulation refers to the living connection between people and their local, grounded environment. After *Old Czech Legends*, the expression of this theme branches off in two directions. In one direction, rootedness becomes earthiness, in which there is an emphasis upon what Mikhail Bakhtin refers to as the 'material bodily lower stratum'.[72] Here, the coarse, rustic humour in evidence as far back as *Song of the Prairie* (*Árie prérie*) in 1949 finds full carnivalesque expression. This trend is most pronounced in Trnka's *Archangel Gabriel and Miss Goose* of 1964, in which a lascivious monk seduces a lady besotted with the Archangel Gabriel by disguising himself with a mask and wings made of goose feathers. The humour in the film is anti-clerical in tone, with jokes made at the expense of the monk's subjugation to his earthbound desires, in spite of the Church's claims of transcendence. Phallic imagery – including visual punning upon a cockerel crowing, long-nosed masks in the *Commedia dell'arte* tradition and the image of the monk himself, his bald head poking out from its sackcloth covering – ensures the film's human figures seem firmly rooted in the fleshy, natural world.

In the opposite direction, Trnka's pastoralism is further refined and aestheticized to the point where civilization and nature stand revealed as correlative to one another. The pinnacle of this mode is Trnka's 1959 adaptation of *A Midsummer Night's Dream* but its origins can be felt in his earlier adaptation of Chekhov's short story *Romance with a Double Bass* (*Román s basou*, 1949) in which the natural beauty of a woman's naked form is elided with the aesthetic beauty of a double bass. In *Midsummer* visual matches similar to the one between the double bass and the naked woman are used to create close metonymic relationships between elements of the natural world and the civilized. The movement of Puck twirling a flower between finger and thumb is matched to Bottom as Pyramus twirling within a red cloth, Robin Starveling's face as Moonshine dissolves to a shot of the moon itself hanging in the sky and the cloth of Titania's train is composed of her fairy entourage. Unsurprisingly, Trnka's vision of Helenic culture is especially amenable to any suggestions of the small, the local and the rooted which exist within a play otherwise 'concerned with the grand affairs of state … in the remote world of classical Athens'.[73]

At this late point of his career, Trnka was still building his films' meanings from visual metonymic associations rather than linguistic metaphors, but he was also moving into a more literary mode, as evidenced by the fact that he was now adapting Shakespeare and Boccaccio rather than fairy tales (*The Emperor's Nightingale, Prince Bayaya*), folk tales (*The Czech Year, The Devil's Mill, Springman and the SS*) or semi-mythic history (*Old Czech Legends*). For the final part of his career Trnka would turn away from adaptation altogether to work within a more consistently allegorical mode, in which his own stories would comment upon Czech society and his position within it as an artist on the eve of the Prague Spring. Despite their political engagement, these works do not merely transform objects into interpretation-ready symbols but demonstrate how political power is embodied at the level of daily life and how humble, domestic objects can help in the artist's individualistic resistance.

Oppressive gestures of 'a hand of state'

By 1965, when *The Hand* had been completed – its fate to remain unseen until the collapse of communist Central-Eastern Europe in 1989 – the KSČ had exercised undisputed control over Czechoslovakia for seventeen years, since the coup d'état of 1948. Under the administration of Antonín Novotný, the governmental system had remained essentially Stalinist, collectivization was still in place, the economic system was experiencing only hesitant and limited reform[74] and policy was still being dictated by Soviet influence in Moscow.[75] Furthermore, the censorship policies of the repressive 1950s would not be significantly altered until the government of Alexander Dubček attempted to establish 'socialism with a human face', leading to the subsequent period of relaxed government control over artistic and press freedom known as the Prague Spring.

Within the realm of visual arts, the Chief Press Inspection Board (Hlavní správy tiskového dohledu) would examine the catalogues and programmes of art exhibitions for expressions of non-conformity.[76] Maruška Svašek details that across the 1950s those works considered ideologically deviant from the tenets of Socialist Realism would not receive distribution, forcing artists to either adapt their style or communicate with other dissidents underground.[77] While by 1965 the influence of Stalinist factions within the KSČ had abated in the wake of Krushchev's second de-Stalinization speech of 1961, Svašek's judgement that 'the dam finally burst in 1964'[78] with the appointment of

Jindrich Chalupecký to the position of Chairman of the Art Union is a little hyperbolic or at least premature. While there was a thawing of dogma in the approach to the censorship under Novotný, in the years preceding the Prague Spring the immediate effect on artists would have been minimal due to their internalization of the previous rules of censorship – a phenomenon Miloš Jůzl refers to as 'auto-censorship'.[79] Jůzl argues that through not knowing precisely what content was allowed by the Party, artists policed themselves, doing the job of the regime's censorship forces, such as the Office for Publishing and Information (Úřad pro tisk a informace) or the aforementioned Chief Press Inspection Board, for them.[80]

This is the argument made by Miklos Haraszt in *The Velvet Prison* (1988) – that the most insidious form of censorship under Soviet communism was the one which artists imposed upon themselves, due to the phantasmal, ever-present fear of the censor; as Haraszt puts it: 'The state is able to domesticate the artist because the artist has already made the state his home.'[81] The hand of the state infiltrates the private sphere and the mind of the artist – insidiously, seductively, coercively – until the artist becomes their own worst censor.

When we imagine the hand of the state how do we imagine it? Do we visualize the phrase nebulously, thinking of the instigation of policies across numberless ministries and departments; their invisible implementation through services, spending and public bodies? Or do we visualize the hand as something concrete, with the ability to put things into place, to count upon its digits, to pat its supporters upon the head, to grasp and to throttle? If we have lived under a totalitarian regime with a cult of personality, we might imagine the specific hand of a specific dictator, real and fleshy and connected to an arm, to a body, to the head of state – a hand that salutes, waves to the masses or pounds in a fist upon podiums. If we are religious, we may believe the hand of the state is dominated in turn by a greater hand, the hand of God and, again, do we imagine this hand as something ethereal and ineffable or emerging benevolent yet powerful from under a whitened robe?

The capabilities of a hand, the weight we afford it, the momentums that characterize it are all indivisible from our knowledge of a hand's physicality. It is difficult to imagine a wholly symbolic and transcendent hand, without investing it with fingers, knuckles, nails and so forth. In Trnka's film, the hand of the state is characterized as a physical repressive force: by turns coercive, placatory and violent. Throughout the short, the titular Hand terrorizes a solitary potter-harlequin, endeavouring to force him into crafting miniature statuettes of itself.

The relationship between the potter-harlequin and the Hand easily offers itself up to symbolic interpretation. For instance, near the start of the film, the Hand attempts to gain entry into the potter's house. First, it leaps in through the shuttered window and then, when driven out, pushes up against the door, attempting to force it open. This sequence of actions is immediately readable as representing the surveillance of the state, under which the public-political realm intrudes into the individual's private space so that their actions, speech and daily life are subject to merciless scrutiny and investigation. Later, when the Hand picks the little potter up by his spherical head, forcing him back down before his potter's wheel, we understand the state can turn to increasingly violent methods to reach its ends, such as imprisonment or the threat of torture.

Considering the above, it should not be surprising *The Hand* has been widely interpreted as an allegorical work. Hames, in an article for both *Sight and Sound* [82] and *Czech and Slovak Cinema*,[83] regards it as such – as do William Moritz,[84] Edgar Dutka,[85] Susan Hayward,[86] Steven Subotnick[87] and William Bernard McCarthy[88] in various published works, not to mention similar readings on blogs and film review sites.[89] In terms of the axes of allegory, these writers position the film as having a singular meaning which is altogether clear. Markéta Dee asserts that *Ruka* 'is clearly Trnka's protest against the conditions imposed by the Czechoslovak Communist state on artistic creation and creative freedom',[90] while Hames states that the film 'remains one of the most overt attacks on Stalinism to have been made in the 1960s'.[91] Hames summarizes the film, thus: 'It tells the story of a happy potter whose simple creative life is ruined by the demands of the state. An enormous hand commissions him to make official works, but he refuses. Initially the hand tries to persuade him, offering him money and women; ultimately it resorts to force.'[92]

Hames, perhaps intentionally, conflates the upper layer of the allegory shown on screen (in which a hand invades a potter's house) with the lower level interpreted by the attentive viewer (the state imposes its demands upon the nation's artists, to the detriment of artistic output and the artist's well-being). Hames's conflation of these two stories usefully illustrates how in allegory, the upper-level meaning exists alongside the lower-level meaning. It is this ever-changing, sometimes confusing relationship between the two layers in *The Hand* – one explicit and diegetic and the other hidden and inferred – that demands special attentiveness to how symbols within the film are embodied. Merely focusing just upon the film's symbols or just upon its objects, without recourse to both, discards the essential fact that the allegory functions via the real hand/Hand existing simultaneously alongside its deeper symbolic meaning.

One need not be a palmist to suggest we can read a hand as we do a face. Frank R. Wilson, in his exhilarating monograph on the evolution, development and social coding of the hand, writes that 'the hand is not merely a metaphor or an icon for humanness, but often the real-life focal point … of a successful and genuinely fulfilling life'.[93] That is to say, a hand does not simply stand in for character, gesturing us to look elsewhere for our understanding of life but is, in its remarkable expressivity, often where we should look first to glimpse life lived in the full. It is as adept as the face at expressing anger, love or fear and, indeed, may often tell the truth of a situation, which the face tries to mask or distort. By this I suggest that, despite the masking of the white glove, the viewer of *The Hand* and its artisan protagonist can read the sinister intentions of the Hand clearly. The Hand is not mere metaphor but powerful in its real embodied incarnation, with its endless potential to smash, throw and throttle. *The Hand* succeeds due to its use of the Hand-in-glove as a *real thing*, not just as a sign functioning within a larger allegory, a characterization typical to previous discussions of the work.[94]

Reading *The Hand*

François Delsarte, in the mid-nineteenth century, developed a systematic and precise approach to the movement and position of hands within the art of oratory.

Delsarte conceptualizes the hand as having three fundamental 'attitudes': the 'normal state' in which the hand is open without strain, the 'concentric state' in which the hand is closed and the 'eccentric state' in which the hand is open with force and tension.[95] Delsarte then further subdivides these attitudes into nine different positions, defined according to the togetherness of the fingers, whether the palm or back of the hand is facing forward, the strain in the muscles of the hand and the movement of the hand, as determined by the movement of the wrist and arm. These variations express one of the following: acceptance, negation, 'lack of will', wilfulness, menace, desire, imprecation, repulsion or tenderness.[96]

Though the Hand of Trnka's film makes a very brief show of decorum upon its entrance, bobbing towards the potter in a movement resembling a curtsey, it wastes no time in adopting a position between wilfulness and menace. Hovering above the potter's wheel, the fingers and thumb are held together in a fist, save the index finger, which is pointed wilfully towards the potter. The Hand then shapes the potter's clay into a small iconographic representation of itself. In doing so, the Hand shifts between a desiring and caressing movement, which is purposeful and possessive, rather than tender. When the potter shapes the clay back into a pot, the Hand returns to its position of wilfulness/menace, jabbing its index finger threateningly towards the potter.

Though it is the Hand's iconographic power that allows us to abstract its meaning to the concept of the 'hand of the state', it is not merely the Hand as icon which communicates the dynamic of power here. The Hand as sign is what alerts us to its allegorical role, but the specifics of Trnka's critique are communicated through its precise, gestural movements. The sequence of courtesy/menace/desire/threat the Hand moves through in the first forty seconds of its on-screen time is a caricature of the emotional position adopted by Soviet governments towards their artists, by turns conciliatory and threatening. Though intruding into the artist's private space uninvited, the Hand immediately establishes itself as a guest, adopting the social ritual of polite greeting to secure this role for itself. From hereon in, any refusal by the potter is transformed into an act of rudeness and incivility, as though it were the potter, not the Hand, being unreasonable. The Hand makes its desires clear and yet is careful to adopt the threatening aspect only momentarily, hinting at the potential for force, rather than becoming explicitly violent. Again, this coercive behaviour allows the Hand to assert its domination while pretending to remain within the sphere of civil relations. Trnka is showing us that the state strikes an emotionally ambivalent relationship with artists, offering plaudits and respect, while all the time reminding the artist – sometimes implicitly, sometimes explicitly – of the fact they are in service to a power which has the ability to destroy their life at any time it chooses.

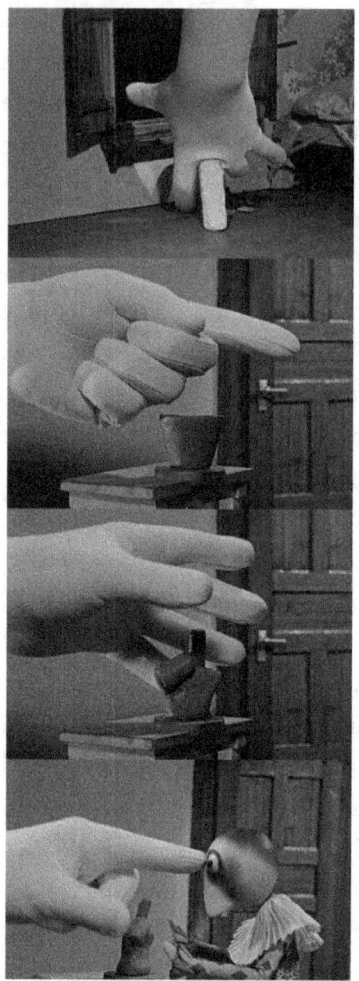

Figure 1.3 Four gestural attitudes in sequence: courtesy, menace, desire and threat in *The Hand* (*Ruka*) (Jiří Trnka, 1965). Images used with permission of the Czech National Film Archive (Národní filmový archive).

However, this power is only hinted at, so the state can retain its mask of benevolence and defend against accusations of tyranny by pointing towards its previous gestures of goodwill.

Neither a static image nor a disembodied signifier could adequately communicate this complex succession of emotional gestures. When the Hand points its index finger it is simultaneously a pointed '*look here*' indicated silently through gritted teeth and also the physical threat of a long, forceful finger that contains threat in itself (rather than pointing to a threat elsewhere) with its power to jab, push or crush the potter to the floor. A sentence from Gilberto Perez's *The Material Ghost* (2001) chimes here with double meaning: 'The photographic image is an index because it is an imprint taken directly from the things represented; and it is also an index because, like a pointing finger, it tells us to look at those things.'[97] If we take the 'pointing finger' to be the very 'thing' represented (as in the example above) the sentence folds in upon itself to become self-recurring. The finger is an icon which points at itself, the thing, which is an icon, etc.

A visual representation of this paradox is M. C. Escher's 1948 lithograph *Drawing Hands*, in which two hands seem to draw each other in an endless loop.[98] Demonstratively, the Hand of Trnka's film is unresolvable as icon or thing, possessing a frightening ambivalence for the viewer, since they can never know for sure at what level of reality (sign or thing) it should be read. This is the irreconcilable difference at the heart of allegory. To quote Elana Gomel: 'The allegorical text is always double, split in the middle by the gap between the literal and the figurative, the wrapping and the message, the husk and the kernel.'[99] That the Hand is possessed of a figurative capacity in its ability to sign and gesture, but is simultaneously a blunt instrument, a fleshy thing, makes it an allegorical figure par excellence, embodying the very sign/thing split that characterizes the allegorical form. Gomel's metaphor of the husk and kernel is apt when we consider that in *The Hand* we only ever see the white glove that houses the Hand itself. Thus, the glove functions like the sign for the Hand, hiding the inner thing, even as it outwardly communicates the Hand's intentions.

Hands have also been used historically to embody abstract ideals, such as power and resistance (the raised fist of the Black Power salute), divine suffering and grace (Christ's stigmata), refined aesthetic sensibility (Michel Sittow's famous portrait of Henry VII *c*. 1500) or peace/victory (the 'V' salute). The latter case is a replicable sign and yet the subtleties of its meaning are dependent upon context. Richard Nixon making a 'V' after a military victory, for instance, carries connotations (unabashed militarism, evocation of Churchill, appeal to populism) very different from the trend for young Japanese women to make the sign in photographs (happiness, friendship, celebration). Moreover, a gesture may be *both* a sign *and* icon. Nixon's 'V' is intended to be read linguistically as signifying 'victory', yet his making of the sign before photographers was also a self-conscious attempt to create an iconic image and a personal signature linked to his public-political persona. Finally, behind all this, may be a simple display of power.

Trnka captures these complexities in a dense montage of images that begins when the Hand, tired of attempting to reshape the potter's clay and having failed in its attempt to bribe him over the telephone, sneaks a television set into his room and bombards the artist with an exultant sequence of pro-Hand propaganda.

Michael Brooke describes this sequence as a 'virtuoso montage' that 'demonstrates the image's potency as a political tool: hands hold scales of justice; the torch of the Statue of Liberty; Napoleon's hand tucked into his waistcoat; a mailed fist; a boxing glove; the accusing finger; the clasped handshake; even the silhouetted rabbit trick'.[100] Not only does this establish in a threatening fashion the omnipotence of the Hand and reassert the previously established gestural motif of the aggressively pointed finger, it also positions the Hand as having omnipotence in language and, as such, a stranglehold on meaning. The hand bearing the torch of the Statue of Liberty, for instance, is both a sign of freedom and, metonymically, America. It marks the entrance to the 'Land of the Free' both figuratively and literally. The Hand holds power over both signifier and signified.

Iconic reminders of violence carry the clear threat of real physical violence, as when the Hand pushes the potter's head down into one of his clay pots. As such, the final pose adopted by the Hand may at first glance seem incongruously playful. It is the shadow puppet of a rabbit, cast by the Hand. However, Stephen Russell-Gebbett perceptively notes this shows the Hand 'is capable of illusion. It can appear to be something that it is not'.[101] In this moment the Hand is shown as phantasmal. The rabbit is the dark shadow of power. At the end of the film the potter is killed not by the Hand itself but by one of his own pots falling upon his head as he accidentally knocks it down from atop a wardrobe. The potter, worked into a frenzy of paranoia, anger and fear, is killed by his own art. Though Trnka needs the embodied Hand to effectively communicate its threat, it is actually the internalized fear of the Hand that is death to the dissident artist.

Allegory's limits

Michal Bregant, director of the Czech National Film Archive, characterizes Trnka's work as not autobiographical, but notes that the concept of the individualistic hero carries personal undertones across his filmography.[102] From the Springman outwitting the SS, to the young lovers of *Midsummer Night's Dream* refusing to acquiesce to the marriage demands placed upon them, to the potter refusing to make tributes to the domineering Hand, it is Trnka's individualism which sets his films at odds with political orthodoxy. While the Soviet state endorsed efficiency, collectivization and progress, Trnka's films celebrate daydreaming, the whims of the individual and tend to be backwards-looking and nostalgic. The potter in *The Hand* makes his ceramics not to be of useful service to the state but merely due to the joy in their own creation. He resists the notion of his art being co-opted towards a larger, political agenda. In such an environment, to make agenda-less art is – ironically – to hold an agenda and renouncing political ideology becomes the artist's message.

This radical individualism can be reconciled with Trnka's more conservative appeal to rootedness through Heidegger's concept of authenticity. Charles Guignon explains that Heidegger's 1927 philosophical treatise *Being and Time* (*Sein und Zeit*) 'attempts to combat the "groundlessness" (*bodenlosigkeit*) of the contemporary world by uncovering enduring values and meanings'.[103] To refuse ideology is not to be without values. In order to live authentically, we must shrug off the concerns of *das Mann* and the codes and conventions they impose upon us[104] and instead root ourselves in the experience of Being.

Trnka's relationship with allegory is problematic because the value he places upon the undifferentiated relationship between the peasant and her local environment or the artisan and his raw materials is potentially disrupted or transformed by the metaphorical register which allegory traditionally operates within. Simile, for instance, opens a rift between signifier and signified through forcing a linguistic comparison between two things that, in reality, are unalike. As has been established, Trnka communicates his theme of rootedness through a visual emphasis upon similitude, not difference.

In *Old Czech Legends* the visual similarity between staffs and tree branches shows the Czechs' civilization is fundamentally rooted in – and not dissimilar to – the natural world. In *Romance with a Double Bass* the heroine's body is not *compared* to a double bass through simile – instead, her form fits perfectly within the instrument's case, becoming a substitute for the missing instrument via its similitude. Likewise, meaning adheres within these cinematic objects themselves (the gestures of the Hand or the song of the nightingale) not through comparisons. Their usefulness derives from their inherent material qualities (the springiness of the springs, the permeability of clay or the digestibility of bread) rather than from ideological abstraction or transformation. Allegory bids us to look beneath the surface of things to unearth the secret meanings hidden there. Trnka's cinema tells us we should meet things on their own terms and adhere to the material surface of things – and yet, he uses allegory to communicate this message, to communicate his spiritual and poetic defence of permanent, nationalistic, traditional values and virtues in the face of ideological abstraction, propaganda and technological advancement.[105] Trnka's films propagate rootedness in the natural world through the artificial, cultivated form of allegory.

In 1962 Trnka produced two films which allegorize the potential dangers of unchecked technological advancement, *The Cybernetic Grandma* and *The Passion*. The critiques made by these films complement and coincide with those made by Václav Havel in works he published as a dissident in the 1960s and 1970s and, later, as president of Czechoslovakia/the Czech Republic – ideas rooted in Havel's academic study of the writings of Heidegger. One of these films, *The Cybernetic Grandma*, makes its allegorical critiques through metonymy, while the other, *The Passion*, does so through abstracted metaphor and simile. Explaining the failure of *The Passion* to sufficiently communicate its allegorical message therefore illuminates the success of Trnka's typical allegorical strategy which, as argued, tends to work by providing microcosmic examples of objects and things used by humans in their local environments, rather than through semantic abstraction or non-pictorial language.

Visual simile in *Passion*

Trnka's *Passion* allegorizes the dangers implicit in unimpeded progress when this progress is untethered to a concrete and collectively rooted system of moral values. The life of the unnamed male protagonist is depicted at various stages of maturity from infancy to old age. As per the title, the protagonist's passion is for speed – an obsession which causes him to experience a series of accidents, the last one of which results in his death. These accidents mark the end of each of the film's vignettes, delineated by the character's age (infant, child, adolescent, adult, pensioner) and vehicle (toy car, scooter, bicycle, motorcycle, electric scooter). The film is marked by its formal playfulness and high degree of visual stylization in its backgrounds.

Boček, in describing *Passion*, puts great emphasis upon the 'compression and economy'[106] with which Trnka communicates his thesis through a series of condensed potent images. Boček states this was a 'new style' for Trnka, incorporating aspects of the animated cartoon into the puppet film.[107] By this Boček means in *Passion* Trnka's approach involves a level of stylization and economy of expression which had only previously been seen in cellular animation. In addition to these aesthetic elements Trnka also uses abstracted and hyperbolic visual metaphor in a way more typical of a Warner Brothers, Disney or Fleischer Studios cartoon than of his own more literal and concrete approach.

To explain: When, in a 'Looney Tunes' cartoon, Wile E. Coyote runs off a cliff, he hangs suspended in mid-air until his realization there is no longer solid ground beneath him. Such a moment follows the magical belief that one's thoughts can influence the external world of things. In doing so it literalizes a series of clichés: 'the power of positive thinking', 'the only thing to fear is fear itself', 'if you believe, it will happen', etc., which would otherwise be rhetorical or abstract. Working within this mode is a marked departure from how Trnka generally communicates meaning in his films, in which concrete examples illustrate evident truths without rhetorical transformation. So, in *The Czech Year* the tradition of baking *koláče* is worth preserving implicitly due to the labour it requires and the pleasure this labour brings. In *Old Czech Legends* the Czech civilization is founded on an agricultural past and we can see this literally in how the peasants' roofs are thatched from the dried stalks of grains. These may be micro examples (baking *koláče* is merely one Czech tradition; homes are just one aspect of civilization) but they stand in for larger ideas (tradition should be preserved; civilization should be seen as an extension of nature, not its enemy) through synecdoche, not simile. *The Hand* works within a more abstract metaphorical register since 'the hand of the state' is already a figure of speech which condenses various non-tangible aspects of sociopolitical power to illustrate the tangible impact such power has upon citizens' daily lives. However, as has been demonstrated, the Hand itself makes recourse to the same means of coercion employed by the state but at a micro level. The

Hand pushing the potter's head down into one of his clay pots isn't a symbolic substitute for physical violence but a real example of physical violence.

By contrast, *Passion* operates at a high level of both visual and metaphorical abstraction. For instance, from 6:08 to 7:23 the protagonist feeds a bust of Beethoven, a volume of Goethe, a bouquet of flowers and some dozen chess pieces into the engine of his vehicle, which magically function as fuel causing the vehicle to accelerate. Clearly, in reality, some of these objects are more combustible than others. In opposition to the *springiness* of the Springman's springs conferring upon him the ability to jump, the material properties of these objects have no bearing upon their use by the racer. Instead, the objects function as symbols representing different aspects of culture which require slow contemplation – classical music and literature, romance, the enjoyment of complex games of strategy. The fact the motorist merely uses these materials to provide his vehicle with fuel represents his inability to appreciate the things in life which require patience and cultivation to enjoy. When the chess knights are shown via cross-section within the belly of the electric scooter's engine, they are depicted leaping up and down in a stampede, producing smoke. Viewers are not being asked to pay any heed to the thermodynamics at work here, but to understand that objects which connote a game of patience have been ironically repurposed as a tool of speed and to enjoy the cartoon illogic and the pun on 'horsepower'.

A potential weakness of Trnka's approach here recalls the flaw of using beautifully wrought artifice to illustrate the limitations of artifice in *The Emperor's Nightingale* – namely, that *Passion* becomes an accidental reaffirmation of the very thing it is attempting to criticize. This is due to more than just the fact that the film moves between its vignettes at a faster speed than in any other film by Trnka, save *The Merry Circus*. Since the objects of the film (chess pieces, bust of Beethoven, etc.) are immediately transformed into symbols, utilized for a quick joke or allegorical riff, the audience is never asked to slow down and contemplate the materiality of these objects or their existence within the film's world. As such, we are not offered an alternative mode of engagement to that practised and enjoyed by the film's protagonist. *Passion* therefore can be considered a curious diversion for Trnka rather than, as Boček states, a 'preparation'[108] for *The Cybernetic Grandma* of the same year, since the latter film extends Trnka's traditional method of illustrating objects' value through metonymic demonstration of their material qualities. Rather, *The Cybernetic Grandma* furthers Trnka's cinematic valuation of rootedness by divesting the concept of some of its mytho-nationalist associations, focusing instead upon rootedness as a form of resistance to technological abstraction – a critique he successfully communicates not via dialogue or narration but through the embodied form of a child's red wooden ball. At this final juncture of his career, Trnka's defence of ontological rootedness complements and coincides with arguments made by Václav Havel in works he published as a dissident in the 1970s and, later, as president – arguments rooted in Havel's study of Heidegger.

Technological abstraction in *The Cybernetic Grandma*

For a film with an often bewildering spatial geography, *The Cybernetic Grandma* has a straightforward plot. A young girl lives alone with her grandma. A message delivered by flying machine prompts the grandma to take the child, who brings with her a red wooden ball, on a journey through the (partially mechanized) countryside to a strange metallic facility. After retrieving a ticket which is hung around the child's neck, the grandmother encourages her granddaughter to enter an elevator-like compartment which brings her onto a moving runway and into a transparent flying pod. The pod transports the girl deep into the facility, where she traverses stark corridors of confusing geometric design, following the path of her rolling red ball. Eventually she finds the titular 'Cybernetic Grandma', a robot created to replace her real grandma. However, the Cybernetic Grandma proves itself altogether too eager to parent its ward, becoming manic and dangerous in the relentless execution of its duties. The girl's real grandma appears and shuts down the Cybernetic Grandma, returning the child to her arms.

Trnka deploys various techniques, some simple and some complex, to leave the viewer in no doubt this technological landscape is dystopian. The sound design matches shrill discordant noises with the artefacts of technology. The flying machine, which resembles a latex hand attached to metal helicopter blades, burbles like a stenograph. In its splicing of the human form with technology, its design recalls the photographic cut-ups of Czech avant-gardist

Karel Teige. His *Collage #225* (1942), for instance, depicts a pale artificial hand sprouting from the landscape. In the foreground a woman in a full-body stocking reclines on the grass before a giant ornament, in which a giant beetle hangs suspended in the air.

In *Cybernetic Grandma*, as in Teige's collage, the countryside has been de-naturalized and rendered strange. Birdsong, overlaid upon dismal organ music, begins to seem eerily repetitive and mechanical. When the girl and grandmother appear to be passing through some kind of heathland, a bird's-eye shot reveals it to fringe an enormous empty motorway of black and white. A dilapidated wooden bridge is one of the only 'traditional' objects passed upon the journey. Made from natural materials, it has been left to fall by the wayside in a world where technological equipment is kept gleaming and clean.

There is a sense, as in Teige, that modernity has alienated people from being rooted within a 'natural' environment, leaving them stranded amid incomprehensible fragments of technology.

This theme of modern man's alienation from nature is returned to repeatedly by Václav Havel in his writings, where it always carries a moral impetus. When in *Summer Meditations* – a manifesto-like work outlining his presidential plans for a newly independent Czechoslovakia – he writes elegiacally about the nation's 'once-picturesque countryside', he implores the Czechs to re-establish a universal harmony with nature, to gather up the fragments of the country and 'renew the old connections between its elements'.[109] Havel appeals to a primordial, ontological rootedness which prefigures the parochial rootedness of Skrodzka's definition of the phrase. His desire for the Czechs is not merely that they attend to *beings* in the sense of the forms and things which constitute their daily lives, but that they reconnect with the unifying *Being* which is the necessary precondition from which all these other beings exist. Technological advancement challenges this rootedness in Being because, according to Heidegger, as it reveals the world to *Dasein*[110] it unfailingly orders what is revealed (including, of course, ourselves) into 'standing reserve' – that is, mere resources to be exploited for their/our instrumental (rather than intrinsic) value.[111] Thus mechanization (or, in Heidegger's terminology, 'enframing')[112] enacts a process of disenchantment by which, in Havel's technophobic philosophy, humans are plucked from the 'experience' of Being and thrown into a world of paltry 'existences'.[113] Since Havel sees this as the existential fate of modern man in post-industrial society, he elevates the figures of the peasant and child to a high moral and spiritual plateaux, since they are, writes Havel, 'more intensely rooted in what some philosophers call "the natural world", or *Lebenswelt*, than most modern adults'.[114] The peasant and child have not experienced the epistemological fall from grace which leads modern man to see himself as separate from Being and thus relate to the natural world as a series of resources to be conquered or exploited. They are thus redemptive figures who experience 'the "worldhood" of the world'[115] on a practical, intuitive and meaningful level.[116]

It is no coincidence therefore that Trnka casts his heroes as a little girl and a peasant grandmother. *The Cybernetic Grandma* is not as clear an allegory as *The Hand*, but it carries a principal moral message, much the same as Havel's. Namely, technology can never replace human relations and alienates us from a stable sense of home and hearth. In this regard, Trnka's career traces an interesting trajectory, moving from the agricultural traditions and pastoralism evident in *The Czech Year* or *Old Czech Legends* towards the fragmented technological future of *The Cybernetic Grandma* and the apartment-dwelling artist of *The Hand*. With this shift comes a change in mise-en-scène and cinematography. Trnka's earlier works are often tranquil, with clearly delineated spaces traced by a slow moving camera, with exceptions only made for battles and celebrations. By contrast, the cinematography of *The Hand* becomes increasingly feverish, splintered and chaotic as the film progresses, as abstract spaces and iconography start to take up more and more of the frame and the artist becomes increasingly panicked.

The Cybernetic Grandma is the apex of such discordance. Some shots are up on screen for mere seconds and are often arranged in an order which makes it difficult for the viewer to make sense of the space being moving through. Some very simple cinematic (or even, proto-cinematic) techniques augment our sense of confusion. One hallway passed through by the little girl is carpeted with tessellating Necker cubes so the girl is literally walking across an optical illusion. The most innovative of these techniques is one also used in several films of the contemporaneous French New Wave. The grandmother carries with her a device that serves as a Polaroid camera and takes several pictures during her journey. Occasionally Trnka will have a photo fill the entire frame and do so unannounced so it seems that the film's action has suddenly come to a stop. The photograph is then moved away from the camera and we realize we were occupying the point of view (POV) of the girl, looking at the photograph, who is now in a different position to that pictured. In one instance, the child looks at a photograph of herself on a swing. The image itself is static, but is moved back and forth across the screen in a movement that resembles the swinging, creating an odd, vertiginous effect, as though reality has been replaced with Baudrillardian simulacra.

The net result is that we lack (visual, spatial) anchorage as viewers. In this way, Trnka seeks to replicate for his audience at the experiential, phenomenological level, the experience of his child protagonist, bewildered by this unnatural, technological landscape. Whenever the camera spins wildly, the film cuts abruptly, the architecture is bewildering, a scene is dimly lit and there are pools of darkness on screen, or else when the frame is treated as an abstract space, with technological objects, symbols and numbers set flying across it, the girl's red ball helps orientate us. It is a simple, unchanging, primary-coloured, ever-recognizable shape, almost a Platonic 'simple object'. It often occupies centre-frame, allowing us to track its movements, giving the viewer anchorage within any especially bewildering space. Its function is as simple as can be. Throughout her journey, the ball becomes the material connection to her previous life within a more stable and rural (although increasingly mechanized) environment.

It is appropriate therefore that when the child finally meets the Cybernetic Grandma, the robot pitches the ball down a seemingly infinite chasm. Symbolically this moment captures the loss of the simple object – the object that knows its place, has a defined function and does not pretend to

Figure 1.4 The ball helps the viewer and child to navigate abstracted, technological interiors, functioning as a point of stability in *The Cybernetic Grandma* (*Kybernetická Babicka*) (Jiří Trnka, 1962). Images used with permission of the Czech National Film Archive (Národní filmový archive).

be a grandma. This incident is equivalent to when Havel's medieval peasant encounters a factory for the first time and drops to his knees, believing it to be the work of the devil.[117] Child and peasant are no longer grounded in a stable sense of 'being' but set adrift 'into the world of "existences"'.[118] The profound influence of Heidegger upon Havel's thinking is evident in such a statement. For Heidegger, along with other 'conservative revolutionaries', technology, 'despite its contribution to the reduction of drudgery, has not solved the main problem of humanity: How to live in an authentically human way?'[119] This sentiment is given its burlesque and parodic fulfilment in the figure of the Cybernetic Grandma, which is unable to be authentically human.

The Cybernetic Grandma is composed of materials metonymically related to a (generic Czech) grandmother – its body is a plush, comfy chair and its wings resemble doilies. The chair, the body of the robot, provides the space where a real grandma would sit, structuring the Cybernetic Grandma around this notable absence. Jean Baudrillard says of robots in *The System of Objects* (1968): 'The robot is a symbolic microcosm of both man and the world, which is to say that it simultaneously replaces ... man and the world, synthesizing absolute functionality with absolute anthropomorphism.'[120] The Cybernetic Grandma is designed to replace a real grandmother, but its excessive functionality renders it perversely *too fit* for purpose. For Baudrillard, as the concept of 'functionality' becomes a selling point, it becomes abstracted to the point of no longer connoting greater ease of use.[121] To explain this, Baudrillard uses the example of the 'tail fin', built into cars in the late 1950s as a mark of style. Baudrillard recalls this as a triumph 'on the part of the object ... the car's fins became the sign of victory over space – and they were purely a sign, because they bore no direct relationship to that victory'.[122] Tail fins are not useful in any practical sense; instead they dramatize the notion of speed. He goes on to assert: 'Tail fins are our modern allegory.'[123]

Baudrillard's notion of allegory here is similar to my own – namely, that of objects encoded with allegorical meaning which transcends their use value. The Cybernetic Grandma is such an object, allegorizing the desire for care and comfort, which it is unable to provide. Alienated from meaningful human relations and community, this hyper-functional object, with its ability to play, skip, talk, clean a child and screen short movies, is useless. Its proficiency at throwing a ball is such that it far exceeds the child's abilities. The movie it shows the child – a bizarre and violent parody of Trnka's own *Two Little Frosts* (*Dva mrazici*, 1954) – scares her. Ultimately, the Cybernetic Grandma cannot offer true love and affection and it falls to the real grandmother to save the day and rescue her granddaughter, restoring familial harmony. Once the grandmother has defeated the Cybernetic Grandma (through turning it off), she settles herself peacefully into its lap. The Cybernetic Grandma is restored to its functional purpose as a chair. The space that signified the missing grandmother is filled and the object is no longer hyper-functional and complex but a simple chair with a single, simple function.

Simple objects and anti-political politics in Týrlová and Trnka

Simple objects with simple functions are accorded great respect in Trnka's work. Normal household springs allow the Springman to defeat the SS, the potter-harlequin's flowerpots are synonymous with art, nature and authenticity in the face of state oppression in *The Hand* and the child's ball offers us a centre-point of stability in a bewildering technological future in *The Cybernetic Grandma*.

Hermína Týrlová shares Trnka's affection for small domestic objects. *A Little Speckle-Ball* (*Míček Flíček*, 1955) concerns a little round ball, similar to the one in *The Cybernetic Grandma*, getting kidnapped by a disturbed kite. The heroes of the film, a kindly grandfather and grandmother, rescue the ball and adopt it as their child. In *Knot in the Handkerchief* (*Uzel na kapesníku*, 1958) a handkerchief saves a house from flooding by alerting the neighbourhood clothes. Not least of course, the heroic toys of *Revolution in Toyland* band together and defeat a Gestapo agent.

The objects in these films exist across a wide spectrum of anthropomorphism. The flowerpots, springs and red ball are not anthropomorphized in the slightest, while some of the toys of *Revolution* resemble tiny people. Yet, however sentient they might look, these objects are not magical but earthbound. Conceivably, Týrlová's knotted handkerchief is blown to life by gusts of wind, the toys are a mere hallucination of the semi-conscious Gestapo agent, the little speckled ball is merely knocked back and forth between people and things.

Figure 1.5 An elderly couple treat a bouncing ball as though it were their infant son in *A Little Speckle-Ball* (*Míček Flíček*) (Hermína Týrlová, 1955). Image used with permission of the Czech National Film Archive (Národní filmový archive).

These are everyday objects depicted within their local environments. Such objects seem to resist ideological imperatives from above by virtue of their everydayness. Partly this is because ideology is a function of power expressed 'top-down' from the state and its apparatus and thus seems incommensurate with the smallness, the humbleness and groundedness of the private domestic realm. Secondly, the everyday world of work and play is always already charged with emotional meaningfulness which connects people to the objects they use and the places they use them within and so refuses to provide the vacuum of meaning expediently filled by ideology. Tautologically, such objects resist being co-opted by ideology because as humble objects they carry such little ideological baggage. These are humble objects, important to children and simple living and, as such, are fundamentally antithetical to political grandstanding or the dogma of Soviet (Socialist) Realism. Artistic works stubbornly focused around such everyday objects are politically provocative by virtue of their seeming refusal to engage with politics.

Havel, in a passage towards the end of his 1984 article 'Six Asides about Culture', maintains:

> Hundreds of examples testify that the regime prosecutes most rigorously not what threatens it overtly but has little artistic power, but whatever is artistically most penetrating, even though it does not seem all that overtly 'political'. The essence of the conflict, that is, is not a confrontation between two ideologies ... but a clash between an anonymous, soulless, immobile and paralyzing ('entropic') power, and life, humanity, being and its mystery.[124]

For Havel, films that show life with all its chance contingencies and imperfections pose a threat to the regime because they illustrate through example that Being is irreducible to any singular truth dogmatically imposed from above, since life can never be fully controlled or predicted, nor its mystery fully understood by humans. In his later 1988 article 'Stories and Totalitarianism', Havel extends this argument further, arguing that 'the totalitarian system is in essence (and in principle) directed against the story'.[125] Havel states his preference for films which are not obviously political but structured loosely around individuals, providing 'a free vision of life as a whole'.[126] He writes: 'I can well imagine a film about nothing more than love and jealousy, yet where this freedom would not be lacking.'[127]

Havel's rhetoric illustrates how the celebration of artisanal labour, simple living and rural life, against the encroachment of alienation via increasing mechanization, in Trnka's work, is politically resistant, despite his films seeming tranquil and non-combative. The objects in these works carry their allegorical meaning not heavily through the abstract symbolism of ideology but lightly through direct and forthright metonymy. The energetic will of the Czech people is contained within the *springiness* of a couple of old springs from a sofa, the labour of the Czech peasantry is embodied in its *koláče* and *vánočka*, the bodies of draft animals return to the soil from which they came to continue the life of the Czechs, the threat of the Hand is *both* phantasmal *and* embodied because of its ability to be icon, symbol and real thing all at once, the Cybernetic Grandma fails to be a grandmother because it is composed of metonymic signs which signal a grandmother's absence – its hyper-functionality rendering it useless. Finally, the little red ball provides visual anchorage for both the viewer and the child protagonist to follow and, in opposition to the complex technology represented by the Cybernetic Grandma, is a near-Platonic idealization of the simple object that gains political resistance precisely because it is so adamantly non-ideological.

The way in which these objects are politically resistant due to their domestic objecthood has something of a parallel in Havel's contentious notion of 'anti-political' or 'non-political' politics.[128] Havel never provided a simple explanation of this concept, despite its repeated usage in his writings. In an address at New York University in 1991, Havel characterized it as politics with a conscience, in which politicians act in good faith, without deceit or recourse to politicking.[129] However, by 1991, Havel was President of Czechoslovakia and his definition of 'anti-politics' had shifted since his first formulation of the concept as a dissident. Reducing anti-politics to just politics without the politicking may have been neoliberal capitulation, simplifying for his American audience a previously more complex metaphysical idea. Earlier in 1984, Havel asserted anti-politics to be the 'politics of man, not of the apparatus ... growing from the heart, not from a thesis'.[130] The parallel with Trnka's allegorical objects is more apparent in this definition since it situates the importance of politics as an authentic engagement with everyday life, rather than an ideology imposed from above.

Elsewhere, scholars and critics of Havel have attempted to clarify the meaning of anti-politics. Popescu argues that anti-politics puts great emphasis upon civil society and civic virtues, while de-emphasizing the role of the state.[131] Simon Smith writes less about Havel's own intentions in developing the idea than in how it was received, claiming Havel's anti-politics found their most 'receptive social milieu' in rural, rather than urban, communities.[132]

Anti-politics, then, concerns itself with how politics might govern and enrich daily life on a micro, individual level as experienced within local (predominantly rural) environments. Popescu explains that this emphasis upon the micro aspects of civic life coincides with a rejection of, or suspicion towards, political ideology:

> Havel's difficulty in considering political institutions comes from the fact that he believes in small associations that are temporary, and dedicated to one goal usually related to a particular community. Individuals involved in such ad-hoc associations are highly motivated problem-solvers rather than the bearers of an overarching ideological creed.[133]

This approach to problem-solving is one applied by the protagonists of Trnka's works in the objects they find ready to hand. The springs in *Springman and the SS* and the little red ball in *The Cybernetic Grandma* are useful objects that serve individuals faced with specific problems. The people these objects serve are the young, the disenfranchised and the rural poor. While the boy racer of *Passion* (who is notably more bourgeois-urban and less rural-working class than most of his fellow protagonists) might be commended for his improvisational approach to the objects he finds – such as his repurposing a clock's wind-up mechanism to power a toy car or blowing a toy windmill against the back wheel of his scooter to get it to accelerate – invariably these items break, malfunction or cause an accident, transforming from useful objects into useless things. Though the relationship between the objects' repurposing and their rebellion against human use is not as clear in *Passion* as it is in *Revolution in Toyland*, *Passion*'s protagonist is punished unwaveringly enough for the viewer to infer that his repurposing of objects is too aggressively in pursuit of speed to fit Trnka's rather more contemplative designs.

Politically non-political objects

There is a tension in discussing Trnka's filmography as simultaneously political and non-political as I have done in this chapter. It seems paradoxical that objects should be both ideologically empty while laden with political meaning. Perhaps this very contradiction is built into Havel's definition as a means for anti-politics to escape being codified within a technocratic framework. If meaning is to be drawn from life then it must be grasped in all of its multivalent irrationality and messy plurality. Such messiness cannot be communicated in a single ideological message or creed but only defined against what it is not. Havel provides his most clear-sighted negative definition of anti-politics in 'Politics and Conscience' (1984) when he writes that it is 'politics not as the technology of power and manipulation, of cybernetic rule over humans or as the art of the utilitarian, but politics as one of the ways of seeking and achieving meaningful lives'.[134]

The Hand is Trnka's stand against 'power and manipulation' and *The Cybernetic Grandma* is his critique of 'cybernetic rule', but Trnka would never so plainly disparage the 'utilitarian' and Havel was mistaken to do so. The simple use of objects can restore us to the state of rootedness which Havel extolled through his career. Trnka's films show us ideology and use-value need not go hand in hand, but that the most useful objects can take on allegorical significance in the quiet fight against oppression.

2

Jan Švankmajer and the network of things

Introduction to Švankmajer

An egg as heavy as a metal weight, a wind-up chicken tethered to a length of rope, a soup spoon peppered with holes, a flapping shoe with hobnail teeth, a dirtied and dilapidated glove puppet of Punch/*Kašpárek*, a chandelier made from human bones, a shoe covered in butter, candy wrappers hiding screws and a swinging pair of dentures tangled up in razor wire – these marvellous and abject things are all from the short films of Czech Surrealist Jan Švankmajer.

Švankmajer's films contain a wealth of *stuff*. It is an irreconcilable tension when engaging with his work that one feels compelled to seek concrete meaning from the dilapidated things on screen, while remaining keenly aware of the futility of this effort, since the meaning these things produce is often proto-linguistic – a 'sense-meaning' that precedes articulation. The gap between the viewing subject and these silent yet expressive things can never be bridged. The textures of the material world remain an alien script, inscrutable to human viewers. However, cinema can allow us the pleasure of experiencing these textures through our eyes and, gradually – if we immerse ourselves in the experience of viewing – through our entire body. Laura Marks refers to this kind of spectatorship as 'haptic visuality', in which 'the eyes themselves function like organs of touch'.[1] If we consider Švankmajer's films to be politically subversive, it is not because they provide a directly political message or slogan with which an audience might resist a given political ideology; rather, the experience of viewing Švankmajer's work can provide a glimpse of a mode of being far removed from the stifling political ideology under which many of his films were made. Instead of thinking dogmatically, functionally or bureaucratically, the viewer is invited to think haptically and sensuously. Švankmajer makes us consider the possibility that artistic resistance in the face of censorship and oppression does not require rhetorical interrogations of specific historical events but feelings, textures and a means of engaging with the world that is not merely visual but tactile. Jonathan Owen offers a concise justification of this mode of engaging with Švankmajer's output, arguing, 'the political quality' of his work 'is as much evident in its aesthetic organization as in the elements of direct critique that it offers'.[2]

Peter Hames asserts the 'anti-Stalinist implications' of two of Švankmajer's most aggressively tactile shorts – *Dimensions of Dialogue* (*Možnosti dialogu*, 1982) and *The Pendulum, the Pit and Hope* (*Kyvadlo, jáma a naděje*, 1983) – are clear even while Švankmajer 'aims at a point beneath such surface realities'.[3] That is to say, though neither film contains any explicitly anti-Stalinist imagery or dialogue, they succeed in expressing a world view which is clearly antithetical to Stalinist orthodoxy.

In terms of the axes of allegory, Švankmajer's films rarely invite clear, singular allegorical readings, but rather, engage pluralistically with universal political conflicts such as the struggle between freedom and oppression– though the ending of *Lunacy* (*Šílení*, 2005) suggests the artist is always inclined towards choosing freedom, even when so doing potentially entails the risk of harm.

Švankmajer and censorship

Švankmajer has been plagued by censorship throughout his career. He was effectively banned from film production from 1972 through to 1979[4] and was only allowed to resume film-making in the 1980s under the instruction he was to produce adaptations of approved literary sources.[5] Švankmajer informs Hames that *The Flat* (*Byt*, 1968) and *The Garden* (*Zahrada*, 1968) were both taken by the regime and locked away in vaults, while *Jabberwocky, or Straw Hubert's Clothes* (*Žvahlav aneb šatičky slaměného Huberta*, 1971) and *Dimensions of Dialogue* were both banned, with the latter used by the government to illustrate precisely the kind of film-making which should not be produced under Socialist Realism.[6] Additionally, *The Ossuary* (*Kostnice*, 1970), *Leonardo's Diary* (*Leonardův deník*, 1972) and *The Pendulum, the Pit and Hope* were all attacked by the censor.[7]

If we agree with Hames[8] and Švankmajer[9] that the latter's work is concerned with themes more intrinsic to civilization than mere transitory phenomena, such as which political party is governing a nation at a given time, what aspect(s) of the artist's animation could have prompted the KSČ to remove so many from public circulation? Since the authorities cannot have been objecting to any specific political messages within the films, we might recall William Moritz's argument that ambiguity *in and of itself* is threatening to regimes which seek to enforce clear, unambiguous ideals upon a compliant populace.[10] For artists working under a totalitarian government, aesthetics can never be divorced from politics. From the regime's point of view, the degree of an artist's stylistic deviation from state-endorsed orthodoxy correlates inversely with their commitment to furthering the ideals of the state.[11] Perhaps the most notorious example of this zero-sum equation being made by the Soviet state came in 1939 when Vsevolod Meyerhold's passionate defence of formalism at the 'Conference of Theatre Directors' resulted in his arrest, torture and subsequent execution.

Even if censors could not pinpoint precisely what was ideologically offensive about Švankmajer's work, they must have experienced with suspicion and distrust that physical sense of anxiety which Švankmajer's juddering, spasmodic editing and harsh, discordant sound design can engender in his audience. The skeletal corpses, the mouldering fruit, the dead insects – all of these motifs communicate something diseased and unhealthy about the artist's outlook that could only be viewed negatively by an ideology, such as communism, that values health and purity of mind and spirit. One can hardly imagine the perfectly synchronized and sculpted gymnasts or the upright and muscular workers of Soviet propaganda enjoying Švankmajer's work.[12] Švankmajer himself has provocatively referred to the output of the Czech Surrealist Group, of which his work is a central part, as being 'an abscess on the body of Czech culture',[13] evoking how unmistakably perverse and visceral such work appears when placed in contrast to his country's mainstream, socially sanctioned culture.

Švankmajer's relationship with Surrealism

Švankmajer has been a member of the Czech Surrealist Group since 1970. Surrealism as an artistic movement offers its practitioners a radical way of living and working that allows the artist to transcend, subvert and evade utilitarian ways of seeing the world. Since the world, for most people, is experienced as a materialist matrix of things and objects all acting upon – and being acted upon by – one another, Surrealism necessarily impacts how the practitioner (and their audience) experiences and understands the physical world as encoded and policed by language and social convention. Much as how Dermot Moran describes the phenomenologist Edmund Husserl attempting to suspend all 'scientific, philosophical, cultural, and everyday assumptions'[14] in his efforts to isolate the experience of pure consciousness, the practising Surrealist wishes to suspend the commonplace moral and metaphysical assumptions about how humans should think and live within society to commune with a more primitive, even infantile, mode of being in the world. Civilization enshrines the injunctions that guard against the artist expressing these archaic desires through the symbolic order of language.

As an artist Švankmajer is engaged in an attempt to wrest himself, his world and his audience from what Antonin Artaud referred to as 'the dictatorship of words'.[15] Owen even goes so far as to argue several of Švankmajer's films can be read as 'implicit polemics against language'.[16] One means of escaping this discursive tyranny is through turning to other senses for one's means of communication, such as touch. In *Touching and Imagining: An Introduction to Tactile Art*, Švankmajer describes the process of his first collaborative investigation into tactile communication, *The Restorer* (*Restaurátéur*, 1975), from which he deduced the strength of tactility lies not in its ability to provoke recognition but in its ability to function as a catalyst for creativity and imagination.[17] Such tactile experimentation is illustrative of Švankmajer's interest in developing forms of communication that do not rely upon language, narrative or speech. It is appropriate therefore to analyse Švankmajer's films from the perspective of 'reading' the objects/things of his work for political messages, in spite of the non-verbal means of this communication.

Surrealism treats objects as conduits for the projected desires of their artist or audience. Say – to borrow an example from Charles E. Gauss – a Surrealist is sold a tomato. He then chooses to exhibit this tomato as a balloon. A Surrealist sensibility insists: 'The tomato has become a balloon for the individual who sees it as such, and that individual is not concerned whether the object is a tomato or a balloon to anyone else. It is a balloon in his imagination.'[18] By this logic the object yields to the transformative power of the mind. As such, while Surrealist activity 'may eventuate in material objects ... the existence of these as material objects is always disregarded by the surrealists. They are reinterpreted as signs of the mental'.[19]

In interview Švankmajer has identified himself as a so-called 'militant surrealist'.[20] Such phrasing evokes an ideologically rigorous approach to the movement, implying the artist is a stalwart adherent of Surrealism as expressed in its official doctrines. Therefore, if we accept Švankmajer's self-characterization, we must – ironically, to understand the ideology-transcending use of objects/things in his work – first assess the role objects/things are assigned within the manifestos and speeches of Surrealism's founder, André Breton, the ideological gatekeeper of the movement.

Objects[21] play a peripheral role within Breton's 'First Manifesto of Surrealism', subservient to the 'psychic automatism'[22] which, for the Breton of 1924, is nothing less than a fountainhead around which the world should be refashioned. Upon this point Breton is explicit, stating that when he writes of automatism he is 'not talking about the poetic consciousness of objects',[23] which he has only experienced with limited success. Contrariwise, when Švankmajer writes of his predilection for objects that 'have some kind of inner life',[24] it is precisely this poetic consciousness to which he is appealing, of which Breton – at the time of the 'First Manifesto' – was sceptical.

Yet if in 1924 Breton regarded metaphysical communion between subject and object as near impossible to obtain, by the time of his *'Qu'est-ce que le surréalisme?'* lecture given ten years later in Brussels, his position on objects had undergone some revision. In contrast to views expressed within the period which Breton, in 1934, refers to as 'the purely *intuitive* epoch of surrealism' in which thought was regarded as 'supreme over matter',[25] he now informs his Belgian audience: 'It is essentially on the *object* that surrealism has thrown most light in recent years.'[26]

Breton gave these ideas their fullest explication six months later in a lecture delivered in Švankmajer's home city of Prague. In this lecture,

'Situation de l'objet surréaliste', Breton contends: 'It is only when we have reached perfect agreement on the way in which Surrealism represents the object in general ... that there can arise the question of defining the place that the Surrealist object must take to justify the adjective Surrealist.'[27] Yet, as in the Brussels lecture the previous year, Breton defers the question – discoursing upon Hegelian aesthetic theory, the death of realism in the arts and Surrealist objets d'art – until the end of his lecture, the last few sentences of which are worth quoting in full:

> Surrealist painting and construction have now permitted the organization of perceptions with an objective tendency around subjective elements. These perceptions, through their very tendency to assert themselves as objective perceptions are of such a nature as to be bewildering and revolutionary, in the sense that they urgently call for something to answer them in outer reality. It may be predicted that in large measure this something *will be*.[28]

In this statement, which verges upon the tautological, Breton seems to suggest that since Surrealist activity has allowed imagination to encroach upon the territory of objects, it is now time for *matter to encroach upon the territory of imagination*. By the principles of dialectical materialism, the Surrealist assertion of 'subjective elements' as 'objective perceptions' demands an equal and opposite assertion from the objective world. The Surrealists have thrust forward ideals and now Breton awaits the world to thrust back matter; 'something *will be*'.

Švankmajer brings Breton's '*will be*' into being through clearing a space for things to be present on screen without their being immediately codified as nameable objects with nameable roles, meanings and functions, as defined by humans in accordance to human needs. Things, for Švankmajer, are not humans' humble servants, to be played with, eaten or otherwise used, but exist resolutely upon their own terms.

Švankmajer expands upon this idea in his 'Decalogue Manifesto' where he instructs the aspiring animator that before they 'bring an object to life' they must 'try to understand it first. Not its utilitarian function, but its inner life.'[29] He continues: 'Never violate objects! Don't tell through them your own stories, tell theirs.'[30] Clearly, Švankmajer is proselytizing here not merely within an aesthetic mode but with an ethical intent. Essential to Švankmajer's creative project is to honour the 'inner life'[31] of things, coaxing their latent content to the surface, while never imposing authorial, anthropocentric authority upon them.

Švankmajer's approach to objects necessitates scepticism towards allegory, since allegory involves imposing a further layer of meaning upon a primary, pre-existing layer. Objects in allegory exist to be read symbolically. They mean other than what they outwardly appear to mean. Consequently, Roger Cardinal argues that a strictly allegorical reading of Švankmajer's work would be fated to over-conceptualize his objects as symbols to be unravelled, thus negating the shock of their tactile immediacy.[32] Švankmajer's things don't stand in for something else but present themselves *as is*. It is along these lines that the head of the Czech Surrealist Group, Vratislav Effenberger – excerpted at length by František Dryje – positions Švankmajer's work in opposition to 'banal allegory'.[33] Instead of operating through symbolism or metaphor, Effenberger argues, Švankmajer's things are essentially metonymic, in that they partake of what they simultaneously represent. Describing a stove on which dolls' heads boil in Švankmajer's *Jabberwocky*, Effenberger writes:

> It is only when the symbol can preserve its original unclouded freshness and its happy lack of restraint that the imagery becomes a great bestower of associative perception ... An old kitchen stove, without losing its objective importance, is at the same time a hell full of sinful souls ... It is not only a comparison with hell; in its everyday use it is a hellish object itself.[34]

The stove does not exist merely as some placeholder in a parable (like Cinderella's pumpkin), interchangeable with any other object that could carry the same symbolic load, but as one of the very subjects of the film with 'objective importance'.[35]

How psychoanalysis is at once a useful tool for reading the objects of Švankmajer while also completely missing the point of the thing

To further illuminate the distinction between things having 'objective' importance and objects having 'symbolic' importance, it is worth examining *Jabberwocky* at greater length, demonstrating how a symbolic (in this case psychoanalytic) reading of the film's objects is at once *both* appropriate *and* limited, since it fails to meet these things upon their own terms.

Jabberwocky is not strictly an adaptation of the Lewis Carroll poem of the same name, though the poem is recited in voice-over at the start of film. What follows, within what appears to be a Victorian playroom, is a succession of stop-motion animated vignettes involving a plethora of objects, mostly antiquated toys – a wardrobe, a rocking horse, building blocks, a gaslight, a doll's house, two irons, a framed photographic portrait of a bearded man, toy soldiers, a chamber pot, a birdcage, porcelain dolls, a pocket knife, a set of dominoes and a suit. Švankmajer himself provides a Freudian model for the narrative of *Jabberwocky*, referring to the film in interview with Geoff Andrews as 'a Freudian record of the development of a child through all its stages: through homosexuality and sado-masochism to rebellion against the father'.[36] Psychoanalysis has historically been linked to Surrealism since the latter's origin. In the 'Second Manifesto' Breton writes: 'Surrealism believes Freudian criticism to be the first and only one with a really solid basis'.[37] Although not all artists who identify as Surrealist work within a psychoanalytic framework, many of the working practices common to Surrealism rest upon basic Freudian assumptions about the nature of the mind. The free associative play of Surrealist games such as 'exquisite corpse' (*cadavre exquis*) and the practice of automatic writing rely upon the belief that an unconscious mind operates beneath all conscious creative acts.

A psychoanalytical reading of the stop-motion animated object vignettes of *Jabberwocky* can be performed with intuitive ease, without resistance. Outwardly this ease seems to contradict Alison Frank's designation of Švankmajer's objects as 'hybrid objects'[38] which 'tend to be resistant to interpretation and simply exist in the film as a focus for a collection of diverse and sometimes contradictory meanings'.[39] However, the films Frank chooses to examine belong – as she notes – to the pre-1970 period before Švankmajer became a member of the Czech Surrealist Group.[40] *Jabberwocky*, produced after Švankmajer had become a member of the group, therefore adheres to the interpretive framework endorsed by the Surrealist movement to a degree to which the 1960s films Frank focuses upon do not. By contrast to these earlier films in which psychoanalytic praxis is simply lacking, in *Jabberwocky* such praxis is excessive to the degree that interpretation becomes redundant.

So, the objects of the film interact and play through certain rituals across the various surfaces of the playroom. A pocket knife flips itself across a table, jumping from table to chair, dramatizing early masturbatory rituals of the male child. The handle of the knife is a carved statuette and when the knife comes to rest on the table, the head of the figure is rubbed back and forth against the embroidered tablecloth. After an extended display of self-mastery, the knife, in a moment of ecstasy, spins itself into the air, then falls to the ground, the blade closing tight upon the figure which bleeds, soaking the white tablecloth in blood. Thus, onanism for the child is bound together with anxiety over damaging the penis – a fear common in puberty, which child psychoanalyst Melanie Klein details in her case studies of 'Bill' and 'Ludwig'[41] and Freud in relation to castration anxiety in his case study of 'Little Hans'.[42]

Other vignettes are amenable to similar interpretation. In another sequence, cloth dolls burrow their way out of the straw-stuffed body of a larger doll, ripping apart its body in the process. This can be seen as playing through anxieties about the mother's body and the children imagined as being inside it.[43] Elsewhere, we bear witness to the oral-sadistic cannibalistic phantasies of the child, as dolls are boiled in little metal saucepans. For the reader of Klein, this might recall the case study of Erna, who chewed up bits of paper, interpreted by Klein as representing, among other things, children.[44] More broadly, to quote David O'Kane, the film represents the 'pure world of transitional phenomena' as experienced by a child.[45]

It would seem that for every episode of the film, a corresponding incident in a case study from Klein or Freud can be found to explicate it. This is not to say that Švankmajer scripted the film with *The Psycho-Analysis of Children* (1932) or *The Interpretation of Dreams* (1899) at hand, but that the games of projection and transference he is playing are clearly lifted from psychoanalytic discourse. However, shouldn't a psychoanalytical reading offer a little more resistance? When reading the above, it feels as though the film is not illuminated but merely described. After all, these meanings are barely latent under the work's surface; they constitute the film's narrative. The film analyst is not unearthing hidden content by such means, since Švankmajer has already brought this content to the surface of the film. Providing a psychoanalytical reading of *Jabberwocky*, however elegant, is about as fruitful as observing that Norman Bates in *Psycho* (1960) is suffering from an arrested Oedipus complex, when the psychiatrist has already told us this at the end of the film.

A psychoanalytic reading, inspired by Klein, can attend to the objects of *Jabberwocky* at the symbolic level but, I would argue, fails to grasp their *objective importance*. Victoria Nelson in *The Secret Life of Puppets* (2001) similarly argues against 'the essential homocentricity of the notion of projection – that is, its assumption that human subjectivity is the source of all phenomena in the universe that cannot be explained by the empirical-materialist rules laid down by science'.[46] 'But of course', the psychoanalyst might argue, 'since objects *are not* subjects they cannot perform acts of projection and so cannot shape the world by their own means'. However, Švankmajer's cinema relies on the notion that objects may become self-shaping thingy subjects (and actively possess the desire to do so). Perhaps, to entertain this, we lose our critical distance and regress from the position of the critic to the level of the child trying to search for the life within their toys, a fantasy Bill Brown admits is 'repeatedly revealed' as 'doomed to exposure'.[47] Perhaps it is sheer childishness to continue to search for meaning within objects, when objects seem so unwilling to yield their secrets; but then, Švankmajer is a self-consciously infantile film-maker. If we are naive in our interpretations, then we are only as naive as the director whose films we interpret.

An alternative in ANT

Which critical approach allows a space for objects to exist and function as things? Psychoanalytical approaches are too insistently anthropocentric. A post-structuralist approach is too dependent upon the centrality of language (however slippery and shifting). Feminist, queer and post-colonial approaches are understandably wary of objectification, foregrounding the danger of applying human ethics to the world of things.

Thing theory is an emergent school with certain limitations. Firstly, it has heretofore generally been associated with the analysis of English and American Victorian literature, as in the work of Bill Brown or Elaine Freedgood. Brown's and Freedgood's objects remain fixed upon the page, transformed only under the gaze of the reader or in relation to their attendant socio-historical contexts. For instance, when Freedgood analyses a mahogany table in Charlotte Brontë's *Jane Eyre* (1847) she also examines the mahogany trade in the mid-nineteenth century and the table's synecdochical relationship to this trade.[48]

Such objects are inextricably bound to their value within systems of human use and exchange. They are objects framed by human desire, transforming only under the different interpretive schemata placed upon them.

An alternative critical approach which confronts the anthropocentric tendencies of the aforementioned theories by respecting that the material world is not a priori compartmentalized by human desires but exists alongside and intertwined with humans as fellow actants is ANT (actor-network-theory) as explicated and developed by Bruno Latour.

Underlying ANT is a basic assumption – that a thing can act upon another thing without there being any necessity for intent or cognition on behalf of that thing. Furthermore, this action is no less significant due to its perceived lack of intentionality. As such, ANT decentralizes the human as the sole site of influence in the world. Latour expresses this when he writes ANT 'does not limit itself to human individual actors, but extends the word actor – or actant – to *non-human, non-individual* entities'.[49] For Latour, the main theorist and proponent of ANT, each and every thing, unique at each given moment, is inextricably intertwined through mediators with other things. Within these systems of mediators and actors (Latour prefers the less anthropocentric 'actants') new combinations are constantly being formed, existing within complex webs of interconnection.

While a human may in some sense facilitate an object's action, this does not mean she/he is the sole party responsible for that action's occurrence. Intention and cognizance do not wholly determine action, for, as Latour reminds us, 'kettles "boil" water, knives "cut" meat, baskets "hold" provisions, hammers "hit" nails on the head'.[50] This radically materialist conception of the world is one that Graham Harman describes as 'a series of negotiations between a motley armada of forces, humans among them'.[51] Therefore, the world as conceived through ANT is inherently political, so long as politics is defined as any site in which there are processes of forceful relations between actants.

Politics can either be defined in terms of its formal institutions (parliaments, law courts, etc.) or else, more holistically, in terms of the interactions achieved through force, negotiation and power within any given system.[52] The lack of formal institutions among objects/things (in spite of Latour's esoteric visions of a future 'parliament of things'[53]), in combination with the fact that Švankmajer's film-making is at once thingy *and* political, predisposes me towards accepting a working definition of politics that is both inclusive and non-institutional. Herein, 'politics' is recognized as a process of power relations and negotiations within and between different assemblances of human and non-human actants. This definition of the political is, in part, a response to Neil Carter's complaint in 'Politics as if Nature Mattered' that, in the majority of attempts to define politics, nature is placed elsewhere, treated as an 'add-on' to civil society.[54] It is also inspired by Jane Bennett's guiding question to herself and other budding vibrant materialists: 'How would political responses to public problems change were we to take seriously the vitality of (nonhuman) bodies?'[55]

Non-human bodies are so central to Švankmajer's films that it would be inappropriate to deny their political centrality, insistently searching for political meaning in the scant range of human subjects who pepper his filmography. A definition of politics when discussing the political meaning of Švankmajer's work must be radically non-anthropocentric.

Carter writes that at the bottom of anthropocentrism lies 'the belief that ethical principles apply only to humans and their relations, and that human needs and interests are of the highest, perhaps exclusive, significance: humans are placed at the centre of the universe, separated from nature, and endowed with unique values'.[56] While a degree of anthropocentrism is still present in the short films of Trnka, in that his objects tend to serve human needs, for Švankmajer, the life of things is just as important as the life of humans and it is this thingy life which his films seek to honour.

The Death of Stalinism in Bohemia: The most explicitly political of Švankmajer's films

The Death of Stalinism in Bohemia (*Konec stalinismu v Čechách*, 1990) is Švankmajer's most overtly political film in the traditional sense of the word. Released after the fall of communism in Central-Eastern Europe, the film was commissioned by the BBC, who asked Švankmajer to produce a reflection upon his country's recent history in the light of the Velvet Revolution. Švankmajer himself acknowledges the film to be a work of 'propaganda' which will 'age more quickly' than his other works.[57] Certainly, much of the film's meaning is incomprehensible without a basic knowledge of twentieth-century Czech history, though photographs and newsreel footage of the principal political players in the drama (Stalin, Klement Gottwald, victims of the Slánský show trials of 1952) ensure the events depicted can be clearly identified by those with recourse to an encyclopaedia. Stephen Russell-Gebbett notes: 'Whatever the metaphorical, allegorical illustration of the political course and its impact on the people, *The Death of Stalinism in Bohemia* is an accurate enough short history of Czechoslovakia from World War II to the end of the Cold War.'[58]

ANT has, as established, a radically non-human-centred view of politics. Moreover, it is resistant to the imposition of interpretive paradigms from outside itself, which allegory necessitates. As such, *The Death of Stalinism in Bohemia* is what we might call an 'edge case' which can function as a critical litmus test. If ideas from ANT help illuminate a political reading of Švankmajer's most conventionally political, anthropocentric film, then it stands to reason that the bulk of his short films, which rarely feature human characters and adhere to a far less traditional definition of politics, will be more, not less, receptive to an ANT-inflected reading.

Stalinism in Bohemia opens with stock footage of a tower block being razed to the ground. It cuts dynamically between this footage and the film's title card and opening credits, forging a direct association between the 'Death of Stalinism in Bohemia' and the image on screen, implicitly suggesting that the tower block is symbolically equivalent to the structure of Stalinism – outmoded, bureaucratic, brutalist – and its demise. Immediately, as viewers, we are keyed into a symbolic reading of the film and its objects. However, even from this first image Švankmajer is working through metonymy, rather than metaphor. The grey, multi-storey apartment building is the concrete embodiment of Socialist Classicism in architecture, which dominated urban design in the post-war communist period. The hyper-functional uniformity of such buildings is the dogma of Stalinism given form, not only metaphorically but literally – the building expresses in and through space the ideology of the state. When such a building is destroyed, we are witnessing Stalinism destroyed in synecdoche.

After the political lives and deaths of Stalin and Klement Gottwalt are depicted in precis – a sequence which ends with portraits of both eaten by a figurative death's-head – a waterfall of grain seems to fill the screen. Victor

Margolin traces the symbolic-historical relationship between grain and the USSR, discussing how grain was exploited by the regime as a symbolic signifier for (fictitious) plenitude under collectivization. In particular, Margolin focuses on a composite portrait of Stalin by A. Zykov published in the Soviet magazine *USSR in Construction* in 1939.[59] The portrait depicts Stalin's face through a collage of different grains – millet, poppy seed, etc. Here, an enticing intersection with Švankmajer's practice is revealed since the picture recalls the composite portraits of Giuseppe Arcimboldo, court painter to Rudolf II – an influence which Švankmajer acknowledges.[60] As with Arcimboldo's paintings, the grain collage can be simultaneously read as a whole or in terms of its constituent parts. Margolin explains: 'The portrait, made up of far too many grains to count, signifies abundance, while their arrangement into an image of Stalin attributes this abundance to him. On another level, each grain might be seen to represent a Soviet citizen, or at least a farm worker.'[61] The grain is at once literally a product of collectivized farming and represents the scheme of collectivization in its totality.

ANT can describe the connection between grain and collectivized farming in functional, objectivist terms, since it allows us to look not merely at the micro level of production (the grain) or at the macro, structural level of organization (collectivization) but allows *both* to be considered simultaneously as existing co-dependently within a network.[62] However, ANT cannot reveal the allegorical connection between grain, collectivization and Stalin's cult of personality produced by Zykov's portrait because it is fundamentally descriptive *but not* interpretive. ANT can provide the material foundation for a symbolic reading but has clear limitations for reading a work of art or film within a specific sociopolitical context.

When, in *Stalinism in Bohemia*, what appeared to be spilling grain in one shot is, in the next sequence, revealed to be merely small fragments of dry pebbles, the sense of lack and depletion this communicates can be linked in the viewer's mind both to the depletion (cultural and material) engendered by the policies of Stalin and Gottwald, and to a certain morbidity – or *dryness* – of the figures themselves. Švankmajer's work here is congruent with the principles underlying ANT since the smallest of things (grain, pebbles) are doing heavy symbolic work, which is reliant upon their placement within a network of cinematic montage.

However, it is not ANT which has allowed me to propose this symbolic reading, even as it allowed me to lay the material foundations which made this reading possible. ANT is descriptive but can never truly be interpretive, which is where it comes into conflict with allegory. This is because the movement from pure description – however detailed – to a symbolic reading always requires an interpretive leap. Typically, Švankmajer ensures in his work that this is never an unbridgeable leap from the material world into pure abstraction by grounding his symbolism in metonymy, not simile.

For example, the Soviet invasion of Czechoslovakia of 1968 – in which soldiers and tanks from Russia and other Warsaw Pact countries occupied Prague to put a stop to the liberalizing reforms of the Prague Spring[63] – is depicted in the film through a sequence in which rolling pins are placed on a hill by a pair of anonymous black-gloved hands. The rolling pins then roll down the hill at speed, leaving crushed objects, such as tin cans, in their wake.

At first this might seem like an absurd instance of comparing two unalike things. Under a conventional understanding, a tin can is not like a person and a rolling pin is not like a tank. However Russell-Gebbett explains beautifully how Švankmajer's sound design enables such objects as rolling pins to function convincingly as tanks and tin cans and rocks to function convincingly as the victimized Czech populace. He writes: 'Amplified and emphasised sounds bring out disgust, rawness and humour, the extra squelch and scrape teasing the inner qualities and thoughts of inanimate objects out. One could say that sound transubstantiates these symbols into what they speak of.'[64] I agree with Russell-Gebbett's implication here that the hyperreal sounds Švankmajer gives to his objects/things provides them with a vividness and tactility that renders them less abstract and more tangible and so easier, on some level, to relate to as subjects.

However, it is also essential these objects are known, domestic objects, familiar to the viewer. The viewer is intimately familiar with the actual violence propagated by rolling pins against hunks of dough or drills against rocks. For Švankmajer it is important we extend our empathy to these objects as well as to our fellow humans. As viewers with an awareness of Czech history, we recognize that the crushed objects recall civilians killed in the Warsaw Pact invasion and it is those people (rather than the film's objects) to whom our sympathy extends. Nevertheless, this pathos is effectively achieved because we have previously known the pathos of a crumpled tin can kicked into the gutter.

Death to anthropocentrism

In an early scene in *Stalinism in Bohemia*, a bust of Klement Gottwald, the first communist president of Czechoslovakia, is extracted through Caesarean section from a bust of Stalin. In the final sequence of the film, the bust of Stalin is brought back into surgery but now, instead of birthing a new leader, his head contains nothing but guts and offal. Russell-Gebbett reads this scene as posing the question of what should fill the cultural space left by the Velvet Revolution and the death of Stalinism.[65] In fact, a document written by Švankmajer in 1990, the same year as the film's release, goes some way towards answering this question.

Švankmajer's 1990 essay 'To Renounce the Leading Role' (*Vzdát se vedoucí role*) is a manifesto that calls for an end to anthropocentrism. In it Švankmajer argues that to survive, humanity must choose to no longer categorize itself as distinct from nature but instead recognize itself as merely one thing among others, no more special or elevated than all the rest of its fellow actants.[66] In doing so, mankind will ensure its own continuation; no longer able to distinguish itself from nature, it will no longer be able to exploit nature as a resource. Moreover, this return to nature will be redemptive since it will reverse mankind's casting off of the natural world in the pursuit of 'civilization', a concept which Švankmajer treats with cynicism.

Švankmajer's radical argument against anthropocentrism is similar to that made by Carter in 'Politics as if Nature Mattered' – that it is essential that humanity reconfigures politics to include nature and so treat the concerns of fauna, flora and things with the same seriousness as its own concerns.[67] Only by so doing will humanity be able to consider nature not as a function of man's desires but as something inextricably intertwined with humanity. Likewise, this is the grand project of Bruno Latour. However, he goes further than Švankmajer since he seeks the abandonment of the very concepts of natural objects and civilized subjects altogether, instead encouraging the reader to think in terms of the 'human' and the 'non-human', if at all.[68] Latour would be hesitant to speak of the ecological necessity of transcending anthropocentrism as Carter does, since he would argue this desire (to avoid ecological collapse) is always already anthropocentric in and of itself. Humanity should not, for instance, be protecting the rainforest for the sake of humanity's survival, but rather should abstain from destroying the rainforest out of respect for the rainforest's own concerns. This does not require us to believe trees are sentient but rather requires us to abandon the concept that sentience or capacity for pain is worthy criteria to judge whether a thing has interests – or indeed rights – to be respected. The summation of this project would be to extend politics to non-human actants. For their interests to be known, not only must these non-humans be 'endowed with speech' but also 'have to be made capable of acting and grouping themselves together in associations'; yet even then, Latour laments, 'there will still be the problem ... of finding a proper body for them'.[69]

One of Latour's ideas for how to achieve this – how to provide a space for non-humans in politics – is to have a number of human spokespeople who speak on behalf of the non-humans' concerns.[70] In many ways, Švankmajer in his manifesto is positioning himself as such a spokesperson – or, in Owen's preferred terminology, a transcriber,[71] since Švankmajer would not wish to *translate* the concerns of objects into human language. Rather, when Švankmajer cautions artists to never speak through objects or impose narratives upon them but to allow things the space to speak for themselves,[72] he is acting as a guardian for these non-human actants, seeking to protect them from the impositions of human artists less respectful than himself.

However, lest we become too lost in fantasies of animism, it is worth considering that objects cannot literally speak. Latour himself reminds us that while politics 'talks and palavers', 'nature does not, except in ancient myths, fables and fairy tales'.[73] Of course, Švankmajer often chooses to work within these modes – his adaptation of Walpole's *Castle of Otranto* (*Otrantský zámek*, 1977) is mythical-Surrealist, while his feature-length film *Little Otik/Greedy Guts* (*Otesánek*, 2000) is a fairy tale adaptation. Švankmajer moves within magical spaces where nature *does* indeed talk. However, the point stands – the layperson is unable to converse with objects, natural or man-made. As Bennett asks of Latour's parliament of things: 'How can communication proceed when many members are nonlinguistic?'[74] In *Picnic with Weissmann* (*Picknick mit*

Weissman, 1968) Švankmajer disquietingly suggests that the desires of these nonlinguistic things may run counter to humans' own, leading to a fatal breakdown in communication between us and them.

A *Picnic with Weissmann* and non-human actants

In *Understanding Animation* (1998) Paul Wells summarizes Švankmajer's filmography in a clear-sighted and vivid litany:

> The tangibility and malleability of clay; the hardness and weight of stones; the fragility and smoothness of china; the living essence of wood; the colour and texture of textiles; and the physical mechanism of the human body become the narrative imperatives of Svankmajer's work and serve as an important example of fabrication, creating stories through rediscovered and redetermined discourses.[75]

Picnic with Weissmann is probably the film that best suits Wells's description of Švankmajer's work. Interspersed with several extreme close-ups of tufts of grass and weeds, a series of increasingly close establishing shots presents the viewer with the host of objects[76] about which the film will revolve: a wardrobe, a bed, a couple of wicker chairs, a white wooden chair, a desk with a drawer, a trowel, a chess game and an antique phonograph, with a few records. These objects are all laid out as though in a bedroom. The juxtaposition between the grass and the domestic objects is immediately apparent, while simultaneously, their very matter-of-factness and the quiet sobriety of their placement neutralize this juxtaposition, rendering it almost banal. It is as though the network that includes both grass and objects assimilates all differences. There is no discordance between the grass and the objects – rather, it provides a surprisingly natural and homely surface for the furniture.

Seemingly, the viewer has stumbled across a rural idyll where things are left to contently exist outside of human influence(s). The film's things are not ensnared in some complex human narrative but simply play through the movements most expressive of their forms – so, the phonograph spins records, the chess pieces move horizontally and laterally across the board, the trowel digs into the earth. These actions literalize Latour's deceptively commonsensical claim that 'kettles "boil" water, knives "cut" meat,'[77] etc. In Švankmajer's vision the tool is quite able to get on with its work without the necessity of a human tool-bearer. Indeed, without the strain of a sweating human, the grass seems more pliant than usual to the trowel's efforts. The movements of all the film's things seem unencumbered and graceful and, most fundamentally, cooperative.[78] Notably, no thing is subjected to desecration, dilapidation or destruction, as is generally par for the course in Švankmajer's work. Even 'natural things' seem to participate alongside the tools and furniture as co-conspirators. A snail works its way across the phonograph and a small stone has replaced one of the pawns in the chess set.

The scene is tranquil. The music from the phonograph is less discordant than Zdeněk Liška's compositions which usually score Švankmajer's early work. The editing is slightly less manic and the frame less cramped. The only visual cues that suggest something more sinister might be afoot reference the human form in some way. A rubber ball is pumped by the desk, the pump's nozzle extending into its drawer. Within the drawer is the cartoon image of a naked woman. The ball inflates as the woman is exposed with the opening of the drawer, providing visual innuendo which sits uncomfortably among an otherwise innocent scene. Perhaps this sequence disturbs because it introduces the notion of sexuality to things. Baudrillard in *The System of Objects* writes that mankind needs robots to be sexless because otherwise their hyper-functionality would be too threatening. Through their asexuality, robots can embody a domesticated and tamed sexuality.[79] As such, the virile rubber ball is faintly threatening, since it is moving into a realm that does not belong to things. Moreover, its expansion/arousal seems to be facilitated by human objectification. The human woman is reduced to the level of an erotic picture postcard, while the non-human ball is elevated to the height of virility. With respect to objectification, Barbara Johnson writes that to 'treat someone like a thing' should be considered negatively if such treatment means to act towards another as though they were 'a tool of one's own desire'.[80] Is, then, objectification even worse when it is a thing that is doing the objectifying?

Equally disconcerting is a shirt and pair of trousers which seem to be mimicking the human form by reclining on the bed and leisurely sucking up plums through an idle sleeve. The fruit is processed within some phantasmal digestive equipment and then a stone pops out of the end of the other sleeve. Not only have the things developed sexual desire, they have also grown appetites.

Indeed, the network of actants, both natural and man-made, functions self-sufficiently without the disruptive presence of human desire. At the end of the film, it becomes apparent this is the conclusion the things themselves have reached. The trowel has dug a sizeable pit and autumnal leaves cover the now unmoving things, heralding the end of their picnic. The doors to the wardrobe swing open and out falls a bound and gagged human (the titular Weissmann) who is dumped unceremoniously into the pit which now serves as his grave. This is perhaps the fate awaiting humanity at the end of a renunciation of anthropocentrism. If humans are not the masters of the world, then objects/things are no longer automatically their slaves.

Picnic with Weissmann illustrates that non-human actants can operate in a network without human intervention. Švankmajer exhibits this magically and cinematically since the blackly comic ending is contingent upon the notion that objects/things are capable of Machiavellian plotting; however, one can easily imagine a more realistic version of the same scenario – a ball blown by the wind against chair legs, dead leaves falling upon a chess set, a record on a phonograph moved by a snail or the wind. After all, intentionality is not the sole determiner of action.

A civilization of stones

In *Picnic with Weissmann* the non-human actants act in symbiotic relationships to defeat the tyranny of anthropocentrism; however, *A Game with Stones* (*Hra s kameny*, 1965) depicts a network of non-human actants which disintegrates into a flurry of violence and destruction. The film provides an allegory of the birth and death of civilization, hinting that with political interaction (i.e. a process of power relations and negotiations) come fragmentation, disorder and an eventual end to the political process. The film also provides a corrective to Barbara Johnson's statement that a 'stone can't defend itself against anthropomorphism without resorting to anthropomorphism'[81] by showing in its early sequences stones engaged in a life project which does not resemble that of humanity. It is only when the stones *do* start collectively depicting the human form that their evolutionary progress comes to a stumbling halt, ending in destruction.

Upon the wall of a dilapidated room is mounted a clock. Suspended from the clock by wire is a bucket and below the face of the clock a tap emerges from the wall. When the hour strikes twelve, two stones issue from the tap into the bucket – one white, the other black. Accompanied by the ringing melody of a music box, the stones then form simple patterns by multiplying and arranging themselves in rows (of the same colour, of alternating colours) and shapes (pyramids, rectangular grids) in a process resembling cell division. It is important to note that the stones are not merely engaged in a facsimile of life but rather are a form of life itself. To claim that the stones, through Švankmajer's animation, *mimic* cell division would be to project a scientific schema upon the film – an epistemological framework derived from a modern understanding of biology that exists outside of the film world. Instead, the film elicits in the viewer a mythologized primitivism that precedes the discoveries of Mendel and Darwin. The stones appear to us self-propelled and self-generating; Švankmajer's interference as an animator is firmly outside the diegesis. This is a depiction and example of animism in its purest state.

At the height of the sequence's complexity, the bucket throws the stones to the floor and upon the hour striking three, more stones are issued into the bucket, of variegated shapes, colours and textures. The sequence that follows depicts the flow of blood, or some other vital life force, through channels of stone, alongside movements of impregnation/fertilization. As Ed Howard writes: 'There is something increasingly sensuous, even sexual, about the subsequent patterns, with stones rubbing against one another, sometimes seeming to birth torrents of smaller rounded stones from the frictive collisions of the larger rocks.'[82] This is a remarkable sequence since the sexual element of these movements is clear without Švankmajer resorting to anthropomorphism. Unlike the rubber ball in *Picnic with Weissmann* that grows firm through a masturbatory pumping movement, the sexuality of the stones in this sequence bears little relation to human sexuality. Švankmajer convinces us that the sensual action of the stones is true to form; in so doing, he accomplishes what Roger Cardinal refers to as a 'rare feat' – namely, 'to elicit higher import from the banal object while still respecting its very banality'.[83] Stones tumbling down mountain sides, or drifting along a river bed, *really do* rub against each other and move in currents. Švankmajer makes the idea that an animistic sexuality exists within the natural world seem commonsensical.

Again, in yet another cycle, the complexity of the interactions increases and we move from engaging directly with the real stones in and of themselves through to pictorial representation and symbolism. In the third movement, stones are arranged to denote simple human bodies, which flex their joints and transform into new humanoid figures. The fourth movement, similar to the third, is the most complex. The stones are broken into shingle, so each fragment of stone is now the tiniest unit of information. Shapes and faces are sculpted from the sediment, depicting dialogue and conflict. The stones, previously the loci of animation (life) in and of themselves, are now pixels/Ben-Day dots/letters/units/cells composing larger, more complex, sites of animation.

Graham Harman reminds us that under Latour's philosophy of the world: 'Nothing is mere rubble to be used up or trampled by mightier actors.'[84] However, at this point in *Game with Stones*, this is exactly what has come to pass. The stones have been reduced to rubble, no longer signifying in and of themselves but merely composing the altogether mightier actants of human faces – arguing, kissing, gobbling each other up. This represents political dialogue, and destruction follows. In the next and final sequence of the film, the stones smash up against and consume one another. This is not, however, a dialectical process leading to greater evolution. Rather, it is war – the breaking point of the political process.[85] The system itself ruptures (the stones smash through the bottom of the bucket) leaving the clock to spit out stones to add to a now ever-increasing pile of rubble. Animation has been reduced to entropy.

A Game with Stones is a perfect illustration of Švankmajer's claim that his films are political but concern currents which run deeper than specific political systems.[86] Although it does not present a symbolically encoded critique of a particular political system, it convincingly sets before the viewer a process of political interaction. Leaving aside the misleading question of their self-cognizance, the stones interact to create increasingly sophisticated patterns – an interaction that necessarily involves conflict as the stones are of different sizes and shapes. This conflict is inevitably destructive and leads to the death of the political system.

Michael O'Pray writes of Švankmajer's career that 'his work is a denial of dialogue, a retreat into the ordered chaos of artefacts and natural objects'.[87] O'Pray is correct to describe the behaviour of the 'artefacts and natural objects' in *Game with Stones* as one of 'ordered chaos', however it does follow that these things thus sit outside of 'dialogue'. Rather, their behaviour is chaotic *because* they (the stones) are engaged in political dialogue. The political dialogue of stones belongs to gestures and actions (attrition, collision, the forming of patterns and erosion into fragments) in a language not translatable to words. Yet Švankmajer's gift is to film this dialogue, showing how it is fundamentally political, while also respecting its fundamental otherness. He is present at the 'parliament of things'[88] and will record its deliberations, without translation. Bertrand Schmitt describes this role as being like a 'ferryman', 'who allows the internal nature of objects and materials to express itself through his actions'.[89] That is to say, the 'ferryman' may galvanize or help facilitate the communication of things, but he does not speak for them.

In his following film – *Možnosti dialogu*, 1982 – Švankmajer turns his focus to humanoid figures, trapped in cycles of futile and destructive repetition. Švankmajer's vision of politics as a violent arena of control and coercion, leading to transformation or degeneration, is as apparent with humanoid actants as it was with the non-human actants of *Game with Stones*.

The political pessimism of *Dimensions of Dialogue*

Hames writes of *Dimensions of Dialogue* that its 'anti-Stalinist implications' are clear.[90] This might seem a contentious claim to make about such a highly abstract work, but according to Švankmajer, the film was used by the Ideological Commission of the Czechoslovak Communist Party Central Committee as 'a deterrent example'.[91] Clearly, the censors recognized political implications in the film which they found highly disagreeable, in spite of – or because of – its high degree of stylization.

Dimensions of Dialogue is composed of three separate movements on the same theme so that analysis of one of these sequences inevitably draws reflections pertinent to the other two. The first sequence, 'Exhaustive Dialogue' (*dialog věcný*), expresses ideas common to ANT more forcefully than the following two less *thingy* sequences and so will be our focus here.

A composite head made of food, with a bulbous lemon nose, sausage lips and two tufty sprigs of garlic for a beard, comes into contact with a head composed of kitchen equipment, with a pastry brush for whiskers, spoons for lips and a ladle for a nose. The head made from these domestic objects violently gobbles down the first head and the film cuts to a montage in extreme close-ups of an eruption of mastication. The component parts of the head of food are pulverized in a frenzy of activity. Scissors slice an apple into pulp, a spoon splatters radishes, keys bore into a lettuce and chicken is dissected by blades. The chaos of this sequence is accentuated by a dense sound design that includes the clatter of metal objects, coarse brushing noises, wet slurping sounds and a flurry of horns.

When the assault has finished, the metallic head vomits up the food, which now looks battered and bruised. The metallic head continues on its way and meets a head comprised of scholastic equipment – textbooks, straight edges, graph paper – recalling Arcimboldo's *Librarian* (1566). This time, it is the paper head that consumes the metallic head and another flurry of violent disorder and frottage bursts forth – lids are crushed between the pages of a book,

Figure 2.1 Two Arcimboldoesque networks of actants fail to communicate in *Dimensions of Dialogue* (*Možnosti dialogu*) (Jan Švankmajer, 1982). Image used with permission of Athanor.

pastry brushes are shattered by graph paper, graters and forks are snapped into pieces. Again, the broken objects that result are vomited back up and the face reconstituted in a more diminished form. The sequence now returns full circle, with the head of food laying waste to the paper head. The cycle continues, with each head sinking further and further into undifferentiated mush and then clay, until every head resembles the others. The movement ends with a sculpted anonymous clay head vomiting up replicas of itself ad nauseam.

Both Michael Anderson and Jack Eason read 'Exhaustive Dialogue' as symbolizing class warfare under communism – with the first head representing agrarian labour and the rural peasantry, the second representing factory work and the industrial proletariat and the third head representing abstract, intellectual labour and the bourgeoisie.[92] Such a reading would suggest that Švankmajer views the class struggle as a dialectic process that repeats until each class is assimilated into the other and the citizen under communism is left anonymous and undifferentiated. Ed Howard offers the alternative reading that 'Exhaustive Dialogue' provides a critique of the processes of cognition and categorization. Howard explains this as follows:

> In this recursive food chain, organic matter is devoured and regurgitated by machinery, masticated to make it finer for digestion, and also dissected, pulled apart in an effort to understand it. This is a continual theme of this section, the way that attempts at understanding inevitably lead to the destruction of the thing under examination.[93]

Howard's reading strikes me as being more congruent with Švankmajer's aims and philosophy than the readings of Anderson and Eason. In the analysis of Eason and Anderson, the specific actants (the foodstuffs, metal objects, paper and books) merely stand in for something else (agrarianism, factory work, the bourgeoisie). As such, their reading suggests a utilitarian approach to the material, i.e. the specific things were chosen by Švankmajer because they could be made to signify. By contrast, Howard's notion that the sequence enacts processes of dissection holds true both symbolically and literally. The heads/actants are literally and symbolically 'pulled apart'[94] in an effort of comprehension which attempts to break each head/actant down into its component parts, open it up or render it flattened and homogenized. To provide a comparative example, when a heart is studied in a biology lesson, the knowledge it contains is symbolically 'opened up' through a literal process of extraction and dissection. The heart is thus brought into the realm of scientific discourse, but the material heart itself is left both severed from the system of its body and broken as a self-contained or functional network.

'Exhaustive Dialogue' suggests that dialogue always fails to maintain things in their state of original wholeness but instead dismembers. The world of 'Exhaustive Dialogue' resembles that of Bruno Latour, in which 'all actants are constructed through numerous trials of strength with others, and all have an intimate integrity that partially resists any attempt to disassemble them'.[95] The dialectical process is, according to Švankmajer's pessimistic view, one of violent conflict in which synthesis does not occur but rather any difference is coercively eradicated through the exercise of power.

In total, Julian Petley's broad political reading of *Dimensions of Dialogue* chimes true: 'Taken as a whole, the three "dialogues" bear witness to humankind's intolerance of otherness, the inhabitual, the non-conformist and the unexpected.'[96] The film is resolutely cynical, suggesting the impossibility of sustained cooperative dialogue, whether personal or political. Latour argues that a network's stability comes not from the strength of any individual actant but through the 'netting, lacing, weaving, twisting of ties that are weak by themselves'.[97] Against these terms, the reason that the dialogues of Švankmajer's film are never sustainable is that each actant is trying to gain ascendency over the other(s). Although the composite faces of 'Exhaustive Dialogue' may originally appear to be tightly woven networks, when the argumentative dialogue with a second face commences, each individual actant (each spoon, sprig of garlic or sheet of paper) ultimately fights alone.

Let the networks be as they are – Švankmajer vs. categorization

Picnic with Weissman and *A Game with Stones* depict networks of objects/things that exist outside the sphere of human influence. *Dimensions of Dialogue* shows that networks of human actants are just as likely to fall into repetition or disarray. By contrast, *Historia Naturae ~ Suite* (*Historia Naturae ~ Suita*,

1967), *The Flat* (*Byt*, 1968) and *A Quiet Week in the House* (*Tichý týden v dome*, 1969) all involve a human actor attempting to exert control over a network of non-human actants. Švankmajer is critical of this urge, his films intimating that objects, things and animals will always exceed or escape human attempts at mastery.

Historia Naturae ~ Suite is an audio-visual suite that, as its title suggests, charts various evolutionary categories in order of ascendency. The zoological categories – aquatilia, hexapoda, pisces, reptilia, aves, mammalia, simiæ, homo – are displayed via densely interwoven montages that combine skeletons, illustrations, anatomical and scientific drawings, stuffed and mounted creatures and living beings. These sequences are edited in time to selected categories of music – foxtrot, waltz, blues, tango, polka, etc. – which heighten the sense that a classificatory schema has ordered the structure of the film. Interspersed between each sequence is a repeated piece of footage in which an anonymous human mouth eats a grey and anonymous piece of cooked meat (presumably belonging to a creature of the category depicted). As such, the editing seems to assert that the carnivorous behaviour of the human is enabled by the preceding acts of categorization. Bruno Latour argues convincingly in *Politics of Nature* that the concept of 'nature' allows humanity to order life within a hierarchy, placing all other flora and fauna beneath itself.[98]

However, Švankmajer makes clear with the conclusion to *Historia Naturae* that this is a delusion. The final sequence in the film is 'homo', thus placing humanity in sequence with all the other creatures. Then, following a montage in which anatomical diagrams flip open to reveal the body's inner workings and the human form is dissected and paraded in precisely the same way as the other creatures before it, a cadaverous skull is shown munching on a piece of grey flesh. Švankmajer reminds his audience that death will eventually consume even the most rational of humans. Try as we might through our desperate hierarchies, we are unable to remove ourselves from the realm of nature.

Historia Naturae, then, forms a Surrealist critique of the rational impulse itself. The desire to place variegated life forms within precise scientific categories is a denial of man's place in nature, a denial of death and, fundamentally, a denial of the richness and variegation of life. For, how can the cacophony of visual data that Švankmajer presents us with possibly be laid to rest within such sober categories? Švankmajer allegorizes this argument by having creatures repeatedly break free from their constraints – a mounted skeletal fish smashes through its glass case, a pair of pinned beetles escape from their fixings and crawl manically about, even shells violently erupt through the black-and-white drawings that depict them, noisily announcing their presence in the world. In *Persons and Things*, Barbara Johnson refers to art as 'a boxing',[99] but we can also say the same of science, academia and pedagogy. In all of these disciplines, subject matter is understood and made readable through categorization. If we think of natural history museums and school textbooks, animals are quite literally put into boxes of pen and ink or wood and glass. Švankmajer makes it clear that this boxing is never an ideologically neutral act, evidencing this through the unpleasant and destructive spectacle of the man eating the creature he has previously categorized. This pedantic ordering, followed by the obsessive consumption, exposes a pathological need for control.

Susan Pearce in her monograph on collecting within the European tradition describes it as 'a dynamic process in which the collector struggles to impose himself and to control outcomes'.[100] The collecting impulse, then, is a fight against chaos and disorder. In *Historia Naturae* the editing process itself exists as a function of the collecting impulse, since it cuts the filmed material into bite-sized chunks. Thus, the very structure of the film (aligned with rationality) is situated in opposition to the content of the film (aligned with irrationality). This is in accordance with O'Pray's invaluable observation that Švankmajer's films, including *Historia Naturae*, create a sense of dynamic conflict by arranging the chaotic and sensuous visual content of the footage according to a rational ordering scheme imposed through the edit.[101] Sometimes order wins the battle in these films – the otherwise ecstatic *Jabberwocky* ends with an ominous slow zoom onto a black suit and trousers – but generally, Švankmajer will end his work on a note of gleeful destruction, in which an ordering system collapses; so, *Game with Stones* ends with a smashed bucket and a malfunctioning machine; in *Picnic with Weissmann*, the human who should be presiding over the picnic is buried alive; and in *Historia Naturae ~ Suite*, man is unable to continue his task of categorization in the face of death. Essentially, to quote Roger Cardinal, 'for all our human methodicality, the world remains alien, irreducible, absurd, fundamentally *unquotable*'.[102] The gawping mouths of fish, the curious eyes of monkeys, the coiling forms of snakes and shells and the absolute strangeness of lobsters – in Švankmajer's vision these things pose a genuine challenge to a rational understanding of the world.

The Flat's network of dissident things

So, in *Historia Naturae* an unseen human influence and the director himself attempt to impose stable categories upon the complex, ever-shifting, variegated network(s) of non-human actants, only to find that this quest is futile, since they too are ensnared within the network. This is a political failure, since it allegorizes human actants' efforts to exert control through dominant discourses of scientific rationalism upon a host of 'natural' actants – shells, crabs, monkeys, beetles, etc. By contrast, in *The Flat* (1968) non-human actants – in this case, domestic objects – persecute a human protagonist (Ivan Kraus).

The man finds himself locked in an apartment. From his very first interactions, the things of the room refuse to cooperate with him. A mirror shows not his reflection but the back of his head. When striking a match, the open stove releases a gush of water which puts it out. When these disruptive events occur, the wistful albeit pensive music on woodwind and string is interrupted with a crash of drums and a series of piano stabs, emphasizing the viewer's sense that these are not unfortunate mishaps but moments of attack. Harman in his work on the metaphysics of Bruno Latour refers to 'trickster objects' that might disrupt proceedings or change the course of events.[103] Harman's point is that even the most seemingly insignificant of actants may yield significant effects, which is why ANT instructs the budding sociologist to attend to every single thing in a given network, no matter how obscure. The absurdity of *The Flat* derives from the accumulation of 'trickster objects' that would seem insignificant in and of themselves, but working within the networked space of the apartment, the objects begin to gain a sinister import.

Unlike the anti-Nazi objects of *Revolution in Toyland* (1946), the things of the apartment persecute a hapless nebbish, more reminiscent of Gregor Samsa or Josef K than a fascist soldier. The apparent animosity of the mirror, stone, egg, picture, etc. is, the viewer might feel, misplaced. As such, it would be more appropriate to consider these items *dissident things* rather than politically resistant objects like the heroic toys of Týrlová's *Revolution in Toyland*. The items that the protagonist of *The Flat* attempts to interact with seem to sabotage the utilitarian function expected of them, asserting instead their hardness, slantedness or porosity – the very qualities that utilitarianism would seek to repress. In the cases of the qualities listed: a boiled egg is so hard that it bends a spoon, a picture insists upon being slanted even when adjusted and a spoon is riddled with porous holes, rendering it impossible to drink soup with.

In *Pandora's Hope* Latour provides a caricatured description of materialism as being a philosophy in which every 'artefact has its script, its potential to take hold of passersby and force them to play roles in its story'.[104] Under such a framework, humans have no agency but merely play out the roles allocated to them by objects/things. If Latour's characterization of materialism is correct, then *The Flat* is a politically materialist film, since it suggests that humans are but the victims of their environment, ensnared by forces beyond their control. Once the utilitarian objects of the apartment refuse to play their roles (i.e. start behaving as dissident things) the human protagonist is plunged into confusion. A black humour derives from the fact that against all odds, the protagonist continues his attempts to engage in the rituals of everyday life, even when non-human actants render his efforts futile. Not only once does he try to drink soup from the porous spoon, but he does so repeatedly, with a certain manic fervour. It is as though the protagonist expects his place in the network of non-human actants to be completely stable and his interactions preprogrammed; when these actants do not behave as he expects them to, he is unable to adapt. Consequently, to quote Ralph Barker: 'The man is reduced to an inanimate body through his subjugated state in the film; he becomes the "object" with which the flat, a supposedly inanimate facet, toys with.'[105] Barker also notes that the pixilation of the actor in the film assists in rendering him object-like.

Barker's observation chimes with Kracauer's gnomic statement that upon the cinema screen the actor is an 'object among objects',[106] except here the non-human objects are imbued with a bustling life that exceeds that of the human. There is a switch between what we as a viewer expect to be the motivating, forceful, directive actant and what we expect to be acted upon, pliant, subject and yielding. The effect is uncanny since the things demonstrating such violent agency are all regular, utilitarian objects. If one is to read *The Flat* as a direct political allegory, it would seem that Švankmajer is critiquing the position of the subject under totalitarianism, manipulated by forces beyond his understanding and control. Barker notes that when the protagonist comes up against a brick wall at the end of the film, among the names of several influential Surrealists graffitied there, is the name of Evžen Plocek, a dissident who, like Jan Palach, committed suicide via self-immolation. Barker writes that the protagonist 'has become as physically inanimate within the flat as Plocek was politically outside of it. Both men attempt to escape from a system that is beyond their control, and must both resign themselves to inevitable fate'.[107]

However, as with the psychosexual reading of *Jabberwocky*, this analysis immediately feels too on-the-nose, failing to grasp from where the affective power of the film derives. As ever, Švankmajer's more interesting political argument is considerably more subtle and universal. Again, it is an argument against anthropocentrism. Man, Švankmajer illustrates, is only able to be the master of his domain if objects acquiesce to his demands. As soon as the objects begin to break, or in any way subvert expectations (thus becoming things), he is thrown into confusion. As such, it is man who is in thrall to objects. Objects/things do not depend on man, nor desire anything from him. Conversely, even the very simplest of man's daily tasks are dependent upon objects, upon which he projects all sorts of desires and anxieties. *The Flat* is, then, a consciousness-raising exercise that instructs the viewer to not be unthinkingly reliant upon objects but rather be attentive to the complex interrelations between humans and non-humans and to always question the assumptions that the humans have absolute sovereignty over non-human actants. Perhaps then the human protagonist, while not a fascist, is punished for an anthropocentric arrogance common to all humans. Alison Frank argues that this complicates the humour of the film: 'When the audience's sympathy leaves room for delight, it is not only because they sometimes take a dark pleasure in the suffering of the protagonist; at some level they are led to feel a complementary sympathy for the objects, and thus they share a defiant pleasure when they see objects, which are usually the slaves of man, refuse their servitude.'[108] It is a credit to Švankmajer's considerable skill as a film-maker that this universal political message can coexist alongside the culturally specific message decoded by Barker.

Although humorous, *The Flat* is also a frightening film. Apart from the brief entrance of a gentleman holding a cockerel (Juraj Herz) who seems sinister due to being rendered in slow motion, all the threats in the film come from non-human actants. This chimes with a startling assertion made by Latour in *Politics of Nature* that the categories of subject and object 'have been created to instil mutual horror'.[109] Over the course of several pages, Latour writes of the monstrousness of objects for subjects, i.e. that humans experience objects as repellent, frightening and abject.[110] The Švankmajer film in which this is most clearly the case is *A Quiet Week in the House* (1969).

Not objects but *things* ~ in defence of indeterminacy

A criminal or government agent makes his way furtively to a grimy and dilapidated house, evidently paranoid that he is being tracked. Once inside, he establishes himself, opens his briefcase, hotwires a light bulb and, using a hand-cranked drill, bores a hole into one of the doors in the corridor. The man peeps through the hole and inside the room a phantasmal spectacle is revealed. Candy wrappers disclose juddering screws that manoeuvre themselves to stand upright upon the keys of a dirty typewriter. Moving away from the door, the man crosses off the day on a calendar he has hung from the wall, makes up a bed from his suitcase and a travel pillow and goes to sleep. The next morning an alarm clock wakes him and he continues about his tasks. Over the course of a week, nightmarish scenes of things interacting reveal themselves in the filthy rooms of the house, all spied upon by the man. A slab of meat licks up the encrusted remnants of leftover food like a tongue, only to feed itself into a mincer, producing coils of shredded newspaper. A colourful clockwork hen, tethered to a rope, tries to reach a bowl of feed, but is pulled back. When the rope breaks, the hen reaches the feed, only to be crushed under a wave of excretal clay. Birds fly from a drawer upwards past the camera and then seem to shed all their feathers. Their plucked carcasses are hung from a hook on the wall and the feathers coat a wooden chair with wings. The chair attempts to fly but tumbles to the ground and is smashed. A rubber hose snakes its way from a black suit to a vase of flowers, whereupon it drains the flowers' water, urinating it back onto the floor. The flowers ignite and burn to a crisp. A coil of wire swings a pair of chattering false teeth, which it binds. A cupboard swings open, revealing a gristly assortment of bound pigs' trotters.

The contrast between the man's bureaucratically tinged subterfuge and the surreal happenings in the closed rooms is heightened startlingly through having the former live-action scenes shot in a sepia monochrome and the stop-motion sequences filmed in colour that seems both garish and diminished all at once. Additionally, the whirr of a camera is constantly present in the live-action scenes, creating a background hum. Although the sound effects are less hyperreal than in much of Švankmajer's work, sounds of the drill boring into wood, the suitcase being opened and the tread of shoes are all present. By contrast, the thingy vignettes are silent, adding to their eerie oneiric quality.

On the last day of the week, the man places a stick of dynamite inside the hole to each room and lights the connective wick. He dashes outside, only to return, since he has forgotten his task of crossing off the day's date on the calendar. He does so, runs outside again and, presumably, the house explodes. The film ends.

A Quiet Week in the House was released in 1969, the year following the apex of the Prague Spring under the liberalizing reform government of Alexander Dubček and the subsequent Soviet-led Warsaw Pact invasion, which ended the Spring. Dubček's government had attempted to introduce so-called 'socialism with a human face', under which censorship was loosened and a free press authorized. Such plans were encompassed by the Action Programme, which also included proposed reforms to the structure of the KSČ that encompassed its central role within Czech society, freedom of the press, economic reform and, more generally, a liberalizing move towards greater political openness, albeit not extending to multi-party democracy.[111] In terms of film history, the Prague Spring was when many of the boldest and most experimental works of the Czech New Wave were produced. In August 1968, Soviet troops with soldiers from other Warsaw Pact countries laid siege to Prague, wounding hundreds of Czech and Slovak civilians. Dubček and other communists deemed 'counter-revolutionaries' were flown to Moscow and in a series of meetings, the 'Moscow Protocol' was drafted, congress was declared invalid and it was agreed that the KSČ would regain control of the media, purge the party and return to a hardline Soviet model of communism.[112]

A Quiet Week in the House allegorizes these events. Simon Field describes the film as 'the paranoid vision of a fugitive able to contemplate his dreams only furtively, through tiny holes in closed doors, the visionary force of what he sees confirming the revolutionary power of the imagination opposed to everyday repression', these visions providing 'a clear message ... about the annihilation of hope'.[113] In a similar vein, O'Pray argues: 'The horrors witnessed in the various rooms ... suggest those of the unconscious mind itself espied by the authorities. Equally, they could be symbolic of the horrors of the Czech state under Soviet domination.'[114] However, I feel we can be more specific about the political meaning of the individual sequences. The screws – giant in close-up – resemble militaristic machinery and recall the occupying Soviet tanks of the invasion. The image of the screws sitting upright upon the typewriter keys can be taken to represent the retraction of press freedom, or perhaps more specifically, the arrest of several dissident authors following the Writers' Congress of 1967.[115] Similarly, the tongue represents freedom of speech, symbolically minced so that we are left with party news speech and dogma. The hen strikes me as representing Czech citizens – perhaps dissident artists especially – straining for personal and creative freedom. Almost as soon as this nourishment is granted (the handful of years in which FAMU film graduates could produce overtly political and experimental films, with less censorship and limited reprisals), the Warsaw Pact invasion and the subsequent purge of reformists from government ensure this freedom is quashed. The plucked birds and the chair that fails to fly are again images of creative and political freedom which is quickly suppressed. Finally, the black suit represents conformity, bureaucracy and the StB stifling the very life of Czechoslovakia. Throughout the film there is no recourse to dialogue or voice-over.

A Quiet Week in the House certainly works as a piece of culturally and temporally specific political critique but, as ever with Švankmajer, there is simultaneously a more universal and perhaps deeper political conflict at work, such as exists between order and chaos in *Historia Naturae*. In this case, the conflict is between ambiguity and certitude.

Kieran Williams writes that the process of Normalization that followed the end of the Prague Spring was essentially concerned with 'restoring extreme predictability, far beyond the certainty provided, for example, by the rule of law'.[116] The Prague Spring, through introducing a greater degree of freedom of speech in the press and within public and political discourse, as well as providing a space for creative expression in the form of the Czech New Wave, introduced a certain amount of unpredictability and novelty into Czechoslovakia that had long been repressed. Williams asserts: 'In an ideal normalized setting, from the point of view of the rulers, all outcomes are intended, desirable, and certain.'[117] This gives credence to Frank's argument that objects of certain Czech New Wave films are politically destabilizing because they are not reducible to any single narrative or symbolic function but instead exist as loci for 'a collection of diverse and sometimes contradictory meanings'.[118] Writing of Němec's *Party and Its Guests* (1966), Frank explains that the film makes its political critique bottom-up, first exposing ambiguities latent in humanity's relationship(s) to the objective world, before demonstrating how ideological/political ambiguities grow out from these 'seemingly innocuous social'[119] ambiguities. Frank's name for these everyday objective elements which, within a film, expose 'ruptures in the seemingly uniform, comprehensible surface of everyday existence' is 'hybrid objects'.[120] While not identical in practice to the 'dissident things' of *The Flat* or *A Quiet Week in the House* – due to the fact that Frank's hybrid object owes part of its hybridity to human psychology[121] while the dissident thing exists resolutely on its own terms separate from humanity – the dissident thing and the hybrid object are united in intent. Both disrupt ideology in their refusal to be tied down to a singular, stable meaning.

The difference between objects and things is one of uncertainty. Bennett argues that objects are things classified through discourse and so stripped of their 'otherness'.[122] Objects have, unlike things, been codified according to human schemata that are imposed upon them. They are permitted, by their human masters, no expression of ambiguity but are defined simply by their functions. Things, on the contrary, exist on their own terms. They are radically non-human, other and uncanny. In many of Švankmajer's films, a human protagonist wants to believe that he is dealing with objects but actually finds himself grappling with things. So, the everyman of *The Flat* wants to have a simple relationship with objects that allows him to go about his daily tasks, but they thwart him at every turn. The unseen ordering curator of *Naturae Historia* wishes to keep his objects and animals in strict categories, but they keep escaping from their boxes, literally and figuratively. In *A Quiet Week in the House*, the agent wishes to record the things that he spies upon before he eventually destroys them, perhaps because they exceed his comprehension. Dryje sees the agent as a surrogate figure for mankind generally, with Švankmajer criticizing man's 'inability to perceive, experience and interpret his ... cultural world not as one-sidedly subservient but as a polyfunctional and multidimensional and transgressive whole'.[123] That is, man has a tendency to experience the world as a categorized collection of functional objects, named by himself and suited to his own needs, rather than as a network of *things* that exceeds any utilitarian system of categorization he seeks to impose upon it.

Schwenger writes: 'The thing can be thought of as the object with the screen removed.'[124] The screen is the human linguistic and comprehensive system that attempts to codify objects according to its own schema. It obscures the vivid, ontological *thereness* of the thing – its fleshy, ineluctable reality. According to the terms of Schwenger's and Bennett's theorizing, the phenomena that unfold themselves in private in the locked rooms of the house are certainly things not objects. They are dirty and hybridized, often in a state of disrepair; aggressively

Figure 2.2 Juddering indeterminate things rather than stable categorizable objects from *A Quiet Week in the House* (*Tichý týden v dome*) (Jan Švankmajer, 1969). Image used with permission of Athanor.

non-functional and sometimes inexplicable in their strangeness. They are almost obscene in their otherness from humanity.

Bill Brown relates how William James would demonstrate that when our habits are interrupted, our sense of things is disturbed in such a way as to allow us to see objects in a new light. James would take a painting from the wall and turn it upside down. When we do this, James contends, we lose our conceptual understanding of the painting while strengthening our sensory perception of it, so that the colours and shapes appear more vital and vivid.[125] In Schwenger's terms, the object drops its veil and its *thinginess* is revealed. In *A Quiet Week in the House*, the disruptive visual practice that Švankmajer employs to disturb our sense of things is to combine his stop-motion trick photography with fluctuating exposure times, meaning that the animated things seem to be in a constant state of transformation, leaving ghostly trails behind them.

Brown writes that things reach being through a process of becoming[126] and refers to things that are 'not so much objects as … congealed actions'.[127] Brown could almost be describing the mysterious *things* of the film, which never seem to settle into a stable state of being and are always in a process of becoming. They are things that we experience in glimpses through their spasmodic, juddering movements. This visual trick is what provides the animated stuff with its potent ambivalence. Since the winged chair, the wire-entangled teeth, the typewriter, etc., are constantly in a state of visual flux, they seem to resist stable categorization. This makes them very threatening to a mindset governed by regularity and dogma – the kind of mindset that Normalization sought to instil in the Czech populace. Furthermore, during these sequences there is only a slight hiss and crackle on the soundtrack, with the things making no noise. This silence strengthens our sense of these things as phantasmal and lacking a stable, singular material presence. They appear and sound more like ghosts of objects than objects.

A political programme as stringent and unwavering as Normalization has no room for objects indefinable in terms of their utilitarian value. If we stop thinking in terms of usable objects and instead think in terms of 'things' or 'non-humans', 'we allow them to enter the collective in the form of new entities with uncertain boundaries, entities that hesitate, quake, and induce perplexity'.[128] Latour is writing here of how objects, if they are to be recoded as non-humans, must be considered actants within ANT, with all the affective power the term implies. However, the things in *A Quiet Week in the House* don't just 'hesitate, quake, and induce perplexity' metaphorically or metaphysically, they also do so literally. As such, not only are they a challenge to a stagnant political order, they also – to borrow a phrase from Harman – 'burst all boundaries of space and time'.[129] It might not even make sense to consider these things in the singular, since one of the effects of the shutter-drag stop-motion is to ensure that the things always look multiple. It is only in our mind that we are able to imagine the singular concrete objects that Švankmajer must have had recourse to in the real world to achieve the effects on screen. I assume, when I see the multiple clockwork hens dissolve into one another on the screen, that behind these phantasms sits a real object purchased from a junk shop or received in childhood, that the animator has on display somewhere in his home. I make the assumption that I could hold this object and that it would have a real tangible presence, as well as a date of manufacture and location, etc.

However, the film itself provides no indication that this should be the case – that these spectacles were ever anything other than fleeting and multiple. Their behaviour is, to quote Bennett's evocation of an idea of Deleuze and Guattari's, 'better imagined through terms such as quivering, evanescence, or an indefinite or nonpurposive suspense'.[130] This idea is politically radical as it holds that structures of power must be constantly open to change, or else they will be rendered moribund in their failure to apprehend indeterminacy. Švankmajer's work gestures towards a system where it would not make epistemological sense to speak of 'revolutionaries' vs. 'counter-revolutionaries', 'reformists' vs. 'regressives', 'dissidents' vs. 'loyal comrades' – such stable binaries would be doomed to failure in attempting to describe an ever-shifting network of multiple, hybridized, unstable actants.

Although Švankmajer foregrounds the indeterminacy of the aforementioned things through the technique of multiple dissolves, indeterminacy is inherent to the stop-motion form itself and animation in general. Indeed, Karen Beckman notes in her edited collection *Animating Film Theory* (2014) that 'animation sometimes makes us question whether true stillness in the world actually exists'.[131] Keith Broadfoot and Rex Butler in *The Illusion of Life* (1991) write lucidly about a paradox central to animation: namely, if a single frame of animation is still, then how does the illusion of movement occur?[132] Broadfoot and

Butler explain this concept with reference to Zeno's paradox of motion, which states that if Achilles were to race a tortoise and give that tortoise a headstart, Achilles could never overtake the tortoise. Once Achilles has reached the point that the tortoise started from, the tortoise will have advanced a certain distance, occupying a further point in space. Once Achilles moves forward to that point, the tortoise will have moved forward yet again and so on. Although the distance the tortoise further travels becomes regressively smaller, this new distance keeps infinitely interposing itself between Achilles and the tortoise, rendering it impossible for Achilles to ever pass the tortoise and win the race.

To apply this paradox to stop-motion animation, as Broadfoot and Butler do, we must think of how stop-motion is achieved. An object or plasticine/clay model is put in place and then a single frame of footage is taken. The object or model is then moved and another frame is taken and so on. When run in sequence, these frames give the illusion of movement due to persistence of vision. Conventionally, film is run at 25 frames per second, which is the rate at which the human eye will start to run images together, rather than perceiving them individually. Between these frames is, of course, movement that goes undocumented. To 'fill in' this gap, one could take more frames, at ever more finite points of movement; like the points between Achilles and the tortoise, frames could be infinitely interposed. However, ultimately, to quote Broadfoot and Butler, 'these points or instants could never give movement because any movement as such – as the paradoxes of Zeno make clear – would always occur in between two points or instances'.[133] As such, there is always an ellipsis between frames, a void that is undocumented and unseen. The implication is that movement belongs to the gap itself. As such, an inherent indeterminacy is built into the very mechanism of stop-motion animation. Indeed, this indeterminacy is also present in live-action film, though stop-motion, especially when not smoothed over in post-production, dramatizes this indeterminacy because it is always clear to the viewer that there has been some manipulation between the frames. As such, Tom Gunning is able to write that the photographic image contains the frozen potentiality for movement, but it is 'the perceptual experience of animation that ressurects time from its grave of immobility'.[134]

One might question whether within the unseen, liminal space between frames where Švankmajer's manipulations take place, objects always adopt the status of things, since they can never be known or seen and thus exceed classification. The idea of a space integral to the very body of the film, but yet unseen by the government censor, is appealing. While I am loathe in a materialist study focusing on objects and things to over-theorize an absence or read too much into a void, I believe there is a certain poetry to the notion that this space that allows movement could be considered as equivalent to the *parallel polis* – the political space theorized by Václav Benda that functions as a safe domain for dissidents, tucked away and hidden within the totalitarian state.[135] This might strike the reader as a fanciful notion, but there is always something unknowable and indeterminate within the very medium of animation itself.

Wells notes that Eisenstein equated the 'apparent freedom of the animated form with personal and ideological freedom'.[136] That is to say, animation's proclivity towards constant transformation and metamorphoses puts it in opposition to rigid and unwavering ideological dogma. This fact, combined with the imaginative scope that not relying on live-action allows, plus the aforementioned hidden space between its frames, makes animation the ideal artistic medium for political dissent.

Concluding remarks: Latour ← → Švankmajer

Across this chapter it has been demonstrated that Švankmajer's political ideas are most often asserted through things which make no recourse to words. His political project strikes me as being very similar in kind to Bruno Latour's – which is not 'to treat humans like objects, to take machines for social actors … but *to avoid using* the subject-object distinction *at all* in order to talk about the folding of humans and nonhumans'.[137]

As such, Švankmajer's cinema is most critical of those humans who refuse to acknowledge that they are inextricably intertwined within networks of non-humans and insist upon their right to use things as objects in purely human, functional terms. The hapless protagonist of *The Flat* finds that he cannot exist within a complex and multiple network of forceful thingy actants when he can only see these things as everyday objects that play their human-directed parts in domestic rituals. The things revolt against him, resisting his attempts at mastery through discordant bouts of violence. Likewise, the unseen ordering curator of *Naturae Historia ~ Suite* is unable to maintain a stark divide between civilization and nature (with himself on the side of civilization and the non-human actants on the side of nature) since he, like the creatures he categorizes, will end up succumbing to the natural process of death and decay. The criminal/agent of *A Quiet Week in the House* is perhaps more successful in his attempts to destroy the hybridized, abject, ambivalent things that reside in the locked rooms in networks outside human influence; however, his pathological need for categorization and control is such that he dashes back into the house to complete a bureaucratic ritual, even at risk of death. Even networks of things that exist outside the influence of humans, like the stones in *A Game with Stones*, can get caught up in their own destructive rituals.

In conclusion, then, the only hope for politics and progress that Švankmajer envisions lies with Bruno Latour's 'parliament of things'[138] and a radical denunciation of anthropocentrism, as outlined in Švankmajer's revolutionary manifesto 'To Renounce the Leading Role'. Ultimately, we – subjects and objects, objects and things, humans and non-humans – are all equal actants that exist on an equal footing. Since these actants are infinitesimally multiple, it is impossible for human actants to control all the variables in any given interaction. We should apply this fact to politics. Communism was predicated upon a notion, its origins in Hegel and Marx, that civilization ascends through an ever-refined, forward-moving dialectical process. A thesis and an antithesis come into conflict, eventually resolving in synthesis, from which a new thesis and antithesis will be produced. A rational, scientific society (as Soviet-style communism viewed itself) can guide these forces towards progressive and fruitful resolution(s) that will reach an ultimate synthesis at the point of Utopia.

However, according to ANT and Švankmajer's films, this is an unobtainable goal, since the interaction between actants is too complex and chaotic for their outcomes to be determined by even the most rational and scientific of methods. In fact, attempting to harness this network of things to run according to human desires will prompt further cycles of destruction and aggression. It is this observation that the world, composed of actants that all wield their own effects upon one another, is chaotic and ultimately uncontrollable, which would have been so disturbing to the Party censors when they viewed Švankmajer's films, resulting in his work being withdrawn from circulation. A view of the world as an inextricably intertwined network does not allow for simplistic configurations of revolutionary or counter-revolutionary, socialist or bourgeois, subject or object. As soon as we make a value judgement against one actant, we find ourselves making a value judgement about those intimately connected with it. Concepts of blame and intention are dispersed and with their loss, the notion that there exist only those people and things that serve the cause of revolution and those people and things that impede revolution becomes untenable.

If politics is the study of how humans can guide progress through micro-managed processes of conflict resolution according to ideals and ideology, then Švankmajer's work is aggressively anti-political, since it regards the political programme as essentially naive and misguided. However, if we choose to regard politics as any process of power relations and negotiations between actants (whether human or non-human), we must regard all of Švankmajer's work as political. His cinema in which things are given a starring role and persons are pushed to the background instructs the human viewer to pay heed to even the most seemingly minute of actants – each stone, nail or leaf with its own desires, fluctuations and singular and unique expressivity – and consider what role they might have to play within a global and holistic parliament of things, in which we are all (humans and non-humans) reliant upon one another.

Jiří Barta and the rhythmic difficulties of living in, or with, time and space

Introduction

Towards the end of the fifth and final chapter of *The Sociology of Marx* (*Sociologie de Marx*, 1966), Henri Lefebvre stops his analysis to reflect on the preceding 160 pages. Lefebvre, who has just explicated Marx's theory of the state, cautions that if his writing were to cease at this point he would have produced 'purely speculative, contemplative knowledge'.[1] This, he makes clear, would only be a partial account of Marx's sociology since 'Marxian thought is not merely oriented towards action' but is also 'a theory of action, reflection on praxis i.e., on what is possible, what impossible'.[2]

Lefebvre's posthumous work *Rhythmanalysis: Space, Time and Everyday Life* (*Éléments de rythmanalyse*, 1992) proposes a method for analysing the ideology encoded in the spaces and times of everyday life in order to interrogate the rhythms of a given city or place. In so doing, Lefebvre seeks to unite speculation with praxis, answering the challenge issued to himself some thirty years earlier in *The Sociology of Marx*. To engage in effective Marxian praxis the rhythmanalyst must be able to internalize environmental rhythms at an experiential, bodily level, while simultaneously maintaining distance from the action of these rhythms, observing them from afar, detached yet receptive.[3] As such, the rhythmanalyst combines the rigorous objectivity of the scientist with the ecstatic subjectivity of the poet.[4] To quote Claire Revol: 'This agent of observation, the rhythmanalyst ... listens to his body as a metronome as he listens to the world.'[5] This comparison illustrates how the rhythms of the body provide the rhythmanalyst with a 'baseline' against which he/she can measure and compare environmental rhythms. In this way, the rhythmanalyst's body acts like a reference oscillator, through and against which external rhythms are processed and defined.

A film viewer is also actively processing rhythms. While the film on screen produces rhythms through its editing, cinematography and the movement of things and actors within the mise-en-scène, in addition to the film's sound design and score, the spectator also has their own specific bodily apparatus (the clarity of their eyesight, the rate of their heartbeat, how they are able to sit, etc.) which will influence and alter their experience of the film. Like the film viewer, the rhythmanalyst is simultaneously aware of their physical enmeshment within the environment, while able to observe the rhythms that surround them. As such, rhythmanalysis (whether conducted outside or inside a cinema) marks a synthesis between observation and experience: the 'felt' with the 'conceived'.[6]

Lefebvre classifies rhythms as being either cyclical or linear, although sometimes what might be taken to be a single rhythm actually contains both cyclical and linear rhythms interacting.[7] Cyclical rhythms are most often observed in nature, such as in the passing of the seasons or the rising and setting of the sun, and are always experienced by the rhythmanalyst afresh, as though new. Linear rhythms, on the other hand, are accumulative and defined foremost by difference and variation. The movement of cars down a street, for example, accords to a linear rhythm of stops and starts. However, this linear rhythm is simultaneously contained within the larger cyclical rhythm of the working day. Sometimes rhythms act in harmonious accordance with one another (as in polyrhythmia) while at other times the interaction of rhythms is characterized by discordance and dissonance (as in arrhythmia).[8] Social rhythms are maintained through agents of the ideological superstructure (the police, law courts, etc.) and 'dressage', the process by which humans are 'broken in' to conform to the rhythms of society through the ritualized repetition of homogenizing movements.[9]

Defined succinctly, rhythm is an expression of variegated but regulated movement through time. For instance, the rhythms of people crossing a street are variegated in terms of how each individual carries himself/herself but regulated by traffic signals, zebra crossings and social codes. While rhythm arises from repetition, temporal or spatial differentiation is what allows this repetition to be perceived. However, if we make recourse to time to analyse the rhythms within a given environment (for instance, within an American nightclub, Soviet factory or Amazonian rainforest), we are confronted with the issue of determining the mode of time under which this environment and its rhythms operate.

We can distinguish between at least three different forms of time which can structure an environment and determine its operations. 'Rational time' is measured by clocks, bells, alarms and calendars and is the model of time which helps structure capitalism and to which the capitalist workforce is expected to conform. As explained by David Harvey, capitalists create the concepts of the working day, week, year, etc., in order to indoctrinate the working class into believing that 'time is not natural at all' and thus control their labour time.[10] Harvey's example of how time can be transfigured by capitalist ideology in order to better wed workers to an industrial mode of production illustrates that time itself (not merely actants within time) can be politically encoded.

Rational time, charismatic time and natural time

In Karel Čapek's *R.U.R.* (1920), the esteemed bourgeois Dr Helman holds the timetable in the highest of regards. 'If the time-table holds good', he pontificates, 'human laws hold good, divine laws hold good, the laws of the universe hold good, everything holds good that ought to hold good'.[11] The ants of the Čapek brothers' *Pictures from the Insects' Life* (*Ze života hmyzu*), written the following year, have even more triumphalist claims to make over time. The ants' chief engineer proclaims that the ants shall 'conquer time', will 'reign over time'.[12] The ant goes on to inform a human visitor that he who 'commands speed' will become the ruler of time and the ruler of time 'will be master of all'.[13] Thus a dialogue between two visions of time is established. Dr Helman positions time as the sovereign rule; it is the divine and moral duty of life to yield to the order of time. Punctuality is the greatest good. By contrast, the ants envision themselves as being able, with sufficient speed, to transcend the timetable. Through industrial efficiency, time itself may be conquered and bent to the will of the worker. Either – as in Dr Helman's conception – time is unsurpassable and life must fall in line accordingly, with work and industry bound unflinchingly to the clock; or else – as the ants believe – a sufficiently resourceful society can make time acquiesce to industry. Time, when tamed, can be made subordinate to work. It is telling that Dr Helman is in the business of manufacture – a scientist of industry and capital. The ants, meanwhile, work for the collective.

These examples from two Czech plays written in the interwar period are illustrative of the divergent tendencies under capitalism and communism regarding how time is conceptualized. Stephen Hanson describes this split in *Time and Revolution* (2000) as follows: 'If the ideal of "bourgeois" economists is a system in which each unit of time is utilized in as productive a manner as possible given scarce resources, the goal of Soviet socialism was to organize production in such a manner as to master time itself.'[14] Hanson refers to the bourgeois conception as 'rational' time and the conception under Soviet socialism as 'charismatic' time.[15] However, we are not dealing with a strict dichotomy; later in his work, Hanson notes that Marx himself 'synthesized charismatic and rational time'.[16] Indeed, charismatic time is something of a propagandistic fiction of Stalin's regime. Clearly, any situation in which workers are required to adhere to a daily, weekly and yearly schedule, adapting their biological rhythms to the demands of a factory or office, owes something to the strictures of clock time. Stalin, no less than a bourgeois industrialist, required his workers to produce as great a yield as possible in as small a time as possible.

Moreover, we must ask, is there a discernible point at which a desire to master efficiency becomes a desire to master time itself? Lefebvre writes in *The Production of Space* (*La Production de l'espace*) that 'the Soviet model has as its starting-point a revision of the Capitalist [*sic*.] process of accumulation, coupled with a good intention – the desire to improve this process by speeding it up'.[17] According to Lefebvre, then, socialism (at least in its Soviet incarnation) defined its conception of time, not in strict opposition to that of industrial capitalism but as an improvement that would exhibit the superior efficiency of the Soviet system. Propaganda may have claimed that this increased efficiency was to be realized through harnessing the collective will of the people, yet as long as this will was conceptualized as a means to an end (rather than the end in itself) it was still the servant, not master, of time. Yet, Hanson argues that the drive under Stalin to fulfil the production quota of a five-year plan (*pyatiletka*) within a four-year period 'meant *literally* overcoming the force of time within the time-bound socioeconomic order'.[18] Hanson makes a provocative leap of faith in asserting that the metaphorical rhetoric of Soviet propaganda should be taken literally at the highest metaphysical level, down to the material realities of production. Achieving a five-year plan in four years might quite simply be a matter of increased speed, as per Lefebvre, or it could mean, as per Hanson, literally compressing five years into four – condensing time through the sheer, collective will of the Soviet workforce.

Further complicating this rhetorical conundrum is the fact that ideology under socialism was often intended to be understood as a literal representation of reality (or what was demanded of reality) and this must be borne in mind even when such a reading seems counter-intuitive to someone living under modern Western capitalism. However, this ambiguity can be circumnavigated (though not wholly resolved) if Hanson's argument is reconceptualized in more limited terms. Even if we don't agree that socialist leaders or workers believed they could *literally* overcome time, there was a qualitative difference between capitalist and socialist rhetoric in relation to time by virtue of the latter's assertion – which may have been only rhetorical, *but to even express the belief is to grant its possibility* – that clock time might be fallible, that there could be another way of thinking about time.

Which, of course, there is – since a rational or a charismatic model is not the only way of conceptualizing time. Though these two concepts of time are different by degrees (humans as subject to time vs. time as subject to humans) they both centralize humanity's position as the ultimate measure of temporality. An anthropocentric conception of time is plagued by the same fundamental mistake as a geocentric model of the universe in assuming that human perception is essential to the existence of time per se.

Hanson provides a third mode of time, more ancient than both rational and charismatic models – that of 'traditional time',[19] by which duration proceeds by the ever-changing flow of natural phenomena, such as the passing of the seasons or the rise and fall of the sun upon the horizon. These things occur without being measured; the Earth would rotate and the trees grow and die without humans bearing witness.

So, there is time as measured by humans (which may be ideologically encoded) and time that exists and continues outside of the human sphere.

Broadly, natural or traditional time tends towards the cyclical (being seasonal in essence) while human time tends towards the linear and accumulative; however, this binary is reductive. To quote Yvette Bíro, 'The present … accommodates an existence of multiple (parallel, criss-crossing) layers and a future that points beyond itself. In other words, the present is not stable at all; it is the dimension of unceasing change.'[20] In short, we must always be wary of speaking of any one singular time and instead be attentive to the various ways in which different modes of time (rational/charismatic/natural/linear/cyclical, etc.) intersect.

Furthermore, time is always intertwined with space, so to speak about one is always inevitably to speak about the other. As with time, we tend to measure space in relation to ourselves as beings temporally and spatially circumscribed within finite boundaries. Euclidean space is comprehensible to us because we are phenomenological creatures who travel through and experience the world through our senses. As with time, space can be ideologically encoded. Lefebvre goes so far as to state that 'space embodies social relationships'.[21] As such, time and space are never neutral but always exist in relation to political structures. Buildings (homes, supermarkets, schools) and the doors, chairs, tables and other objects within them tend to be ergonomically constructed to best fit the bodily dimensions of an able-bodied human. This is a literal embodiment of anthropocentric, ableist hegemony. Polling stations only reachable via stairs, without access to persons in wheelchairs, simultaneously reflect an ideology that only able-bodied persons are legitimate political citizens and structurally enforce this ideology at the level of material relations. Not merely architecture alone but also the way architecture is used helps reinforce messages and rhythms encoded within a given space or place. For instance, certain benches in Manchester and London come fitted with retractable spikes to prevent their use by the cities' homeless populations.[22] Whether non-homeless citizens pay to use these benches themselves (or, instead, provide homeless citizens with the change to use them) then impacts upon the degree to which the hostile architecture is able to condition and control the rhythms of the environment it is intended to police.

Of course, benches and stairs are objects within the space(s) they occupy; so, while they impact spatial rhythms, they are fundamentally politically encoded things. The movement from politically encoded objects/things to objects/things treated as actants within political networks in time and space, to time and space *themselves* as politically encoded, does not describe a causal relationship but an expansion in praxis. So, the domestic objects of Trnka and Týrlová are political by virtue of their stubbornly non-ideological objecthood, but they are also metonymically linked, through allegory, to an idealized, rural Czech past, which can be treated in itself as a politicized temporal-spatial construction.[23] Likewise, while it has been argued that Švankmajer's things forge a dissident political space in the interstice between his films' frames, one could shift the focus of argumentation from the on-screen things to the absent space-time itself. The issue is one of where to contract and where to expand analysis.

The stop-motion films of Jiří Barta are suited to this expanded temporal-spatial analysis because they return repeatedly to the motif of the clock, constantly interrogating the notion that space and time are non-political. Barta's cinema illustrates that only through better acquainting themselves with the variegated, heterogeneous rhythms of natural time might citizens of Czechoslovakia (or, indeed, any society) free themselves from the stifling strictures of human-centred time, whether rational clock time under capitalism or charismatic time under socialism. Likewise, Barta suggests, predictable, rectilinear spaces will only ever produce citizens who live according to predictable, rectilinear rhythms. For a revolution to transform everyday life, the people must produce new, radical spaces and live according to a rich variety of times.

Jiří Barta: An ambivalent animator

Jiří Barta's films are not as recognizably the works of an auteur as those of Jan Švankmajer. While Švankmajer's thematic concerns are viscerally tangible throughout his films – the grossness of food and consumption, the strangeness and violence of childhood, the petty animal self-interest that lies behind human behaviour, etc. – Barta's themes are, generally, more nebulous. His films often deal with ritual and repetition, purging and sacrifice; yet these may be seen as formal structuring elements, rather than artistic or personal obsessions. Jenny Jediny lists 'changing social climates, myths and legends, and the organic'[24] as representative of the animator's themes but notes this makes an anomaly of *The Vanished World of Gloves* (*Zanikly svet rukavic*, 1982). I would add that neither *Riddles for a Candy* (*Hadanky za bonbon*, 1978) nor *The Last Theft* (*Poslední lup*, 1987) deal with these concerns, which, considering Barta's non-commercial output is less than a dozen films, indicates the difficulty in fitting his work within a limited number of descriptors. Perhaps the only indisputable theme of Barta's career is that of greed, which operates throughout many of his films as the ultimate vice, discernible behind every act of human evil. Thematic concerns aside, while we may recognize Švankmajer's films from their distinctive aesthetic tropes – intrusive, hyperreal sound designs, the bulging, googly eyes of his stop-motion creations, high-speed editing composed of extreme close-ups, etc. – Barta shifts stylistically between his films, choosing to work within a different mode of animation (whether stop-motion, traditional 2D forms or CGI) for each of his projects.

Another difference between the two animators is that Barta never worked under the more formal system of censorship that existed in Czechoslovakia prior to 1968, his first film being released in 1978. While many of the changes of the Prague Spring were rolled back over the 1970s, censorship during the period known as Normalization was enforced through bureaucratic processes, such as requests for post-production edits, or via self-censorship, rather than through the direct threat of legal sanction or persecution. As such, Barta may have felt less personal and artistic impetus to be a consistently political director than an artist like Švankmajer who experienced a greater degree of censorship throughout his career. While it will be argued that several of Barta's films function as political critiques – especially of certain socially licensed models of time and space – taken as a whole, his filmography does not comprise a politically radical body of work but a series of provocative and brilliant reflections upon a variety of themes. His films are as much formal reflections upon the medium of animation as they are political works. Of course, since animation was a comparatively marginal art form under Normalization, it allowed for a greater degree of stylistic experimentation than live-action film-making. As ever, the formal aspects of animation as a medium cannot be wholly extricated from the political content of a given animated film.

In short, Barta's filmography resists generalized, all-encompassing judgements and each of his films must be discussed by turn. It may seem perverse, then, to be discussing the bulk of Barta's filmography with a view to demonstrating a specific argument – namely, that time and space can be politically encoded on film. It is therefore important to note that time and space are not simply thematic concerns of Barta's but essential elements of the very medium in which he works. An analysis of the political encoding of time/space could potentially be performed on the films of any director or animator. In the case of the majority of cinema, however, the conception of time/space provided by the film will also be that of the dominant ideology. So, for example, a Hollywood action movie, such as *Die Hard* (1988) or *Mission Impossible* (1996), will generally possess a rationalistic conception of time, congruent with the capitalist production process under which the film was made. The concern of these films is to pack increasing amounts of novelty and spectacle into increasingly shorter times at increasingly faster speeds. Chases in cars, trains and aeroplanes are present to accentuate the audience's sense of speed and acceleration. Count-down clocks and bomb-timers remind the audience of the protagonists' need to complete their world-saving tasks as efficiently as possible. Conversely, the propagandistic pro-Soviet cinema of Eisenstein and Dziga Vertov is committed to a charismatic conception of time. Time is presented as dynamic, forced into acceleration by revolutionary or industrial practice. Time is measured not by the clock but by the actions of workers.

By contrast, Barta's work self-consciously circles the theme of society's relationship to time. His films are either structured around natural rhythms and repetitions or, more often, concern how rational/charismatic time has warped natural sensibilities, leading to the corruption of human society. Barta is not unique in these concerns as a Czech film-maker. For instance, much of Vojtěch Jasný's filmography – most notably, *All My Compatriots* (*Všichni dobří rodáci*, 1968) – comprises a lyrical celebration of rural Czech/Moravian life, while the changing of the seasons is a central structuring element of Jiří Menzel's *Seclusion Near a Forest* (*Na samotě u lesa*, 1976) and, to a lesser extent, *The Snowdrop Festival* (*Slavnosti sněženek*, 1984).

It might be tempting to regard Barta as a champion of lost Czech pastoralism, continuing in the same tradition as Trnka. However, while Trnka's work tended to contain simple, unidirectional messages, Barta's films tend towards the obfuscatory and multiple end of the allegorical spectrum.

Their moral impetus is often clear, yet the viewer's experience of assembling a coherent message is often fragmentary, gleaned through partial glimpses and momentary revelations. This likely stems from Barta's working method, which he has explained in interview. Rather than taking a complete story as his point of departure, or starting from a message that he wishes to impart, Barta develops his films from scattered pictures and images. By these means, he explains, he is able to 'fill animated shots not only with proper movements but also with metaphors, symbols and hidden meanings usually seen in still pictures'.[25] These symbols, metaphors and meanings may not always coalesce into allegory proper but rather reach towards a multiplicity of possible allegoresis – some political, others not.

Barta's films exemplify a form of cinematic engagement which Pasi Väliaho argues is invoked by all cinema – 'a mode of consciousness not as a homogeneous sphere but as a disjunctive assemblage of moving contents that waver on an uncertain threshold and remain constantly susceptible to falling into the unconscious'.[26] Väliaho argues that cinema as a medium has a unique relationship to space and time. Since cinema induces a state of consciousness in its audience that is wholly unique to its form, it also requires viewers to adopt a certain way of seeing the world that honours the singularly disjunctive flow of the medium. We must, urges Väliaho, 'avoid recurring traditional notions of the substance of the immutable being and, instead ... think of the world as dynamic and temporally constituted, and conceive of things in their eventful and processual nature'.[27] This is congruent with how Lefebvre instructs the budding rhythmanalyst to experience the world, understanding that if one looks out upon a landscape 'each plant, each tree, has its rhythm, made up of several: the trees, the flowers, the seeds and fruits, each have their time'.[28]

Clearly, then, the rhythmanalyst (or indeed, Väliaho's cinema-goer) must look further than the realm of abstract clock time to internalize the polysynchronous rhythms of nature, on screen or off. The polysynchronicity of natural time exists in a conflictual relationship with capitalist industry, which requires the multiplicity of natural rhythms to be subordinated to an unwavering timetable. Natural time is in a constant state of flux and shift; the lengths of days stretch out and then contract, while the flowering and decay of trees and flora are variegated and move in fits and starts. Yet labour under capitalism requires that the workers' circadian rhythms be dictated by their working hours, despite the fact that sleep cycles naturally shift with the seasons and the rising and setting of the sun. Time is artificially portioned into even, ever-forward moving increments to which the worker is forced to adapt.

As for charismatic time, Lefebvre notes that 'the cyclical, repetitious spacetime of death and of life, has nothing in common with Marxist time – that is, historically driven forward by the forces of production and … oriented by industrial, proletarian and revolutionary rationality'.[29] There is a gross arbitrariness about natural time from a state socialist perspective, since it is not dictated by the drive towards progress. The repetitions of natural growth and decay do not build towards some teleological end but recur across millennia, insensate and undirected. Nature does not *make use* of time and space in any conventional sense; rather, nature and time and space *are one and the same*. The rings in the trunk of an oak only become a means of measuring time once they are 'read' by a forester or lumberjack; left within the oak, unseen by humans trained in either rational or charismatic time, they are *not a signifier of time but the spatial embodiment of time itself*. Unwatched and undisturbed by humans, nature has rhythms of its own. Barta evokes and pays tribute to these rhythms in his stop-motion animated short *A Ballad about Green Wood* (*Balada o zeleném drevu*, 1983). Honouring natural rhythms at the expense of charismatic or rational time, Barta offers a vision of the world in thrall neither to communism, nor capitalism, but the rhythms of nature.

The loss of *Green Wood* and the defeat of natural time

It would perhaps be a misnomer to describe *A Ballad about Green Wood* as having a narrative in the conventional sense, though the film does consist of a distinct series of rhythmic movements which may be understood sequentially. The first movement depicts a brief montage of wood chopping in extreme close-up. We begin, then, with the world of human labour encroaching upon nature. The second movement depicts – in time-lapse footage – thawing, gushing and sprouting, as spring passes over the land. The third movement depicts, through still images, freezing and ossification, winter spreading death and cold. The fourth movement returns us to spring as the yearly cycle begins anew. Finally, the fifth movement returns us to the human sphere as the chopped wood is burnt for fuel. So, a narrative depicting the human use/exploitation of the natural world frames the ecstatic depiction of a natural fertility cycle analogous to the passing of the seasons.

Two figures in the film seem to be linked metonymically to the summer solstice and the winter solstice, respectively – metonymically, in the sense that they are at once both the harbingers *and* the embodiments of summer/winter, figuratively and literally ushering in the seasons they represent. The figure which appears to be a summer deity is a split piece of wood with the face of a beautiful woman carved into it. She is destroyed by the winter deity mid-way through the film, yet at the film's end is reincarnated and sprouts grass, which consumes the winter deity, who is sacrificed, allowing the cycle to begin again. Meanwhile, the deity associated with the winter solstice is a shard of wood with wings and a death's head in its most stable incarnation; however, it moves through a series of transfigurations. At first the figure is a raven, then a hybridized figure between a raven and a piece of dead wood, then an icicle and then, once again, the hybridized figure. The figure is also, of course, winter itself. The equivalent of this figure in Slavic folklaw is Koliada, associated with the winter solstice.[30] Its bird-like form recalls human-bird hybrids, such as the Sirin bird, also from Slavic folklaw.[31] The shard of wood with the maiden's face is equivalent to Kupalo, a deity of summer/spring, although traditionally Kupalo is a male figure.[32] However, it is hardly necessary to match Barta's creations onto corresponding figures from Slavic folk traditions, considering his collaged approach to narrative. Indeed, mythological figures that embody the seasons can be found in folk traditions from across the globe. Rather, what is worth noting in these regards is that Barta is drawing inspiration from ancient myths that not only predate both communism and capitalism but are transnational rather than specifically Czech. This gives the film a universal aspect which protects it not only from accusations of specific political critique but also from being co-opted by the regime as were the works of the National Revival under Gottwald's 'Jirásek Action'.

The temporal location of the film is, for the purposes of the film-maker, a mythic time – or more precisely, a time *outside of time*. Since the film enters into a natural cycle which exists outside of human influence, it would be erroneous to pin this cycle down to a specific calendar year. However, just as

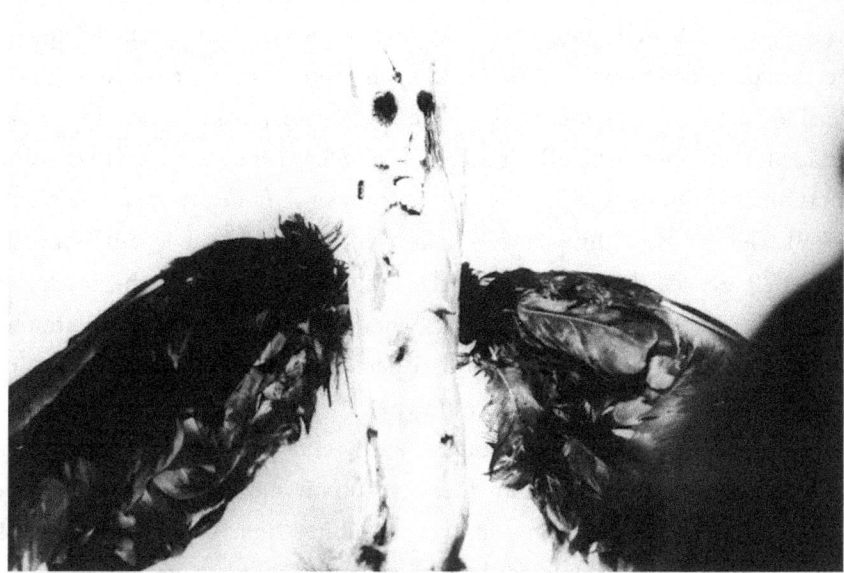

Figure 3.1 A puppet-object-thing that is at once Koliada, a death's head, a bird and a piece of wood in *A Ballad about Green Wood* (*Balada o zeleném dřevu*) (Jiří Barta, 1983). Image used with permission of Krátký film Praha.

the mechanization of nature in *The Cybernetic Grandma* (1962) suggests the near-future, the verdancy of the 'Green Wood' of Barta's title, which unfurls to the rhythms of Vladimír Merta's folk music, suggests a date prior to the film's release. By the end of the 1980s, approximately 30 per cent of the forests in Bohemia had been destroyed by acid rain, while, of the remaining 70 per cent, about half had been partially destroyed.[33] Concern over these affairs was not merely limited to environmentalists. Maria Dowling reports that a survey of 400 Czech citizens, carried out in November of 1989 into problems affecting the nation, found that 98 per cent of those canvassed considered the environment a primary issue of concern.[34] So, at the start of this 1983 film, when we are shown extreme close-ups of wood being cut to pieces by an axe, we should consider that a Czech audience watching the film in a cinema upon its release would not have been indifferent to the topic under representation.

Intriguingly, Barta seems to hint that not all of the woodland is willing to acquiesce to its own destruction. After a series of six brief shots (intercut with credit/title cards), in which logs of wood are split, the axe swings down upon a piece of wood that does not yield to the blade. Instead, the axe blade becomes embedded in the icy wood and the log is smacked repeatedly against the chopping slab until it splits. At this point in the film, the wood might be considered to be a dissident thing, like the egg or porous spoon that assail the hapless protagonist in Švankmajer's *The Flat* (1968) or those mysterious unclassifiable things spied upon by the agent in *A Quiet Week in the House* (1969). The dissident thing asserts its mute otherness in the face of a human subject. It evades the utilitarian designs thrust upon it. For the frustrated human the stubbornness of the thing (whether a back-firing car, a computer failing to start or a frozen log of wood) is perceived as a challenge. It is refusing to behave as it ought. It will not acquiesce.

While the first chunks of wood are easily chopped into pieces and thus turned into nothing more than fuel for human subjects (i.e. transformed into pure use value), this final log resists subjugation. When, eventually, it is split, the splitting is depicted through stop-motion photography as the log splinters into a dozen smaller pieces. As with the abrupt use of stop-motion to depict an effect that might have been achieved with live-action in *Revolution in Toyland* (1946), here the use of stop-motion signals a shift into a different mode of phenomenological reality – one of animism and pagan ritual.

Václav Havel writes, in an essay collected in *Living in Truth* (1989), that without social time humanity is cast back into a more primitive mode of existence, in which time is measured 'by the cosmic and climatic patterns of endlessly repeated annual seasons and the religious rites associated with them'.[35] Or, to reverse Havel's statement but retain its meaning, Stephen Hanson argues that Stalinism assured a loss of natural rhythms as the Russian *muzhik* were uprooted to work in factories.[36] More broadly we might argue that labour alienates man from nature, even as nature furnishes the 'material substratum'[37] which labour works and transforms. Man and labour are simultaneously *of* nature and *against* nature. Since labour is a 'nature-imposed necessity'[38] required by man to live, he must always already be engaged in the work of transforming the world around him into use value. This might be considered a Marxian account of the fall of man.

Though such symbolism may be unintentional, it is interesting to note that the first shot of *Green Wood* is an extreme close-up of the rings of a severed piece of tree trunk, which, after an outwards zoom, is split into two by the fall of the axe. Thus, an embodiment of natural time is violently broken to pieces by human labour. The steady fall of the axe, marking the spaces between the credits, keeps beat. The regular and monotonous rhythm of human work, ever linear, is introduced.

However, once the wood begins to protest, we are plunged outside of the sphere of human work into a medley of natural rhythms. The camera, which had been static save for the opening outwards zoom, becomes far looser, panning across the fallen shards of wood. Streams gush and burble, ice thaws and the splints of wood appear to dance in an ecstatic, merry circle. Immediately, then, the circular rhythms of nature interpose themselves. The shards of wood not only dance in a circle but also spin, moving in circles within a circle. This creates a vertiginous and dizzying effect. In contrast to the predictable and stable rhythms of the chopping, these rhythms are unshackled to linear time.

Through cutting between stop-motion footage of the wood and close-ups of water flowing, the viewer experiences a multitude of rhythms. These rhythms are harmonious, yet chaotic. The water is shown flowing in different directions, across the screen from right to left, then from left to right, then from screen top to bottom. As such, the water appears not to have a linear progression (we are clearly not following these streams from source to sea) but rather embodies a natural eruption of life, unharnessed and spilling over with energy. The diegetic sound of the rushing water heightens our sensory immersion in the scene. As viewers we are placed at the centre of this jumble of busily intersecting currents.

To return to Bíro's remark about 'the present' – it 'accommodates an existence of multiple (parallel, crisscrossing) layers and a future that points beyond itself'.[39] The present is not a single, static moment but contains a multiplicity of different rhythms, with each having its own time. It is difficult for the individual human to access this 'multiple present' since we are locked into a linear forward moving experience of time. However cinema, due to the freedom that editing gives to the manipulation of time, can allow the viewer to experience time in a non-linear fashion. At this moment in the film, the repetition of the nature shots and the circularity of the dance create the impression of occupying a multiple present. Rather than progressing sequentially, this gushing forth of nature is occurring all at once in some ecstatic moment outside of rational, linear time.

A fluke in the film-making process serendipitously contributes to this impression. In an interview with Jeremy Clarke, Barta speaks of the difficulty in filming stop-motion on location, since it is impossible to regulate the light.[40] The sun keeps changing its position in the sky and the intensity of the light dips and wanes. This creates a flickering effect of rapidly changing dimness and brightness during the stop-motion sequences. This adds to the impression that what is unfolding is not taking place at any one time of day but instead represents the passing of an entire season. Väliaho notes that 'cinematic rhythms' are 'not measures of time but rather contribute to our perception of time and the duration of things and events'.[41] When our eyes dart across a painting, we do not assume – save in the case of cabinet paintings – that the order in which we pick out objects and moments from the landscape necessarily represents the order of their occurrence. Rather, we tend to assume that a painting crystallizes a moment, idea or a span of time, but one in which many rhythms and alternate times are contained. Certainly, we do not assume that each painting is a still life and the subjects and objects depicted always static. Paintings rarely function as photographs – they generally depict not frozen moments but overlaid tableaux of different moments and actions of indeterminate duration. Likewise, the 'spring awakening' montage in *Green Wood* captures ecstatic simultaneity. All at once spring has arrived and wood dances, water gushes, doors blow open and ice thaws.

As Barta's montage continues, it starts to depict more variegated phenomena of nature at alternate speeds. Mud is shown rising up and bubbling open, seeds sprout and an earthworm, in extreme close-up, burrows through the earth. Some of these shots are composed of time-lapse footage of micro phenomena. Some appear murky and abstract and merely evoke pulsing or thrumming, without a clear sense of the actants moving on screen. Our sense of duration is, as in the first half of the montage, not concrete but symbolic. That is to say, the montage does not depict a literal series of events in sequence. We are being presented with an idea, an experience of the breath of nature. Such a reading chimes with Vicky Smith's contention that time lapse, when used in experimental cinema – unanchored from human characters or documentary voice-over narration – allows natural objects the time-space to express their own agency independent from human control or oversight.[42] In the case of *Green Wood*, we do not follow a human protagonist walking

Figure 3.2 The world spins and the ground heaves with innumerable actants surging, flowing, thrusting and thawing in *A Ballad about Green Wood* (Jiří Barta, 1983). Images used with permission of Krátký film Praha.

along the bank of the river, but neither are we provided with a static long take of the environment via time lapse (as per many of the films Smith discusses). Instead, the footage is unanchored from an anthropocentric position through being edited – in no discernibly logical order – into a montage of differing speeds of motion, direction of movement and shot length.

We start to internalize these rhythms at the level of our body as the film transports us to what could be assumed to be the POV of one of the shards of wood. The camera weaves dizzyingly around in circles, moving up and down in waves as on a carousel. The image blurs and the sensation induced by watching the footage is exhilarating, yet queasy. That this is the POV of one of the shards of wood is communicated by the viewer's ability to match movement they first viewed from the outside of the dance, looking in, to movement they now experience from the inside, looking out. Of course, unless we are a firm believer in universal animism, the notion of a POV from a piece of wood seems immediately incongruous, absurd. As such, one might posit that the POV is not from the wood per se but shot from the position of the rhythm itself. That is to say, the shot portrays the inner experience of the dance of nature as felt on a gut-level by the audience.

At this juncture, it may be apposite to introduce the concept of 'vitality affects'.[43] The phrase originates in the work of developmental psychologist Daniel Stern and refers to dynamic sensations that accompany many of the activities of daily life. Väliaho radically repurposes Stern's original idea to consider vitality affects not in terms of the everyday but as embodied sensations elicited in the film viewer by certain cinematic sequences or techniques. Väliaho describes vitality affects as being 'characterized in dynamic and kinetic terms such as surging, fading away, fleeting, explosive, accelerating, decelerating, bursting, reaching, and hesitating' and concerning 'the force, intensity, quality, form, or rhythm of experience'.[44]

Vitality affects, then, are not so much properties of things in themselves as they are qualities which belong to the movement of things and the sensations of subjects entangled with those things. Lefebvre writes that a rhythm 'is not a thing, nor an aggregation of things, nor yet a simple flow. It embodies its own law, its own regularity, which it derives from space – from its own space – and from a relationship between time and space'.[45] Perhaps, then, vitality affects should be conceptualized as varieties of rhythm. This succeeds in bridging the gap between Stern's conception of vitality affects as relating to bodily activities such as 'breathing, moving, sucking, defecating, and swallowing' and Väliaho's sense that they are a form of 'cinematic embodiment'.[46] When Väliaho refers to embodiment, this embodiment is not merely that of the objects on screen (as might be implied by 'cinematic embodiment') but that of the audience member as the rhythms of their body harmonize and/or clash with the rhythms on screen.

So, the vitality affects of *Green Wood*'s 'spring awakening' sequence should be positioned at the intersection between what transpires upon the screen and the inner sensations this elicits in the viewer's body. Some potential vitality affects (which will differ from viewer to viewer) of the montage are a feeling of release and exhalation, a desire for growth and movement, dance and dizziness, wave-like plunging and a sense of 'entering into' the world. The soundtrack of flute, string and horns also intensifies the atmosphere and feelings of renewal and vitality.

The rhythms of spring are soon modified, however, by the coming of winter. The music shifts to more ominous tones as the raven enters and pecks the shard of wood with the maiden's face to pieces. After this, a shot of the raven standing upon the snowy grass, wings outstretched, dissolves to a shot of the raven with a wooden death's head. As this creature then flies across the landscape, shots of grassland cut abruptly to static images of the now frosted landscape in monochrome. It is as though the vitalist pulse – the very rhythms of nature – has been sucked from the land. Winter has ossified the landscape.

Time lapse is cinema *in excess*, exhibiting its ability to accelerate the rhythms of life. By contrast, still photography has the ability to freeze life and remove all movement from a vital, living landscape. The transition from the former to the latter in *Green Wood* provides an exemplary illustration of Siegfried Kracauer's belief that film acts as a gateway from the outer world to the inner, providing a means by which the 'emanations' of an environment can be internalized by the viewer.[47] To speak holistically, as Kracauer often does, cinema allows an audience to reconnect with the 'vitalist pulse' of the world. In the movement from time lapse to still photography, Barta has allegorized – caricatured, even – the transition from spring to winter as it occurs and is experienced within a rural environment.

Lefebvre writes that 'everyday life remains shot through and traversed by great cosmic and vital rhythms: day and night, the months and the seasons, and still more precisely biological rhythms'.[48] Lefebvre's *Rhythmanalysis* and *The Production of Space* are predominantly urban texts. When 'everyday life' is spoken of, it tends to be the life of the city – life that is criss-crossed by the hustle and bustle of people. Perhaps then, *Green Wood*, through its lyrical, ecstatic and vitalist rendering of the Czech countryside, helps reacquaint its viewers with these great cosmic and vital rhythms, already muted by the destruction of northern Bohemia's forests and only dimly perceptible within a town or city cinema.

These rhythms having stilled, the wood-raven hybrid alights in a cave, where it hangs upside down from the ceiling like a bat. This image then dissolves to a shot of an icicle hanging at the cave's entrance. There is a match between the two shots on the form of the creature and the form of the icicle. It is not merely a parallel that is drawn here but a visual means of capturing the magical thinking of mythology. The crow's body *is* winter, *is* dead wood and *is* an icicle. They are related via similitude, not difference.

The sun rises and an exultant fanfare of horns begins on the soundtrack. A knight carved from light wood appears. His design distinctly mirrors the recognizable aesthetic style of Trnka. Heroic figures in Barta's films tend to be reminiscent of Trnka's. This, of course, could merely be a nod of respect to the great animator; however, the reference to Trnka may also represent the simplicity and virtue of peasant life as celebrated in his works. This is the class we tend to believe to be best acquainted with natural time. The knight, then, represents the unfreezing of natural time from its slumber and the coming of spring. Soon the wooden raven is defeated and the icicle falls from the mouth of the cave. In celebration, the wooden maiden, newly reborn, ignites the funeral pyre of the fallen creature, which then teems with and is consumed by verdant grass.

Bruce Kawin asserts that 'primitive man' learned from the rejuvenation of the earth in spring that the harms caused by winter were not permanent.[49] It is not that primitive man was in denial of winter but that he had to understand death as a cyclical process, or else the harsh losses of winter would have imposed too heavy a toll upon his psychological and social well-being. Hanson expresses this idea succinctly: 'Birth and death in traditional cultures tend to be seen not as the finite endpoints of a lifespan conceived in linear terms but instead as passages in a natural process of generational renewal.'[50]

It is clear from the ecstatic music cues and sheer vitalist energy of the central portion of *Green Wood* that Barta believes this cyclical vision of time to possess aesthetic value. The abrupt violence and lifelessness of the opening and closing sections of the film also hint that there is an added moral dimension to Barta's interests. At the start of the film, an axe chopped up wood with monotonous regularity. Now, at the end of this seasonal fertility ritual, all joy and animism is stripped away from the wood with the maiden's face upon it. Clanging, machine-like noises enter the soundtrack and the film cuts to a shot of a chimney, smoke rising from its top. It lasts but a couple of seconds and then the screen fades to credits. Nature's cyclical rhythms of purging and rebirth have been violently interrupted by the encroachment of civilization. In Lefebvre's terminology, cyclical cosmic rhythms have been superseded by human linear rhythms. The wood was part of a larger natural cycle of birth, decay, death and rebirth, but in being burnt for fuel, it has been removed from this eternal cycle merely for transient gain.

A Ballad about Green Wood becomes a eulogy mourning the loss of both the woodlands of Bohemia and natural time. On the wrist of the man who collects the wood and strips it clean is a watch. The wood, the embodiment of natural time (with its tree rings), has been thrown to the fire, sacrificed and exploited by human subjects with emblems of rational clock time upon their wrists. Esther Leslie explains, after George Lukács, that 'attached to pockets and wrists, time is spatialized ... [S]uch a spatialization is synonymous with reification or alienation of the self, from nature, from other beings, from the outputs of one's energies'.[51]

There is a moral dimension to this notion that through binding ourselves to rational time we sever ourselves from a vital connection with nature. Moreover, charismatic time cannot remedy this state of affairs since it is merely a modification of abstract time that centralizes human will. Reconnecting with natural time means forgoing civilization. The project is – like Havel's and Trnka's – essentially reactionary since it requires a return to a previous state of being. However, when the KSČ was engaged in a process of Normalization – reversing the liberalizing reforms of the Prague Spring and seeking to implement, through bureaucracy and censorship, what the Stalinist regime of the 1950s had achieved through terror – nostalgic, reactionary thinking became a means of envisioning a semi-mythic past Utopia neither reducible to capitalism or communism. It is the loss of this non-political realm of embodied natural time that *A Ballad about Green Wood* mourns, expressing through images, music and rhythms what Lefebvre expresses here in words:

> In nature, time is apprehended within space – in the very heart of space: the hour of the day, the season, the elevation of the sun above the horizon, the positions of the moon and stars in the heavens, the cold and the heat, the age of each natural being, and so on. Until nature became localized in underdevelopment, each place showed its age and, like a tree trunk, bore the mark of the years it had taken it to grow. Time was thus inscribed in space, and natural space was merely the lyrical and tragic script of natural time ... With the advance of modernity time has vanished from social space. It is recorded solely on measuring-instruments, on clocks, that are as isolated and as functionally specialized as this time itself ... Our time, then, this most essential part of lived experience, this greatest good of all goods, is no longer visible to us, no longer intelligible. It cannot be constructed. It is consumed, exhausted, and that is all. It leaves no traces. It is concealed in space, hidden under a pile of debris.[52]

Designing uniformity in *The Design*

So, according to Lefebvre, time, under modernity, has been used up and violently severed from space. Increasing abstraction has removed time from lived experience and displaced it to clocks and measuring devices, which convert time into space. However, this is not to say that space is invulnerable to being distorted and diminished. Two of Barta's early films, *The Design* (*Projekt*, 1981) and *Disc Jockey* (*Diskzokej*, 1980), illustrate that space is closely linked to human lived experience and that human interactions are flattened and reduced by topographical thinking exercised through space.

The Design provides a short, effective critique of Soviet housing projects in communist-era Czechoslovakia. From the coup of 1948 through to the late 1950s, 'the doctrine of socialist realism (*sic*) changed the tone and direction of architectural practice'.[53] The individual vision of a single architect was de-emphasized and concordantly there was a dwindling in avant-gardist experimentation. A more efficient mode of factory production based on the Soviet model was introduced, leading to greater uniformity in design as exemplified by the pre-fabricated apartments known colloquially as *panelák*. Later, in the 1970s, these panel buildings spread to non-urban areas as the Husák administration constructed thousands of new housing estates throughout the country. Barta, then, in *The Design*, addresses a contemporaneous phenomenon with roots as far back as his childhood.

The building designed and constructed in *The Design* is a forty-room *panelák* apartment. The film begins as the architect's tool kit is opened and the implements systematically laid upon a work surface. The implements are positioned in a row, every object evenly spaced apart and horizontally aligned. The rectilinear thinking of our unseen architect protagonist has been quickly established. The kind of design that is to be drawn has already been subtly determined by his means of production. Barta's film illustrates the concept that a diagram not only describes but brings reality into being.[54] At the microcosmic level of the drawing board, ideology (superstructure) and material reality (substructure) are already determining one another. The architect's straight-edged tools and measuring devices are only ever going to produce rectilinear designs because they are ill-suited to drawing curves or irregular shapes – they merely reflect the utilitarian and rectilinear world view of their designer. The

Figure 3.3 The tools of the architect and his ideological world view predetermine both design and material reality in *The Design* (*Projekt*) (Jiří Barta, 1981). Image used with permission of Krátký film Praha.

functional, utilitarian thinking that the architectural process demands, ensured by the precise, rational and quantitative scales and measures used for the job, predetermines the functional design of the building. There is no gap between the ideology that dictates how buildings are designed and the material facts of their existence when built.

While the foundations of the building and its framework are sketched out on screen, the sounds of a construction site are heard. Clearly, these are non-diegetic sounds, but they are not disconnected from what we see on screen; rather, they fuse the present moment of design with the future moment of construction. Since *The Design* is a graphical drawn animation, there is no discernible point at which the drawing of the apartment block becomes 'the real thing', a confusion which is only amplified by the sound design.

The skeleton of the building has been sketched out in black ink. The architect opens a series of envelopes from which he takes small paper cut-outs of household objects and consumer goods, as well as residents for the apartments, and places them within their respective homes. What we took to be a mere representation of space is now being treated as a 'real' place in which people can live. The fact that the schematic has become indistinguishable from the very thing it depicts highlights that it was never a neutral representational tool. Because as a means of representation, the blueprint is airless and unimaginative, so too is the apartment it depicts.

In contrast to the design, each resident or family retrieved from the envelope is drawn in their own distinct style matched to their specific taste in furnishings. There is a scholarly gentleman who sits at his desk alongside a bookcase and elegant grandfather clock. An artistic couple is drawn in a cubist style reminiscent of Picasso. As each of the rooms of the apartments is furnished, a distinct piece of music plays on the soundtrack, matched to the style of the individual or family. So, the artistic couple is accompanied by modern piano music. A man, who seems to embody the traditional, rural values of an older generation, is placed in his apartment to the accompaniment of an accordion. The music builds; the past layers sink into the background and are overlaid with the music associated with each new resident. This creates a cacophonous but densely interwoven soundscape, indicating the variegating rhythms of apartment life.

However, concessions are made in the name of progress, ensuring not all individuality is honoured. The man who seems to be a Czech or Slovak peasant brings with him a goat. The goat's horns and udders are promptly snipped off, transforming it into a dog. Likewise, a traditional stove is removed since the apartment is already fitted with an oven. At first, some of these concessions seem ideologically neutral since a number of the objects simply do not fit the dimensions of a single flat. The scholarly gentleman has the greater portion of his bookcase snipped away, for instance, since it does not fit the room. However, this sense of innocent happenstance is contingent upon the naive idea that the design itself was only ever neutral and non-ideological. However, designs do not merely describe reality; they actively construct it. Lefebvre expresses this idea as follows: 'The graphic elements involved (in drawings, sections, elevations, visual tableaux with silhouettes or figures, etc.) which are familiar to architects, serve as *reducers* of the reality they claim to represent – a reality that is in any case no more than a modality of an accepted (i.e. imposed) "lifestyle".'[55] That is to say, an architectural blueprint provides a specific socially constructed version of reality, which necessarily omits certain details and includes others.

The homogeneity of design under Socialist Realism and Normalization ensures the uniformity of not just *panelák* buildings but also their inhabitants. Soon enough, the individuality of the film's residents is erased. A second sheet of paper is placed on top of the first. The ink roller is taken and rolled across the second sheet which, when removed, reveals the inhabitants of the apartments now stripped of colour, their furnishings all alike. However, there are still some discrepancies and a couple of rooms have yet to be fully assimilated. A third sheet of paper is rolled down. Then a fourth. Now, all that remains, demarcating a final room from all the rest, is a lone portrait of a couple. The hands peel the paper portrait from the design and crumple it up into rubbish. The bossa nova music slows and stops and all is quiet. A diminishment of space has taken place and, with it, the daily lives of the inhabitants of space have been hollowed and abstracted. 'The reduction with which we are concerned', writes Lefebvre,

> is directed towards the already reduced dimensions of Euclidean space; as we have already seen, this space is literally flattened out, confined to a surface, to a single plane. The person who sees and knows only how to see, the person who draws and knows only how to put marks on a sheet of paper ... contribute in their way to the mutilation of a space which is everywhere sliced up.[56]

The topographical mode of thinking engaged in by the architect has literally defined the urban space, abstracting it, so that the individuals within experience no *depth* to their lives – both literally and figuratively. By the end of Barta's film, the music, once vibrant and densely layered, has been reduced to a low wind or perhaps the roar of traffic. The camera zooms out and we see that the panel building was just one of many, arranged in endless rows, like flat-pack furniture. The original blueprint design, measured and scored so precisely with exacting implements, could only ever produce conformity.

Finally, as a nasty juxtaposition to the crisp whiteness before us, the sound of a fly buzzing enters intrusively onto the soundtrack, continuing beneath the credits. The sense of abjection this introduces cements the viewer's feeling that there is something fundamentally perverse, deathly and life-denying about the entire architectural project. The very geometrical cleanliness of the design work disguises the ideological rot at the heart of a scheme that values making space cheaper, more efficient, over individual human vitality and life and, in so doing, diminishes both space and human life.

Repeating uniformity in *Disc Jockey*

Disc Jockey, produced a year before *The Design*, is less politically astute than *The Design*, yet there are some interesting affinities between the two films. While *The Design* is a live-action film with stop-camera effects and *Disc Jockey* is a traditionally animated two-dimensional work, both might be considered 'graphical animations', in the sense that both adopt a topographical view, which reduces objects to their elementary shapes and forms. In *The Design*, the structuring element is the square. In *Disc Jockey*, it is the circle. Both films are concerned, at a thematic level, with how the rhythms and practices of everyday life are modified by design. In *The Design* the argument is made specifically in relation to Soviet-style housing projects. In *Disc Jockey*, the broader argument is made that the daily rituals which compose life in a late-period communist society are determined by advertising and design. So, there are very fast, abrupt cuts between advertisements for products and the products themselves being used.

Rarely do we see any actual spaces or places in the film. Instead, locations are signalled for the viewer through their familiarity with ubiquitous icons, signs and logos. A driving sequence provides a brief establishing shot of a road, before reducing the journey merely to common road signs, the speedometer and roadside advertisements. Usually, these are elements that might help navigate or determine a journey; but here, they have superseded the journey itself. These signifiers – which can be read but not inhabited or experienced – seem to dominate a landscape without things. The film is rigorously pessimistic, since any potential means of transcending this topographic emptiness – drugs, music or natural time – are shown to be easily co-opted or diminished. Natural time is represented at the start of the film by the sun moving across the sky, but this is overshadowed by an enormous alarm clock in the foreground, with a circular form that seems to both mirror and parody that of the sun. During a sequence in which the disc jockey plays records at a club, the wild flights of fantasy evoked by the music merely end up reduced to banal domestic routines or the ubiquitous circle. Images that feature in the montage are meat being sliced, a combine harvester spitting out bales at regular intervals, soup boiling, a stack of tumbling cans and boxing gloves punching forward, but never connecting. The images would be surreal in their juxtaposition, but the way in which they all conform to the same circular forms renders them banal. Even fantasy does not break from the regular patterns and rhythms circumscribed

Figure 3.4 A world reduced to flattened signs without depth or differentiation in *Disc Jockey* (*Diskzokej*) (Jiří Barta, 1980). Image used with permission of Krátký film Praha.

by the material relations of everyday life. All of the different records even sound alike, just variants on the same tired old tune.

Eventually, the disc jockey starts placing pill after pill into his disembodied mouth, an action that was shown at the start of the film to be part of his morning routine. With the consumption of each pill, the ink around the mouth becomes smudged and the drawing cruder and more diminished. There are two potential readings, both bleak. Either, drugs can deform or distort the content of cycles, but ultimately the cyclical forms which house this content will continue unabated; or else, the eating of each pill represents the beginning of a new day of routines and repetition, which eventually diminish and deform the individual.

Twisted spirals and swollen shards: The sickened rhythms of Hameln

If Barta seems deterministic in *The Design* and *Disc Jockey* about the ability of people to escape the influence of determining rhythms (whether spatial or temporal) in their daily lives, his stop-motion retelling of 'The Pied Piper of Hamelin', *Rat Catcher* (1985) is more pessimistic still in depicting a society structured by rhythms that have become so warped and corrupted by greed that any persons displaying goodness or charity therein are destroyed. Barta demonstrates throughout the film how repetition can allow sick, unhealthy rhythms to become naturalized and socially sanctioned.

Barta's film is an adaptation of a 1915 novel by Viktor Dyk, which itself is an adaptation of the famous German folk tale with origins in Backhaus's *Hameln Chronicle*.[57] The most notable inclusion from Dyk for a viewer best acquainted with English versions of the story (such as Browning's) is a romantic subplot between the piper and a young maiden named Agnes. A viewer most familiar with Browning's poem will also note the absence of children from the town. Indeed, the only child is a small infant, cradled by a fisherman who floats on a boat in a river outside the borders of the town. The fisherman himself, named Sepp Jörgen in the novel, is another addition by Dyk. Hameln itself is – of course – plagued by rats, which terrorize the citizens and consume the town's produce. The piper, a mysterious and robed figure in the film, offers to rid the town of the vermin, for a sum. He succeeds in this, but the town elders refuse to pay him. In Barta's version of the story, this insult is compounded by the horror of Agnes's rape and murder, which drives the piper to transform the townspeople into rats and, through the means of his music, send them plummeting into the river, where they are drowned. Only the fisherman survives with the infant he has rescued.

It is, perhaps, familiarity with the basic structural elements of the story of 'The Pied Piper' that lends to the experience of watching the film a sense that things are unfolding to a predetermined design. However, this sense of predetermination also derives from Barta's notable inclusion of motifs associated with abstract clock time and a self-conscious use of repetition in his editing. The impression that the tragic and grotesque unfoldings of the plot conform to some inner mechanism and proceed like clockwork serves the impression given by the film that the immorality of the townspeople is habitual and derives from repetitions encoded in the very space of the city.

At the start of *Rat Catcher*, an extreme long-distance establishing shot of Hameln is intercut with extreme close-up shots of a clock mechanism – cogs turning and a pendulum swinging. An intimate connection is immediately established between the city and the mechanized forward-march of abstract clock time. Although the shots of the mechanism are soon matched to a great clock tower rising up from the city, the connection is not made immediately apparent, so that the first impression is that the city *itself* is mechanized and that we are to watch unfold the drama of a clockwork Hameln. As with the shot in *Disc Jockey* that pairs the rising of the sun with the rotating arms of an alarm clock, the passing of a metallic sun affixed to one of the clock hands seems to prompt the rising of the sun in the sky, an indication that abstract time has superseded natural time.

Kawin notes that 'a clock can tell about time but cannot express or be time'.[58] Since a clock has an indexical relationship to time, it cannot be time itself. It can merely defer to time, point towards it. As such, clocks take us outside of a lived experience of time because they always posit that time is 'elsewhere'. Thus, by associating Hameln so closely with the image of a clock, Barta communicates something of the city's arrogance. Hameln has attempted to position itself outside of natural time, as though the city's clock which measures the beginning and end of the working day is the only form of time worth conforming one's rhythms to. Hameln literalizes the notion of clock*work*. As soon as the bells above the city chime in accordance with the clock, the inhabitants of Hameln poke their heads out of windows, resembling cuckoos, which stick out their heads on the hour, every hour. They are tethered to and unable to think outside of a routine which, in turn, is connected unfailingly to ever-standard, unchanging clock time. Consequently, they are unable to think or act for themselves and, in turn, are incapable of internal change, unless imposed from outside. In this regard, anyone who labours under capitalism is not dissimilar to the citizens of Hameln. Harvey remarks that to the extent that we have internalized the hegemonic ideology of clock time, 'we learn to live by it almost without thinking ... captive to a certain way of thinking about temporality and the practices that attach thereto'.[59]

This notion of the inhabitants of Barta's Hameln being slaves of clock time makes considerable sense of a rather cryptic remark made by Barta in interview in which he refers to the Pied Piper as 'a symbol of nobody, of death, of time, destiny and so on'.[60] Barta risks speaking in vague generalities in order to communicate a sense of *that which exceeds clock time*. The Pied Piper is not reducible to quantifiable measures, production quotas or monetary value. He is an absent symbol. He sits absolutely outside of the system of production and consumption of the city and its endless chain of commodity exchange. He is also, perhaps, a romantic symbol of the sublime artist who transcends the banal and mean drudgery of daily working life. It is essential that he comes from outside of the city since this indicates that he does not belong to its mechanical rhythms. Visually, his design differs from the inhabitants of the town – his face is more naturalistic and well defined, less warped and grotesquely stylized. However, his moral ambivalence is signalled by the fact that he is carved from the same dark walnut as the corrupt citizens, rather than the lighter wood of Agnes and the fisherman, which signals their innocence.[61]

This reading is congruent with Barta's statement that

> Agnes represents a world of purity the same world as the fisherman … They are two main persons; the other belongs to the city, which is the city of evil. The person of the Pied Piper is somewhere in the middle, because he belongs to the world of time, of Saturn.[62]

Barta does not characterize the Pied Piper as a moral force, as per Lefebvre's description of time as the 'greatest good of all goods',[63] but rather as a neutral figure, positioned between the absolute innocence of Agnes and the fisherman and the absolute corruption of the city's other inhabitants. Furthermore, Barta explicitly calls the city itself, 'the city of evil'.[64] How, then, is the city coded as evil and how is this evil passed onto its inhabitants?

The most immediately striking aspect of the town is its slanted and stylized design, inspired – according to Barta – by both German medievalism and German Expressionism.[65] Both are modes of artistic expression which tend towards allegory, in which the form of a depicted city and its inhabitants is reflective of their moral or social status.

Writing of German Expressionist cinema, Lotte Eisner remarks: 'What is internal and latent, hidden and coded is rendered external. The interior becomes the exterior.'[66] What is hidden and coded is made tangible and visible. So, this influence, cited by Barta, gives artistic precedence to the fact that in *Rat Catcher* the harsh, angular forms of Hameln – the way in which buildings lean and sag, seem to sprout from one another or are stacked haphazardly in piles – embody the moral warping of the city. Likewise, the dark and gloomy colouration of the walnut wood indicates the city's spiritual darkness. The fact that the inhabitants are composed of the same angular, jutting, coarse shapes as the city and are carved from the same wood indicates their shared corruption, especially when we realize that Agnes and the fisherman are carved from softer, lighter wood.

Two spatial forms ubiquitous throughout Barta's Hameln signify, embody and arguably predetermine this moral degradation – the spiral and the spire. The spiral conforms to an inward-moving rhythm towards ever-greater perversity and corruption and is to be found within the very foundations of Hameln, in the catacombs and underground networks upon which the city has been built. It can be glimpsed in the image of a rat chasing its own tail or an obscenely coiled string of sausages. It is a regressive, anal symbol. The sausages, coiled, appear excretal. Spires, meanwhile, rise from many of the buildings of Hameln, either pursed together thinly or bulgingly splayed apart. Spires have a 'phallic aspect', to quote Lefebvre's appraisal of monuments and, like towers, 'exude arrogance'.[67] They capture the gross hubris of the city and the greed of its inhabitants. In contrast to regressive spirals, they embody misguided and grotesquely unchecked progress. Spirals (with their inward-moving rhythms) and spires (with their outward-moving rhythms) spatially embody the corruption of the city and, so doing, ossify it, forging paths that further predispose its inhabitants towards corruption.

The forms of the spire and the spiral are foregrounded through match cuts and camera movements which emphasize and mirror the shapes present on screen. A clear example of the former occurs at around four minutes into the film's running time, where a tailor raises a pinched corner of fabric into the shape of a spire and then cuts the thread that holds it. On the 'cut' of the scissors, the film cuts to an exterior shot of the building which itself takes the form of a conical spire. Repeatedly, the form of the city's inhabitants and their labour closely mirrors the form of the buildings in which they work and live, as though they exist in a dialectical relationship. Regarding the recurring motif of the spiral, the aforementioned sequence then cuts to a bird's-eye view of the city, which resembles a warped spiral of broken shards. As the camera moves into this spiral, it rotates and the screen fades across several brief shots of spirals and openings, as though moving into the heart of the city. Naturally, moving spatially, we are also moving through time. Smriti Saraswat argues that the spiral is a form uniquely suited to expressing time. Saraswat sees the spiral as representing simultaneously a cyclical vision of time and an image of time as growth,[68] a repetitive ascension of ever-spiralling progress as per Hegel's teleological conception of history. Saraswat considers the spiral to be an essentially progressive, not regressive, form. However, the spiral, like a clock face, has the potential to be read both ways. If we trace a spiral from its centre and move upwards and outwards, then it is a form that communicates ever-increasing freedom and expansion. However, if we trace a spiral from its outer rim through to its centre, moving ever-downwards and inwards, it is transformed into a regressive form, representing a deterministic descent to a point of absolute limitation and constriction. As Amelia Groom points out, the line of the spiral 'curves hypothetically towards microcosmic infinity at one end and out to macrocosmic infinity at the other'.[69] It is the direction in which we choose to trace the spiral which determines whether it becomes a symbol of the micro or the macro: the regressive or the progressive. Through having the spirals rotate in the opposite direction to that of a clock face and creating the sensation of descent in the viewer, Barta utilizes the spiral as a regressive shape that evokes the stagnation of Hameln.

In the Japanese manga *Uzumaki* (1998–9) by Junji Ito, the inhabitants of the small town of Kurôzu-cho become increasingly obsessed by the form of the spiral. Men collect shells and coiled springs, inhabitants begin to contort their bodies into spirals, pupils and teachers transform into snails and the town is plagued by hurricanes. Eventually, the cursed citizens of the town, under the absolute thrall of the shape, reassemble the town in the shape of an enormous spiral labyrinth. When the project is finally completed and all the inhabitants' bodies compose spirals themselves, Ito's narrator recounts:

> And with the spiral complete, a strange thing happened. Just as time sped up when we were on the outskirts, in the centre of the spiral it stood still. So the curse was over the same moment it began ... and it will be the same moment when it ends again ... when the next Kurôzu-cho is built amidst the ruins of the old one.[70]

For Ito, time stops at the centre of the spiral. It is a point of both utter stagnation and eternal recurrence, since it is the point at which progress is impossible: the apex of absolute repetition, a degree zero[71] of time.

In *Uzumaki*, it is the inhabitants of the city themselves who eventually become the centre of the spiral, but in *Rat Catcher* it is money that sits at the spiral's centre, which is minted in the black heart of the city. The mayor of the city, with his angular pointed face and skeletal figure, is sat at a table marking the insignia of the city into coins. The symbol is an iconographic representation of Hameln itself, composed of a couple of towers and shards. An extreme close-up of the coin fades to a bird's-eye view of the city's central 'square' (actually, more circular in form) and for a second, the coin appears superimposed upon the square and the tiny figures milling about inside. The film then cuts to a market scene.

The symbolism here suggests this is a city determined by the lust for money, its very architectural form utterly in thrall to the demands of capital. However, Marx and Engels remind us repeatedly in *The German Ideology* (1932) that the zeitgeist of a given place and time is not determined top-down by the consciousness of individuals but by the material relations of production existing between different classes.[72] Similarly, in *Capital* (*Das Kapital*, 1867–83), Marx is at pains to stress that money arrives at its unique status as the universal equivalent only through already being a commodity embodied with value. Those writers who hold that 'the value of gold and silver is imaginary'[73] forget that the value of gold – no less than of any other commodity – is the embodiment of socially necessary labour. Money may often bewitch us with its seemingly magical metaphysics, but beneath 'the ideal measures of values there lurks the hard cash.'[74]

When Lefebvre writes about gold, he theorizes it as the *stuff* that anchors capitalism, always positioned at the end of the chain of commerce.[75] Gold is literally the material foundation of the city of Hameln – it composes its very heart; it is found at the end of the spiral. However, as *Uzumaki* illustrates, at the centre of a spiral can only be stagnation, since it is the point at which spatial and thus temporal progress is impossible. As such, the money everminted in Hameln's heart blocks, rather than guarantees, progress, locking its citizens into a pathologically greedy cycle of endless buying and bartering that is presented by the film as being deeply morally ugly. In *The Production of Space* Lefebvre writes – somewhat cryptically – that 'in the absence of any dialectical movement, a given logic … may generate a space by generating a spiral or vicious circle'.[76] The spiral form of Hameln combined with the greed of its citizens ensures the impossibility of social, political or psychological development, so the town and its inhabitants are stuck within a vicious cycle of endless consumption. Barta shows us precisely how vicious this cycle is in the market scene that follows.

The film cuts, moving through the market, between various transactions taking place – people bartering for a pear, a chicken and a pastry. The bartering is depicted by a series of paired figures standing either side of a set of scales or the bartered-for object. The customers offer a price represented by a coin (or several) issuing from their mouths and the sellers offer their own price, again represented by coins issuing from their mouths. However, with each transaction, the buyer and seller are unable to come to a harmonious agreement and barely budge from their original amounts. The faces of both become coarser and more deformed. The lips inflame and the teeth buckle, while the head grows increasingly red. The figures communicate in animalistic grunting noises which become more insistent and discordant as the bartering becomes more heated. Notably, as the buyer and seller squabbling over the chicken become increasingly enraged, their voices degenerate into clucking and gobbling noises.

Thus, these transactions of commercial exchange transform tradesman and customer alike into the objects of purchase. This recalls Georg Lukács's argument, after Marx, that a process of reification (*verdinglichung*) occurs to subjects under capitalism[77] – though the terms of Lukács's argument allow the concept to be extended to any rationalized system of commodity exchange, as – for instance – also existed in late communist Czechoslovakia. When the worker is compelled to sell his capacity to work upon the market, he is alienated from his objectified labour, which is transformed into a commodity *belonging to* him rather than some quality *of* himself. For Marx, whether we are dealing with the worker selling his labour power, the prostitute selling her body or the merchant selling his wares,[78] at the marketplace buyer and seller 'exist for one another merely as representatives of … commodities'.[79] This process may be attributed to the division capitalism cleaves between use value and exchange value, but Lukács intimates that reification does not only take place under capitalism, but it is under capitalism that it achieves its most developed form.[80]

Marx and Engels argue that the philosophy of utilitarianism (far from having metaphysical origins) arises specifically out of 'modern bourgeois society' in which 'all relations are subordinated in practice to the one abstract monetary-commercial relation'.[81] However, Švankmajer's systematic critique of utilitarianism throughout his work (both under capitalism and communism) arises from a disavowal of anthropocentrism which the artist locates within human civilization, rather than any of its specific political incarnations. That is to say, the tendency to see the world in terms of its use values incites a level of objectification, which may be attributed to capitalism after the fact.

Moreover, in *Rat Catcher*'s market sequence, the townspeople's partial transformation into objects might also be attributed to the repetitive nature of the bartering, which has a mechanical quality. The process of bartering enforces monotonous, regular rhythms and so fatally reduces rhythmic diversity, which marks individuals out from one another. Forced by the rhythms of commerce into the objectifying roles of buyer and seller, they become little more than objects, since they become functions of capital, component parts that facilitate trade, rather than individuals in control of their transactions. Just as workers in a factory become labouring machines, the townspeople of Hameln, who we rarely see working, are buying and selling machines.

Just as previously indicated, greed is the most unpardonable sin within Barta's filmography – as gold anchors capitalism, so greed anchors all immorality. However, the obscenity of gold and the greed it produces would not register with viewers if kept abstract. It is hard to be disgusted at something wholly intangible. As such, Barta constantly emphasizes the *objectness* of gold to increase the sense that it is not transcendent or an ideological ideal but mere *stuff* that humans lust after and hoard.[82] One of the ways in which Barta emphasizes the *objectness* of gold is through substituting the language of trade for money itself. Through having coins, rather than words, issue from the mouths of the traders, the capitalist relations of production in which exchange is housed are brought down from the lofty heights of ideology to ugly material reality. When the arguing reaches its zenith, one of the customers fires coins from her mouth like bullets, literally spitting coins in anger. This is exponentially more effective than dialogue would have been, since by emphasizing the physical damage that the coins could do through their cold, metallic hardness, Barta bluntly reminds the viewer of the violence of money. Cutting someone's wages or stealing from someone's purse – these are not abstract injustices but on a *real* physical level can deprive an individual of material sustenance. Money is used to disguise and soften our sense of the violence inherent to a consumerist system.

Emphasizing the object status of gold in order to communicate the material horror of greed is a device used strikingly by Barta in *The Last Theft*. The film concerns a thief (Frantisek Husák) who, while on a job, stumbles into a crypt of aristocratic vampires, who deceptively allow him to win a game of cards, before leading him into a back room where they drain his blood. The pace of the film is slow and stagnated, as though glutted with greed. The use of a wide-angle lens and shallow depth of focus makes objects and characters bulge obscenely towards the screen, creating the sense of a warped moral vision. Many objects in the film (particularly jewellery and golden trinkets) are given an incandescent after-image, as though illuminated by the glow of long-frozen labour. Likewise, there is something obscene about the soft focus of the camera – something gauzy, pornographic and over-decadent.

The most arresting visual device is borrowed from Erich von Stroheim's *Greed* (1924) in which golden objects are tinted yellow. Rather than painting or printing directly onto the film, Barta projected the already shot footage and then phased colour into it.[83] Visually, this causes images to appear sickly and diminished, looking both too gaudy and drained of vitality all at once.

Figure 3.5 Decadent corruption is rendered palatable through gauzy lighting, pallid skin tones and unusually placed wide-angle shots in *The Last Theft* (*Poslední lup*) (Jiří Barta, 1987). Image used with permission of Krátký film Praha.

As in *Greed*, objects which are the focus of unwholesome desire (an elegant carriage clock, for instance) glow, as though radiating and reflecting the greed projected by the subject. Reflecting on *McTeague* (1899) by Frank Norris, the novel upon which *Greed* was based, Bill Brown writes of the hoarder, Trina: 'Her mode of possession – her habitual interaction with the coins – preserves the gold from being a function and maintains its status as a thing.'[84] This is the effect that Stroheim's colouration achieves, as later used by Barta. Gold is enshrined as material stuff, which instructs the viewer that greed is a base desire for base things. Even the carriage clock appears not to be signalling the restrictive hegemony of abstract time – as typical of clocks in Barta's work – but has been reduced to a desirable commodity. Even a symbol of time has been ossified by greed.

Greed is contaminative. By the end of the film, the thief's body glows golden. It has become the unwholesome and glutted body of greed. When his body is then drained of blood, Barta tells us that greed is also parasitic. It is no coincidence that the vampires resemble French aristocrats from a cheap dramatic performance of *Les Misérables* (1899). In life these creatures sucked the blood from the living and now they do the same in death. Kawin makes a curious aside about vampires. 'Unable to die', he writes, 'they are doomed to repetition'.[85] Repetition is, for Barta, that which encodes greed within the material structure of the city and ensures its propagation. This argument is made forcefully in *Rat Catcher*, partly through having the citizens of Hameln repeat their daily gestures (sticking their heads out of windows upon the hour, for instance), but also through having the rats imitate these behaviours.

So, the mayor and his cohorts gobble chunks of meat, while, under the table, rats do the same. A man and a woman are shown courting, but as the man gropes the woman's breast the woman reaches out for the man's purse. The film cuts to a rat sniffing the bottom of another rat, following it into a burrow. The rats are shown in sleeping, drunken stupor; so are the town dignitaries. It is not merely that equivalences are being drawn between the rats and the inhabitants of Hameln but that the rats are shown to merely repeat the rhythms encoded by the evil city. They are not a cause of the city's degradation but a symptom.

Indeed, the same might be said of the citizens of Hameln – that they merely follow rhythms already imposed by their environment. After a montage

Figure 3.6 Rats and the corrupted inhabitants of Hameln are just symptoms of the same architectural-ideological disease in *Rat Catcher* (*Krysař*) (Jiří Barta, 1986). Image used with permission of Krátký film Praha.

in which the film cuts between images of rats scavenging and the people of Hameln sleeping, the day begins anew and the shots that were used at the start of the film, when the bells rang and the citizens of Hameln awoke, are repeated. The people appear to wake in the same order, cross the same paths through the city and go about the same business. At the market people work through the same motions, as though preordained, slotting themselves into the roles of buyer and seller. These socially sanctioned and regulated rhythms conform to the codified behaviours imposed by consumer society. The process by which these rhythms become ubiquitous is referred to by Lefebvre as *dressage*. Joe Kember provides the following definition:

> Dressage tends to stand in for our initiative, since it makes each unique moment in our lives appear to be the repetition of another, and enables us to respond to these in an equally repetitive socially sanctioned manner. At the same time it gives us a use value coordinated with that of other individuals, one that is today most often tied to capital.[86]

Kember indicates that dressage tends to be associated with predetermined behaviour, though not in such a way as is ideologically neutral but in such a way that the repeated behaviour conforms to the demands of capital. So, the townspeople at the market play through the rehearsed gestures of haggling – they raise their arms, shout down prices and make the tiniest of concessions – and can be expected to do this every time they go to market. The specific products they are buying and the amounts of money exchanged are, ironically, immaterial. The process itself – one that requires both a buyer and a seller – is one that endorses and enables a consumerist society, founded on greed.

These repetitive tasks are 'homogenizing factors'[87] that maintain the status quo – such factors often take the form of repetitive tasks and may be linked to law, regulation, clock time or bureaucratization. By contrast, the rats function as 'fragmenting factors'[88] that interrupt the cyclical rhythms of commerce. They spill barrels and knock open cages, steal food and break eggs. Despite the fact that the rats' rhythms mirror those of the people of Hameln, the over-layering of the two rhythms creates disruption and chaos. The Pied Piper, by charming the rats into the sea, is able to preserve the homogenous rhythms of Hameln. However, it becomes quickly apparent that these rhythms are inherently sick and founded upon greed.

Ultimately, the Pied Piper decides that the townspeople should endure the same fate as the rats and the sequence of the rats' drowning is repeated but now with the townspeople in their place. A city that was characterized by the repetition of corrupt rhythms is finally purged by an act of absolute repetition. This evokes a passage by Kawin, in which he expresses a visionary conception of repetition. 'Repetition', Kawin propounds, 'is also the objective correlative of sin and purgation, of stopped time and the intense investigation of time: the ultimate trap, and at the same time the way out of that trap; the cage and its key; the labyrinth and its solution'.[89] Repetition (as embodied by the spiral form of the city and the spiralling movements of rats beneath it) enabled the corruption of Hameln and prevented its moral growth – it was a trap. Yet repetition as induced by the Pied Piper (the symbol of cosmic time) allows for the purging of the city and the potential for its rebirth in the form of the innocent fisherman and his rescued child. It provides the key to escape from the cage of greed and corruption. Barta provides us with two visions of repetition, one positive and one negative. The repeated rhythms of consumerism are negative, since they operate through dressage, which encourages reactive, unreflective and greedy behaviour. The repetition of cosmic rhythms which are truly cyclical (in the way that human-imposed rhythms fail to be) is positive, since it returns life to a prelapsarian natural order of things that precedes the existence of ideology. Clock time and the emblems thereof (such as the giant clock tower that shadows over Hameln) should be treated with suspicion, since they enable the rhythms of work and commerce, which are almost invariably corrupt. Natural time (in the form of the sun and the Pied Piper) should be respected and adhered to, since it transcends the egocentric desires of humans and so is not ideologically in thrall to either labour or consumerism.

It should perhaps come as little surprise, considering the previous analysis of *A Ballad about Green Wood*, that the film ends with clock time (as embodied by the great clock tower) finally ceasing. After the townspeople have been transformed into rats and drowned, the fisherman with the child in his arms enters a painted landscape first glimpsed when the Pied Piper played his pipe for the maiden Agnes and disappears along a long, winding road into a frozen pastoral scene of natural, bucolic promise, free from the greed of consumer society and the strictures of clock time.

Repeating the past in *The Club of the Laid-Off*

Ivana Košuličová in *Kinoeye* expresses the belief that *Rat Catcher* reflects the decay and decline of late-period Czech socialism.[90] However, Barta in interview with Jeremy Clarke refutes the notion that the film has anything specific to say about Czech society, but rather is a universal parable of the destructive quality of greed, which he envisions as common to all human societies.[91] A repetition of this process of critics reading a specifically Czech political meaning into one of Barta's films, while Barta refutes such a reading in interview, occurs when we turn to articles and interviews on *The Club of the Laid-Off* (*Klub odložených*, 1989). Jenny Jediny in a retrospective piece on Barta's work unambiguously refers to *The Club of the Laid-Off* as an 'expression of the Velvet Revolution'.[92] However, in interview with Phil Ballard, Barta repeatedly stresses that the film was completed *before* the Velvet Revolution, stating: 'Of course, this is a metaphor for the Prague society we were living in. It was a society before the Revolution; it was a conformist system, and everything was very boring, everything was very empty, everything was very average and closed in rooms and boxes.'[93] Later he repeats this fact: 'We finished this film in 1989 and it was before the Revolution.'[94]

However, Jediny can hardly be accused of naivety when the film seems so explicitly to concern the transition between a socialist-style society and a capitalist one. For such a film to be released in Czechoslovakia in 1989, it seems counter-intuitive *not* to read it as an allegory of the Velvet Revolution. Yet, Barta stresses that the film was completed before those historic events transpired. Are we then to accuse him of clairvoyance? Perhaps the riddle can be partially resolved by turning to Kierkegaard's visionary understanding of repetition. Edward Mooney explains that repetition, for Kierkegaard, 'means getting our cognitive and moral bearings not through prompted remembering, but quite unexpectedly as a gift from the unknown, as a revelation from the future.'[95] This statement points towards what Lisa Trahair calls the 'aporetic relation'[96] between repetition and difference; as Trahair explains: 'The problem with the concepts of repetition and difference is that you cannot know difference without repetition nor repetition without difference.'[97] Trahair, like Broadfoot and Butler in the same volume, deploys Zeno's paradox to elucidate this notion. If we think of animation cells taken in series, each cell seems to repeat the image of the cell preceding it; however, there are subtle differences in the repetition, so that progress is made. However, say we wanted our animation to be smoother and the illusion of life more real, then we might draw some additional cells between those cells, or take some extra stop-motion stills between those already taken, to 'fill the gap'. But now there are new gaps between those additional cells/stills and so more must be drawn or taken, ad infinitum. As such, this renders progress through repetition a philosophical impossibility. So, we may indeed be moved like Kierkegaard to invoke prophecy to explain repetition, for there is something inscrutable in the metaphysically impossible fact that movement and change can arise through stagnation.

Yet this is precisely what happened in the case of the Velvet Revolution. There was no violent uprising, but rather the giving way of a system that had stagnated. By 1980 the net hard currency of Czechoslovakia stood at £3.6

billion and with the economy no longer growing, money was spent simply on sustaining the standard of living that had increased in the early 1970s. The hundreds of thousands of *panelák* apartments and the consumerist lifestyles of their inhabitants needed to be maintained, diverting money away from modernizing processes of further industrialization.[98]

By 1989, the year *The Club of the Laid-Off* was released, economic stagnation was so dire that the State Planning Agency recommended that 30 per cent of Czechoslovakia's enterprises cease production on account of being unprofitable. This was perhaps unsurprising, since earlier in the year 100 enterprises had been declared bankrupt by the government.[99] However, as with the barely imperceptible changes between animation frames, surface-level stagnation can disguise subtle shifts. By 1989 there were signs of growing unrest. Dowling notes: 'Student discontent and dissent' grew 'in a subdued manner throughout the year' culminating in the violent police suppression of a 15,000-strong student protest on 17 November on the anniversary of the funeral of anti-Nazi student protester Jan Opletal.[100] More generally, 'loss of international support from a powerful military ally, the fall of neighboring Leninist states, eroding legitimacy of the old regime', all contributed to a growing sense of the state's vulnerability.[101] John Glenn's choice of words to describe those factors that undermined the security of the regime – 'loss', 'fall', 'eroding' – evokes a structure worn away by a multitude of factors, both internal and external, perhaps unseen to the eye but holistically creating an impression of the potential for change. We need not subscribe to the mystic powers of art to suggest that Barta may have suspected a gathering paradigm shift, without precisely putting his finger on the revolution that would have occurred by the end of the year.

The Czech title of Barta's film is *Klub odlozenyc*. The translation provided by the 2006 Kino Video collection *Labyrinth of Darkness* is *The Club of the Laid-Off*. Elsewhere on the *Cartoon Noir* DVD anthology from 1999 the title is translated as *The Club of the Discarded*. Alternatively, we might translate *odlozenyc* as 'delayed' or 'postponed'. Clearly, all possible translations are suggestive of uselessness – of this being a club of used-up things – but they have different temporal implications. Both 'laid-off' and 'discarded' suggest that something has been left behind and are backward-looking words; meanwhile, 'delayed' or 'postponed' suggests a suspension or arresting of progress, looking forward to a delayed future. Thus, the paradox of temporal movement inherent in repetition (that difference is generated through sameness) is contained within the very title of the film itself. The protagonists of the film are at once remnants of the past and figures that may yet catch up with the future.

The protagonists of the film are mannequins – those peculiar hybridized figures beloved by the Surrealists that occupy the uncanny region halfway between humans and objects. These particular mannequins have been left in storage and have become worn, dirtied and corroded. However, despite their dilapidation, they move stiffly through grotesque parodies of domestic routines, which one imagines they have been repeating for months, if not years, on end. The first fifteen minutes of the film are given to the display of the mannequins' repetitive routines. A husband rises from bed and bids farewell to his wife, striding to work, where he sits motionless at a desk. The wife stands in the kitchen and monotonously stirs a pot, until a later part of the routine, in which the paint from the pot is poured over crumpled balls of newspaper on plates, which the family mime eating but never actually consume.

Some of the more fetishistic rituals are cued to evoke tactile sensations in the audience. It can be assumed that the intimacy of the camera with filthy and dilapidated surfaces provokes a sense of abjection in the viewer (a physical tensing, withdrawal from the screen, distaste or even nausea) on the precondition that the viewer is immersed within the film – and so experiencing the camera's eye as their own, feeling 'drawn in' to the film world, physically and emotionally. Human instinct combined with social taboos around hygiene and dirt ensure that few people would bring their face into close proximity to such contaminated surfaces in the real world and this inner prohibition is likely to persist even when the surfaces are on screen.

Plastic fingers caress the coarse, broken, rusted strings of a harp in obscene close-up. A mannequin's neck squeaks unpleasantly as it turns in jagged stop-motion, the sound like nails down a blackboard. An elderly mannequin holds a single white feather with which she makes sewing motions, despite the futility of this action. A mannequin pokes a phallic finger through a piece of fabric to spy voyeuristically upon another mannequin's bathing rituals.

If these rituals seem pathological, they have also been rendered banal through repetition. In a paper collected in *Beyond the Pleasure Principle: And Other*

Writings (2003), Freud recounts his grandson playing a game in which he repeats the trauma of his mother's absence by throwing away a toy only to retrieve it and once again throw it away. From this, Freud makes the inference that, for the child, choosing to repeat an undesired experience creates the comforting impression of having control over the experience.[102] Brown expresses this concept thus: 'By doing the same thing with the same things you create the illusion of sameness and continuity over and against the facts of disorder and change.'[103] If the mannequins sense in any way that revolution is in the air, they are determined not to admit as much through the alteration of their domestic routines.

These routines are cyclical in form in as much as they repeat almost exactly, over and over. While Lefebvre often equates cyclical rhythms with natural time, he makes it clear that dressage is also able to forge cyclical rhythms. Lefebvre strikes a warning tone when discussing dressage, as though advising the reader not to underestimate its insidious influence. 'Dressage can go a long way', he informs us, 'as far as breathing, movements, sex. It bases itself on *repetition*. One breaks-in another human living being by making them repeat a certain act, a certain gesture or movement'.[104] Dressage is the means by which humans are induced to follow the social contract and can extend as far as, Lefebvre argues, bodily rhythms. The term implies adherence to an ideology. In this case, I would argue, the mannequins are living in accordance with the rational ideology of clock time and the rhythmic conformity this implies. The way in which the husband rises in the morning, the time at which he rises, the position of his body as he embraces his wife – all of these are in accordance with social codes, which have become ossified through repetition. If there is pathology in this habitually ingrained behaviour it is in the way in which it subsumes human will. As such, the repetitiveness of everyday life is, in a sense, morbid.[105] This morbidity is communicated visually by Barta through his choice of mannequins as protagonists, which are less than human. They are deathly in their pale, unchanging countenances and corpse-like in the stiffness of their movements and their absolute stillness in sleep.

Although the daily routines of the mannequins are broadly cyclical, the minutiae of their behaviour within these cyclical rhythms is often linear and variegated. One mannequin plays on a broken stringed instrument. She may play the instrument at precisely the same time within her routine, but her fingers will cause the strings to vibrate in different ways; the instrument will gradually become more dilapidated and the sounds it produces will change. Likewise, upon entering the room he uses as an office, the father mannequin shoos away gathered pigeons. Inevitably, the amount of pigeons in the room and where they have settled themselves will subtly determine his actions. This produces an uncertainty in the viewer regarding the cognizance of the mannequins with respect to their environments. While they seemingly proceed through their routines unthinkingly (the futility of many of which – such as cooking without the possibility of eating or the fact that the father enters the office each day and does no work – suggests this), they can also be seen to react to external stimuli. Most dramatically, the mannequins freeze when they hear a cat entering the apartment until one of the mannequins takes the initiative of throwing a spoon to scare it off. Clearly, our plaster protagonists are not wholly insensate.

Perhaps the most interesting case of difference through repetition within the film is the descent of the father down a flight of stairs leading to the office room. Each time this process occurs, the mannequin trips and he tumbles down the steps. However, upon each repetition, he also progresses a step or two further down the staircase before he trips. This recurrent sequence almost dramatizes the process of stop-motion animation, by which movement is accomplished through small incremental changes that pass virtually unseen. However, the entire process only works due to the viewer's own persistence of vision and memory. We are able to step, light-footed, between one frame and the next without tripping over. The failure of the mannequin's repetition is reliant upon the success of the repetition inherent to the film medium. Of course, in a sense, the mannequin both succeeds *and* fails in his repetition. He succeeds in the repetition of his failure (he trips in the same manner every time) while simultaneously failing to achieve an exact repetition (the trip, while identical in form, occurs at a different temporal-spatial point in each repetition). Put more simply, the mannequin succeeds in navigating the previous step, seemingly having learnt from his mistake, but subsequently fails in then tripping over in the same way as on his previous descent. Brown notes that 'the failure of repetition can call attention to what we might call the thingness of the object'.[106] This is to say, the mannequin's ungraspable otherness presents itself through the failure of its repetition. However, simultaneously, its/his humanness is foregrounded by the learning process and the fact that it/he seems to be slowly but surely mastering the staircase, suggesting the mannequin is possessed of a rudimentary memory.[107] This vacillation between our understanding of the mannequins in the film as humans or objects increases the sense of their uncanniness and also drives home the point previously made in *Rat Catcher* that humans can be rendered object-like through a monotonous adherence to the banal repetitive rhythms of daily life.

As with *Rat Catcher* the daily rituals of the humanoid characters seem to be triggered primarily by clock time, although there also seems to be a rhythmic connection between the timetabled passing of electric trams outside the apartment and the routines of the mannequins inside. The father mannequin first hoists himself out of bed when the vibrations of a tram knock an alarm clock onto the floor, setting the daily ritual in process. This occurs later a second time in a near-exact repetition of the first instance, but with the sun now setting outside. Clearly, the adherence to (what is taken to be) clock time has no relation to natural time – or indeed, the working routines of the world outside of the apartment.

On the third repetition of the 'daily cycle', the father mannequin has been in bed for all of a second. The bedcovers have become trapped under the cabinet on which the alarm clock is placed. Pulling the covers shakes the cabinet, causing the clock to fall to the floor, forcing the mannequin to start his routine all over again. This highlights the absurdity of a strict adherence to clock time. It also ironically reverses the relationship between man and time. In this instance, the mannequin has inadvertently dictated the start of his day and the moment at which his alarm clock 'goes off'. It would be a stretch to argue that we shift at this point in the film from a system dictated by rational, clock time to a system dictated by wilful, charismatic time; however, the sequence neatly demonstrates that both a mode of existence in which humans are in thrall to clocks and a mode of existence in which clocks are in thrall to humans are equally absurd. It would be better, perhaps, if the mannequins were outside, where the sun might dictate their routines.

Though some fleeting intrusions interrupt the mannequins' routines, they resume their cycles unabated until the arrival of a new group of figures. These are brought in a crate up to the loft apartment by a couple of workmen and resemble cyborgs, with silver and gold bodies, bedecked with American apparel. Perhaps Barta is critiquing a Westernization of late-period Czech socialism. Bradley Adams notes that the number of citizens who owned consumer goods such as a colour television or an automatic washing machine rose throughout the country across the 1970s, but that by the 1980s many citizens still owned the same items they had purchased in the preceding decade and the rate of purchase had, for many items, slowed.[108] As such, if Barta is critiquing a sudden influx of American-style consumer goods into Czechoslovakia, then his critique may have come a decade too late.

In a dynamic montage composed of close-ups and POV shots, the two groups of mannequins fight and dismember each other in the process. However, when the daily ritual begins again, it becomes clear that the mannequins have reassembled themselves into hybridized figures and while some of the qualitative elements of the routines they enact may have changed, their essential cyclical form has not. Allegorically, instead of dissolving into fragments, the social body has simply assimilated the new pieces and resumed its old routines. So, the father is now plastered with stickers for various brands and wears leopard-print shorts, but he still rises from his bed and embraces his wife precisely as before and again trips upon the staircase, this time beginning once again from the top stair. Barta's argument seems to be that the progress of civilization is illusionary; any change in a political regime or social upheaval (such as the shift from a socialist to a capitalist society) will soon be rendered banal through repetition. The behaviour of the mannequins is determined primarily by dressage and their unthinking adherence to clock time not by ideology or any form of political engagement. The moment of historic resistance (the fight between the two groups – certainly more outwardly violent than the Velvet Revolution was to be) is quickly forgotten and the socially sanctioned rhythms of everyday life, resumed.

It strikes me that here Barta extends Václav Havel's 'principle of outward adaptation'[109] across ideological borders. Havel's theory was that communist conformity functioned as a series of social gestures. As such, what was important under communism if one wished to preserve 'the quiet life' was essentially dressage – to follow the rhythms of state-sanctioned behaviour, going to party meetings on occasion, not complaining too loudly, not reading *samizdat* literature, etc. Inwardly one could rebel as much as one desired, as long as one's outward, social gestures were in accordance with the state. *The Club of the Laid-Off* suggests that these behaviours of 'outward adaptation' cannot be easily thrown off, but will stick fast even in the face of a dramatic political or ideological shift.

Lefebvre's fundamental argument in *The Production of Space* is that in order to change our way of relating to one another and how we behave as social animals, it is not enough to change ideology; we must alter our very rhythms and to do that our relation to time and space must be changed. As long as Barta's mannequins are living in accordance to clock time, taking the same old paths down the same old broken stairs, then any revolutionary behaviour they display will only ever be a temporary aberration, quickly normalized by a return to comforting, social and domestic rituals that have been hard-wired through repetition.

Brown asserts, in a somewhat gnomic statement, that 'repetition is the mode of becoming historical'.[110] If Brown is correct, then it is fallacious to think that revolutions and uprisings define history or to speak of the 'return to history' to Central-Eastern Europe after communist rule – a phrase that Abby Innes critiques eloquently in her prologue to *Czechoslovakia: The Short Goodbye* (2001).[111] Rather, history is composed of the dullness of routine, of things being repeated and repeated until they hold true in our memories. In the face of such repetition, political engagement can begin to seem futile. We might become locked within – to borrow a phrase from Merlin Coverly – an 'eternal stasis that renders all political engagement redundant'.[112] Coverly is writing about the notion of eternal return. Barta's vision seems decidedly less transcendent. His films provide us with a weary prophecy that humans are destined to eternally return to the same tired routines, the same greedy vices and the same old times and spaces.

A hopeful repetition for the future?

However, repetition might yet be liberating. Kawin notes that while repetition 'can lock us into the compulsive insatiability of neuroses' it can also 'free us into the spontaneity of the present tense'.[113] Repetition as defined by rational, clock time fails to promise a sense of renewal. It is merely accumulative, working towards targets and end points that are endlessly deferred. The repetition in *Club of the Laid-Off* appears so futile because it accomplishes so little; it is repetition without growth. However, the fertility cycle of *A Ballad about Green Wood* is no less repetitious; yet, because it adheres to natural time, it seems verdant and ecstatic. Moreover, the film immerses us in the variegated rhythms of nature (vegetation budding and sprouting, ice thawing, water running) to create symphonic vitality affects. Without a clock to measure time by, we are taken out of time, to experience the eruption of life, holistically, in and of itself.

Hope, in Barta's films, arises from the human potential to return to these rhythms and cast off the alienation of abstract time. This is an evolution of Havel's invocation of *rootedness* as displayed decades earlier in Trnka's films and the notion that humans should cast off technological advancement and return to the simple life of immediate phenomenological existence as enjoyed by children and peasants. It is a more evolved form of this thinking, since Havel and Trnka's vision is essentially static and reactionary – it seeks to simplify rhythms until they are manageable. This is why objects in Trnka's films so rarely transform, but are appreciated best when they are functional and easily defined. By contrast, Barta's films show us that adhering to singular, simple rhythms is nullifying at best (*Club of the Laid-Off*) and leads to vice and corruption at worst (*Rat Catcher*). The simple, cyclical, repetitive rhythms of these films are likely so destructive because they are encoded within spaces (such as Hameln, the *panelák* apartment or the isolated loft of the mannequins) that are cut off from nature and that restrict the potential for complex movement and play. Hameln with its warped spires and regressive spirals elicits greedy, competitive and destructive behaviour. The flattened, cuboid form of the *panelák* apartment flattens the lives of its inhabitants, until they are all alike.

Wooden figures that move like clockwork and dusty mannequins are ideal subjects for dressage. Their forms dictate their restricted lives. They are spiritually imprisoned by the stiff, constricted rhythms of their bodies. Michel de Certeau's *The Practice of Everyday Life* (*L'invention du quotidien*, 1984) evokes through difference the human void at the heart of Barta's cinema. Though de Certeau, like Lefebvre, believes that human social relations are determined by the space(s) in which they live, he is often optimistic about the potential for humans to transform this space and the way they inhabit it. After all, while one might be 'put in one's place', it is equally possible to 'forge a space' for oneself. De Certeau's faith in the common man allows him to imagine tactics such as *la perruque*[114] (in which an employee uses her time at the office or factory to accomplish her personal work rather than that of the company) which a person can make recourse to in order to resist the predeterminations of space. We can choose to walk along the wall of a building, rather than the path. We can secretly grow vegetables in the soil of a communal park or sit backwards, facing away from the screen, at the cinema. Barta's humans fail to have recourse to such tactics because they are fundamentally unplayful. They are too rhythmically bound by dressage to move outside of the routes and paths that spaces and places have predetermined for them. The most imaginative attempt to escape this predetermination among Barta's humans is the Disc Jockey's drug taking, but this merely diminishes and distorts experience, rather than renewing it.

Perhaps the only playful figures in all of the work Barta produced under communist rule in Czechoslovakia are the wooden shards in *A Ballad about Green Wood*. Their rhythms are genuinely unpredictable and, as they whirl and dance, they seem at play. Barta's adherence to natural time in *Green Wood* is not just incompatible with the values of communist society; it is also at odds with the predominant values of capitalism. It would be presumptuous to expand the conclusions taken from a single film to be indicative of an artist's general philosophical outlook. Yet, it is worth noting that while Barta's other films do not serve as outright celebrations of natural time, the absence of natural time in *Club of the Laid-Off* and *Rat Catcher* (an absence reinforced by the presence of the sun-lit world outside the attic in the former and the pastoral vision conjured by the piper's music in the latter) seems to be connected to these societies' stagnation and essential lifelessness.

However, returning to a wholly pastoral existence is not the only way in which we can radicalize our relationship to time and space. Writing during the period of late communism, Lefebvre speculated about a society that was neither capitalist nor socialist but found the notion impossible to concretize. 'What might an "alternative society" be', he asked rhetorically, 'given the difficulty of defining "society", and given that all such words lose any clear meaning if they do not designate either "capitalism" or "communism" – terms which themselves have now become equivocal?'[115] After the Velvet Revolution, animators in the Czech Republic – including Jiří Barta – continued to make films, despite struggling for funding under a system that was now privatized. Many of these films reflected upon the city of Prague and how its residents might go about forging new relations with time and space within its walls. The next chapter looks to these films, holistically taking the city (with all its variegated intercrossing movements and rhythms) as its object of enquiry.

4

Animators reconstructing Prague and Czech identity after the Velvet Revolution

Portrait of a city

Pavel Koutský's *Portrait of the Man in the Street* (*Portrét*, 1989) depicts the (ubiquitously male) Czech citizen on the eve of the Velvet Revolution as a figure who comprises irreducible multitudes. Koutský's animated short presents his anonymous pedestrian as everything from a benevolent do-gooder, to a harshly scribbled thug, to a softly drawn romantic. While through most of the short it appears as though these starkly caricatured figures are all separate characters, at the end they coalesce into a solitary rotoscoped individual, the 'Man in the Street' of the animation's title.

Koutský's film may have been intended as a universal portrait of the vicissitudes of men the world over, or it may have been intended as a more specific examination of the moral make-up of the Czech citizen circa 1989. The difficulty in making this distinction with any certainty is due to the fact that the film's vignettes unfold against a series of blank anonymous backgrounds. The concluding live-action footage suggests retrospectively that all the film's action has taken place within a shopping district in Prague, but for the majority of the short we could be watching citizens from almost any European city. Of course, the absence of geo-temporal markers leaves room for interpretive supposition – the very fact that the viewer cannot discern the city which the street belongs to might hint at the fact that, by the end of the communist era, increased commercialization and Gorbachev's policies of *glastnost* and *perestroika* led to Central-Eastern Europe becoming slowly less distinguishable from Western Europe.

Intentionally or otherwise, Koutský's film indicates that a portrait of a city's populace is incomplete if removed from the physical, spatial and architectural context of the city. After all, a city is composed not only of its inhabitants but of its buildings, streets, spaces, signs, etc., as well as the seasonal, daily and hourly interactions between all of these things. If you wish to construct an accurate portrait of the man in the street, then you must remember to include the street.

This chapter considers Czech animations (and partially animated films) produced from 1989 to the present, examining how film-makers have depicted, embodied and inhabited the city of Prague on screen during a period in which many of the ideological taken-for-granted presuppositions of the twentieth century continue to be undermined or subverted. By necessity this chapter is broader and more diffuse than the three preceding due to covering the work of many more film-makers over a greater period of time. It is the city of Prague – or perhaps, rather, the *idea* of Prague – that helps bind these otherwise disparate works together into a cohesive whole. Indeed, the myth of a collectively shared *polis* can provide citizens with a perception of unity in the face of ideological fragmentation – a tendency that can easily curdle into fascism once certain 'Others' are designated as being outside the city, state or country. As with Trnka's Bohemian pastoralism, we might question whether it is possible to make art within a mythic mode that upholds local concerns and strengthens community ties, while simultaneously ensuring that a certain plurality of thought, behaviour and belief is safeguarded. Is it possible to celebrate difference within similitude?

In the years immediately following the Velvet Revolution there were many disparate ideas within Czech politics as to the direction in which the country should, or would, develop after stultifying decades of Normalization. To have some indication of the fracturing of consensus among seemingly homogeneous political groups in this period, one must only consider the fact that across the summer months of 1991, Civic Forum (Občanské forum) – the dissident movement which evolved into Czechoslovakia's governing political body after 1989 – splintered into five separate groups: the Citizens Democratic Party, the Citizens Democratic Alliance, the Citizens Movement, the Club of Social Democratic Orientation and the Club of Independence, despite their common repudiation of the KSČ.[1] The sheer number of similarly named parties with markedly similar goals and beliefs testifies to a cultural-political difficulty in the immediate post-communist period with containing small, but legitimate difference. It is not merely that politicians had differing ideas about the direction the country should take after communism, but that they were unpractised in how to allow space for political disagreement. Bernard Wheaton and Zdeněk Kavan express this problem eloquently:

> The installation of democracy in circumstances of radical economic change is extremely difficult. It is not only concerned with the rule of law and formal democratic structures and human rights but also with developing a political culture to encourage a democratic mind-set. This implies not simply establishing a spirit of tolerance but setting limits to legitimate disagreement, providing a framework for the expression of conflicting interests sufficiently broad to cater to all major groups in society and allow for their resolution or management by a constant process of bargaining.[2]

In view of the above, it strikes me as understandable – if not necessarily desirable – that Czech citizens in the early 1990s, including artists and film-makers, would turn to national myths, pre-communist history, traditions or a renewed interest in the country's capital city to explore questions of national and personal identity. After all, not only were these artists experiencing change and dislocation at the macro level, on a personal level they also faced the difficulties implicit in the shift from a state-funded system of film production to one of competing for corporate or private funding within a market economy.

For the film-makers discussed in this chapter, the matter of determining a specifically Czech post-communist cultural identity is linked to Prague itself, the city where they have predominantly worked. Through setting their films within the city's public and private spaces, these artists consider what it means to be a citizen of Prague and how this identity is negotiated with and against the material reality of the city. The human and non-human actors of the films are shaped by the city, just as they in turn shape the environment around them. The films discussed enact a dissident repossession of the tactile world through forging a tangible space which the viewer can imaginatively inhabit, at a time in history when Czechoslovakia/the Czech Republic had been wrested from hegemonic political control through a popular revolution.

In these works, each director seems to take the city into their hands – like a lump of clay – and mould it according to an idiosyncratic view of what it is to be Czech, emphasizing some aspects of the city, while neglecting others. As such, each work considered here presents a highly subjective portrait of Prague in spite of dealing with what is ostensibly the same city documented (or illustrated) in broadly the same place and time. In each work the city – on the one hand – yields to the director's moulding as it is pressed into a shape that embodies their vision of Prague post-1989, while – on the other hand – resisting such moulding through its own irrevocable materiality.

Methodological multiplicity

A city is a complex network of intersecting people and things. As such, a methodology that seeks to encompass an entire cinematic city must be flexible and multifaceted. It makes sense therefore to move here between all three of the methodologies employed over the preceding three chapters in a loose (even unruly) synthesis.

Recourse to thing theory is justified by the *thinginess* of cities and the fact that stop-motion depictions of Prague necessarily ensure the manipulation of real objects. ANT reminds us that each city is a network of bustling actants in which interactions are often negotiated with and between human and non-humans. Rhythmanalysis illustrates that cities are rhythmically complex, combining both cyclical and alternating rhythms in harmonies which sometimes synchronize and sometimes clash. All three of these methodologies are fundamentally materialist in approach, privileging the physical stuff of the world. As such, they are well suited to grasp the material city itself, treating the streets, bricks and spires of Prague as objects and things that have a tangible relationship with one another.

However, it must not be forgotten that the subject of this chapter is filmed and animated representations of the city. When I write here about the rhythms of Prague, what is being discussed is the way in which the city's rhythms have been interpreted through cinematography or constructed through editing. Films cannot provide pure, unmediated access to the material city, despite their notable tactile and haptic qualities.

Historicization of the objects of Prague

Any given city is made up of a plethora of objects that develop layered, sometimes contradictory, meanings and associations through time. Prague is exemplary in this regard, with its history so rich in material fascination – home to Rudolf II's *kunstkammer*, the junk dealers of Gustav Meyrink's *The Golem* (*Der Golem*, 1913–14), the astronomical clock (*orloj*), the statues on Charles Bridge and, of course, after 1989, a whole new array of consumer goods. The historicization of objects involves, firstly, the means by which objects gain iconographic status and, in so doing, become historical things; and, secondly, the way in which the meanings of objects shift and change through time, acted upon by material, historical processes. Objects must be considered not merely *in* but also *through* time.

Objects that occupy public spaces are almost always easier to historicize than their private counterparts due to their comparative ease of access for the historian. For instance, information about the Prague *orloj* – subject of Garik Seko's *About Master Hanus* (*O mistru Hanusovi*, 1976) – is readily available in the public domain due to the interest it holds for tourists visiting the city. By contrast, the provenance and history of specific props within a given film might only be known to a film's art director or set designer, or else recognizable by the viewer already acquainted with the object in question due to its branding or circulation within other film texts.

The cinema of Jan Švankmajer provides some rare examples of the latter tendency. A viewer can track the specific histories of some of the artist's objects/things due to the way in which they circulate within his work. For example, the hybrid bone animals of *Alice* (1988) originally belonged to Švankmajer's encyclopedic *Kunstkamera* project, begun during his period of tactile experimentation in the 1970s. They then persecuted Alice in the 1988 film and, more recently, have appeared on display as art objects in the exhibition 'Jan Švankmajer: The Inner Life of Objects' at the University of Brighton in 2013.

Jiří Barta, meanwhile, makes reference to some specifically Czech objects within a few of his works. For example, his CGI short *Cook, Mug, Cook!* (*Domečku, vař!*, 2007) contains the fleeting image of a box labelled 'The Key: Safety Matches', a real Czech brand of matches. The film concerns the loss of traditional Czech ways of life (chopping wood by hand, wearing peasant costume, cooking broth, etc.) in exchange for those modern consumer goods available under capitalism (represented by pornography, computers and soy sauce). The film was released in 2007, one year before the company that manufactured 'The Key' matches – Wooden Solo – was forced to close its production plant in Sušice due to falling profits, relocating abroad. A *Radio Praha* piece on the closure described the safety match as 'an immediately recognisable symbol first of Czechoslovakia and later the Czech Republic'.[3] A 1993 article from the graphic design journal *The Eye* contrasts the 'unsophisticated and crude designs' produced by Solo Sušice for private companies in the post-communist period to the originality of those earlier designs which championed state initiatives. The authors note that 'matchbox labels from the former Eastern bloc may display a certain naïvety, but nonetheless demonstrate a remarkable ability to communicate across language barriers. Produced for the most part as propaganda and controlled to a large degree by the state, they provide a fascinating insight into the operation of a fast-disappearing society'.[4] While it is unlikely that Barta knew the manufacturer was soon to cease production, his reference to a specific Czech brand of matches manufactured within the country since 1834 signals his nostalgia for a past before electric ovens and the loss of state-supported manufacturing in the modern Czech Republic.

Cook, Mug, Cook!, which will be returned to later in the chapter, uses a traditional fairy tale as a structuring device for Barta to make his critiques of contemporary Czech society around. The use of a traditional fairy or folk tale to comment upon the present is a technique employed in several post-communist Czech films, including Švankmajer's feature-length *Little Otik* (2000) and his adaptation of the myth of Faust, which both function (in part) as critiques of post-communist consumerism in Czechoslovakia/the Czech Republic and also Prague specifically.

Undermining the 'magic city' of tourism in *Faust*

Švankmajer's *Faust/A Lesson from Faust* (*Lekce Faust*, 1994) is a modern retelling of the story of the scholar-magus Faust (Petr Čepek), who sells his soul to the devil in exchange for occult knowledge and magical power.

Victoria Nelson remarks that over the course of its history, the 'Faust' story has 'ricocheted from popular legend and puppet show to high drama and back to puppet show'.[5] Švankmajer's film features actors in giant puppet costumes modelled upon marionettes used in those folk versions of the Faust myth that have been performed as puppet theatre in the country since at least 1851.[6] Perhaps the use of traditional Czech puppet designs in the film is a gesture of nostalgia that seeks to arrest the decline of a national tradition at the point where Czech national identity was at the greatest risk of fragmentation. However, Švankmajer's *Faust* also quotes from Marlowe's late sixteenth-century play, Goethe's epic *Faust, Part I* and *II* (1806 and 1832), Gounod's opera of 1859 and Grabbe's *Don Juan und Faust* (1829).

North and Pavel Drábek characterize Švankmajer's *Faust* as a bricolage of unassimilated fragments.[7] This highlights not only the disjointed nature of the film's script, which jumps between these different historical texts, but also the film's architectural/spatial form. It is not just the real, geographic city of Prague but, rather, the mythic idea of Prague that helps bind these fragments together, an idea associated with the sixteenth-century Prague of Rudolf II, a time remembered in the popular imagination as one of alchemists, magic and the Golem, the mythic protector of the Jewish people.

Early in *Faust* our everyman protagonist follows a map to an area Alfred Thomas identifies as *Josfov*,[8] perhaps magically preserved from the late nineteenth century, just before the ghetto was razed.[9] Here he descends some stairs to enter a mysterious cellar and dressing room, where he picks up a script for Goethe's *Faust*. From thereon in scenes taken from various iterations of the Faust myth tend to unfold in underground spaces, connected by corridors and tunnels, while dialogue-less linking scenes take place above ground in contemporary Prague.

These scenes, which include interludes that occur within pubs and cafés, conform to everyday spatial logic. Thus the door to an apartment opens onto an apartment foyer and stairwell, an outdoor pub backs onto a street, etc. While the editing patterns themselves do not change in those sequences set underground, the spatial logic of these sequences is more dream-like and associative in comparison to those set in contemporary Prague. Drábek and North argue that 'by interpolating the spaces of the city and the puppet theatre … Švankmajer confronts Prague with an interpretive realm that grafts the old Faustus myths onto the modern city and reveals them as a summation of the challenges facing the contemporary subject'.[10]

'Grafts' however strikes me as suggesting too neat a joining. Despite the two being somewhat integrated, scenes in the modern city have a notably different tone to scenes in the puppet theatre and its surrounding environs. Not least, as discussed, the modern city is depicted as a space conforming to conventional architectural, spatial logic, while the puppet theatre is connected to its diverse environs magically and associatively. The impression is of a commercial, contemporary city that obscures its mythic double – which exists in the (underground) collective subconscious of its inhabitants where the myths, stories and legends of a place survive – while simultaneously exploiting this double for commercial and economic gain. Drábek and North better evoke this impression when they refer to a 'Magic Prague' that lives 'alongside, even within, the real city'.[11] The 'real city' is necessary for this 'Magic Prague' to exist, but the two do not quite intersect, since Magic Prague is more of an internal state than an external reality, belonging to the associative spaces and blurred borders of dream and imagination. By contrast, real Prague, at the end of the twentieth century, is depicted in *Faust* as homogeneous, banal and devoid of magic, especially when divorced from an awareness of the city's mythological and cultural history.

Hames notes that, in *Faust*, 'Švankmajer avoids any exotic images of "tourist Prague", preferring nondescript streets and down-at-heel cafés serving nauseous food'.[12] The fact that Švankmajer's shooting script describes the opening shot as being of an 'ordinary busy street'[13] testifies to Hames's sense that, when it comes to Prague in the 1990s, Švankmajer's focus is upon the mediocre and the mundane. Charles Bridge, statues of religious martyrs, the astronomical clock, Prague Castle – none of these feature in the film. Rather, the streets filmed are gloomy back alleys, pedestrian crossings and grey high streets lined with concrete buildings. As Derek Sayer says of Prague, 'the city has hitched its economy and its identity to marketing its magic'.[14] Avoiding a tourist's-eye view of Prague is not simply a matter of neglecting to show its iconic sights or monuments; it also requires ensuring that the streets and cafés that the film does show are intentionally presented as plain and dingy.

Marie Zemanová's choppy editing, the general lack of establishing shots and the sheer lack of colour or vitality in Svatopluk Malý's footage, prevents a contemplative gaze or tone of reverie[15] from ever being established. Moreover, the frame is – during these exterior scenes – often densely crowded, making Prague's citizens seem in uncomfortably close proximity to one another and the city itself claustrophobic and dirty. The film rejects the marvellous not merely through its unromantic view of the city but also in how Švankmajer chooses to frame his own stop-motion puppeteering and trick photography.

In *Faust*, Švankmajer constantly undermines his own spectacle. A fiery carriage that strikes us as a dark portent, summoned by a black magic ritual, is 'put out' with a fire extinguisher. The magicians Valdes (Jan Kraus) and Cornelius (Vladimír Kudla) appear to have pupil-less eyes, until it is revealed they are wearing trick contact lenses. This technique of undercutting the film's own special effects emphasizes Švankmajer's unromantic view of the city. Perhaps this represents a cynical reaction to the promise of hope brought by the Velvet Revolution. Interviews with Švankmajer from the period of *Faust*'s production reveal a deep cynicism about the utopian potential of the new Czech Republic. In interview with Hames, Švankmajer speaks derisively of capitalism as a system that, through advertising, creates 'unified consumers' devoid of free will, happy to lick up 'any old scum'.[16] This criticism surfaces in *Faust* when we first encounter Valdes and Cornelius, handing out maps on the street which direct Faust to the underground puppet theatre where the major events of the film unfold. Faust is lured to his doom, not through a desire for greater knowledge or through the acquisition of some fabled grimoire but by taking a photocopied street flyer. Later, hidden among a sheaf of junk mail, the map is indistinguishable from the pamphlets and advertisements it is sandwiched between. At the end of the film, we see a new 'Faust' entering the same courtyard that our protagonist entered at the start of his diabolical journey, holding the same flyer, suggesting an endless stream of consumers willing to sell their soul to the devil. Seemingly, in a land of infinitely exchangeable consumers and consumer objects, one 'Faust' is as good as any other.

In conclusion, Švankmajer's vision of Prague circa 1994 appears pessimistic. Its citizens are characterized as easily manipulated consumers, who exist within an increasingly banal, homogenized environment. This everyday Prague obscures what might be termed the collective subconscious of the city, where myths and history freely intermingle. The architecture that belongs to mythic-historic Prague has been co-opted by tourism, erased through regeneration and redevelopment and simply ignored and forgotten by contemporary citizens. However, one should be open to the possibility that the rhythms encoded by the city (either through its spatial architecture or through its myths and legends) determine at some level the behaviour of its citizens and their inner lives. Such a reading would hold that the people of Prague are Faustian figures not merely due to the vicissitudes of post-communist capitalism but also due to cultural myths deeply entrenched within the material foundations of that gloomy, magical and eminently marketable city.

Networks of desire in *Conspirators of Pleasure*

'Desire paths' are those paths trodden into the ground by a repeated decision on the part of pedestrians not to follow the 'official' state-sanctioned route to their location. Instead they take a short cut, motivated by their desire – likely for greater expediency, but sometimes because crossing a field or patch of grass is simply more pleasant, more *desirable*, than sticking to the footpath.[17] Švankmajer's third feature, *Conspirators of Pleasure* (*Spiklenci slasti*, 1996), tracks the desire paths of six secret fetishists, whose routes through the city cross and intersect over a few days. These individuals live their lives furtively, dedicating all their spare time to the collection and assembly of objects which they use in highly idiosyncratic masturbatory rituals.

The two central characters of *Conspirators* are Mr Pivoine (Peter Meissel) and Mrs Loudalova (Gabriela Wilhelmova) – the secretly sadistic and mutually desiring neighbouring tenants of a *panelák* apartment building. They cross paths with Mrs Malkova (Barbora Hrzánová), a postmistress who delivers parcels to their apartment. Meanwhile, two other characters – Mrs Beltinska (Anna Wetlinská), a newsreader, and Mr Beltinska (Pavel Nový), a police inspector – live together in a modest house. Finally, Kula (Jiří Lábus), a newsagent, is only ever seen within his shop or its back room, where he builds a robotic masturbation machine to caress him while watching Mrs Beltinska's news broadcasts. The secret lives of these characters, built around obscure desires, masturbation aids and fetish objects, pose a challenge to the homogeny of their surroundings, which recall the grey apartment blocks criticized in Barta's *Design* (1981) or the unremarkable, crowded streets of

Švankmajer's *Faust*. Indeed, at least three commentators maintain that the conspirators' sexual perversity is politically rebellious since these characters are all engaged in the pursuit of erotic freedom in the face of dull, unyielding reality.[18] Although each character is beholden to their own individual fetish, the commonality of their shared pursuit ensures that their lives become entangled, though sometimes only in the most incidental of ways, crossing each other in the street or in shops.

Indeed, each of the so-called conspirators of the film enables the others' erotic activities, as noted by Stephen Holden.[19] Mr Pivoine purchases the pornographic magazines with which he coats his chicken mask from Kula's store. Mrs Malkova delivers to Mrs Beltinska the bread balls with which she feeds her fish. Only during the erotic activities themselves do the characters seem to move outside the social network into spaces of private, clandestine desire – Mrs Loudalova secretes herself in an inconspicuous chapel, Mr Pivoine escapes to the countryside, while Mr Beltinska hides himself away in his shed. Only Kula and Mrs Beltinska seem to transcend their isolation. During her television broadcast, Mrs Beltinska is indulging her fetish for having her feet sucked by *koi* carp, while Kula watches this broadcast on the screen of his masturbation machine. The rapid editing between close-ups of the two characters' faces in sexual ecstasy, alternating with close-ups of the 'arm' of the machine as it pleasures Kula, creates a unity of man, woman and thing in pleasure. In its visceral and comic immediacy, this sequence transcends, if only momentarily, the mediated basis of their encounter, offering a glimpse into communality between subject and object, human subjects and the non-human machine, founded upon erotic desire.

My utopian reading of this scene stands in contrast to Gary Morris's argument that the absence of any binding 'social fabric' in the Prague of the film 'has inspired some of the more driven of the citizenry to weave a new kind of fabric, one where they can replace human warmth and interplay with a mocking mechanical version'.[20] Morris's comment might be read politically, namely that the citizens of Prague, no longer ideologically united under communism, are free to pursue their own personal desires but, in so doing, become little more than desiring machines in a network of mutual exploitation. Under such a reading, Švankmajer's political message is ultimately acerbic – condemnatory, even. This is the reading offered by Bertrand Schmitt, who sees the film as a 'denunciation of the scourges and perversions represented by television and technological enslavement'[21] and insists that the film's characters are governed by 'false desires, false beliefs and false exchanges'.[22] Contrariwise, I would question whether desire itself can be *false* – it strikes me that the conspirators' desires provide a locus of undeniable truth within an alienated and fragmented civilization. However ludicrous the labyrinthine and pernickety preparations, at the moment of orgasmic release the conspirators are all invariably awarded a look of absolute satisfaction that is enviable and undeniable.

Arguing along the same lines as Schmitt, Michael Brooke[23] and David Sorfa[24] both agree that while the film offers an affirmation of sexual liberty, it condemns the acts of perversion as ultimately destructive. While this may be true for those practices that involve the ritual debasement of humanoid puppets in the film, the masturbation machine creates a serendipitous moment of sexual communion between Mr Kula and Mrs Beltinska. Of course, the fact that Mrs Beltinska happens to reach sexual pleasure at the same moment as Kula may just be a matter of coincidence, since the former is completely unaware of the latter's existence. However, such a moment of miraculous coincidence (synchronicity) is the very germ of Surrealism – the ecstatic heart of the Surrealist impulse. There is unarguably a ludicrous side to the scene, but it feels like a triumph nonetheless. While Mr Kula bangs his head up against a television screen, sweat pouring form his face, and Mrs Beltinska orgasms from the pleasure given to her from two sucking fish, it is we – as viewers and critics – who are locked outside this sublime moment of enjoyment, forced into the unenviable role of smirking voyeurs. Surely, it would be better, more pleasurable, to be invited into the network of desire than forced to merely observe it through a screen – which, as it happens, makes us rather like Mr Kula, but without his orgasmic pleasure, depending upon how one chooses to watch the film.

Steven Shaviro does not stop at seeing Mr Kula and Mrs Beltinska as being united by Kula's machine but goes further, asserting: 'The conspirators themselves are also parts or components of these machines that they have constructed … Their orgasms are functions of the machine, parts of its functioning, rather than autonomous ends for which the machines would be simple means.'[25] Švankmajer's use of close-ups when we might expect mid-shots, the lack of establishing shots that situate characters in clearly defined space and his/Zemanová's fragmentary editing style that cross-cuts regularly between disparate scenes ensure that the protagonists of the film always feel somewhat less than fully realized characters. One might consider this a weakness of the script, or indeed performance, but the lack of identification we feel for the film's characters appears to be congruent with Švankmajer's professed approach to live-action film-making and his treatment of actors as 'inanimate objects'.[26]

Shaviro frames his conception that *Conspirators* depicts a network of isolated yet interconnected actors in political terms, as follows:

> Svankmajer proposes a strange new sort of social bond, one that is irreducible either to Communist solidarity … or to capitalist atomism. There is no common interest, no togetherness; but also no competition of rationally calculating, autonomous individuals in the marketplace … Everything is irreducibly particular; but all these particularities are incomplete and uncontained, not to mention too compulsive and too partial to be recuperated as attributes of a 'self'.[27]

While *Faust* depicted the city as a banal reality that retains a sense of magic through its mythic subconscious, *Conspirators* depicts Prague as a network of competing desires that pose a challenge to consumer capitalism, even while their fulfilment is dependent upon the exchange and sale of goods. The pornographic magazines, pots and pans, fish, brushes and umbrellas bought and stolen in the film are not used for the purposes for which they were intended, but neither are they banished from the network. Likewise, each of the individuals in the film may be pursuing their own idiosyncratic, unique and ultimately selfish desires, yet they cannot but form an ad hoc community in this pursuit. Even in the absence of collectivizing ideology, humans and non-humans alike cannot help but remain entangled.

Consumption as a desire older than consumerism

Little Otik is based upon a Czech fairy tale (known in English as 'The Wooden Baby') published by Karel Erben in 1865. In this tale, a childless man chances upon a log resembling a baby, which he presents to his wife who treats it as a real infant. Consequently, it comes to life, consuming all food given to it and eventually devouring its own adoptive parents. Making its way through the Bohemian countryside – gobbling as it goes – it eventually meets an old woman hoeing cabbages, which the wooden baby eats. The old lady strikes the wooden baby with the hoe, splitting its stomach open, releasing the people and animals trapped therein. *Little Otik*'s plot broadly follows these events, with Erben's own version also interpolated within the body of the film as a two-dimensional animated short illustrated by Eva Švankmajerová.

The film has typically been read as an allegorical critique of contemporary Czech consumerism.[28] Such readings draw from the fact that Švankmajer includes within the film many banal, everyday aspects of contemporary Czech life in a consumer capitalist society, with characters watching television commercials, shopping, going on holiday, etc. At first Otik is integrated into this world by his parents – taken in a pram to the supermarket with his mother and fed with milk bottles – but once his size and appetite have grown, he is locked away in the basement, as though he were the embodiment of some shameful desire – the desire, perhaps, to consume.

Otik's movement from the family home and surrounding community to his status as a monstrous pariah imprisoned in the cellar mirrors the disintegration of the apartment as a locus for community over the course of the film. At the start of the film Otik's parents are charitably lent the use of their neighbours' – the Štádlers – guest home with Mr Štádler's assurance: 'We're neighbours. Today I help you and tomorrow you help me.' By the film's end the apartment dwellers are either dead or otherwise isolated from one another, with the Štádlers barricading themselves in their front room. Any sense of neighbourly sympathy has all but disintegrated, as one resident comments: 'People are disappearing and nobody's interested.' This progression from community to dissolution hints darkly that any sense of shared kinship experienced in the wake of the Velvet Revolution might have been precarious and short-lived. As soon as people face a crisis, Švankmajer seems to warn, every man and woman are left fending for themselves. The only exception to this rule within the film is the young pre-teen Alzbetka (Kristina Adamcová) who seeks to protect Otik, but she does so at the expense of her family and neighbours, feeding them to her gluttonous wooden friend.

While it might seem at first glance that *Little Otik* is positioned towards the uncomplicated end of the allegorical spectrum, with a singular meaning clearly communicated (i.e. that consumerism is infantile, monstrous and rampant in self-centred contemporary Czech society), as an allegorical figure and symbolically encoded thing, Otik himself is surprisingly hard to tie down. Otik cannot be said literally to be a product of Czech consumerism since his appetite develops before his exposure to the living-room television or socialization. Likewise, if this were the symbolic meaning Švankmajer intended, he could easily have strengthened it through having Otik's parents, Karel (Jan Hartl) and Bozena (Veronika Zilková), ply their child with plastic, non-traditional toys or having Otik consume food more uniquely ubiquitous to post-communist consumer capitalism than broth and hunks of meat, both of which were common staples under communism. More importantly, Otik, as an animated creature, is not *experienced* by the viewer as a product of modern consumerism. Aga Skrodzka notes perceptively: 'The awkward movement that animates the organic monster in stop-motion is pre-industrial, made possible by careful manipulation of the animator's hand. Cinematic technology is used here by the filmmaker to lead the viewer beyond the technological vision, into the slow optics that intentionally fails to master the unknown, instead preserving its horrifying alterity.'[29]

Consumer capitalism may have worked as a catalyst upon Karel and Bozena's desires for a baby or Otik's desires to consume, but such desire is primal, predating the fairy tale form. Otik thus seems less an embodiment of consumer capitalism and more like the embodiment of *desire itself* – the same pure desire that motivated the protagonists of *Conspirators of Pleasure*. The fact that Otik is devoid of all sensory organs, save a mouth, is telling. Otik's primary mode of engaging with the world is through devouring it, incorporating the external 'Other' into himself in a process of endless consumption. While the film critiques consumerism for being a grotesque hyper-embodiment of this desire to consume, the consumerist desire itself (as staged by the pre-civilized Otik) must be recognized as one of those phenomena that moves below any transitory, surface manifestation of political ideology (such as capitalism or communism) with which Švankmajer is concerned.[30] Anikó Imre notes judiciously that 'all of Svankmajer's films have an almost universal allegorical dimension that cannot be reduced to a representation of the Communist regime'.[31] More specifically, she writes of *Little Otik* that the horror of the film is in 'the difficulty of pinning down the meaning, the origin of the horror'.[32]

This argument borders on the circular, but its evasive, twisty reasoning rings true. Otik as an allegorical figure (or politically encoded thing-subject) cannot be easily contained or pinned down, either literally or figuratively. To quote Skrodzka again: 'If one chooses to view Švankmajer's images in their palpable, multisensory richness, the allegorical perspective becomes harder to grasp … The material texture, so important in all the filmmaker's works, short-circuits the allegory.' Skrodzka's point here is similar to that made by myself in Chapter 2 where I demonstrate the inadequacy of a purely symbolic reading of Švankmajer's *Jabberwocky* (1971) to account for the affective power of the work. The haptic pleasures of the artist's films subsume their allegorical content, as demonstrated – in this case – by the squirming, chomping, cannibalistic body of Otik himself.

So, at one level, Švankmajer is employing the same artistic strategy as Trnka with *The Czech Year* (1947) and *Old Czech Legends* (1953) by turning to national myths and legends that predate both modern capitalism and communism in order to reaffirm Czech identity. Barta attempted something similar with his *Ballad about Green Wood* (1983). However, what Švankmajer accomplishes in *Little Otik* is closer still to Barta's achievements in *Rat Catcher* (1986) since he does not merely evoke a Central-Eastern European folk tale to forge a link between a mythic, pre-modern Czech identity and the present but also illustrates how that folk tale can be used to critique modern Czech society. Importantly, both these rhetorical strategies are achieved simultaneously and in dialectical relation to one another, though never in complete synthesis, as per the relationship between modern and mythic Prague in *Faust*.

So, 'Little Otik' can, as both a figure and a story, be recontextualized to modern Prague, but he and the story simultaneously resist this recontextualization. 'The Wooden Baby' both fits and does not fit the Czech Republic of the late twentieth century, since fairy tales are always already 'a rebellion of the imagination against the way things are'[33] in the present. As such, Švankmajer indicates that the Czech people can never fully return to some mythic culture that existed before communism and consumer capitalism. However, at the same time, pre-modern myths continue to pulse darkly under contemporary Czech culture in such a way resonances between the past and the present can still be found.

While *Little Otik* might be nominally set within the city, 'Otik' as a character can never become a naturalized, urban citizen, with a home in Prague; his roots are in the now pollution-decimated forests of Northern Bohemia and small villages and towns like Knovíz, the home of Švankmajer's animation studio and the place where the cherry tree wood used to sculpt the Otik puppet was found.[34] The kind of desire embodied by Otik is too unrestrained, primordial even, to be assimilated into the network of modern Czech civilization. It is telling that the film ends with Otik's defeat at the hands of an old lady protecting her cabbages. Urban bourgeoisie like Otik's adopted parents are too ill-acquainted with their country's rural folklore to know what to do when faced with an ancient monster of Old Bohemia; only the old woman – who resembles a traditional Bohemian peasant – retains a connection to her country's pre-communist past strong enough to ensure her survival.

Jiří Barta has offered his own critique of Prague under consumer capitalism in his aborted adaptation of Gustav Meyrink's novel *The Golem* (1915). The project – for which only a pilot exists – explores the connection between the country's history and the individual Czech citizen's sense of national identity and suggests, like Švankmajer's *Faust* and *Little Otik*, that old myths still inform the collective subconscious of contemporary Prague, even while such myths and stories are offered up for tourists at the altar of capital.

The Golem is Prague and Prague is the Golem

In 1991 Barta began work on his adaptation of Meyrink's *The Golem*; as of 2019, the project still remains incomplete due to lack of financial investment. In interview with Phil Ballard, Barta has wryly noted that while under communist rule, film-makers had access to state funding but found themselves with limited artistic freedom due to censorship; under capitalism, artists can theoretically produce any work they choose but find themselves unable to realize their vision without the funding and distribution previously provided by the state.[35] Barta's *Golem* – of which only a pilot dating from 1996 exists – has attracted the attention of several producers but, following an initial expression of interest, each has withdrawn from the project. One of the reasons Barta suggests for this is that he is not interested in producing an adaptation of the 'traditional' Golem legend, in which a clay homunculus is raised to serve the Jewish people of Prague, only to run amok. Such a project would be in the vein of Paul Wegener's *The Golem: How He Came into the World* (*Der Golem, wie er in die Welt kam*, 1920) or Julien Duvivier's *The Golem* (*Le Golem*, 1936) and likely more commercially viable than the film Barta intends to direct. The director envisions his Golem not as a singular figure but as 'one shape' that 'forms something which is everywhere'.[36] Barta's esoteric statement suggests a unity between the Golem itself and the city in which he is birthed. After all, the Golem's clay, it is said, comes from the banks of the river Vltava that runs through Prague. Barta illustrates this merger of Prague with the Golem in the film's pilot through having the brick buildings of Josefov (first shown in live-action footage) transform into huge clay animated figures. This notion of the Golem and Prague (and, more specifically, the Jewish ghetto and its people) being inextricably interlinked, expressed through the anthropomorphization of the city's buildings, is clearly lifted from Meyrink's novel, where the writer describes a 'half house, crooked, with a receding forehead'[37] and, later, houses with black doors like 'gaping mouths in which the tongues had rotted away'.[38]

In Barta's film, houses, rendered in clay, stretch themselves upwards and outwards with great groans of exertion, revealing toothed mouths in doorways. An ear spins up a spiral staircase and torsos bulge from walls. It is not merely that these buildings resemble people but that they too partake, in a bodily sense, in the sensory life of the city, as though Prague itself were some great sensorium – a living, breathing organism in which humans reside like parasites within a host. This is not quite congruent with the premises of actor-network-theory, since Barta is not precisely demonstrating that a city is composed of a multitude of actants, the movements of which are all interconnected. The film's visuals are too murky for this to be the case. The claymation sections of the pilot consist almost entirely of different shades of brown. The lines in the clay marking out windows and doors are often crudely and imprecisely scored to the point where it is hard to ascertain precisely the moment at which a door becomes a mouth or a wall a shoulder. The impression given is one of writhing, organic, undifferentiated clay, which at times resembles a city, but always remains first and foremost the primordial clay itself.

While the unification of the Golem and the city is a vision of incorporation and subsumption, it is worth noting that Barta's pilot begins with a shot portraying spiritual, if not physical, exclusion. An elderly Jewish rabbi walks down Maiselova Street, identifiable through a POV shot in which both the distinctive Old-New Synagogue (Staronová snagoga) and the Jewish Town Hall (Židovská radnice) are seen. Rob Humphreys identifies Maiselova as the thoroughfare of Josefov. He notes: 'The sheer volume of tourists … that visit Josefov has brought with it the inevitable rash of souvenir stalls flogging dubious "Jewish" souvenirs, and the whole area is now something of a tourist trap.'[39] Some of these stalls can be seen in Barta's opening shot, including racks of souvenir postcards, near which tourists take photographs.

Touring Prague in April 2014, I visited Josefov in order to locate the real streets that appear in Barta's pilot. Having made my way to the district, I discovered that much of the 'Jewish Museum in Prague', far from being a single building with accompanying exhibitions, actually consists of several streets and synagogues of the Jewish district themselves – or rather, the location of many of the museum's objects in these buildings makes certain streets inaccessible to the non-paying member of the public. The Old Jewish Cemetery (Starý židovský hřbitov), with its overwhelmingly dense collection of collapsed and crooked gravestones, is cordoned off from the surrounding area by a high wall. With many of the main streets of Josefov lined with shops selling items by Gucci and Prada, one has the sense of being kept outside the authentic 'heart' of the district. Indeed, the very architectural layout of the district, with the most preserved sites cordoned off for paying visitors, almost forces the pedestrian into assuming the role of the voyeuristic tourist. It is prohibited, for instance, to take photos within the cemetery, unless one has paid a nominal price to do so. However, as my friend who accompanied me on the trip wondered, 'What happens if you are a Czech Jew, visiting the grave of an ancestral relative?'

In *Golem*, the rabbi is shown to be more familiarly acquainted with Josefov than the crowd of tourists. After the establishing shot that shows the rabbi walking down the street towards the camera, the film cuts to a close-up of the rabbi's shoes upon the cobblestones. The intimacy of this shot – the rabbi's hand, arm and right leg are very close to the camera lens – provokes a sense that these are stones that the rabbi has walked across many times before. The rabbi, however, whose face is now shown in close-up, looks with confusion at the scene. At first his knotted brow seems to be in response to the commercialization before him, but then his POV fades into a sepia-toned photograph and back again. A possible reading of this sequence might build upon an assertion made by Susan Sontag about the nature of photography, quoted by Suzanne Buchan: 'As photographs give people an imaginary possession of a past that is unreal, they also help people to take possession of a space in which they are insecure.'[40] Under this reading, the rabbi feels insecure faced with the commercialization of the Jewish district and its bustling crowds of tourists and so summons a photograph in his mind, depicting a period in which Josefov was still predominantly Jewish, to enable him to take back 'possession' of a district from which he has been spiritually dispossessed. For, even though the oldest rabbi in the late twentieth century would have been born long after the old Jewish ghetto was demolished, the rabbi cannot be considered a tourist since he inhabits a role as ancient as the ghetto.

A relationship between a citizen and his/her city fostered within the imagination bolstered by myths and legends should not necessarily be dismissed as inauthentic, even while it is mediated by fictions. Aviezer Tucker reminds us: 'Home is usually a multilevel structure that combines several single-level homes, such as an emotional home, a geographic home, a cultural home, etc.'[41] The perception of a city as one's home is, like the architectural city itself, a palimpsest.[42] Cultural and historical images, ideas and memes about a city densely intermingle with one's own personal experiences. In a strictly geographic and temporal sense the rabbi does not belong to Josefov of the nineteenth century, although architectural elements of that period do still remain intact, preserved for tourism. However, the reflective, contemplative attitude he strikes as he walks down Maiselova Street as images from distant history are conjured in his mind attests to the validity of the concept of an enduring 'emotional home'.

It is, perhaps, this kind of home that Franz Kafka experienced when walking through Josefov with the poet Gustav Janourh, reflecting to his friend: 'The unhealthy old Jewish Town within us is far more real than the hygienic town around us.'[43] Kafka gives ontological pre-eminence to the spiritual Josefov that supersedes the architectural Josefov of the present. In this way, the writer is more optimistic than the Švankmajer of *Faust*. For Švankmajer, living in the late twentieth century, the magic of Old Prague has been swallowed up by the banality of the present. Ironically, the kitsch marketing of Kafka to tourists has played none too small a part in this. Yet, as the quotation from Kafka illustrates, 'Old Prague' was always something of a construct, more felt than real in any objective-materialist sense. Derek Sayer makes the acute observation that 'Magic Prague is not just a projection of foreigners' desires for the esoteric and exotic ... Gustav Meyrink ... and many other Prague authors accreted just as generously in both Czech and German to the ghetto's mystique, which lent itself equally well to the fecundity of the decadent or the expressionistic imagination'.[44] Through adapting Meyrink, Barta is not reaching back to a historically real Prague that existed before the advent of communism (even if we imagine this is his intent) but, rather, to a Prague that is always already literary and cinematic.

If the Golem of Barta's film is the memory of the ghetto itself,[45] then it follows logically that it should consist of 'mutating layers',[46] considering the mutable nature of memory. The grotesque clay transformations of the houses are not baroque formalism, but an embodied metaphor for how a place and the memories of that place are not static, but contingent upon each other as they shift and mutate through time. Wood buckles and the clay warps and shifts. When the houses seem to birth/contort into sense organs (a mouth, a tongue, an ear) the effect is fragmentary and heterogeneous – a kind of visual heteroglossia, a collage of sense-memories and images belonging to the historic-mythic ghetto. In this light, it is perversely (though sadly) fitting that Barta's film remains unfinished. If the Golem is not a singular creature but the ghetto itself, the film that bears the title 'Golem' must also never be finished, since such a project must keep transforming, accruing new layers of meaning as financial investors come and go and Josefov itself changes under the weight of commercialism and tourism.

At the end of Barta's pilot, all the non-human actants of the ghetto crumble into a sucking whirlpool of undifferentiated mud. Objects with defined names and functions – a doll, a chair – break into pieces to become mere *things*. Perhaps, they become even something less, more primordial – mud; sediment; residue; *humus*, the void from which all things, objects and humans are birthed and to which they will all, eventually, return.

In a motif typical to Barta, as per Chapter 3, a grandfather clock succumbs to the sucking gravity and is pulled to pieces, disappearing into oblivion.[47] The human conception of abstract, sequential time – of one thing following another – cannot hold in the face of nothingness. The Golem belongs to this liminal, uncanny space that exists before and after meaning. Josefov can never be destroyed because it was always already absent. The Jewish people were never permitted a home in Prague. The high, locked walls of the ghetto disclose nothing.

Just orbiting bodies in abstract space

While Barta's 2007 short *Cook, Mug, Cook!* (otherwise known as *Sweet Porridge*) prominently features a woman cooking at a pot, she is not the only figure whose work routine is depicted in the film. Among others, an author is shown working at a typewriter; a lumberjack cutting through a log; a collector foraging for mushrooms; a bank robber cracking a safe. All these characters are subsequently shown in extreme long shot as minuscule particles of dust floating in the air under a light bulb. Their mechanical character is emphasized as an angel, a devil and a figure of death glide close to the screen, figures that clearly recall the clockwork characters that mark the hour for Prague's astronomical clock.

In the fairy tale 'Sweet Porridge' (*Der süße Brei*) – from which the film takes its name – a girl is given a cooking pot that will create an infinite supply of porridge when the user says the magic word 'cook'. The girl's mother tells the pot to do so, but does not know the word to stop it. As a result, chaos ensues as the town is consumed by porridge. In Barta's loose film adaptation of the tale, it is not merely cooking porridge but the whole host of domestic and everyday routines depicted that run out of control, prompted by the substitution of newer, modern and more diverse objects in the place of traditional ones. So, following the appearance of the clock figures, we see the lumberjack cutting through his log with an electric chainsaw. The cook shakes oriental seasoning and soy sauce into her broth. A digital clock replaces a mechanical pocket watch. Then, a drunken man in traditional Bavarian costume stumbles into a golfer, sending his golf ball careening into a television set. A car smashes into a tree. The angel and devil are hurled against one another, so that their heads switch bodies – possibly a symbolic jibe at moral relativism. Money from the bank heist rains down upon a homeless busker. The music increases in speed and, as the tempo changes, so does the pitch, the sound becoming increasingly manic and intense. Social order has been thrown into disarray and the simple, predictable daily rituals that help comprise this order are wholly disrupted. Eventually it appears that the whole society is a simulation running within a computer programme, which a police officer desperately tries to shut down, like the mother in the fairy tale trying to stop the overflowing porridge. The computer system crashes, the light bulb is smashed and the film ends.

The first thing one notices when watching *Cook, Mug, Cook!* – if one has watched Barta's previous filmography – is that real objects have been replaced with CGI. Instead of the solid materiality of stop-motion animation, which allows the viewer to imagine grasping the tangible stuff on display, computer-generated shapes, resembling household objects, hang suspended in abstract space. Patrick Crogan asserts that the computerization of special effects in film means that special effects no longer equal 'the making of something out of something else in an immense labour of the transformation of materials'; instead, special effects become 'the transformation of materiality per se'.[48] To a degree, Crogan is confusing what CGI *affects* with what it actually *is*. CGI may appear to be pure, self-willed 'potentiality', able to transform itself into any 'amorphous'[49] form, but in actual fact there is always physical hardware behind the software and a team of digital animators directing the form the CGI takes. However, in terms of their affective impression upon the viewer, the objects of *Cook, Mug, Cook!* certainly look less like real items that might be found about the home and more like abstract, potentially amorphous forms that are being used to represent objects without actually *being* those real objects themselves. It is hard to imagine cooking with the perfectly cylindrical blue pot upon which the film centres. Many of the 'objects' are textured, but one never has the sense that we are intended to believe that, say, the CGI tree is a real living tree. This is, in part, due to the lack of any background or environmental details that might help anchor these objects or provide a sense that they are rooted in a real living environment.

While there are clearly myriad actors at work within the tiny society depicted in the film, they do not appear – at least superficially – to be networked. One might be reminded of the pleasure seekers of *Conspirators of Pleasure*, each one isolated in their own singular pursuit of erotic gratification. However, as was demonstrated, the fulfilment of the desires of the characters in that film was at least contingent upon the interaction of myriad different actants. By contrast, the figures in *Cook, Mug, Cook!* seem to exist within their own private universes. This atomized society, composed almost exclusively of private and domestic rituals, finds its perfect expression in CGI since, to quote Lefebvre, 'Computerized daily life risks assuming a form that certain ideologies find interesting and seductive: the individual atom or family molecule inside a bubble where the messages sent and received intersect.'[50] Lefebvre goes on to explain: 'Users, who have lost the dignity of citizens now that they figure socially only as parties to services, would thus lose the social itself, and sociability.'[51]

In Barta's film, society breaks down in the face of computerized abstraction and domestic isolation.[52] The fact that the events of the film are ultimately revealed to be a digital simulation is a way for the director to signal that his film occurs in 'no place'. Barta's message could be that routines unanchored from space and place lose their social meaning, which ultimately leads to the disintegration of traditions. Without an environment for the film's characters to occupy, there can be no community between them. Without shared experience(s) rooted in the physical world, they are merely orbiting bodies. The absence of Prague (or any other material environment) in *Cook, Mug, Cook!* – like the absence of the Old Jewish Ghetto in the modern Josefov of Barta's *Golem* – is the central absence about which the meaning of the film is structured. After a period of political transition, such as that experienced after the Velvet Revolution, it is not enough to just maintain the traditional rituals and routines of a national culture to ensure a national revival; the spaces where the revolution has taken place must be newly revitalized and engaged with anew for the society to hold together as a stable, flourishing network.

Life among the dead in *One Night in One City*

Jan Balej's stop-motion feature *One Night in One City* (*Jedné noci v jednom městě*, 2007) provides a similarly atomized portrait of Czech society to Barta's

CGI short, with the fragmentation extending from the often solitary lives of its characters to the very form of the film itself. *One Night* is a effectively a portmanteau film, composed of several short films released independently by Balej over the years 2000 to 2006, with a few additional segments written with Ivan Arsenjev. As such, the film as a whole does not provide a cohesive, overarching narrative. Instead, the shorts are thematically arranged. The one factor uniting these disparate strands is the working-class district of Žižkov, the location where all the film's characters reside.[53]

Gin (*Džin*, 2000), the first of the shorts to be released, focuses upon the antics of two drunkards who summon a genie from a bottle of gin. *Mr. Fin and Mr. Twig* (*Větvička a Ploutvička*, 2006) depicts the friendship of an apartment-dwelling tree and fish through the changing seasons. *Stopped Time* (*Zastavený Čas*), previously unreleased, is set in a haunted café. Finally, *Shells* (*Ulity*, 2003), the short with which *One Night in One City* begins, depicts the isolated lives of a group of eccentric residents of an apartment building.

Most of the apartment dwellers in *Shells* never leave their flats. Each concerns himself or herself with some obsessive, idiosyncratic hobby – conducting miniature circus performances with a cast of dead insects, taking photographs of terrified dogs before a mock furnace, dressing their dog in a lion costume and then pretending to be a big game hunter or snorting lines of sugar/cocaine filled with living ants – that other characters find disturbing, ridiculous or alienating. These activities often constitute tiny self-contained microcosmic worlds within the already domestically divided apartment, such as an insect circus or fake jungle. Yet these are dead worlds composed of dead things. The insects, even when passed through a hoop or loaded into toy cannon, are always obviously, pathetically dead. The jungle's grass is clearly carpeting, while the little dog is awkwardly unconvincing in his bearskin costume. When real life, in the form of ubiquitous black ants, enters the frame, it is immediately brushed aside or snuffed out. The man with the circus batters an ant with a newspaper. The safari hunter finds an ant on his toy gun, which he sweeps to the floor. More starkly, the dog photographer has a toy crematorium within his own flat, alongside fake urns and memorial photography. These apartment dwellers can only cope with life when it is ossified, mortified and, to preserve this ossification, most pursue their hobbies in isolation.

Jean Baudrillard argues that the private, personal worlds of hobbyists and collectors 'bear the stamp of solitude'.[54] 'Because he feels alienated and abolished by a social discourse whose rules escape him', Baudrillard writes, 'the collector strives to reconstitute a discourse that is transparent to him, a discourse whose signifiers he controls and whose referent *par excellence* is himself'.[55] The morbidity of the hobbyists in *One Night* is befitting since such a person is already dead, their objects performing 'the work of mourning',[56] like the burial treasures of an Egyptian pharaoh. Rather than engage with the outside world, the hobbyists of the film have created stagnant microcosms, over which they can exert ultimate control and, in doing so, ensure a lack of change.

What might have led these fictional citizens of Žižkov to their sequestered, lonely lives? Johnson, Hraba and Lorenz assert in their article 'Criminal Victimisation and Depression in the Czech Republic' that crime levels in the Czech Republic rose after the fall of communism and that this, combined with a growing belief in the ineffectuality of the police, led, in some cases, to an increased adoption of avoidance strategies, by which citizens avoided leaving the house at night, or visiting certain streets, due to their fear of victimization.[57] Furthermore, the number of pensioners in the Czech Republic has been on the increase since 1997 which, combined with a sizeable growth in unemployment in the latter part of the 1990s,[58] has led to an increase in the number of citizens of all ages remaining within the home for longer periods, adopting avoidance strategies, such as 'not going out after dark'.[59] Finally, it might be worth considering that Žižkov, the district where this first part of the film is set, was, to quote Ivana Edwards, 'a cauldron of local Communist Party support'[60] for most of the twentieth century. Neil Wilson and Mark Baker in their *Prague City Guide* (2010) also characterize Žižkov as a working-class area with strong left-wing political sympathies.[61] One might imagine that for many citizens of Žižkov, the decline and eventual overthrow of the KSČ and the subsequent loss of certain state institutions and securities was a shattering, potentially traumatic experience. Perhaps the citizens of Balej's Žižkov have retreated into their stagnant, solitary, domestic lives in response to the loss of employment, local party meetings or more broadly defined ideological certainties.

In *Cityscapes* (2005) Ben Highmore reminds us: 'Nature in all its forms is present in the city, but one of its forms predominates – its human form.'[62] In the section of *One Night* that concerns the friendship of a tree, Mr Twig, and a fish, Mr Fin, nature has adopted humanoid form and exists in a curious balance between natural and human rhythms. So we observe a tree living according to the rhythms of clock time. He rises in the morning and gets dressed, but he also sheds his leaves according to the seasonal cycle. Mr Fin and Mr Twig observe the ritual of Christmas, dressing Mr Twig with tinsel and baubles so he can stand as a Christmas tree; however, this has also been enabled by the fact that Mr Twig has, quite naturally, lost his fruit and leaves across the autumn and winter months, leaving him prime for decoration. The section's tone is charming and whimsical, but there is also a sense that nature (in the form of the tree and the fish) has been modified by human rhythms. The linear rhythms of the social world – Lefebvre calls linear rhythms 'the daily grind'[63] – have imposed themselves upon the natural order. We might think of Barta's filmography and his critique of abstract clock time in favour of cyclical natural rhythms that express themselves in terms of variegated decay and transformation. However, the tone here is far less cynical. The viewer is presented with a fantasy Utopia in which trees and fish can live in perfect harmony with the human world. The absence of soil or salt water from the network of their lives is not shown to be important. The city can provide a living, vibrant ecosystem of its own.

Indeed, Balej's interest in actants out of place from their usual network has continued in his adaptation of Hans Christian Anderson's *The Little Mermaid* (1837) (*Malá z rybárny*, 2015), with the girl of the title literally a fish out of water. The little mermaid (or 'Little from the Fish Shop', to translate Balej's and Arsenjev's title) is characterized as a 'displaced immigrant'.[64] A parallel is drawn in the film between the intersection/clash of different cultural rhythms and the intersection/clash of the rhythms of nature with and against the rhythms of human society. The film's English-language trailer states that Little is 'driven by her desire' to venture into the seedier districts of the city only to discover that her 'Prince Charming' is the owner of a nightclub, with little interest in monogamy. The film is ultimately tragic, with Little dying on the streets of the city – Balej and Arsenjev positioning romantic love as fundamentally at odds with the more commercial drives of the city.

Desiring rhythms in *Tram*

Kyna Morgan, in interview with Michaela Pavlátová, describes Pavlátová's animation *Tram* (2012) as being about the pleasures of rhythms.[65] The rhythms in the film are those of a tram journey through Prague, which take on an erotic quality as they harmonize with the bodily rhythms of the driver. The mechanical rhythms of the tram as it travels through the city, and the repetitious rituals of the driver's job, interact with her bodily rhythms creating libidinal pleasure and leading to an orgasmic fantasy sequence. The film thus enacts a transformation, revealing an erotic playfulness in a commuter journey that might otherwise be seen as dull or banal. The tram chugs along slowly, bouncing gently as it moves, with the stamping of tickets creating a regular 'chunking' sound that interpolates the rhythm.

Although the route of the tram is likely cyclical, the two-dimensional animation style (in which the tram is shown moving horizontally across the screen), combined with the staccato rhythm of the passengers boarding the tram and stamping their tickets, provides an impression of linear, rather than cyclical, travel. Lefebvre, in *Rhythmanalysis*, expounds upon the concept of linear rhythms as follows: 'The linear … consists of journeys to and fro: it combines with the cyclical, the movements of long intervals … The linear is the daily grind, the routine, therefore the perpetual, made up of chance and encounters.'[66] Lefebvre reference to 'the daily grind' hints at the potential tediousness imbued inside linear rhythms in contrast to the more restorative and rejuvenating potential of cyclical rhythms. Indeed, the tram driver's job is initially depicted as tedious. Her customers are grey and humourless and all look alike. The 'chance encounters' to which Lefebvre refers provide only momentary diversions – a screeching halt before a busy intersection and a stop at a zebra crossing while a kitten licks itself idly in the path of the tram – which seem to annoy and frustrate the homogeneous mass of commuters. In a review of the film, Ali Deniz describes the protagonist as being 'stuck in her job'.[67] It is the tram driver's erotic imagination that is ultimately able to transform the banal repetition of her work into a sexual fantasy. Deniz provides an impressionistic inventory which charts this transformation: 'Tram, roads, male passengers on tram, "stick" of tram's panel board, vibrating driver chair become objects of sexual desire for the main character … The tram becomes an organic extension of the character.'[68]

It remains obscure as to whether the rhythms of the tram, despite outward banality, are possessed of some innate eroticism or whether the imagination of the tram driver is such that she is able to transform even the most banal of rhythms. Is the driver's erotic reverie an escape from the rhythms of daily lived reality or an extension of them? Lefebvre helps illuminate the answer to this question through his reflection that rhythm 'appears as regulated time, governed by rational laws, but in contact with what is least rational in human being: the lived, the carnal, the body'.[69] Deniz's statement that the tram 'becomes an organic extension of the character' is precisely right. There is a harmonious intermingling of mechanical and organic rhythms so that the body of the driver is not easily distinguished from the body of the tram.

Over the course of the film, the tram's levers – which the driver grasps and rubs her hands up and down in a masturbatory fashion – become increasingly fleshy and phallic, as though responding to her touch. At the start of this chapter, I spoke of directors picking up the city of Prague like a lump of clay and moulding it according to their desires. In *Tram* it is as though the erotic imagination of the driver is able to transform part of Prague's transportation network into an erogenous extension of her body. Even the commuting businessmen are wholly consumed by the driver's fantasies, transformed into faceless pink phalluses, which she cavorts among and joyfully grasps and mounts. They are finally dehumanized into a pink seething mass of phallic cilia that move in caressing waves – the commuters' movements, once mechanical, staccato and linear, are transformed into organic, orgasmic, cyclical rhythms.

When Lefebvre writes about the body, he tends to stress its 'polyrhythmic' and 'eurhythmic' qualities.[70] In short, our bodies are never one single, unitary entity but a complex harmony of different rhythms, all interlinked. The beat of our heart keeps a different time to the rhythm of our breathing. As an animator, Pavlátová is aware of this polyrhythmia, which extends to her working methods. *Tram* was animated in the computer software 'Flash' in a series of stacked visual layers. Pavlátová informs Laura-Beth Cowley that as she was working on the film, she 'realised that everything is moving and bopping and all the movement is happening one after the other'.[71] To animate the tram driver, she separated her body up into different sections. Each leg and each breast were animated separately, yet they move together rhythmically on screen. Pavlátová states that this was 'difficult to sequence' while maintaining 'that feeling of bouncing on the tram, even though it was only one woman and the same men being driven along'.[72]

As partially determined by her use of Flash, Pavlátová honours a Lefebvrean conception of the body as being ineluctably intertwined with the rhythms of the city. Citizens of Prague do not merely ride its transportation network; they *partake* of it, bodily. The poetics of *Tram* are in harmony with Lefebvre's contention that 'there is neither separation nor an abyss between so-called material bodies, living bodies, social bodies and representations, ideologies, traditions, projects and utopias. They are all composed of … rhythms in interaction'.[73] The tram driver's fantasies do not merely take place within her head but within the public-social arena of Prague's transportation system. The rhythms of the tram and the Czech commuters each play their part in contributing to her erotic experience, intentionally or otherwise. The imaginary lives of a city's inhabitants are never fully divorced from the material reality of the city and its rhythms.

Surviving Life as an *Insect*

In her music video for Dominika Truban's *Different Kinds of People* (*Rôzne druhy ľudí*, 2015) Pavlátová envisions the city as a chaotic system of endlessly over-layered planes of repetitive everyday rituals. The different kinds of people in the video (school children, businessmen, nuns, etc.) go about their daily activities in predictable uniform formations until – seemingly at random – individuals are thrown flailing into the air, as though subject to a glitch in the matrix. The animation is then looped for a second time, but now with the different kinds of people replaced by different kinds of animal (pigs, sheep, cows, etc.), repeating the previous rhythms of their human counterparts.

Švankmajer's final two features, *Surviving Life: Theory and Practice* (*Přežít svůj život*, 2010) and *Insect* (*Hmyz*, 2018), are each similar to the *Different Kinds of People* video but in distinctly different ways. *Surviving Life* also treats the city as a series of flat overlapping planes, in which citizens constantly cross paths but never quite meet. *Insect*, on the other hand, depicts a great deal of interactions between its human characters, but they are each shown to be, in essence, animals (specifically insects) acting in accordance with their genus and class.

Surviving Life ostensibly unfolds among the streets of Prague. Occasionally street signs can be glimpsed, so the viewer can recognize that a given scene transpires, for instance, in Žižkov. One might, then, imagine that *Surviving Life* would provide a very rich site of analysis for the thing theorist, actor-network-theorist or rhythmanalysist seeking to understand better the relationship between the citizen of Prague and the city in all its material detail.

However, one reaches into the film armed with these critical theories and comes back empty-handed. Why? My view is that the reason for this critical failure is due to an aspect of the film's form unprecedented in Švankmajer's feature films – although the technique may be seen in shorter works like his 1977 adaptation of Walpole's *Castle of Otranto* (1977) or, briefly, in *Virile Games* (*Mužné hry*, 1988) – namely, that *Surviving Life* is animated through the use of paper cut-outs in a style reminiscent of Terry Gilliam's contributions to *Monty Python's Flying Circus* (1969–74). As a result, the thing theorist lacks any tangible, thingy objects at which to grasp. There are barely seconds of stop-motion animation in the film.

The actor-network-theorist is confronted with a beguiling sparseness. Rarely do the static backgrounds – photographs of city streets – feel *occupied* in any real sense. Their monochrome colouration gives them the feel of frozen memories and their two-dimensionality precludes them from feeling 'lived in'. Likewise, the film lacks actants. Whole scenes might involve two characters talking within a frozen street, absent of any objects. *Surviving Life* is easily the Švankmajer film with the least amount of *stuff* on display. It is uncharacteristically uncluttered.

The rhythmanalysist is stumped by the immobility of the flat backgrounds. There is very little movement and so very little rhythm. Someone wishing to talk about the depiction of Prague in the film could do little more than namecheck places from street signs and discuss the city as a heterogeneous, postmodern and fragmentary space. An illustrative quote from Lefebvre, which almost sounds as though it could have come from a review of the film, reads: 'We are confronted by an indefinite multitude of spaces, each one piled upon, or perhaps contained within, the next.'[74] The technique of paper

Figure 4.1 The flattened and monochrome city of Prague as depicted in *Surviving Life: Theory and Practice* (*Přežít svůj život*) (Jan Švankmajer, 2010). Image used with permission of Athanor.

cut-out animation means that architectural backgrounds are often assembled from a jumble of different buildings that may, in reality, be geographically separated. The main thing that unites the spaces of the film – besides from the combination of architectural monumentality and crumbling plaster that characterizes the city – is the ubiquitous graffiti that marks so much of the brickwork. The Prague of *Surviving Life* matches Ripellino's description of the city as 'a heap of singed and stained rubbish'.[75]

The protagonist of the film, Evzen (Václav Helsus), spends much of his running time asleep. Evzen's dream life is rich and wild (humans exist with chicken heads, dogs walk upright wearing suits, giant hands appear through windows, etc.) but it only ever imposes itself upon, rather than achieving a full integration with, the city. His imagination is personal, obsessive and idiosyncratic, but it is not shared. When Evzen's wife tries to enter his dream world, he rejects her. Švankmajer strikes an ambivalent position towards Evzen's decision to choose imaginative disconnect over waking life at the end of the film, but it is clearly a position he has some sympathy for, considering his tendency towards infantile/intrauterine regression in his work.[76]

Troublingly from a materialist perspective, Evzen's decision appears to be a retreat from community and a retreat from personal relationships that exist outside of his mind. It is a solipsistic position, even while the character of his dreams is necessarily influenced to some degree by the environment of Prague. Indeed, perhaps the nature of his retreat has been subtly determined by the city itself. In the introduction to *Cities after the Fall of Communism* (2009), Czaplicka, Gelazis and Ruble note:

> In the Soviet period, new cities were built alongside the old, with little or no relationship to the structures of the past. The 'historic' city was often neglected ... it is an irony of history that such neglect, which meant to make history vanish, would ultimately help to conserve the historical 'substance' that now literally invites attempts to return to some 'radiant past'. It is the once modern and subsequently dilapidated Socialist city that now belongs to history.[77]

The monochrome monuments of *Surviving Life* seem to be resolutely stuck in the past. There is no sense of a living, breathing, present city but merely a forgotten historical city, frozen in time. I would contend that this impression is due to the flatness of the cut-out animation style in which the animated figures are placed on top of rather than within the landscape. This is true of planar animation generally (including traditional cellular animation) in which – as characterized by Sean Cubitt – the animated figure is set 'against an environment that is palpably separate from them'.[78] Cubitt's ecocritique of this form of animation is that it estranges characters from their environment, working against a sense of rootedness, which reflects and embodies modernity's tendency to see the individual as outside and above nature. Since this anthropocentrism is arguably the ideology Švankmajer most consistently critiques, Evzen's alienation from his environment (and a lack of condemnation of that estrangement) might indicate Švankmajer abandoning this project in despair at the 'flattening' of Prague by the commercial and reifying imperatives of tourism. If Evzen lacks a living city in which to exist, it is little wonder that he retreats to the vibrancy of his dreams.

A more optimistic reading of the film would hold that Švankmajer is engaged in the Surrealist project of disrupting the viewer's understanding of Prague as a stable, homogeneous space, consisting of identifiable landmarks and historical sites. David Sorfa argues that in 'a political sense the work of the Czech Surrealists ... can be seen as undermining the concept of a rational city that could be perfectly designed and planned'.[79] However, ultimately, this rings more true of *Faust* than it does of *Surviving Life*. The Prague of *Surviving Life* does not disclose irrational spaces – rather, irrational fantasies are superimposed upon a banal, flattened city of grey brick and lacklustre graffiti.

This emphasis upon the unconscious mind is continued in *Insect*, but coupled with a renewed fascination with the materiality of things lacking in *Surviving Life*. *Insect* is, on one level, a film of the Capeks's *Insect Play*, but it is also, simultaneously, a portrait of the rehearsal process of the actors within the film staging the play, as well as a document of Švankmajer's own direction of the film (and thus the play within the film), with all three layers often blurred and intermingled with one another.

Švankmajer's interest in the workings of the unconscious mind is clear in scenes in which the various actors working on the film recount their dreams to camera. On the surface these scenes are provocatively counterbalanced, even undercut, by Švankmajer's repeated assertions, both in direct address to the audience and while directing his actors, that the film is intended to be free from any psychological depth. However, these dreams are not selected for their richness or potential receptivity to psychological analysis. Indeed, a couple of the actors either cannot remember their dreams or recount dreams which are stupefyingly dull. Rather than prove some special depth which would otherwise be hidden, the dreams are just actants alongside other actants which have gone into the making of the film. They are no different therefore from any of the 'documentary' sequences integrated into the body of the film which include what would normally be classified as out-takes, such as a dog walking onto set, crew members in discussion with Švankmajer and sequences in which the production of various 'special effects' is shown, such as the cooking up of the soup later used as fake vomit. Through including these aspects of the process of film-making, not as DVD extras or downloadable content but as integral aspects of the finished text itself, Švankmajer comes the closest in his career to honouring the fundamental project of ANT, achieving this not least in the mode of production itself. Approximately $300,000 of *Insect*'s budget was raised through the crowdfunding website Indiegogo. Having not merely consumed the film as a finished product, but been part of its process of production through contribution to this campaign, I can also count myself as part of the network of actants that composes *Insect*.

We don't see much of Prague in *Insect* until a curious sequence at the end of the film, in which two of the film's characters (now completely indistinguishable from the 'real' actors who play them) greet good morning to various pedestrians who pass them on the street. Two construction workers and a tourist both cheerily offer greetings. Among these actors, citizens of Prague mill, seemingly unaware they are on camera. Even a homeless person seems to have his own special role to play in the city (just as every insect had his/her own role within the play within the film), commenting that the day has turned out well as he salvages food from a bin. Suddenly the camera whip pans across to Švankmajer sat in his director's chair. 'I told you', he remarks – eyebrows raised – and the film ends. The rhythms of the everyday world stand revealed as no less constructed than those of the theatre. Dressage ensures that the citizen in the street is conditioned into a repetitious playing through of polite but inauthentic gestures, such as wishing a homeless man good morning, in spite of having no intention of changing the material circumstances of his existence. In the face of a Hobbesian universe of ritualized conformity, the individual must seek personal transformation through imagination and the unconscious.

The citizen's inner life is collective, public and dependent upon myths and stories

So, with *Surviving Life: Theory and Practice* and *Insect* we come back to the city as mere backdrop for the psychological portrait of the individual citizen as witnessed at the beginning of the chapter with Pavel Koutský's *Portrait of the Man in the Street*. However, the other films discussed thus far in this chapter engage in depth with the city of Prague. Sometimes this is in a concrete sense, as in Švankmajer's *Faust* and *Conspirators of Pleasure* or Barta's *Golem*; sometimes this is in a more abstract mode, such as with Barta's *Cook, Mug, Cook!* Taken as a whole, this body of films provides two possible responses to the increased homogenization of Prague due to tourism and consumer capitalism. One is to retreat from the city like the apartment dwellers in *One Night in One City* or Evzen in *Surviving Life* and fixate on one's own personal obsessions in isolation; however, this can lead to loneliness and dysfunction. The alternative is to enact one's imaginative fantasies within the public space of the city itself, like the perverts of *Conspirators* or the protagonist of *Tram*. This necessitates social interaction in which other citizens become part of the fulfilment of one's fantasies and sometimes unwitting actors in each other's games. Anxiety about increased tourism, consumerism and the subsequent homogenization of the city characterizes the work of all the film-makers discussed; and yet, there is a recognition among these artists that the city of Prague was always already mythic and constructed through stories such as that of Faust or the Golem, or even the fairy tale of 'Sweet Porridge' as recounted in *Cook, Mug, Cook!* According to these films, the entry of the Czech Republic into Western consumer capitalism, along with the increased tourism this has brought to its capital, cannot wholly efface the meaning the city has for its inhabitants, as long as these stories and myths persist and the citizens of Prague choose to engage with their collective history rather than retreat from it.

Twenty-first-century Czech animation

Critical commentators writing about the condition of Czech animation at the end of the first decade of the twenty-first century regarded it as being in a state of decline. Lucie Joschko and Michael Morgan cite three possible reasons for this downturn in fortunes: '(1) the disappearance of the common enemy (the communist government); (2) the fragmentation of the Czech audience; and (3) the arrival of economic censorship',[80] with the third working in combination with the removal of state funding. After the privatization of Kratky Film in 1992, production by the Trick Brothers Studio and the Studio of the Puppet Film dramatically decreased.[81] As with their live-action counterparts,[82] instead of working upon original Czech films with local themes, animators found employment with international co-productions attracted to the lower overheads of working in a post-communist country with newly available resources, equipment, staff and studio space.[83] Recounting her visit to the Trick Brothers and Puppet Film studios in 2008 (then occupying only a single building in Barrandov), Lucie Joschko describes debris piled up in disused rooms, being surprised when she chanced upon a camera-shy Jiří Barta working upon *In the Attic* (*Na Pude*, 2009), having otherwise encountered only empty corridors.[84]

Indeed, *In the Attic* was the only Czech animated feature film in cinemas in its year of release. Notably, in Peter Hames's review of the state of the Czech film industry in 2006, Švankmajer, Barta and Pavlátová comprise three out of only four animators mentioned[85] – all directors who had also produced films within the twentieth century and all already mentioned in the preceding chapters here. The only 'new' animator Hames singles out as worthy of note is Aurel Klimt. Klimt's harshly expressionistic films (with the exception of his exquisitely delicate contribution of stop-motion and shadow puppetry to the 2008 children's film *Mozart in China*) tend to be coarsely funny, morbid and occasionally melancholy illustrations of human cruelty and weakness. In his professional debut short *The Fall* (*Pád*, 1999) an elderly woman hangs from the roof of a house in a Moscow street while various public servants fail to help her, while others fall to their death unnoticed and unmourned. While the short might be read as a Kafkaesque allegory for the Russian state's treatment of its citizens under Lenin (or that of the human condition more broadly), it comes closer to the absurdist approach used by Roy Andersson in showing the isolated iniquities of human life by which selfishness and self-absorption easily tear through any kind of social fabric. Klimt's starkly varied puppet designs help enforce this impression, as with the failure of characters to connect or truly interact with one another. This stands in contrast to the non-human figures in some of Klimt's other films, such as the balletic glass figures that dance together in motion-capture synergy in *The Glassworks* (2005) or the animals that band together to defeat the human scientists in *Laika* (*Lajka*, 2017). Klimt's work is also defiantly (arguably offensively) against political correctness, with the deaths in *The Fall* played for morbid humour, as with the rapes committed by the villain in his student pixilated short *Bloodthirsty Hugo, an Eastern* (*Krvavý Hugo*, 1997), a parody of silent film Westerns.

This gleeful (and occasionally puerile) disregard for good taste, occasionally expressed in the form of racial caricature, is also present in the animations of Michal Žabka, whose work presents a Bakhtinian view of the world, though often with emasculated male characters dominated by – or in the thrall of – voluptuous female characters, as in *Baballoon* (*Babalon*, 1997), *Premammals* (*Prasavci*, 2001) and *Mrs. G* (*Paní G.*, 2007). Like Klimt, Žabka has also worked on children's animations (including three films about 'Čtyřlístek', a group of four animal friends created by Jaroslav Němeček) and commercials (for Alka Seltzer, MasterCard, Vodafone, Famous Grouse, etc.) to fund his adult projects. Notably, *Lucky Four in the Service of the King* (*Čtyřlístek ve službách krále*, 2013) draws upon Czech history and legend in the form of Rudolf II and his search for the philosopher's stone (*kámen mudrců*). Meanwhile, Klimt is best known for his work upon the *Fimfárum* (2001) and *Fimfárum II* (2006) – anthology films based upon adult fairy tales by Jan Werich, which themselves also draw from traditional aspects of early modern Bohemian culture.

Sections of *Fimfárum II* were also directed by Jan Balej, Vlasta Pospíšilov and Bretislav Pojar (with art direction by Pavel Koutsky) – all animators covered elsewhere in this volume. Michal Žabka has also contributed to an anthology film in the form of his section of *Car Fairy Tales* (*Autopohádky*, 2011). Anthology films – as also seen with Balej's *One Night in One City* – proved a viable format for the animated feature film to take in the early twenty-first century. The anthology format allows a production company or director to bring together short films which might have been independently commissioned or financed, releasing them in a form that can bring sales on DVD. Short films collated within such a feature may have already won awards at film festivals – awards which can then be used to advertise the feature. Some such anthology films – such as *Car Fairy Tales* – employ a frame narrative to bring the potentially disparate shorts together with greater cohesion, while others – like *Fimfárum I* and *II* – already have a degree of unity due to being based upon stories in the same collection by a recognized author. The films in *One Night in One City*, meanwhile, have shared directorial authorship, which provides a degree of tonal and aesthetic consistency; additionally, the title somewhat artificially suggests that the short films within all take place within the same night in Prague.

Perhaps the most innovative of these anthology films is the 2016 release *Murderous Tales* (*Smrtelné historky*) directed by Jan Bubenicek. *Murderous Tales* collects a trilogy of shorts (two of which were made for the feature) and then interpolates another short between them. This tripartite short, *Charge the Dragon* (*Na Draka*), stages three comically fatal encounters between a diminutive knight and three different, but equally deadly dragons, in a style reminiscent of Chuck Jones's 'Wile E. Coyote and the Road Runner' cartoons (1949–64). The three other shorts – *Antonio Cactus* (*Antonio Cacto*), *The*

Lighthouse (*Maják*) and *The Big Man* (*Velký Chlap*) – all deal in some way with geographical and spiritual displacement, with the latter being a road trip centred around miscommunication, *The Lighthouse* being an ecological fable from a worm's-eye view and *Antonio Cactus* featuring the 'soul' of a cactus that wishes to return to Mexico. This sense of displacement is reinforced by the form of the film, which places live-action puppets within real and CGI-augmented locations (among other compositing devices).

While only one or two animated feature films like *Murderous Tales* are released in the Czech Republic per year, this is not ultimately a significant decline to the period Joschko and Morgan refer to as the 'Golden Age of Czechoslovak Animation' of 1945 to 1989 and, more specifically, the 1950s and 1960s.[86] Indeed, while the early 2000s witnessed a significant decline in the amount of Czech animated films being made, in the last decade there has been a notable increase in the amount of independent Czech animated films being made (albeit without the critical and commercial recognition received within the 'Golden Age'). One of the reasons for this is likely the establishment of the Czech Film Fund in January 2013,[87] which expanded in 2017 to incorporate both the Czech Film Commission[88] and the Czech Film Center.[89] New independent studios like Alkay Animation, along with non-profit organizations like the Association of Czech Animation Film (ASAF), have begun to provide infrastructural support and lobbying power for what remains – even with the advent of graphics tablets, CGI and motion capture – a labour-intensive industry. However, an analysis of the current state of the Czech animation industry by the ASAF indicates that cooperation between public institutions like the State Cinematography Fund and the private sector is still behind that of most other European countries, with films very rarely extending beyond the domestic market to reach international audiences.[90] Compounding this problem is that recent animation graduates lack specialization (as compositors, riggers, VFX programmers, etc.) due to having worked mainly upon small-scale, individualized short films, rather than upon larger collaborative projects.[91] As such, while there is a wealth of animated shorts produced by students at institutions like Film School Zlín and FAMU, these students rarely seem to establish themselves as animation directors post-graduation. Those post-grads who do pursue such a career either finance their independent projects through working upon the visual effects of larger (generally Western European or American) films – as in the case of Stepán Batousek, director of the charming *Thamauturgic Miniworld* (*Divotvorný pidisvět*, 2004) and *Lullaby* (*Uspávanka pro Aničku a Batathua s počítáním oveček*, 2001) – or else produce mainly children's animations, which is the path taken by Kateřina Karhánková with such films as *The New Species* (*Nový druh*, 2013), *Tony and Mr. Illness* (*Tonda a bacil*, 2014) and *Fruits of Clouds* (*Plody mraků*, 2017), which combine digital animation, live-action photography and children's drawings to produce stories that appeal to young audiences upon their own terms.

Since 2013 such student and short animated films have been screened within the '*Magazín studentského a krátkého filmu*' magazine strand on ČT art, Česká televize. However, broadcast around midnight, viewership is limited. The rise of video streaming platforms like YouTube and Vimeo has further reach beyond the nation's borders. Particularly encouraging in this regard is the recent 2016 establishment of Aniont.com, a curated internet portal of student and short film animations. Aniont exhibits too wide an array of work to be adequately covered here, but of particular note are the stark and haunting low-resolution animated line drawings by Soňa Jelínková – *Dedicated to*

Figure 4.2 One of the many disturbing and inscrutable visions that make up the morbid erotic fantasy spirit quest of *Dedicated to Darkness* (*Věnováno tmě*) (Soňa Jelínková, 2010), rendered in Jelínková's characteristic scratchy style. Screenshot taken from Anioint.com.

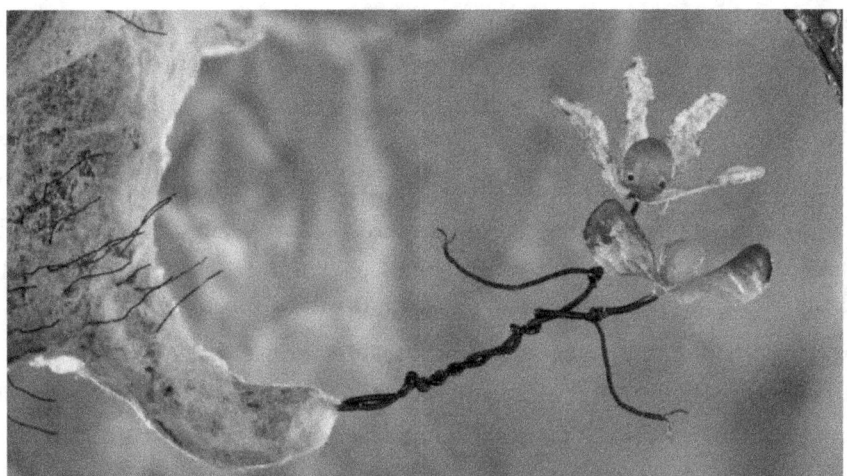

Figure 4.3 Thrumming and twitching insectoid-floral actants intertwined in *The Entangled* (*Zápletka*) (Standa Sekela, 2014). Screenshot taken from Anioint.com.

Darkness (*Věnováno tmě*, 2010), *Never Ending Desire* (*Nedokáže si říct dost*, 2011), *Comely Face* (*Sličná tvář*, 2012) – and the pessimistic allegories of power relations directed by Aleš Pachner. Pachner's *A King Had a Horse* (*Jeden král měl koně*, 2011) is an especially major work, staging a steampunk panopticon of clearly articulated figures. As such, as viewers we are always aware not only that each actor-object in the film is an actant among actants but that each actor-object is *in itself* a network of linked components. This concern with interconnectedness is also present in the ecological themes of many twenty-first-century Czech animations, from family entertainment like Jan Svěrák's *Kooky* (*Kuky se vrací*, 2010) to student films like Milan Ondruch's and Jaroslav Mrázek's *The View* (*Výhled*, 2011) and avant-garde shorts like Standa Sekela's *The Entangled* (*Zápletka*, 2014).

Finally, many of the key figures from the Golden Age of Czech animation continue to wield a material influence upon a newer generation of Czech animators. One of Michal Žabka's most recent shorts, *The Christmas Ballad* (*Vánoční balada*, 2016), was based upon an unproduced script by the late Břetislav Pojar. Meanwhile, Jiří Trnka's grandson, Matyáš Trnka, has produced several shorts and gallery installations which display a tendency towards visual abstraction (*Absurp*, 2009) and a willingness to experiment with new digital technologies (*Another World*, 2012) not present in his grandfather's more traditionally representational and picturesque work. It is interesting to note, however, that this could be seen as a continuation of a new tendency that emerged in Jiří Trnka's later work, building upon the departures of *Passion* (1961), *The Cybernetic Grandma* (1962) and *The Hand* (1965). Jan Švankmajer's son, Václav Švankmajer, has departed stylistically from his father's work with the metallic and forbidding *The Torchbearer* (*Světlonoš*, 2005), which recalls the Brothers Quay in its clockwork-like precision. However, he more recently worked as the art director upon *Insect*, taking up the role previously carried out by his late mother, perhaps showing willingness to 'take up the torch' of his parents' artistic practice. Whether these new animators will restore Czech animation to past critical glories will not, ultimately, come down to a question of talent, but whether public and private organizations prove willing to invest in the country's animation industry.

Political messages from past to present

At its outset this book posed the question, What are the political messages communicated by Czech stop-motion, animated and partially animated films from the end of the Second World War to the present day? Secondly, how are these messages communicated to the viewer? The central argument of this book has been that these political messages are not 'spoken', in the sense of being conveyed through dialogue or voice-over, but are instead communicated via non-human objects/things – both individual and intertwined, static and in flux – and their rhythms, on screen (through editing) and off (through nature and dressage).

The answer to *what* political messages the films communicate is dependent upon the historical period in which any given film was produced. Those films created by Jiří Trnka (and, to a lesser extent, Hermína Týrlová) in the immediate post-war period provide simple messages of national unity in the wake of Nazism's defeat. Trnka's later films, produced during communist rule in Czechoslovakia, celebrate small-scale artisanal work and simple, grounded relationships between humans and their environment over the abstractions of ideology[92] and technological progress. They constitute a defence of the quiet life, unmolested by political power.

Jan Švankmajer's films, meanwhile, suggest that even if dominant forms of political power *were* to be done away with, the stubbornly anthropocentric self-awarded position of humanity in relation to its non-human others would ensure the continuation of cycles of repetitious violence, leading invariably to entropy and destruction. Švankmajer's central political argument is that humans must not be considered as more 'important' than non-human actors. One of the ways in which humans express their power over non-human others is through the imposition of systems of classification and control (such as language or science). Švankmajer's films suggest that these systems are doomed to failure. Instead, reciprocal networks must provide space for a parliament of things. As such, Švankmajer offers a corrective to Trnka's and Týrlová's work. It is not enough for the individual citizen to live a quiet life surrounded by simple domestic objects if the relationship between the humans and the objects is merely one of functional servitude.

If Švankmajer offers an antithesis to Trnka's thesis, the films of Jiří Barta can be seen as staging a synthesis of their two positions. Like Trnka, Barta eulogizes a direct, grounded relationship between humanity and nature in the face of social and individual alienation. However, while Trnka's work positions technological advancement as the major cause of alienation, Barta's films seem to argue that the primary causes of alienation under modernity are, firstly, society's adherence to rational clock time and, secondly, the flattening of space through urban planning and commercialization. It is not enough for people to live simply and humbly alongside objects that anchor the individual to their environment. The environment itself must also be reshaped and the human conception of time reimagined.

Like Švankmajer, then, Barta submits that humans should not differentiate themselves from – or set themselves outside of – nature. Švankmajer sees the existence of utilitarian objects to be most symptomatic of this tendency (i.e. humans are alienated from their tools), while Barta is most suspicious of the clock (i.e. humans are alienated from the natural rhythms of life). Both are politically more radical than Trnka since neither proposes some kind of return to the prelapsarian life of the peasant class but, rather, a restructuring of ideology through a changed relationship to material reality. To help accomplish Švankmajer's vision, one might construct non-rational, non-utilitarian things (as indeed Švankmajer, as a sculptor, does). To help accomplish Barta's vision, it would be necessary to construct new non-rational built environments that implicitly foster healthy, community-building rhythms. However, Barta is more idealist/reactionary than Švankmajer since nature in his works is envisioned as an uncomplicated idyll corrupted by humanity. Švankmajer problematizes this view in films like *A Game with Stones* (1965) which suggest that games of dominance and destruction adhere within nature itself. Both Barta and Švankmajer urge through their work that people must be more attentive to the variegated rhythms of the non-human. Humans should not live like clockwork mannequins in a darkened attic but be receptive to the ways in which time ebbs, flows and repeats irrespective of human clocks or calculations. However, Švankmajer's cinema pessimistically hints that even if humanity were to achieve this, the rhythms of existence (and all its material actants) would remain in violent disharmony with and against one another.

Švankmajer and Barta have both produced works that use Prague as a setting in which to envision and interrogate the relationship(s) between citizens and the city. The central political message of those Czech animated (and partially animated) films made and set in Prague since the Velvet Revolution is that consumer capitalism has led, in the Czech Republic, to isolation and alienation, in which individual citizens pursue their own desires irrespective of the greater good of their community. Moreover, escalating tourism in the city has increased the potential for residents to be alienated from their own built environment(s) and transformed the myths and legends of old Bohemia into kitsch commodities. The films variably propose two potential solutions to this malaise. The first solution is to retreat into the collective subconscious of the city, as in *Faust* (1994) or *Golem* (1996), or the obsessive life of the hobbyist, as in *One Night in One City* (2007) and *Conspirators of Pleasure* (1996). Evzen in *Surviving Life* (2010) combines both of these approaches through making a hobby out of the exploration of his own imagination, as to a certain extent do the actors of *Insect*. The other solution – more potentially transgressive, but also more engaged with the rhythms of everyday life – is to ensure that one's personal pleasure is contingent upon a networked relationship with other urban actants, as achieved (however problematically) by the protagonists of both *Tram* (2012) and *Conspirators of Pleasure*. Those individuals that fail to do either, such as Otesánek or the citizens of *Cook, Mug, Cook!* (2007), are not merely ostracized or alienated but destroyed.

The messages and themes in those short and student films made over the last twenty years but *not* set in contemporary Prague are unsurprisingly more varied. However, across numerous different animation forms, including new digital technologies, emerges a common theme of individuals pursuing spiritual and/or geographical freedom often in defiance of their society, with sometimes fatal results. Many of these works also seem engaged in ecological consciousness-raising through placing focus on the radical otherness of non-human beings.

While the ideas expressed through all these films are political, they are specific to a Czech cultural and historical context. Trnka's pastoralism, for instance, is inextricable from the rural folk customs of Old Bohemia and the Czech National Revival. The reason it is possible to trace affinities between Trnka's film-making and the political rhetoric of Václav Havel is that both build upon a semi-mythic agrarian folk history in which the ancestry of the Lands of the Bohemian Crown can be traced back to the dynasty of Přemysl the Ploughman. The close relationship between the Czech people and their lands is a foundational myth which underpins both Trnka's and Havel's work. Their political ideas are closely tied to an idealized conception of 'Czechness'. Likewise, the film-makers in this chapter are specifically interested in the notion of Czech identity in the wake of the Velvet Revolution. Though their political messages may sometimes hold universal relevance – especially since dismantling anthropocentrism and the rhythms of consumer capitalism[93] are vital to avoiding the worst excesses of global warming – it is the concept of what it means to be Czech that is among their foremost concerns.

As Ewa Mazierska noted in her 2010 review of Hames's *The Cinema of Jan Švankmajer: Dark Alchemy*, despite the sheer quality of Czech and Slovak cinema in the 1960s and the continued cinematic production of both countries, 'this is not reflected in the quantity of work published in this area'.[94] It is hoped that this book has, in its own modest way – restricted as it has been by my own lack of fluency in the Czech language – addressed the lack of academic attention given to Czech animation, providing impetus for others to produce work upon their Slovak counterparts.

Communication of political messages

So, the political messages of the films have been defined; as for *how* these messages are communicated, it is through a combination of editing, cinematography and sometimes the use of exaggerated, hyperreal sound effects. These are generally cinematic techniques, rather than techniques purely specific to animation, although animation can allow for a greater degree of manipulation of specific objects. For instance, Trnka makes the simple, functional red ball in *The Cybernetic Grandma* (1962) eminently attractive to the eye through editing the surrounding technological landscape in a disjunctive, disorienting way and including optical illusions like Necker cubes as part of the film's visual design. As such, the bright red ball provides a point of visual stability within the film's confusing mise-en-scène, which affirms the film's commitment to rootedness.

The things in *A Quiet Week in the House* (1969) appear uncategorizable and nameless due to Švankmajer's exploitation of exposure length, meaning that these things each trail an after-image, ensuring that they look less like stable objects and more like ever-transforming and unstable phenomena, reflecting Švankmajer's conception of the world as always already in conflict and in motion.

Barta edits the spring awakening sequence in *A Ballad about Green Wood* (1983) to undermine the viewer's stable perception of the forward march of linear clock time. The river flows backwards, forwards, up and down; buds sprout; the earth breathes. The use of a choppy editing rhythm, with real-life footage interspersed with brief sequences of time-lapse photography, gives rise to vitality affects in the viewer, such that they feel immersed in simultaneously experienced moments of time.

Finally, Otesánek's movements are filmed through jerky primitive stop-motion, overlaid with harsh, hyperreal rustling noises on the soundtrack. As such, he viscerally feels uncivilized and uncivilizable. Long before Otesánek is destroyed, we intuitively know that he will not be assimilated into the network of consumer capitalism of modern-day Prague.

These four examples from the four chapters of this work exemplify some of the cinematic strategies a film-maker has recourse to when seeking to communicate a political message, which either transcends language or leads to censorship and persecution if detected by authorities.

A materialist turn

An essential aspect of this work has been to build my symbolic analysis from the material objects on screen, rather than simply translating these filmed things into abstract symbols, as though the objects were mere placeholders for meaning. This has followed in the footsteps of such thing theorists as Bill Brown and Elaine Freedgood; yet while these writers have primarily focused upon the literary object – with a couple of exceptions made by Brown for *Toy Story* (John Lasseter, 1996) and *Bamboozled* (Spike Lee, 2000)[95] – my own writing has focused upon the cinematic thing.

While this book makes academic headway into the comparatively under-explored areas of Czech cinema and animation studies more generally, it does not propose a new grand theory with which one might approach the analysis of films. That said, the similarities between the three materialist methodologies used herein have been mapped out in the Introduction and, it is hoped, this chapter has illustrated how each of these theories can work in dialogue with one another.

It would be instructive to see film historians and theoreticians using thing theory to consider objects/things within live-action films with the scrutiny that I have attempted to apply to the objects/things in the animated films of this study. Some notable work is already being done in the area. University College London's 'Autopsies Project', for example, examines obsolete objects in films and literature, as well as possessions of the student researchers themselves.[96] Much of Hollie Price's academic writing, such as her chapter 'Furnishing the Living Room in Film Noir: Disillusion and the Armchair' in *Spaces of the Cinematic Home: Behind the Screen Door* (2015), is highly attentive to the cultural dialogues that circle and encode material things at different stages of their histories.

Although ANT may prove most appropriate for use in those studies in which a researcher has access to ground-level production, as in Anita Lam's remarkable *Making Crime Television* (2013), its use in this book has illuminated political ideas implicit in Švankmajer's work and addressed most comprehensibly in his manifesto 'To Renounce the Leading Role' (1990). Giving focus to Švankmajer's critique of anthropocentrism reveals a later film like *Conspirators of Pleasure* to be the fulfilment of the decentred networks of desire first glimpsed in *A Games with Stones*, *The Flat* (1968) or *A Quiet Week in the House*. While in these shorter works human actors are either not present or are in direct conflict with non-human actors, in *Conspirators of Pleasure* non-human and human actors become intertwined and inseparable in the creation of masturbation machines.

Rhythmanalysis, meanwhile, can provide a poetic augmentation to current analyses of editing patterns. Previous works of rhythmanalysis, or those that use the ideas of Henri Lefebvre more broadly, tend to simply consider the material city as experienced at the level of the street, unmediated. Of course, one might usefully explicate the rhythms of Berlin without once considering Wim Wenders's *Wings of Desire* (*Der Himmel über Berlin*, 1987), but film is also able to probe areas of a city that the citizen, city-planner or tourist are unable to reach. Moreover, films can provide that balance between distance and immersion that Lefebvre considers necessary for the budding rhythmanalyst. Such analysis need not be political, but due to the ways in which time and space are regularly exploited in the name of political power – or help structure and uphold political hegemony – it is likely that politics will often be a contributing factor to work performed in this area. It is hoped that this book demonstrates that film-making can be political even without the involvement of human actors on screen and, moreover, that politics need not always be centred upon the human. A political reading of a film can be rooted in the things within a scene that might otherwise appear non-political. We need not abandon politics, but must expand our notion of the political in order to have an adequate intellectual, emotional and ethical mode of engagement and critique as academics, students and readers within the Anthropocene.

A silent language

'Cosmologies, myths, and mythologies', writes Lefebvre, 'are turned into ideologies only when they become ingredients in religion … Then the images and tales are cut off from the soil that nourished them … marked on the one hand by abstractness and by loss of their original local flavor'.[97] Praising a 2018 touring retrospective of Trnka's restored filmography, Michael Sragow remarks that the animator 'didn't craft his puppet-cartoon shorts and features merely to imitate life. His endlessly original and inventive movies incorporate life, or transcend it ... The whorls of nature and the wrinkles of human experience come together in his flexible, robust style'.[98] It is this attentiveness to material reality in Trnka's work that ultimately poses a challenge to the ideology of the state because, as both Marx and Lefebvre understand, the state is always *representative* and representation 'is always abstract in relation to concrete human beings'.[99] This is why any allegory that seeks to challenge political ideology imposed from above must root its symbolism in metonymy, not abstract metaphor. The resolute silence of objects and things cannot be assimilated by the dissemblage of ideology.

At the end of this study, it is perhaps this very silence that proves most articulate. The SS officer of Trnka's *Springman and the SS* (1946) may attempt to arrest innocent objects as political dissidents, forcing upon them ideological readings; but ironically, it is the sheer *springiness* of the Springman's springs – their essential material reality – that enables his defeat. Likewise, in *The Cybernetic Grandma*, the silent, dependable, eyeline-guiding red ball is placed in eloquent contrast against the chattering banality of the technological robot-grandma hybrid. The gloved Hand and television set in *The Hand* (1965) perform a flurry of gestural and symbolic significations, but neither possesses the simple, utilitarian beauty of the artist's flower pots. Likewise, in Švankmajer's *The Flat*, *A Quiet Week in the House* and *Naturae Historia* (1967), it is the tendency of humans to attempt to impose linguistic categorizations upon mute things, trying to tie down abject and unspeakable *stuff*, which proves their undoing. That same anthropocentric desire for structured meaning comes under attack in Barta's filmography, with clock time shown to be hopelessly reductive in comparison to the ecstatic rhythms of natural time in *A Ballad about Green Wood*. The citizens of *Rat Catcher* secure their own demise through their greedy tendency to translate everything into monetary value, as preconditioned by the brutalizing design of their city. In this chapter, film-makers like Barta and Švankmajer seem to express their dismay at a constant rearticulation of certain national stories and myths for the benefit of tourists flooding to a newly Europeanized Prague.

In short, the materialist methodologies of thing theory, ANT and rhythmanalysis emphasize the material world over the semiotic – a valorization present in the work of the film-makers themselves, who have sought to use objects and things, not words, to express their meanings. Paradoxically, I have been required to use words to discuss this materialist turn away from the semiotic. Yet this book stands as a thing in itself. Printed and bound or rendered digitally upon the screen of your e-reader it has a certain weight in your hand – a look; a smell; a feel – a materialist reality eluded by the awkward, stumbling words you are reading that gives voice to the political fervour within everyday and miraculous things.

Epilogue

A materialist, not idealist ecocriticism

Over the last year of finalizing this book for publication, I have been simultaneously involved in Extinction Rebellion (XR), a group which protests against governmental inaction on climate change. During this period Rupert Read – one of the principal spokespeople and strategists of the group – also released his monograph *A Film-Philosophy of Ecology and Enlightenment* (2018), a work that in many respects intersects with my own. Read, after Wittengenstein, argues for philosophy as a transformative *process* rather than as a set of truth statements or hypotheses. From this he argues that films themselves can be considered works of philosophy – providing viewers immerse themselves in such a way as to be receptive to the wisdom embodied and enacted by a film. Read selects case studies, such as Lars von Trier's *Melancholia* (2011) and James Cameron's *Avatar* (2009), that he believes enact an eco-philosophy *through* film and, in so doing, 'midwife a personal or inter-personal, philosophical and even political *aware-ing*, by means of which we no longer take ourselves to be superior to or alienated from the rest of life'.[1] As might be imagined, I am hugely sympathetic to Read's resistance to critical superiority in the form of imposing critical theory 'from above' onto texts, rather than working upwards from the texts themselves.[2] Here we are, I believe, united with Suzanne Buchan when she writes – after David Bordwell and Noël Carroll – in defence of so-called 'micro-analysis' and 'piecemeal theorizing' as a means by which it is possible to work 'bottom-up' from a detailed description of a film's cinematic language to 'develop sustained discussions about the experiential complexity' of a given case study.[3]

However, where I part company with Read is in his willingness to transition from rejecting the imposition of ideology in the realm of aesthetic analysis[4] to rejecting ideological praxis within the personal-political sphere. In his 2017 essay 'This Civilisation Is Finished ... ', much of which sows the seeds for ideas developed further in *A Film-Philosophy*, Read criticizes 'extreme identity politics' as staging 'a systematic retreat into the present, and into the self', critiquing the Combahee River Collective for organizing politically around their identity as black women.[5] While Read recognizes that it 'may have been fine, even perhaps entirely necessary, for that group of black women at that time trying, understandably and rightly, to make feminism more representative',[6] he does not recognize the way(s) in which identity politics remain necessary for oppressed groups engaged in collective struggle due to such groups being *already ideologically encoded from above* by what bell hooks refers to as 'imperialist, white supremacist, capitalist patriarchy'.[7] It is, in part, this refusal to engage constructively with identity politics that has led Anupama Ranawana and James Trafford to condemn Extinction Rebellion as relying 'upon an amalgamation of liberal universalism with a kind of anti-politics in sync with contemporary populism', arguing that 'calls to single-issue politics and simplicity of message can easily become a cover for universalising parochialism'.[8] Despite the progressive initiatives of groups like XR Liberation, Extinction Rebellion Youth, XR Disabled Rebels and XR Scotland, a lack of attentiveness to the material realities of those persons already the worst impacted by air pollution and global warming has led protestors within XR to engage in actions – such as giving a thank you note and flowers to the institutionally racist Brixton police force[9] and disrupting the Underground in one of the most economically deprived boroughs in London[10] – which have been criticized for further entrenching the systematic inequalities inextricably intertwined with climate justice.[11] It must be noted that Read has – in clear-sighted and non-equivocal terms – expressed regret for the Tube protest in interview with *The Times*.[12] However, if the incident is symptomatic of an absence of attention within XR to how material relations impact different people's everyday lives – such as the largely working-class residents of Canning Town – in unequal and unquest ways, then such incidents seem likely to continue.

In warning against the danger of neglecting these material realities, I had originally planned to warn against depending upon ideas – 'any bigger than the things that surround you'. However, I then recalled that Timothy Morton has theorized global warming as a 'hyperobject' so big that we, as humans, do not realize that we exist inside of it.[13] So, instead, I will caution against two strands of idealism that, as I see them, function as two sides of the same coin within both academia and activism and should be approached with trepidation.

The first temptation is to insist upon the perfection of a political ideology imposed from above, misrepresenting material reality in order to make it fit that pre-ordained ideology. Symptomatic of this tendency is when Baudrillard, in a section on narciccism in *Symbolic Exchange and Death* (1976), misrepresents Brigitte Bardot in a scene from Jean-Luc Godard's *Contempt* (*Le Mepris*, 1963) as gazing at her own buttocks in the mirror so as – consciously or not – to fit his Freudian/Lacanian schemata.[14] It is this tendency (attempting to reshape reality to accord to an ideological model) that Barta critiques in *The Design* and Trnka in *The Cybernetic Grandma*. It is the ideological process that subjugates everyday people under 'the People' under communism.[15] It is the danger of seeing the world as you wish it to be rather than the world as it is.

However, the inverse tendency must also be guarded against – that of believing that ideology (often finding expression in variegated forms of power and politics) can be eternally displaced elsewhere or neglected. As we see with Heidegger's Nazism[16] or Jung's fascistic sympathies[17] attempting to bypass the complexities of politics in favour of an idealistically envisioned pure ontology may lead to a quasi-mystical metaphysics[18] which fascism can easily co-opt.[19]

Indeed, Josie Sparrow cautions, several writers we might align with the academic resurgence of interest in vitalism, such as Jane Bennett and Graham Harman (writers I have quoted uncritically across this book), often risk elevating the figure of the central philosopher-subject, purportedly attuned to the experience of pure Being, at the expense of social relations perceived collectively. This can reiterate and reinforce structures of colonial oppression through imposing an individualist white European stranglehold over questions already grappled with philosophically, culturally and socially by indigenous subjects and thinkers.[20]

Many of Read's case studies, for instance – in particular the *Lord of the Rings* films (2001, 2002, 2003) with which much of the book is concerned – are structured in terms of the 'Hero's Journey', modelled by Joseph Campbell (1949) in accordance to his understanding of Jung. Read interprets the 'Hero's Journey' undergone by Frodo in these films as akin to that of the individual awakening to the ecological and climate emergency and thus to a re-awakened connection to the Earth, prompting the individual to action.[21] Read writes: 'The hero/heroine is reborn, returning to share "the elixir of life" which, in Jungian terms, is the reward of individuation (which is not at all the same thing as individualism, quasi-solipsism), of becoming who one is.'[22] However, in a published sermon entitled 'Home, Individuation, and the Tower', the Reverend Lewis Connolly has laid out a troubling argument that 'seeking one's own self-actualisation is at least to some degree in conflict with what is in the interest of humanity ... collectively'.[23] Connolly argues that marking out one's own territory is intrinsic to self-actualization – yet, upon a planet with limited resources, this psychological desire can only be realized by some. Connolly concludes:

> If it is fair to set our own self-actualisation up against the longevity of the planet and the human race in general ... then it's worth considering, given that stark choice, which of those two options you would choose. I already know which I would choose: I would choose the meaning of life over life itself. I would choose self-actualisation, and my own individuation, over self-denial for the sake of longevity for longevity's sake. I do not, however, choose ignorance. My lot is to seek my own self-actualisation, while at the same time wholly recognising the harm and damage I am necessarily causing in the process.[24]

As has hopefully been made apparent through this book, I would choose self-denial in favour of the betterment of the collective; Read, he makes clear, would choose the same.[25] However, such individual sacrifice – and we return now to where we began, with the figure of Jan Palach, who sacrificed more that I should like to believe will be necessary of us – is only meaningful if engaged in collectively, with one foot stuck firmly in the material world and the other foot within the political world – for it is then that we recognize that we are in actual fact standing upon common ground, the Earth.

The resurgence[26] of eco-facism[27] over the past few years ensures that these concerns are not merely academic, but neither are they divorced from the academy. Writing that seeks to resist anthropocentrism on one hand, while recognizing everyday experiences of human oppression with the other, needs to strike a material balance between these two poles of idealism (both of which can misrecognize themselves as materialist). Likewise, animated allegories that seek to communicate ideas to an audience need to strike a balance between specificity towards real objects, settings and actors, and a broader universalism that allows abstract meaning to emerge. Such films – whether drawn, stop-motion or CGI – need to be rooted in the everyday stuff of the world, charting their rhythms and interconnections, while not being so purely descriptive that they merely reify that world, leaving themselves open to regressive or oppressive narrative(s) and meaning(s) to be projected onto them. The most accomplished Czech animations – Trnka's *Cybernetic Grandma* and *The Hand*, Barta's *Ballad about Green Wood* and *The Club of the Laid-Off*, much of Švankmajer's work and, I would argue, Aleš Pachner's *A King Had a Horse* and Kateřina Karhánková's films for children – manage to balance describing the world attentively with transforming the world imaginatively. It is hoped that the newly ecologically conscious Czech animations to be released over the coming difficult decades ahead are able to hold this delicate ambiguity and, in so doing, show us how to sit with ambiguity and resist the temptation to retreat into the comforting certainties of anthropocentric idealism.

Notes

Prologue

1. Josef Hlavatý, Jan Zajíc, Evžen Plocek, Josef Hlavatý, Miroslav Malinka, Jan Bereš and Ilja Rips, among others.
2. Blažek, 'Hrob Jana Palacha/Jan Palach's Grave'.
3. Ibid.
4. Ash, 'Prague – A Poem, Not Disappearing', 214.

Introduction

1. Torre, *Animation – Process, Cognition and Actuality*, 151.
2. Brown, *A Sense of Things*, 76.
3. Ibid.
4. Brown, 'Thing Theory', 4.
5. Heidegger, *Being and Time*, 73.
6. Ibid., 75.
7. Ibid., 73.
8. A distinction outlined in the previous section.
9. Lam, *Making Crime Television*, 3.
10. Indeed, I do not think much can be accurately or usefully said 'about' Barta's work *as a whole* because I am sceptical of the premise that such holistic, author-centred analysis is appropriate in the case of a film-maker like Barta who works with such variegated forms of animation with such large gaps of time between releases. Not every film-maker is an auteur and this fact does not detract from the quality or importance of their work.
11. Skrodzka, *Magic Realist Cinema in East Central Europe*, 111–12.
12. Frey, 'No(ir) Place to Go', 76.
13. Freedenberg, 'One-Minute Boogie Woogie', 15–21.
14. 'Actant' is a term commonly used by ANT practitioners. The term is defined in the *Encyclopedia of Social Theory: Volume I* as 'any agent, collective or individual, that can associate or disassociate with other agents'. Crawford, 'Actor Network Theory', 1.

15 d'Axa, 'Us'.
16 Bendazzi, *Animation: A World History, Volume 1*, 165.
17 Colpan and Nsiah, 'More Than Product Advertising', 114–30.
18 Czech National Film Archive, 'IRE-Film'.
19 Wright, *Animation Writing and Development*, 26.
20 Ibid.
21 Bellano, *Václav Trojan*, 6.
22 Ibid., 14.
23 Bendazzi, *Animation: A World History: Volume 1*, 166.
24 Mertová, 'Czech Animated Film before 1989'.
25 Palonkorpi, 'Mole Holes in the Iron Curtain', 147.
26 Ibid.
27 Ibid., 150.
28 Joschko and Morgan, 'Learning from the Golden Age of Czechoslovak Animation', 68.
29 Palonkorpi, 'Mole Holes in the Iron Curtain', 152.
30 Joschko and Morgan, 'Learning from the Golden Age of Czechoslovak Animation', 67.
31 Palonkorpi, 'Mole Holes in the Iron Curtain', 148.
32 Joschko and Morgan, 'Learning from the Golden Age of Czechoslovak Animation', 69.
33 Bendazzi, *Cartoons*, 170.
34 Dutka, 'Jiri Trnka – Walt Disney of the East', 1.
35 Fraňková, 'Jiri Trnka: An Artist Who Turned Puppets into Film Stars', *Radio Praha*.
36 Hames, *Czech and Slovak Cinema*, 189. Hames notes that in the 1840s there were at least seventy-nine travelling puppet theatre troupes in Bohemia and that far from being a marginal cultural force, puppet theatre has been immensely popular throughout the country's history and has performed the mainstream role normally occupied by non-puppet theatre, helped preserve the Czech language across the seventeenth and eighteenth centuries and contributed to political resistance during Nazi occupation.
37 Hames, 'Czechoslovakia', 55.
38 Liehm and Liehm, *The Most Important Art*, 110–11.
39 Ibid., 111.
40 Kundera, 'Candide Had to Be Destroyed', 258.
41 Havel, 'The Power of the Powerless', 81–3.
42 Bellano, *Václav Trojan*, xxi–xxii.
43 Balz, 'The Puppet Films of Jiri Trnka'.

44 Hames, 'Introduction to the First Edition', 2.
45 Ibid., 37.
46 Cardinal, 'Thinking through Things', 73.
47 Švankmajer with Hames, 'Interview with Jan Švankmajer', 127; Švankmajer with Jackson, 'The Surrealist Conspirator'; Švankmajer with Stafford and Sélavy, 'Interview with Jan Švankmajer'.
48 Švankmajer in *The Animator of Prague* (James Marsh, 1980) quoted in Rickards, 'Uncanny Breaches, Flimsy Borders', 28.
49 Rickards, 'Uncanny Breaches'. Rickards convincingly argues that the uncanny generally tends towards disturbing dogmatic binaries, forging spaces in which other modes of politics can develop; however, she does not illustrate the political ends to which Švankmajer more specifically uses the uncanny and why his particular use of the uncanny is of 'grave socio-political import'.
50 Jenny Jediny, 'The Animation of Jiří Barta'.
51 Košuličová, 'The Morality of Horror'.
52 Hames, *Czech and Slovak Cinema*, 200.
53 Zipes, *The Enchanted Screen*, 213.
54 This book does not cover all animations produced in Czechoslovakia/the Czech Republic. It is also restricted to Czech rather than Slovak animators. As such, work by Slovakian animators, such as Viktor Kubal, Ondrej Rudavsky, Noro Držiak, Ivana Zajacová or Jaroslav Baran, is not covered, such work requiring its own book-length study.
55 In her 2003 monograph *Cinema of the Other Europe*, Dina Iordanova authoritatively asserts: 'The concept of European cinema is still more or less synonymous with West European film-making, and the teaching of European cinema barely covers Central-Eastern European traditions.' Iordanova, *Cinema of the Other Europe*, 1. That said, while the hegemony of Western European cinema may hold true as a general trend within the discipline, academic journals such as *Kinoeye* and *Studies in Eastern European Cinema* have forged a significant niche for the study of Eastern/Central European cinema within film studies.

Chapter 1

1 Gambarato, 'Methodology for Film Analysis', 105–15.
2 Gambarato and Malaguti, 'Objects of Desire', 164.
3 Gambarato, 'Talking Objects of Denys Arcand', 2–3.
4 Ibid., 3.

5   Ibid., 2.
6   Ibid.
7   I use the term 'associative editing' rather than 'intellectual montage' after Eisenstein since Trnka is not working within a dialectical mode.
8   Kelley, *Reinventing Allegory*, 2.
9   Tambling, *Allegory*, 2.
10 Xavier, 'Historical Allegory', 337.
11 Moritz, 'Narrative Strategies for Resistance and Protest', 39–47.
12 Copeland and Struck, 'Introduction', 10.
13 Koresky, 'Eclipse Series 32: Pearls of the Czech New Wave'.
14 Ibid.
15 Hames, *The Czechoslovak New Wave*, 240.
16 Xavier, *Allegories of Underdevelopment*, 16.
17 Moritz, 'Narrative Strategies for Resistance and Protest', 39.
18 Xavier, *Allegories of Underdevelopment*, 16.
19 Petrov, 'Socialist Realism (Sotsrealizm)', 575.
20 Holý, *The Little Czech and the Great Czech Nation*, 62.
21 Brown, *A Sense of Things*, 6–7.
22 Havel, 'Politics and Conscience', 136, in Tucker, *The Philosophy and Politics of Czech Dissidence*, 150.
23 Havel, *Summer Meditations*, 111.
24 Tucker, *Philosophy and Politics of Czech Dissidence*, 98, making reference to the ideas of Czech dissident Jan Patočka.
25 Miller, *The Comfort of Things*, 25 and 195.
26 Brown, 'Thing Theory', 3–4.
27 Schwenger, *The Tears of Things*, 77.
28 Bennett, *Vibrant Matter*, 2.
29 Brown, 'Thing Theory', 3–4.
30 Merleau-Ponty, 'Eye and Mind', 163, quoted by Brown, 'Thing Theory', 4.
31 de Sola Pool, 'Public Opinion in Czechoslovakia', 16.
32 Jack is identified as being the subject of Victorian penny dreadfuls by Dunae, 'Penny Dreadfuls', 133; Springhall, 'Disseminating Impure Literature', 571. He existed alongside figures such as Varney the vampire and Turnpike Dick.
33 Eisenstein, *Eisenstein on Disney*, 64.
34 Ibid., 30.
35 The same distinction Bennett makes between her concept of 'material vibrancy' and 'traditional' vitalism; see Bennett, *Vibrant Matter*, xiii.
36 Švankmajer with Hames, 'Interview with Jan Švankmajer', 110.

37 Hames, 'The Film Experiment', 38.
38 Bendazzi, *Cartoons*, 170.
39 Heimann, *Czechoslovakia: The State That Failed*, 99.
40 Hilmar-Jezek, 'Jiří Trnka and the Czech Year'.
41 Boček, *Jiri Trnka: Artist and Puppet*, 97.
42 Martin, *Czechoslovak Culture*, 161–6.
43 Dutkova-Cope, 'Texas Czech Ethnic Identity', 663.
44 Ibid., 662.
45 Šemíková with Meyer, 'In 2015, Czech Koláče Is Trendy Worldwide'.
46 Roberts, *A Dictionary of Czech Popular Culture*, 79.
47 Celenza, *Hans Christian Andersen and Music*, 62.
48 Bendazzi, *Cartoons*, 168.
49 Anderson, 'The Nightingale', 133.
50 Crowther, 'The Screen in Review; "Emperor's Nightingale"'.
51 *Prague Puppet Museum*, 'About'.
52 For example, Grob, 'Císařův Slavík (The Emperor's Nightingale)'; Simels, 'Video Review: "The Emperor's Nightingale"'; Meyers, 'The Emperor's Nightingale'; Borroughs, 'Nice to Look at for a Few Minutes but I Found It Dull'.
53 Crowther, 'The Screen in Review'.
54 Boček, *Film a doba* 5, quoted in Liehm and Liehm, *The Most Important Art*, 108.
55 Holý, *The Little Czech and the Great Czech Nation*, 37.
56 Auty, 'Language and Society in the Czech National Revival', 241.
57 Underhill, *Creating Worldviews*, 110.
58 Ibid., 102.
59 Hames, *Czech and Slovak Cinema*, 191.
60 Underhill, *Creating Worldviews*, 124.
61 Hames, *Czech and Slovak Cinema*, 193–4.
62 Ibid., 194.
63 Dutka, 'Jiri Trnka'.
64 Hanáková, 'The Hussite Heritage Film', 474.
65 Underhill, *Creating Worldviews*, 110.
66 Skrodzka, *Magic Realist Cinema*, 23.
67 Ibid., 31.
68 Ibid., 21.
69 Ibid., 45.
70 Jirásek, 'Father Čech', 5.
71 Ibid., 6.

72 Bakhtin, *Rabelais and His World*, 62, 78, 81, 82 and 86ff.
73 Wall, 'Why Does Puck Sweep?', 67.
74 Narayanswamy, 'Czechoslovakia: Reforming under Pressure', 1112.
75 Skilling, 'Czechoslovakia's Interrupted Revolution', 409.
76 Svašek, 'The Politics of Artistic Identity', 399.
77 Ibid., 390–1.
78 Ibid., 401.
79 Jůzl, 'Music and the Totalitarian Regime in Czechoslovakia', 46.
80 Ibid.
81 Haraszti, *The Velvet Prison*, 5.
82 Hames, 'The Hand That Rocked the Kremlin'.
83 Hames, *Czech and Slovak Cinema*, 193.
84 Moritz, 'Narrative Strategies for Resistance and Protest', 40–1.
85 Dutka, 'Jiri Trnka'.
86 Hayward, *Cinema Studies: The Key Concepts*, 20.
87 Subotnick, *Animation in the Home Digital Studio*, 17.
88 McCarthy, 'Trnka, Jiří (1912–1969)', 1054.
89 Such as Power, 'Antidote Art #1'; Stettner, 'Thank You Jiri Trnka'.
90 Dee, 'Jiri Trnka – "The Walt Disney of Eastern Europe"'.
91 Hames, 'Hand That Rocked the Kremlin'.
92 Ibid.
93 Wilson, *The Hand*, 14.
94 See, for instance, the reviewers and critics quoted throughout this section who provide short effective summaries of the allegorical meaning of *The Hand* and its historical import, but without being fully attentive to what the hand is *doing* at a scene-by-scene, shot-by-shot level.
95 Delsarte, *Delsarte System of Oratory*, 472–4.
96 Ibid.
97 Perez, *The Material Ghost*, 395.
98 Allegories functioning as a 'strange loop' (as per Douglas Hofstadter's 2007 publication *I Am a Strange Loop*) is not unique to Czech culture. James Thurlow has explored this tendency in relation to Iranian cinema. Reflecting upon the function of the apple in Samira Makhmalbaf's 1998 film of the same name, he writes: "[L]et us say that the apple symbolizes the object or objects of desire. But the apple can only symbolize this because, in reality, it is an object of desire. Thus we have a kind of circle of: apple (reality 1)/symbol of desire/ apple (reality 2), where the first image of the apple is the bare fact of the apple

in the narrative ... the second is it's symbolic meaning ... and the third place, the understanding that the apple can only symbolize what is good in the world because *an apple really is good* (and thus can be an object of desire)." James Thurlow, 'Iranian Cinema', 16.

99   Gomel, 'The Poetics of Censorship', 89.
100 Brooke, 'The Hand'.
101 Russell-Gebbett, '8. The Hand'.
102 Bregant with Jůn, 'Jiří Trnka: 100th Anniversary of the Birth of a Great Czech Animator'.
103 Guignon, 'Heidegger's "Authenticity" Revisited', 322 (italics own).
104 Sherman, 'Martin Heidegger's Concept of Authenticity', 2.
105 Boček, *Film a doba* 5, quoted in Liehm and Liehm, *The Most Important Art*, 108.
106 Boček, *Jiri Trnka*, 250–1.
107 Ibid., 251.
108 Ibid., 253.
109 Havel, *Summer Meditations*, 111.
110 'There-being', i.e. us as self-reflective being(s)-in-the-world.
111 Heidegger, 'The Question Concerning Technology', 27.
112 Ibid.
113 Havel, 'The Power of the Powerless', 206.
114 Havel, 'Politics and Conscience', 136.
115 Watts, *The Philosophy of Heidegger*, 45.
116 Ibid., 46.
117 Havel, 'Politics and Conscience', 136, quoted in Tucker, *Philosophy and Politics of Czech Dissidence*, 150.
118 Havel, 'The Power of the Powerless', 206.
119 Tucker, *Philosophy and Politics of Czech Dissidence*, 68.
120 Baudrillard, *The System of Objects*, 129.
121 Ibid., 123–6.
122 Ibid., 62.
123 Ibid., 64.
124 Havel, 'Six Asides about Culture', 133.
125 Havel, 'Stories and Totalitarianism', 333.
126 Ibid., 347.
127 Ibid.
128 Popescu, *Political Action in Václav Havel's Thought*, 105–34.
129 Havel, 'New York University'.

130   Havel, 'Politics and Conscience', 157.
131   Popescu, *Political Action in Václav Havel's Thought*, 105.
132   Smith, 'Civic Forum and Public against Violence', 43.
133   Popescu, *Political Action in Václav Havel's Thought*, 127.
134   Havel, 'Politics and Conscience', 155.

Chapter 2

1   Marks, *Touch*, 2.
2   Owen, *Avant-Garde to New Wave*, 190.
3   Hames, 'The Film Experiment', 37.
4   Ibid.
5   Švankmajer with Hames, 'Interview with Jan Švankmajer', 108.
6   Švankmajer with Koepfinger, '"Freedom Is Becoming the Only Theme"'.
7   Švankmajer with Hames, 'Interview with Jan Švankmajer', 107–8.
8   Hames, 'The Film Experiment', 37.
9   Švankmajer with Hames, 'Interview with Jan Švankmajer', 127.
10 Moritz, 'Narrative Strategies for Resistance and Protest', 38–47.
11 Liehm and Liehm, *The Most Important Art*, 39.
12 Of course, such theorizing is highly speculative. There are few published or archival sources regarding film censorship in Czechoslovakia. This is due to the fact that there was no formal censorship body during the period that consistently dealt exclusively with film; instead, censorship involved members of the Party functioning like executive producers, making suggestions as to the nature of the work that should be produced. For example, Jiří Purs, director general of Czechoslovak film from 1969, and his deputy, Bohumil Steiner, were both members of the central committee of the Czech Communist Party. In the absence of any recorded correspondence or documentation from the likes of Purs or Steiner, one can but hypothesize about the reasons why any given film of the period was censored or banned.
13 Švankmajer with Peter Hames, 'Bringing Up Baby'.
14 Moran, *Introduction to Phenomenology*, 11.
15 Artaud, *The Theatre and Its Double*, 28.
16 Owen, *Avant-Garde to New Wave*, 199.
17 Švankmajer, *Touching and Imagining*, 13–25.
18 Gauss, 'The Theoretical Backgrounds of Surrealism', 43.

19 Ibid., 42.
20 Švankmajer with Brooke, 'Makers: Free Radical'.
21 'Object' being the common translation of Breton's *objet*.
22 Breton, 'Manifesto of Surrealism', 26.
23 Ibid., 34.
24 Švankmajer with Hames, 'Interview with Jan Švankmajer', 118.
25 Breton, 'What Is Surrealism?', 157.
26 Ibid., 184.
27 Breton, 'Surrealist Situation of the Object', 258.
28 Ibid., 278.
29 Švankmajer, 'Decalogue Manifesto', 140.
30 Ibid., 141.
31 Ibid., 140.
32 Cardinal, 'Thinking through Things', 76.
33 Effenberger, 'Žvahlav/Jabberwocky', extracted in František Dryje, 'The Force of Imagination', 160.
34 Ibid., 159.
35 Ibid.
36 Švankmajer with Andrews, 'Malice in Wonderland', 16–17.
37 Breton, 'Second Manifesto of Surrealism', 160.
38 Frank, *Reframing Reality*, 92–8.
39 Ibid., 21.
40 Ibid., 92.
41 Klein, *The Psycho-Analysis of Children*, 83.
42 Freud, 'Analysis of a Phobia in a Five-year-old Boy', 1–122.
43 Klein, *Psycho-Analysis of Children*, 174–5.
44 Ibid., 38.
45 O'Kane, 'Seeking Švankmajer', 17.
46 Nelson, *The Secret Life of Puppets*, 222.
47 Brown, *A Sense of Things*, 7.
48 Freedgood, *The Ideas in Things*, 30–54.
49 Latour, 'On Actor-Network Theory', 369.
50 Latour, *Reassembling the Social*, 71.
51 Harman, *Prince of Networks*, 13.
52 Leftwich, 'Thinking Politically', 2.
53 Latour, *Politics of Nature*, 227.
54 Carter, 'Politics as if Nature Mattered', 188.
55 Bennett, *Vibrant Matter*, viii.

56 Ibid.
57 Švankmajer with Hames, 'Interview with Jan Švankmajer', 109.
58 Russell-Gebbett, '31. The Death of Stalinism in Bohemia'.
59 Margolin, 'Stalin and Wheat', 14–16.
60 Švankmajer with Hames, 'Interview with Jan Švankmajer', 116.
61 Margolin, 'Stalin and Wheat', 16.
62 Latour, 'On Actor-Network Theory', 372.
63 As detailed in Korbel, *Twentieth-Century Czechoslovakia*, 305–8; Williams, *The Prague Spring and Its Aftermath*, 112–18; Eidlin, '"Capitulation," "Resistance" and the Framework of "Normali-Zation"', 319–32. Davy details some of the political consequences of the invasion in 'Soviet Foreign Policy and the Invasion of Czechoslovakia', 796–803.
64 Russell-Gebbett, 'The Death of Stalinism in Bohemia'.
65 Ibid.
66 Švankmajer, 'To Renounce the Leading Role'.
67 Carter, 'Politics as if Nature Mattered', 182–95.
68 Latour, *Politics of Nature*.
69 Ibid., 71–2.
70 Ibid., 64–5.
71 Owen, *Avant-Garde to New Wave*, 208.
72 Švankmajer, 'Decalogue', 140–1.
73 Latour, *Politics of Nature*, 62.
74 Bennett, *Vibrant Matter*, 104.
75 Wells, *Understanding Animation*, 90–1.
76 At first the viewer recognizes these items as objects. They are not immediately estranged from their everyday objecthood.
77 Latour, *Reassembling the Social*, 71.
78 This is not merely a side effect of the stop-motion technique since often the movements of Švankmajer's object-puppets are harsh, juddering or spasmodic.
79 Baudrillard, *System of Objects*, 130.
80 Johnson, *Persons and Things*, 2.
81 Ibid., 17.
82 Howard, 'A Game with Stones/Punch and Judy/Historia Naturae (Suita)'.
83 Cardinal, 'Thinking through Things', 74.
84 Harman, *Prince of Networks*, 15.
85 Crick, 'Politics as a Form of Rule', 67.
86 Švankmajer with Hames, 'Interview with Jan Švankmajer', 127.
87 O'Pray, 'In the Capital of Magic', 218–19.

88 Latour, *Politics of Nature*, 227.
89 Schmitt, 'The Artworks of 1958–1968', 110.
90 Hames, 'The Film Experiment', 37.
91 Švankmajer, 'Freedom Is Becoming the Only Theme'.
92 Eason, 'Dimensions of Dialogue: moznosti dialogu'; Anderson, 'Dimensions of Dialogue'.
93 Howard, 'The Ossuary/Dimensions of Dialogue'.
94 Ibid.
95 Harman, *Prince of Networks*, 63.
96 Petley, 'Dimensions of Dialogue', 223.
97 Latour, 'On Actor-Network Theory', 37.
98 Latour, *Politics of Nature*, 25.
99 Johnson, *Persons and Things*, 130.
100 Pearce, *On Collecting*, 181.
101 O'Pray, 'Jan Švankmajer: A Mannerist Surrealist', 46.
102 Cardinal, 'Thinking through Things', 70.
103 Harman, *Prince of Networks*, 21.
104 Latour, *Pandora's Hope*, 177.
105 Barker, 'Jan Švankmajer – The Psychological Švankmajer'.
106 Kracauer, *Theory of Film*, 97.
107 Ibid.
108 Frank, *Reframing Reality*, 97–8.
109 Latour, *Politics of Nature*, 77.
110 Ibid., 73–9.
111 Williams, *The Prague Spring*, 15–27.
112 Korbel, *Twentieth-Century Czechoslovakia*, 305–14; Williams, *The Prague Spring*, 29–59.
113 Field, 'A Quiet Week in the House', 378–9.
114 O'Pray, 'Jan Švankmajer: A Mannerist Surrealist', 50.
115 Barley, *Czechoslovakia: A Short History*, 192.
116 Williams, *The Prague Spring*, 41.
117 Ibid.
118 Frank, *Reframing Reality*, 21.
119 Ibid., 80.
120 Ibid., 70.
121 Ibid., 68.
122 Bennett, *Vibrant Matter*, 2.

123 Dryje, 'Jan Švankmajer, Surrealist', 254.
124 Schwenger, *Tears of Things*, 47.
125 Brown, *A Sense of Things*, 75, with reference to William James, *Principles of Psychology*, 727.
126 Ibid., 60.
127 Ibid., 146.
128 Latour, *Politics of Nature*, 76.
129 Harman, *Prince of Networks*, 65.
130 Bennett, *Vibrant Matter*, 55.
131 Beckman, 'Animating Film Theory: An Introduction', 5.
132 Broadfoot and Butler, 'The Illusion of Illusion', 263–98.
133 Ibid., 267.
134 Gunning, 'Animating the Instant', 51.
135 Palous, 'The Parallel Polis after 12 Years', 53.
136 Wells, *Understanding Animation*, 22, with reference to Eisenstein, *Eisenstein on Disney*.
137 Latour, *Pandora's Hope*, 193–4.
138 Ibid., 227.

Chapter 3

1 Lefebvre, *The Sociology of Marx*, 160.
2 Ibid.
3 Lefebvre, *Rhythmanalysis*, 27.
4 Ibid., 23–4.
5 Revol, 'Rue Rambuteau Today'.
6 Ibid.
7 Lefebvre, *Rhythmanalysis*, 8.
8 Ibid., 16.
9 Ibid., 38–45.
10 Harvey, 'Class 06 Reading Marx's Capital Vol I with David Harvey'.
11 Čapek and Čapek, *R.U.R. and The Insect Play*, 54–5.
12 Ibid., 156.
13 Ibid., 157.
14 Hanson, *Time and Revolution*, viii.
15 Ibid., x.

16 Ibid., 53.
17 Lefebvre, *The Production of Space*, 421.
18 Hanson, *Time and Revolution*, 152.
19 Ibid., 1.
20 Bíro, *Turbulence and Flow in Film*, 10.
21 Lefebvre, *Production of Space*, 27.
22 Andreou, 'Anti-homeless Spikes'.
23 Wilson, 'Nostalgia as a Time and Space Phenomenon', 478–92.
24 Jediny, 'The Animation of Jirí Barta'.
25 Barta with Sarto, 'The Magical Junk-Filled World of Jiří Barta'.
26 Väliaho, *Mapping the Moving Image*, 58.
27 Ibid., 187.
28 Lefebvre, *Rhythmanalysis*, 31.
29 Lefebvre, *Production of Space*, 22–3.
30 Kononenko, *Slavic Folklore*, 11.
31 Ibid., 9.
32 Ibid., 11. Elsewhere Koliada is known as Morana/Morzanna and Kupalo as Jarilo. Slavic mythology has an unstable pantheon and names differ between the Slavic countries.
33 Dowling, *Brief Histories: Czechoslovakia*, 143.
34 Ibid., 150.
35 Havel, 'Letter to Dr Gustáv Husák', 26.
36 Hanson, *Time and Revolution*, 208.
37 Marx, *Capital: A New Abridgement*, 17.
38 Ibid., 19.
39 Bíro, *Turbulence and Flow*, 10.
40 Barta with Clarke, 'Jiri Barta and The Pied Piper'.
41 Väliaho, *Mapping the Moving Image*, 12.
42 Smith, 'Experimental Time-Lapse Animation', 79–99.
43 Ibid., 92, with reference to Stern, *The Interpersonal World of the Infant: A View from Psychoanalysis and Development Psychology*, 54, and Stern, *The Present Moment in Psychotherapy and Everyday Life*, 64–5.
44 Ibid.
45 Lefebvre, *Production of Space*, 206.
46 Väliaho, *Mapping the Moving Image*, 92.
47 Kracauer, *Theory of Film*, 35 and 287.
48 Lefebvre, *Rhythmanalysis*, 73.

49 Kawin, *Telling It Again*, 91.
50 Hanson, *Time and Revolution*, 3.
51 Leslie, 'Animation's Petrified Unrest', 85.
52 Lefebvre, *Production of Space*, 95–6.
53 Zarecor, *Manufacturing a Socialist Modernity*, 71.
54 Väliaho, *Mapping the Moving Image*, 11.
55 Lefebvre, *Production of Space*, 338.
56 Ibid., 313.
57 Košuličová, 'The Morality of Horror', with reference to Humplíková, 'Kronika Krysaře', 115–19.
58 Kawin, *Telling It Again*, 184.
59 Harvey, *A Companion to Marx's Capital*, 147–8.
60 Barta with Ballard, 'Magic against Materialism'.
61 A dated and potentially offensive way of marking moral difference through colour.
62 Barta with Ballard, 'Magic against Materialism'.
63 Lefebvre, *Production of Space*, 95.
64 Barta with Ballard, 'Magic against Materialism'.
65 Barta with Clarke, 'Jiri Barta and The Pied Piper'.
66 Eisner, *The Haunted Screen*, 15.
67 Lefebvre, *Production of Space*, 49.
68 Saraswat, 'Studying the Spiral', 24–6.
69 Groom, 'This Time Around'.
70 Ito, *Uzumaki: Volume 3*, 218.
71 To appropriate the title of Barthes's 1953 work.
72 Marx and Engels, *The German Ideology*, 37, 41, 42, 46 and 47ff.
73 Marx, *Capital: A New Abridgement*, 55.
74 Ibid., 64.
75 Lefebvre, *Critique of Everyday Life Volume 3*, 55.
76 Lefebvre, *Production of Space*, 374.
77 Lukács, 'The Phenomenon of Reification', 83–109.
78 These gendered assumptions being Marx's own. Lefebvre's assertion that in a post-slavery society only prostitution has the ability to transform the worker into a commodity rests upon the assumption that during prostitution it is the woman being bought and not her labour. Lefebvre, *Sociology of Marx*, 100.
79 Marx, *Capital: A New Abridgement*, 51.
80 Lukács, 'Phenomenon of Reification', 83–6.

81 Marx and Engels, *The German Ideology*, 109.
82 Marx draws a distinction between a naive form of hoarding in which surplus use value is hoarded and the hoarding of the capitalist who does so for social power. Marx, *Capital: A New Abridgement*, 83–5. When hoarding occurs in Barta's films it is of the former, naive kind.
83 Barta with Clarke, 'Jiri Barta and The Pied Piper'.
84 Brown, *A Sense of Things*, 66.
85 Kawin, *Telling It Again*, 49.
86 Kember, 'Child's Play: Participation in Urban Space in Weegee's, Dassin's, and Debord's Versions of *Naked City*', 75.
87 Lefebvre, *Critique of Everyday Life: Volume 3*, 61.
88 Ibid.
89 Kawin, *Telling It Again*, 83.
90 Košuličová, 'The Morality of Horror'.
91 Barta with Clarke, 'Jiri Barta and The Pied Piper'.
92 Jediny, 'The Animation of Jirí Barta'.
93 Barta with Ballard, 'Magic against Materialism'.
94 Ibid.
95 Mooney, Introduction to *Repetition and Philosophical Crumbs*, by Soren Kierkegaard, viii.
96 Trahair, 'For the Noise of a Fly', 196.
97 Ibid.
98 Adams, 'Buying Time: Consumption and Political Legitimization in Late-Communist Czechoslovakia', 401, with reference to Brown, *Eastern Europe and Communist Rule*, 507.
99 Dowling, *Brief Histories: Czechoslovakia*, 142.
100 Ibid., 146.
101 Glenn, 'Competing Challengers and Contested Outcomes to State Breakdown', 193.
102 Freud, 'Beyond the Pleasure Principle', 53–4.
103 Brown, *A Sense of Things*, 64.
104 Lefebvre, *Rhythmanalysis*, 39.
105 Lefebvre, *Critique of Everyday Life: Volume 3*, 65.
106 Brown, *A Sense of Things*, 73.
107 Of course, an animator like Jan Švankmajer and a theorist like Peter Schwenger would argue that objects do indeed have material memories.
108 Adams, 'Buying Time', 405–6.
109 Havel, 'Letter to Dr Gustáv Husák', 9.
110 Brown, *A Sense of Things*, 73.

111 Innes, *Czechoslovakia: The Short Goodbye*, x.
112 Coverly, *Psychogeography*, 127.
113 Kawin, *Telling It Again*, 5.
114 de Certeau, *The Practice of Everyday Life*, 25.
115 Lefebvre, *Production of Space*, 381.

Chapter 4

1   Wheaton and Kavan, *The Velvet Revolution*, 134.
2   Ibid., 184.
3   Velinger, 'Famous Match Manufacturer to Close Down Czech Plant'.
4   Richmond and Fendley, 'Propaganda for the Pocket'.
5   Nelson, *Secret Life of Puppets*, 76.
6   McCormick and Pratasik, *Popular Puppet Theatre in Europe, 1800–1914*, 174.
7   North and Drábek, 'What Governs Life', 525–42.
8   Thomas, *Prague Palimpsest*, 172.
9   Paces, *Prague Panoramas*, 250.
10 Drábek and North, 'What Governs Life', 539.
11 Ibid., 532.
12 Hames, *Czech and Slovak Cinema*, 181.
13 Švankmajer, *Švankmajer's Faust: The Script*, 1.
14 Sayer, *Prague: Capital of the Twentieth Century*, 102.
15 We are firmly *not* inhabiting the wandering gaze of Walter Benjamin's or Louis Aragon's *flâneur*.
16 Švankmajer with Hames, 'Interview with Jan Švankmajer', 127.
17 Luckert, 'Drawings We Have Lived'.
18 Neff, 'Conspirators of Pleasure'; Heilman, 'Conspirators of Pleasure (Jan Svankmajer) 1997'; Holden, '"Conspirators of Pleasure": Manipulating Characters like Cartoons'.
19 Ibid.
20 Morris, 'A Crazy Cake: Jan Svankmajer's *Conspirators of Pleasure*'.
21 Schmitt, 'Detailed Biography with Commentary (III) 1990–2012', 349.
22 Ibid.
23 Brooke, 'Conspirators of Pleasure: DVD Video Review'.
24 Sorfa, 'The Object of Film in Jan Švankmajer', 13–15.
25 Shaviro, 'Conspirators of Pleasure'.

26 Švankmajer with Jackson, 'The Surrealist Conspirator'.
27 Ibid.
28 Zipes, *The Enchanted Screen*, 352; Mitchell, 'Little Otik (2000) Film Review'.
29 Skrodzka, *Magic Realist Cinema*, 114.
30 Švankmajer with Hames, 'Interview with Jan Švankmajer', 127.
31 Imre, *Identity Games*, 208.
32 Ibid.
33 Smalley, '125. Little Otik (2000)'.
34 Švankmajer, 'An Alchemist's Nightmares'.
35 Barta with Ballard, 'Magic against Materialism'.
36 Ibid.
37 Meyrink, *The Golem*, 42.
38 Ibid., 51.
39 Humphreys, *The Rough Guide to Prague*, 99.
40 Sontag, *On Photography*, 17, quoted in Buchan, *The Quay Brothers*, 92.
41 Tucker, *Philosophy and Politics of Czech Dissidence*, 253–4.
42 de Certeau, *Practice of Everyday Life*, 202.
43 Kafka, quoted in Janourh, *Conversations with Kafka*, 80, in Ripellino, *Magic Prague*, 125.
44 Sayer, *Prague*, 63–4.
45 Thomas, *Prague Palimpsest*, 50–1.
46 Ibid., 43.
47 Interestingly, this image is reversed in Barta's *In the Attic/Who Has a Birthday Today?* (*Na pude aneb Kdo má dneska narozeniny?*, 2009), which reaches its climax with a pocket watch that opens onto a sucking vortex, which pulls all the surrounding objects – and nearly two of the film's heroes – inside.
48 Crogan, 'Things Analog and Digital'.
49 Ibid.
50 Lefebvre, *Critique of Everyday Life*, 151.
51 Ibid.
52 Interestingly, what seemingly triggers this social disintegration is not the lack of communal bonds between the actors but rather an increased speeding up of the rituals of everyday life and the insertion of newer and more diverse actants into the system (chainsaws, soy sauce, television sets, etc.) As such, it is possible to read the film as a reactionary allegory for technological advancement, multiculturalism, shifting gender roles and, generally speaking, the increased complexity of the modern Czech Republic. While my fondness for Barta's cinema

leads me to want to reject this reading, it is important to be mindful of the tendency to see in allegory a reflection of the politics you wish the artist to hold.
53 Cockrell, 'One Night in One City'.
54 Baudrillard, *System of Objects*, 114.
55 Ibid.
56 Ibid.
57 Johnson, Hraba and Lorenz, 'Criminal Victimisation', 195–209.
58 Rabušic, 'Why Are They All So Eager to Retire?', 324.
59 Johnson, Hraba and Lorenz, 'Criminal Victimisation', 196.
60 Edwards, *Praguewalks*, 202.
61 Wilson and Baker, *Prague City Guide*, 129.
62 Highmore, *Cityscapes*, 152.
63 Lefebvre, *Rhythmanalysis*, 40.
64 Falvey, 'Animator Jan Balej Wins Record Subsidy for New, Gloomier Little Mermaid'.
65 Morgan with Pavlátová, 'Sundance, Day 7: Interview with Filmmaker-Animator Michaela Pavlátová'.
66 Lefebvre, *Rhythmanalysis*, 40.
67 Deniz, 'Tram by Michaela Pavlátová'.
68 Ibid.
69 Lefebvre, *Rhythmanalysis*, 18.
70 Ibid., 77.
71 Pavlátová with Cowley, 'Interview with "Tram" Director'.
72 Ibid.
73 Lefebvre, *Rhythmanalysis*, 51.
74 Lefebvre, *Production of Space*, 8.
75 Ripellino, *Magic Prague*, 18.
76 Švankmajer interviewed with Hagemann, 'Who Is Jan Svankmajer?'; Hagemann, 'Jan Svankmajer, Birth Trauma, and the Gesture toward Touch'.
77 Czaplicka, Gelazis and Ruble, 'Introduction: What Time Is This Place? Locating the Postsocialist City', 7.
78 Cubitt, 'Ecocritique and the Materialities of Animation', 100.
79 Sorfa, 'Architorture: Jan Švankmajer and Surrealist Film', 103.
80 Joschko and Morgan, 'Learning from the Golden Age of Czechoslovak Animation', 78.
81 Ibid., 75.
82 Hames, 'A Business like Any Other: Czech Cinema since the Velvet Revolution'.

83 Joschko and Morgan, 'Learning from the Golden Age of Czechoslovak Animation', 77.
84 Joschko, 'A Journey to the Heart and Soul of Czech Animation', 27–8.
85 Hames, 'A Business like Any Other'.
86 Joschko and Morgan, 'Learning from the Golden Age of Czechoslovak Animation', 67.
87 'Czech Film Fund', *Czech Film Commission*.
88 'About Us', *Czech Film Commission*.
89 'Czech Film Center', *Czech Film Commission*.
90 Association of Czech Animation Film, *Analysis of the current state of Czech animation/Analýza současného stavu animované tvorby*, 8–30.
91 Ibid., 42.
92 I am sympathetic to this project, while ultimately being sceptical that ideology (as a top-down human imposition) can be meaningfully transcended within a post-Feudal political system – perhaps this is why Trnka so often has to look towards the past or to the future to stage his allegories. The pragmatic Leftist in me feels that it is often when one claims to be done with ideology that ideology is most at risk of sneaking through the back door.
93 Just one of the reasons why environmental activism is inherently political.
94 Mazierska, 'The Cinema of Jan Švankmajer: Dark Alchemy', 735.
95 Brown, 'How to Do Things with Things (A Toy Story)', 935–64; Brown, 'Reification, Reanimation, and the American Uncanny', 175–207.
96 Autopsies Research Group, *Autopsies Project*.
97 Lefebvre, *Sociology of Marx*, 79.
98 Sragow, 'Deep Focus: The Puppet Master'.
99 Lefebvre, *Sociology of Marx*, 137.

Epilogue

1 Read, *A Film-Philosophy of Ecology and Enlightenment*.
2 Ibid., ix.
3 Buchan, 'Animation, in Theory', 116.
4 From my personal perspective, the limitations of this approach are apparent in Batkin, *Identity in Animation: A Journey into Self, Difference, Culture and the Body*. Despite some stretches of clear-sighted analysis, Batkin concludes her monograph with the observation that 'the medium used, whether it is 2D, stop

motion or 3D, is irrelevant', 171. My analyses throughout this book demonstrate that this is far from being the case, as do observations by Torre and Torre, in 'Materiality, Experimental Process and Animated Identity', 85–101.
5. Read, 'This Civilisation Is Finished ...'.
6. Ibid.
7. hooks, *Feminist Theory: From Margin to Center*, xv.
8. Ranawana and Trafford, 'Imperialist Environmentalism and Decolonial Struggle'.
9. Blowe, 'It Is Not Just a Bunch of Flowers'.
10. Poulter, 'Extinction Rebellion's Tube Protest Isn't the Last of Its Problems'.
11. XR Scotland, 'On Class and Climate Struggle: Decolonising XR'.
12. Read, quoted by Ball, Webster and Webber, 'Extinction Rebellion Apologises after Commuters Drag Protester Off Train'.
13. Morton, *Hyperobjects*.
14. Baudrillard, *Symbolic Exchange and Death*, 133.
15. Lamarre, 'Coming to Life: Cartoon Animals and Natural Philosophy', 136.
16. Faye, Watson and Golsan, 'Nazi Foundations in Heidegger's Work'.
17. Mishra, 'Jordan Peterson & Fascist Mysticism'.
18. That is to say, metaphysics which seems to disclose the magnetic pull and gravity of *something* powerful, while simultaneously hiding that powerful *something* outside of human reach or comprehension. I am thinking here of Heidegger's near-mystical 'thing-in-itself', which Bill Brown (*Other Things*, p. 33) describes as 'the absence' around which a jug, say, is formed, or even Jung's 'collective unconscious'.
19. Read's film philosophy is absolutely not fascist in and of itself. My concern is similar to that of Sparrow's with Bennett's and Harman's writing.
20. Sparrow, 'Against the New Vitalism'.
21. Read, *A Film-Philosophy*, 126–68.
22. Ibid., 119.
23. Connolly, 'Home, Individuation, and the Tower'.
24. Ibid.
25. Read, *A Film-Philosophy*, 207.
26. Manavis, 'Eco-fascism: The Ideology Marrying Environmentalism and White Supremacy Thriving Online'.
27. Wilson, 'Eco-fascism Is Undergoing a Revival in the Fetid Culture of the Extreme Right'.

Bibliography

'About'. *Prague Puppet Museum*. Last updated 2015. Accessed 19 September 2017. http://www.praguepuppetmuseum.com/about.

Adams, Bradley. 'Buying Time: Consumption and Political Legitimization in Late-Communist Czechoslovakia'. In *The End and the Beginning: The Revolutions of 1989 and the Resurgence of History*, edited by Vladimir Tismaneanu and Bogdan C. Iacob, 399–422. Budapest: Central European University Press, 2012.

Anderson, Hans Christian. *Andersen's Fairy Tales*. Ware: Wordsworth Editions, 2003.

Anderson, Michael, J. 'Dimensions of Dialogue'. *Tativille*, 11 August 2005. Accessed 19 September 2014. http://tativille.blogspot.co.uk/2005/08/dimensions-of-dialogue.html.

Andreou, Alex. 'Anti-homeless Spikes: "Sleeping Rough Opened My Eyes to the City's Barbed Cruelty"'. *The Guardian*, 18 February 2015. Accessed 12 July 2018. https://www.theguardian.com/society/2015/feb/18/defensive-architecture-keeps-poverty-undeen-and-makes-us-more-hostile.

Andrews, Geoff and Jan Švankmajer. 'Malice in Wonderland'. *Time Out*, 19–26 October 1988.

Aragon, Louis. *Paris Peasant*. Translated by Simon Watson Taylor. Boston: Exact Change, 1994.

Arnott, Peter. *Plays without People: Puppetry and Series Drama*. Indiana: Indiana University Press, 1964.

Artaud, Antonin. *The Theatre and Its Double*. Translated by Victor Corti. London: Calder Publications, 2005.

Ash, Timothy Garton. 'Prague – A Poem, Not Disappearing'. In *Václav* Havel *or, Living in Truth*, edited by Václav Havel and Jan Vladislav, 213–21. London: Faber and Faber, 1989.

Association of Czech Animation Film/Asociace animovaného filmu, 2016. *Analysis of the current state of Czech animation/Analýza současného stavu animované tvorby*, 1–71. Accessed 23 October 2019. http://www.asaf.cz/co-delame/strategie-animace.

Autopsies Research Group, 2011. *Autopsies Project*. Last modified 2012. Accessed 1 June 2015. http://www.autopsiesgroup.com.

Auty, Robert. 'Language and Society in the Czech National Revival'. *The Slavonic and East European Review* 35, no. 84 (December 1956): 241–8.

Aveni, Anthony. *Apocalyptic Anxiety: Religion, Science, and America's Obsession with the End of the World*. Boulder: University Press of Colorado, 2016.

Bakhtin, Mikhail. *Rabelais and His World*. Translated by Helene Iswolsky. Bloomington: Indiana University Press, 1984.

Ball, Tom, Ben Webster and Esther Webber. 'Extinction Rebellion Apologises after Commuters Drag Protester Off Train'. *The Times*, 18 October 2019. Accessed 30 October 2019. https://www.thetimes.co.uk/article/commuters-clash-with-extinction-rebellion-climate-protesters-on-london-underground-v25z5gmnn.

Ballard, Phil and Jiří Barta. 'Magic against Materialism'. *Kinoeye* 3, no. 5 (September 2003). Accessed 25 September 2014.

Balz, Adam. 'The Puppet Films of Jiri Trnka'. *Not Coming to a Theatre Near You*, 17 June 2007. Accessed 13 September 2014. http://notcoming.com/features/jiritrnka.

Barker, Ralph. 'Jan Švankmajer – The Psychological Švankmajer'. *Applied Imagination*, 8 August 2012. Accessed 19 September 2014. http://artandculturecritic.com/2012/08/08/jan-svankmajer-the-psychological-svankmajer.

Barley, J. F. N. *Czechoslovakia: A Short History*. Edinburgh: University of Edinburgh, 1971.

Batkin, Jane. *Identity in Animation: A Journey into Self, Difference, Culture and the Body*. Abingdon-on-Thames: Routledge, 2017.

Baudrillard, Jean. *Symbolic Exchange and Death*, rev edn. Translated by Iain Hamilton Grant. New York: Sage, 2016.

Baudrillard, Jean. *The System of Objects*. Translated by James Benedict. London and New York: Verso, 1996.

Bažant, Jan, Nina Bažantová and Frances Starn, eds. *The Czech Reader: History, Culture, Politics*. Durham: Duke University Press, 2010.

Beckman, Karen. 'Animating Film Theory: An Introduction'. In *Animating Film Theory*, edited by Karen Beckman, 1–23. Durham: Duke University Press, 2014.

Bellano, Marco. *Václav Trojan: Music Composition in Czech Animated Films*. Abingdon-on-Thames: Taylor & Francis, 2019.

Bendazzi, Giannalberto. *Animation: A World History, Volume 1: Foundations – The Golden Age*. Abingdon-on-Thames: Routledge, 2016.

Bendazzi, Giannalberto. *Cartoons: One Hundred Years of Cinema Animation*. Bloomington and Indianapolis: Indiana University Press, 1994.

Benjamin, Walter. *Illuminations*. Translated by Harry Zorn and introduced by Hannah Arendt. London: Pimlico, 1999.

Bennett, Jane. *Vibrant Matter: A Political Ecology of Things*. Durham: Duke University Press, 2010.

Bíro, Yvette. *Turbulence and Flow in Film: The Rhythmic Design*. Bloomington: Indiana University Press, 2008.

Blažek, Petr. 'Hrob Jana Palacha/Jan Palach's Grave'. *Charles University Multimedia Project*. Last modified 2009. Accessed 13 September 2014. http://www.janpalach.cz/en/default/mista-pameti/hrob.

Blowe, Kevin. 'It Is Not Just a Bunch of Flowers'. *Medium*, 16 October 2019. Accessed 26 October 2019. https://medium.com/@copwatcher_uk/it-is-not-just-a-bunch-of-flowers-bc5078b899e4

Boček, Jaroslav. *Jiří Trnka: Artist and Puppet Master*. Translated by Till Gottheiner. Prague: Artia, 1965.

Borroughs, D. B. 'Nice to Look at for a Few Minutes but I Found It Dull'. *IMDB*. Last modified 27 April 2008. Accessed 20 September 2017. http://www.imdb.com/title/tt0043410/reviews?ref_=tt_urv.

Bregant, Michal and Dominik Jůn. 'Jiří Trnka: 100th Anniversary of the Birth of a Great Czech Animator'. *Radio Praha*, 28 February 2012. Accessed 25 September 2014. http://www.radio.cz/en/section/czech-history/jiri-trnka-100th-anniversary-of-the-birth-of-a-great-czech-animator.

Breton, André. *Manifestos of Surrealism*. Translated by H. R. Lane and R. Seaver. Michigan: University of Michigan Press, 1972.

Breton, André. *What Is Surrealism? Selected Writings*. Edited and translated by Franklin Rosemont. Atlanta: Pathfinder Press, 1998.

Broadfoot, Keith and Rex Butler. 'The Illusion of Illusion'. In *The Illusion of Life: Essays on Animation*, edited by Alan Cholodenko, 263–98. Sydney: Power Institute of Fine Arts, 1993.

Brooke, Michael. 'Conspirators of Pleasure: DVD Video Review'. *The Digital Fix: Film*, 27 February 1999. Accessed 22 September 2014. http://film.thedigitalfix.com/content/id/3381/conspirators-of-pleasure.html.

Brooke, Michael. 'The Hand'. *Closely Watched DVDs*, 27 July 2006. Accessed 16 September 2014. http://filmjournal.net/czech/2006/07/27/the-hand.

Brooke, Michael. 'Makers: Free Radical'. *Vertigo Magazine* 3, no. 5 (Spring 2007). Accessed 22 June 2015. https://www.closeupfilmcentre.com/vertigo_magazine/volume-3-issue-5-spring-2007/free-radical.

Brown, Bill. 'How to Do Things with Things (A Toy Story)'. *Critical Inquiry* 24, no. 4 (Summer 1998): 935–64.

Brown, Bill. *Other Things*. Chicago: University of Chicago Press, 2019.

Brown, Bill. 'Reification, Reanimation, and the American Uncanny'. *Critical Inquiry* 32, no. 2 (Winter 2006): 175–207.

Brown, Bill. *A Sense of Things: The Object Matter of American Literature*. Chicago: University of Chicago Press, 2004.

Brown, Bill. 'Thing Theory'. *Critical Inquiry* 28, no. 1 (Autumn 2001): 1–22.

Buchan, Suzanne. 'Animation, in Theory'. In *Animating Film Theory*, edited by Karen Beckman, 111–29. Durham: Duke University Press, 2014.

Buchan, Suzanne. *Quay Brothers: Into a Metaphysical Playroom*. Minneapolis: University of Minnesota Press, 2011.

Čapek, Karel and Josef Čapek. *R.U.R. and The Insect Play*. Adapted by Clifford Bax and Nigel Playfair and translated by Paul Selver. Oxford: Oxford University Press, 1969.

Cardinal, Roger. 'Thinking through Things: The Presence of Objects in the Early Films of Jan Švankmajer'. In *The Cinema of Jan Švankmajer: Dark Alchemy*, 2nd edn, edited by Peter Hames, 67–82. London: Wallflower Press, 2008.

Carroll, Rachel, ed. *Adaptations in Contemporary Culture: Textual Infidelities*. London and New York: Continuum, 2009.

Carter, Neil. 'Politics as if Nature Mattered'. In *What Is Politics? The Activity and Its Study*, edited by Adrian Letwich, 182–95. Cambridge: Polity Press, 2004.

Caygill, Howard. 'Walter Benjamin's Concept of Allegory'. In *The Cambridge Companion to Allegory*, edited by Rita Copeland and Peter T. Struck, 241–53. Cambridge: Cambridge University Press, 2010.

Celenza, Anna Harwell. *Hans Christian Andersen and Music: The Nightingale Revealed*. London and New York: Routledge, 2017.

Cholodenko, Alan, ed. *The Illusion of Life: Essays on Animation*. Sydney: Power Publication, 1991.

Cholodenko, Alan, ed. *The Illusion of Life 2: More Essays on Animation*. Sydney: Power Institute of Fine Arts, 2007.

Clarke, Jeremy and Jiří Barta. 'Jiří Barta and the Pied Piper'. *Animator Mag* 23 (Summer 1988): 24–6. Accessed 25 September 2014. http://www.animatormag.com/archive/issue-23/issue-23-page-24.

Cockrell, Eddie. 'One Night in One City'. *Variety*, 18 July 2007. Accessed 24 September 2014. http://variety.com/2007/film/reviews/one-night-in-one-city-1200557735.

Colpan, Sema and Lydia Nsiah. 'More than Product Advertising: Animation, Gasparcolor and Sorela's Corporate Design'. In *Films that Sell: Moving Pictures and Advertising*, edied by Patrick Vonderau, Bo Florin and Nico De Klerk, 114–30. London: BFI, 2016.

Connolly, Lewis. 'Home, Individuation, and the Tower'. *Lewis Connolly Blog Archive*, 27 October 2019. Accessed 30 October 2019. https://www.lewisconnolly.com/post/2019/10/27/home-individuation-and-the-tower.

Copeland, Rita and Peter T. Struck. 'Introduction'. In *The Cambridge Companion to Allegory*, edited by Rita Copeland and Peter T. Struck, 1–13. Cambridge: Cambridge University Press, 2010.

Coverly, Merlin. *Psychogeography*, 2nd edn. Harpenden: Pocket Essentials, 2006.
Cowley, Laura-Beth and Michaela Pavlátová. 'Interview with "Tram" Director Michaela Pavlátová'. *Skwigly*, 22 January 2014. Accessed 24 September 2014. http://www.skwigly.co.uk/michaela-pavlatova.
Crawford, Cassandra S. 'Actor Network Theory'. In *Encyclopedia of Social Theory: Volume I*, edited by George Ritzer, 1. London: Sage, 2005.
Crick, Bernard. 'Politics as a Form of Rule: Politics, Citizenship and Democracy'. In *What Is Politics? The Activity and Its Study*, edited by Adrian Leftwich, 67–85. Cambridge: Polity Press, 2004.
Crogan, Patrick. 'Things Analog and Digital'. *Senses of Cinema* 5 (April 2000). Accessed 14 September 2014. http://sensesofcinema.com/2000/conference-special-effects-special-affects/digital.
Crowther, Bosley. 'The Screen in Review; "Emperor's Nightingale," Fantasy Made in Czechoslovakia, at 60th St. Trans-Lux'. *New York Times*, 14 May 1951. Accessed 18 September 2017. https://www.nytimes.com/1951/05/14/archives/the-screen-in-review-emperors-nightingale-fantasy-made-in.html.
Cubitt, Sean. 'Ecocritique and the Materialities of Animation'. In *Pervasive Animation*, edited by Suzanne Buchan, 94–114. Abingdon-on-Thames: Routledge, 2013.
Czaplicka, John, Nida Gelazis and Blair A. Ruble. 'Introduction: What Time Is This Place? Locating the Postsocialist City'. In *Cities after the Fall of Communism: Reshaping Cultural Landscape and European Identity*, edited by John Czaplicka, Nida Gelazis and Blair A. Ruble, 1–16. Baltimore: Johns Hopkins University Press, 2009.
Czech Film Commission. 'About Us'. Last modified 2019. Accessed 22 October 2019. https://www.filmcommission.cz/about/mission.
Czech Film Commission. 'Czech Film Fund'. Last modified 2019. Accessed 22 October 2019. https://www.filmcommission.cz/about/czech-film-fund.
Czech Film Commission. 'Czech Film Center'. Last modified 2019. Accessed 22 October 2019. https://www.filmcenter.cz/en/home.
Czech National Film Archive. 'IRE-Film'. *Portal*. Last modified 2018. Accessed 6 October 2019. https://www.filmovyprehled.cz/en/person/127381/ire-film+&cd=1&hl=en&ct=clnk&gl=uk.
'Czech Republic incl. Český Ráj, Jičín & Prague Holidays'. *Holiday 'N' Adventure*. Last modified 2014. Accessed 22 September 2014. http://www.holiday-n-adventure.co.uk/czech-republic-tours/prague-holidays.htm.
d'Axa, Zo. 'Us'. Translated by Mitch Abidor. *L'En-Dehors*, 1896. Last modified 2004. Accessed 12 May 2015. https://www.marxists.org/reference/archive/zo-daxa/1896/us.htm.
Davy, Richard. 'Soviet Foreign Policy and the Invasion of Czechoslovakia'. *International Journal* 33, no. 4 (Autumn 1978): 796–803.

de Certeau, Michel. *The Practice of Everyday Life*. Translated by Stephen Rendall. California: University of California Press, 1988.

Dee, Markéta. 'Jiri Trnka – "The Walt Disney of Eastern Europe"'. *Bohemian Connection*, 25 February 2012. Accessed 25 September 2014. http://bohemianconnection.wordpress.com/2012/02/25/jiri-trnka-the-walt-disney-of-eastern-europe/.

Delsarte, François. *Delsarte System of Oratory*, 4th edn. Translated by Abby L. Alger. New York: Edgar S. Werner, 1893. Accessed 16 September 2014. http://www.gutenberg.org/ebooks/12200.

Deniz, Ali. 'Tram by Michaela Pavlátová'. *Nisi Magazine*, 6 June 2012. Accessed 26 September 2014. http://www.nisimazine.eu/Tram.html.

Dowling, Maria. *Brief Histories: Czechoslovakia*. London and New York: Bloomsbury Academic, 2002.

Dryje, František. 'The Force of Imagination'. In *The Cinema of Jan Švankmajer: Dark Alchemy*, 2nd edn, edited by Peter Hames, 143–86. London: Wallflower Press, 2008.

Dryje, František. 'Jan Švankmajer, Surrealist'. In *Jan Švankmajer: Dimensions of Dialogue/Between Film and Fine Art*, edited by Bertrand Schmitt and František Dryje, 219–320. Prague: Arbor Vitae, 2013.

Dunae, Patrick A. 'Penny Dreadfuls: Late Nineteenth-Century Boys' Literature and Crime'. *Victorian Studies* 22, no. 2 (Winter 1979): 133–50.

Dutka, Edgar. 'Jiri Trnka – Walt Disney of the East!'. *Animation World Magazine* 5, no. 4 (July 2000): 1–2. Accessed 25 September 2014. https://www.awn.com/animationworld/jiri-trnka-walt-disney-east.

Dutkova-Cope, Lida. 'Texas Czech Ethnic Identity: So How Czech Are You, Really?'. *The Slavic and East European Journal* 47, no. 4 (Winter 2003): 648–76.

Eason, Jack. 'Dimensions of Dialogue: moznosti dialogu'. *Cinelogue*, 17 November 2010. Accessed 21 June 2013. http://www.cinelogue.com/reviews/dimensions-of-dialogue.

Edwards, Ivana. *Praguewalks*. London: Boxtree, 2004.

Eidlin, Fred H. '"Capitulation," "Resistance" and the Framework of "Normali-Zation": The August 1968 Invasion of Czechoslovakia and the Czechoslovak Response'. *Journal of Peace Research* 18, no. 4 (December 1981): 319–32.

Eisenstein, Sergei. *Eisenstein on Disney*. Edited by Jay Leyda and translated by Alan Upchurch. Calcutta: Seagull Books, 1986.

Eisner, Lotte. *The Haunted Screen: Expressionism in the German Cinema and the Influence of Max Reinhardt*, 2nd edn. Translated by Roger Greaves. California: University of California Press, 2008.

Falvey, Christian. 'Animator Jan Balej Wins Record Subsidy for New, Gloomier Little Mermaid'. *Radio Praha*, 18 May 2009. Accessed 23 September 2014. http://www.

radio.cz/en/section/curraffrs/animator-jan-balej-wins-record-subsidy-for-new-gloomier-little-mermaid.

Faye, Emmanuel, Alexis Watson and Richard J. Golsan. 'Nazi Foundations in Heidegger's Work'. *South Central Review* 23, no. 1 (2006): 55–66.

Field, Simon. 'A Quiet Week in the House'. *Monthly Film Bulletin* 55, no. 659 (1988): 378–9.

Frank, Alison. *Reframing Reality: The Aesthetics of the Surrealist Object in French and Czech Cinema*. Bristol: Intellect, 2013.

Fraňková, Ruth. 'Jiří Trnka: An Artist Who Turned Puppets into Film Stars'. *Radio Praha*, 12 June 2011. Accessed 14 April 2015. http://www.radio.cz/en/section/czech-history/jiri-trnka-an-artist-who-turned-puppets-into-film-stars.

Frey, Mattias. 'No(ir) Place to Go: Spatial Anxiety and Sartorial Intertextuality in "Die Unberührbare"'. *Cinema Journal* 45, no. 4 (Summer 2006): 64–80.

Freedenberg, Eitan. 'One-Minute Boogie Woogie: Rhythmanalysis and Landscape Cinema'. PhD paper, University of Rochester (Spring 2013): 1–25.

Freedgood, Elaine. *The Ideas in Things: Fugitive Meaning in the Victorian Novel*. Chicago: University of Chicago Press, 2006.

Freud, Sigmund. *Beyond the Pleasure Principle: And Other Writings*. Translated by John Reddick. London: Penguin Classics, 2003.

Freud, Sigmund. *The 'Wolfman' and Other Cases*. Translated by Louise Adey Huish. London: Penguin Classics, 2002.

Gambarato, Renira Rampazzo. 'Methodology for Film Analysis: The Role of Objects in Films'. *Fronteiras* 12, no. 2 (May/August 2010): 105–15.

Gambarato, Renira Rampazzo. 'Talking Objects of Denys Arcand'. *Lumina* 3, no. 2 (2009): 1–12.

Gambarato, Renira Rampazzo and Simone Malaguti. 'Objects of Desire. Methodology for Film Analysis in the Sense of Peircean Semiotics and Intermedial Studies'. *Kodikas/Code* 29, nos. 1–3 (2006): 155–74.

Gani, Aisha. 'More Than Half Unemployed Young People Anxious about Life – report'. *The Guardian*, 14 January 2015. Accessed 25 June 2015. http://www.theguardian.com/society/2015/jan/14/more-than-half-unemployed-young-people-anxious-about-life-report.

Gauss, Charles E. 'The Theoretical Backgrounds of Surrealism'. *The Journal of Aesthetics and Art Criticism* 2, no. 8 (Fall 1943): 37–44.

Glenn, John K. 'Competing Challengers and Contested Outcomes to State Breakdown: The Velvet Revolution in Czechoslovakia'. *Social Forces* 78, no. 1 (September 1999): 187–211.

Gomel, Elana. 'The Poetics of Censorship: Allegory as Form and Ideology in the Novels of Arkady and Boris Strugatsky'. *Science Fiction Studies* 22, no. 1 (March 1995): 87–105.

Graffy, Julian, Richard Taylor, Nancy Wood and Dina Iordanova, eds. *The BFI Companion to Eastern European and Russian Cinema*. London: British Film Institute, 2000.

Grob, Gijs. 'Císařův Slavík (The Emperor's Nightingale)'. *Dr. Grob's Animation Review*, 25 September 2013. Accessed 20 September 2017. https://drgrobsanimationreview.com/2013/09/25/cisaruv-slavik-the-emperors-nightingale.

Grob, Gijs. 'The Hand (Ruka)'. *Dr. Grob's Animation Review*, 14 May 2011. Accessed 25 September 2014. http://drgrobsanimationreview.com/2011/05/14/the-hand-ruka.

Groom, Amelia. 'This Time Around'. *AmeliaGroom.com*, April 2012. Accessed 25 September 2014. http://ameliagroom.com/?p=319.

Guignon, Charles B. 'Heidegger's "Authenticity" Revisited'. *The Review of Metaphysics* 38, no. 2 (December 1984): 321–9.

Gunning, Tom. 'Animating the Instant: The Secret Symmetry between Animation and Photography'. In *Animating Film Theory*, edited by Karen Beckman, 37–53. Durham: Duke University Press, 2014.

Hagemann, Jessica. 'May I Touch Your Meat? Jan Svankmajer, Birth Trauma, and the Gesture toward Touch'. *Bright Lights Film Journal*, 31 October 2012. Accessed 23 July 2018. http://brightlightsfilm.com/may-i-touch-your-meat-jan-svankmajer-birth-trauma-and-the-gesture-toward-touch.

Hagemann, Jessica and Jan Švankmajer. 'Who Is Jan Svankmajer? [And What's with His Claim That We're All a Bit Sadistic?]'. *Cider Spoon Stories*, 6 September 2016. Accessed 23 July 2018. http://www.ciderspoonstories.com/blog/2016/9/6/who-is-jan-svankmajer-and-why-does-he-claim-that-were-all-a-bit-sadistic.

Hames, Peter. 'A Business like Any Other: Czech Cinema since the Velvet Revolution'. *KinoKultura* Special Issue 4 (Winter 2006). Accessed 20 October 2019. http://www.kinokultura.com/specials/4/hames.shtml.

Hames, Peter. 'Bringing Up Baby'. *Kinoeye* 2, no. 1 (January 2002). Accessed 25 September 2014. http://www.kinoeye.org/02/01/hames01.php.

Hames, Peter, ed. *The Cinema of Jan Švankmajer: Dark Alchemy*, 2nd edn. London: Wallflower Press, 2008.

Hames, Peter. 'The Core of Reality: Puppets in the Feature Films of Jan Švankmajer'. In *The Cinema of Jan Švankmajer: Dark Alchemy*, 2nd edn, edited by Peter Hames, 83–103. London: Wallflower Press, 2008.

Hames, Peter. *Czech and Slovak Cinema: Theme and Tradition*. Edinburgh: Edinburgh University Press, 2009.

Hames, Peter. *The Czechoslovak New Wave*, 2nd edn. New York: Columbia University Press, 2005.

Hames, Peter. 'Czechoslovakia'. In *The BFI Companion to Eastern European and Russian Cinema*, edited by Richard Taylor, Nancy Wood, Julian Graffy and Dina Iordanova, 54–7. London: BFI, 2000.

Hames, Peter, ed. *Dark Alchemy: The Films of Jan Svankmajer*, 1st edn. Connecticut: Greenwood Press, 1995.

Hames, Peter. 'The Film Experiment'. In *The Cinema of Jan Švankmajer: Dark Alchemy*, 2nd edn, edited by Peter Hames, 8–39. London: Wallflower Press, 2008.

Hames, Peter. 'The Hand That Rocked the Kremlin'. *Sight and Sound* 22, no. 4 (April 2012). Accessed 25 September 2014. http://old.bfi.org.uk/sightandsound/feature/49844.

Hames, Peter. 'Jiří Trnka'. In *The BFI Companion to Eastern European and Russian Cinema*, edited by Richard Taylor, Nancy Wood, Julian Graffy and Dina Iordanova, 237. London: British Film Institute, 2000.

Hames, Peter and Jan Švankmajer. 'Interview with Jan Švankmajer'. In *Dark Alchemy: The Films of Jan Švankmajer*, 1st edn, edited by Peter Hames, 96–118. Connecticut: Greenwood Press, 1995.

Hames, Peter and Jan Švankmajer. 'Interview with Jan Švankmajer'. In *The Cinema of Jan Švankmajer: Dark Alchemy*, 2nd edn, edited by Peter Hames, 104–39. London: Wallflower Press, 2008.

Hanáková, Petra. 'The Hussite Heritage Film: A Dream for All Czech Seasons'. In *A Companion to Eastern European Cinemas*, edited by Anikó Imre, 466–82. Chichester: Wiley-Blackwell, 2012.

Hanson, Stephen E. *Time and Revolution: Marxism and the Design of Soviet Institutions*. Chapel Hill and London: University of North Carolina Press, 1997.

Haraszti, Miklos K. *The Velvet Prison: Artists under State Socialism*. Translated by S. Landesmann and introduced by George Konrád. London: I.B. Tauris, 1988.

Harman, Graham. *Prince of Networks: Bruno Latour and Metaphysics*. Melbourne: re.press, 2009.

Harvey, David. 'Class 06 Reading Marx's Capital Vol I with David Harvey'. *YouTube*. Last modified 19 January 2011. Accessed 11 July 2018. https://www.youtube.com/watch?v=_EP7N2VtFz0.

Harvey, David. *A Companion to Marx's Capital*. London: Verso, 2010.

Havel, Václav. 'Letter to Dr Gustáv Husák, General Secretary of the Czechoslovak Community Party'. Translator unknown. In *Living in Truth: Twenty-two Essays Published on the Occasion of the Award of the Erasmus Prize to Václav Havel*, by Václav Havel and edited by Jan Vladislav, 3–35. London and Boston: Faber and Faber, 1990.

Havel, Václav. *Living in Truth: Twenty-two Essays Published on the Occasion of the Award of the Erasmus Prize to Václav Havel*. Edited by Jan Vladislav. London and Boston: Faber and Faber, 1990.

Havel, Václav. 'New York University', October 1991. *VaclavHavel.cz*. Last modified January 2012. Accessed 27 October 2014. http://www.vaclavhavel.cz/showtrans.php?cat=projevy&val=273_aj_projevy.html&typ=HTML.

Havel, Václav. *Open Letters*. Edited by Paul Wilson. London: Faber and Faber, 1992.

Havel, Václav. 'Politics and Conscience'. Translated by E. Kohák and R. Scruton. In *Václav Havel or, Living in Truth*, by Václav Havel and edited by Jan Vladislav, 136–57. London: Faber and Faber, 1989.

Havel, Václav. 'The Power of the Powerless'. Translated by P. Wilson. In *Václav Havel or, Living in Truth*, edited by Václav Havel and Jan Vladislav, 36–122. London: Faber and Faber, 1989.

Havel, Václav. 'Selected Speeches and Writings'. *Prague Castle*. Last modified 2003. Accessed 22 September 2014. http://old.hrad.cz/president/Havel/speeches/index_uk.html.

Havel, Václav. 'Six Asides about Culture'. Translated by E. Kohák. In *Václav Havel or, Living in Truth*, edited by Václav Havel and Jan Vladislav, 123–35. London: Faber and Faber, 1989.

Havel, Václav. 'Stories and Totalitarianism'. Translated by P. Wilson. In *Open Letters*, by Václav Havel and edited by Paul Wilson, 328–50. London: Faber and Faber, 1992.

Havel, Václav. *Summer Meditations: On Politics, Morality and Civility in a Time of Transition*. Translated by Paul Wilson. London: Faber and Faber, 1992.

Hayward, Susan. *Cinema Studies: The Key Concepts*, 3rd edn. London and New York: Routledge, 2006.

Heidegger, Martin. *Being and Time*, rev edn. Translated by Joan Stambaugh and revised by Dennis J. Schmidt. Albany: State University of New York Press, 2010.

Heidegger, Martin. *The Question concerning Technology and Other Essays*. Translated by William Lovitt. New York City: Harper & Row, 1977.

Heilman, Jeremy. 'Conspirators of Pleasure (Jan Svankmajer) 1997'. *Movie Martyr*, 19 December 2001. Accessed 22 September 2014. http://www.moviemartyr.com/1997/conspirators.htm.

Heimann, Mary. *Czechoslovakia: The State That Failed*. New Haven: Yale University Press, 2011.

Highmore, Ben. *Cityscapes: Cultural Readings in the Material and Symbolic City*. Basingstoke: Palgrave Macmillan, 2005.

Hilmar-Jezek, Kytka. 'Jiří Trnka and the Czech Year (aka Špaliček)'. *Très Bohèmes*, 10 June 2017. Accessed 28 August 2017. https://www.tresbohemes.com/2017/06/jiri-trnka-and-the-czech-year-aka-spalicek.

Hofstadter, Douglas. *I Am a Strange Loop*. New York: Basic Books, 2007.

Holden, Stephen. '"Conspirators of Pleasure": Manipulating Characters like Cartoons'. *The New York Times*, 22 August 1997. Accessed 22 September 2014. http://www.nytimes.com/library/film/pleasure-film-review.html.

Holý, Ladislav. *The Little Czech and the Great Czech Nation: National Identity and the Post-Communist Social Transformation*. Cambridge: Cambridge University Press, 1996.

hooks, bell. *Feminist Theory: From Margin to Center*, 3rd edn. Abingdon-on-Thames: Routledge, 2014.

Howard, Ed. 'A Game with Stones/Punch and Judy/Historia Naturae (Suita)'. *Only the Cinema*, 27 January 2009. Accessed 19 September 2014. http://seul-le-cinema.blogspot.co.uk/2009/01/jan-svanmajer-shorts-game-with-stones.html.

Howard, Ed. 'The Ossuary/Dimensions of Dialogue'. *Only the Cinema*, 2 June 2008. Accessed 19 September 2014. http://seul-le-cinema.blogspot.com/2008/06/62-ossuary-dimensions-of-dialogue.html.

Humphreys, Rob. *The Rough Guide to Prague*. London: Rough Guides, 2011.

Illner, Michal. 'The Changing Quality of Life in a Post-Communist Country: The Case of Czech Republic'. *Social Indicators Research* 43, no. 1/2 (February 1998): 141–70.

Imre, Anikó. *Identity Games: Globalization and the Transformation of Media Cultures in the New Europe*. Cambridge: MIT Press, 2009.

Innes, Abby. *Czechoslovakia: The Short Goodbye*. New Haven: Yale University Press, 2001.

Iordanova, Dina. *Cinema of the Other Europe: The Industry and Artistry of East Central European Film*. London: Wallflower Press, 2003.

Ito, Junji. *Uzumaki: Spiral into Horror, Vol. 3*. Translated by Yuji Oniki. San Francisco: VIZ Media, 2002.

Jackson, Wendy and Jan Švankmajer. 'The Surrealist Conspirator: An Interview with Jan Svankmajer'. *Animation World Magazine* 2, no. 3 (June 1997). Accessed 14 September 2014. http://www.awn.com/mag/issue2.3/issue2.3pages/2.3jacksonsvankmajer.html.

Jarvis, Helen, Andy C. Pratt and Peter Cheng-Chong Wu. *The Secret Life of Cities: The Social Reproduction of Everyday Life*. Harlow: Pearson Education Limited, 2001.

Jediny, Jenny. 'The Animation of Jiří Barta'. *Not Coming to a Theatre Near You*, 17 June 2007. Accessed 25 September 2014. http://notcoming.com/features/jiribarta.

Jirásek, Alois. *Old Czech Legends*. Translated by Marie K. Holeček. London: Forest Books, 1992.

Johnson, Barbara. *Persons and Things*. Cambridge: Harvard University Press, 2010.

Johnson, Lee, Joseph Hraba and Frederick O. Lorenz. 'Criminal Victimisation and Depression in the Czech Republic'. *Czech Sociological Review* 8, no. 2 (Fall 2000): 195–209.

Joschko, Lucie. 'A Journey to the Heart and Soul of Czech Animation'. *Society for Animation Studies Newsletter* 21, no. 1 (Spring 2008): 26–30.

Joschko, Lucie and Michael Morgan. 'Learning from the Golden Age of Czechoslovak Animation: The Past as the Key to Unlocking Contemporary Issues'. *Animation: An Interdisciplinary Journal* 3, no. 1 (2008): 66–84.

Jůzl, Miloš. 'Music and the Totalitarian Regime in Czechoslovakia'. *International Review of the Aesthetics and Sociology of Music* 27, no. 1 (June 1996): 31–51.

Kawin, Bruce. *Telling It Again and Again: Repetition in Literature and Film*. Ithaca: Cornell University Press, 1972.

Kelley, Theresa M. *Reinventing Allegory*. Cambridge: Cambridge University Press, 1997.

Kember, Joe. 'Child's Play: Participation in Urban Space in Weegee's, Dassin's, and Debord's Versions of Naked City'. In *Adaptations in Contemporary Culture: Textual Infidelities*, edited by Rachel Carroll, 72–84. London: Continuum, 2009.

Kierkegaard, Soren. *Repetition and Philosophical Crumbs*. Edited by Edward F. Mooney and translated by M. G. Piety. Oxford: Oxford University Press, 2009.

Klein, Melanie. *The Psycho-Analysis of Children*. Translated by Alix Strachey and H. A. Thorner. London: Vintage, 1997.

Koepfinger, Eoin and Jan Švankmajer. '"Freedom Is Becoming the Only Theme": An Interview with Jan Švankmajer'. *Sampsonia Way*, 5 June 2012. Accessed 18 September 2014. http://www.sampsoniaway.org/blog/2012/06/05/freedom-is-becoming-the-only-theme-an-interview-with-jan-svankmajer.

Kohák, Erazim. 'After the Revolution'. In *The Czech Reader: History, Culture, Politics*, edited by Jan Bažant, Nina Bažantová and Frances Starn, 493–9. Durham: Duke University Press, 2010.

Kononenko, Natalie O. *Slavic Folklore: A Handbook*. Westport: Greenwood Press, 2007.

Korbel, Josef. *Twentieth-Century Czechoslovakia: The Meanings of Its History*. New York: Columbia University Press, 1977.

Koresky, Michael. 'Eclipse Series 32: Pearls of the Czech New Wave'. *Current*. Last modified 25 April 2012. Accessed 23 June 2015. http://www.criterion.com/current/posts/2269-eclipse-series-32-pearls-of-the-czech-new-wave.

Košuličová, Ivana. 'The Morality of Horror: Jiří Barta's *Krysař* (*The Pied Piper*, 1985)'. *Kinoeye* 2, no. 1 (January 2002). Accessed 25 September 2015. http://www.kinoeye.org/02/01/kosulicova01_no2.php.

Kracauer, Siegfried. *Theory of Film: The Redemption of Physical Reality*. New Jersey: Princeton University Press, 1997.

Kundera, Milan. 'Candide Had to Be Destroyed'. Translated by K. Seigneurie. In *Václav Havel or, Living in Truth*, edited by Václav Havel and Jan Vladislav, 258–62. London: Faber and Faber, 1989.

Lam, Anita. *Making Crime Television: Producing Entertaining Representations of Crime for Television Broadcast*. New York: Routledge, 2014.

Lamarre, Thomas. 'Coming to Life: Cartoon Animals and Natural Philosophy'. In *Pervasive Animation*, edited by Suzanne Buchan, 117–42. Abingdon-on-Thames: Routledge, 2013.

Latour, Bruno. 'On Actor-Network Theory: A Few Clarifications'. *Soziale Welt* 47, no. 4 (1996): 369–81.

Latour, Bruno. *Pandora's Hope: An Essay on the Reality of Science Studies*. Cambridge: Harvard University Press, 1999.

Latour, Bruno. *Politics of Nature: How to Bring the Sciences into Democracy*. Cambridge: Harvard University Press, 2004.

Latour, Bruno. *Reassembling the Social: An Introduction to Actor-Network-Theory*. New York: Oxford University Press, 2007.

Lefebvre, Henri. *Critique of Everyday Life Volume 3: From Modernity to Modernism (Towards a Metaphilosophy of Daily Life)*. Translated by Michel Trebitsch. New York: Verso, 2005.

Lefebvre, Henri. *The Production of Space*. Translated by Donald Nicholson-Smith. Malden: Wiley-Blackwell, 1991.

Lefebvre, Henri. *Rhythmanalysis: Space, Time and Everyday Life*. Introduced by Stuart Elden and translated by Stuart Elden and Gerald Moore. London: Continuum, 2004.

Lefebvre, Henri. *The Sociology of Marx*. Translated by Norbert Guterman. Middlesex: Penguin, 1972.

Leftwich, Adrian. 'Thinking Politically: On the Politics of Politics'. In *What Is Politics? The Activity and Its Study*, edited by Adrian Leftwich, 1–22. Cambridge: Polity Press, 2004.

Leslie, Esther. 'Animation's Petrified Unrest'. In *Pervasive Animation*, edited by Suzanne Buchan, 73–93. Abingdon-on-Thames: Routledge, 2013.

Liehm, Antonin J. and Mira Liehm. *The Most Important Art: Eastern European Film after 1945*. California: University of California Press, 1977.

Luckert, Erika. 'Drawings We Have Lived: Mapping Desire Lines in Edmonton'. *University of Alberta*. Last modified 2012. Accessed 5 May 2018. https://journals.library.ualberta.ca/constellations/index.php/constellations/article/download/18871/14659.

Lukács, Georg. *History and Class Consciousness*. Translated by Rodney Livingstone. Cambridge: The Merlin Press, 1971.

Macura, Vladimír. *The Mystifications of a Nation: The 'Potato Bug' and Other Essays on Czech Culture*. Edited and translated by Hana Pichová and Craig Cravens. Madison: The University of Wisconsin Press, 2010.

Manavis, Sarah. 'Eco-fascism: The Ideology Marrying Environmentalism and White Supremacy Thriving Online'. *The New Statesman*, 21 September 2018.

Accessed 26 October 2019. https://www.newstatesman.com/science-tech/social-media/2018/09/eco-fascism-ideology-marrying-environmentalism-and-white-supremacy.

Margolin, Victor. 'Stalin and Wheat: Collective Farms and Composite Portraits'. *Gastronomica: The Journal of Food and Culture* 3, no. 2 (2003): 14–16.

Marks, Laura U. *Touch: Sensuous Theory and Multisensory Media*. Minneapolis: University of Minnesota Press, 2002.

Martin, Pat and John Zug, ed. *Czechoslovak Culture: Recipes, History and Folk Arts*. Iowa City: Penfield Press, 1989.

Marx, Karl. *Capital: A New Abridgement*. Edited by David McLellan. Oxford: Oxford World Classics, 2008.

Marx, Karl and Frederick Engels. *The German Ideology*. Edited by C. J. Arthur and translated by W. Lough, C. Dutt and C. P. Magill. London: Lawrence & Wishart, 2007.

Mazierska, Ewa. 'The Cinema of Jan Švankmajer: Dark Alchemy. 2nd edn. Directors' Cuts by Peter Hames'. *The Slavonic and East European Review* 88, no. 4 (January 2010): 734–6.

McCauley, Justin. 'The City of a Thousand Spires'. *The Vienna Review*, March 2011. Accessed 22 September 2014. http://www.viennareview.net/on-the-town/on-the-road/the-city-of-a-thousand-spires.

McCarthy, William Bernard. 'Trnka, Jiří (1912–1969)' In *Folktales and Fairy Tales: Traditions and Texts from around the World*, 2nd edn, edited by Anne E. Duggan, Donald Haase and Helen J. Callow, 1053–4. Westport: Santa Barbara, 2006.

McCormick, John and Benny Pratasik. *Popular Puppet Theatre in Europe, 1800–1914*. Cambridge: Cambridge University Press, 2005.

Mertová, Michaela. 'Czech Animated Film before 1989'. *Animateka*, 2013. Accessed 6 October 2019. http://animateka.si/2013/en/focus-on-czech-animation.html.

Meyer, Jacy and Hana Šemíková. 'In 2015, Czech Koláče Is Trendy Worldwide'. *Expats.cz*, 5 August 2015. Accessed 29 August 2017. https://www.expats.cz/prague/article/for-foodies/in-2015-czech-kolac-is-trendy-worldwide.

Meyers, Ryan. 'The Emperor's Nightingale'. *Letterboxd*. Last modified 16 January 2016. Accessed 20 September 2017. https://letterboxd.com/rcmeyers/film/the-emperors-nightingale.

Meyrink, Gustav. *The Golem*. Translated by Mike Mitchell. Sawtry: Dedalus Limited, 1995.

Miller, Daniel. *The Comfort of Things*. Cambridge and Malden: Polity Press, 2008.

Mishra, Pankaj. 'Jordan Peterson & Fascist Mysticism'. *New York Review of Books*, 19 March 2018. Accessed 26 October 2019. https://www.nybooks.com/daily/2018/03/19/jordan-peterson-and-fascist-mysticism.

Mitchell, Elvis. 'Little Otik (2000) Film Review; Demand-Feeding Becomes Another Extreme Sport'. *The New York Times*, 19 December 2001. Accessed 22 September 2014. https://www.nytimes.com/2001/12/19/movies/film-review-demand-feeding-becomes-another-extreme-sport.html.

Mooney, Edward F. 'Introduction'. In *Repetition and Philosophical Crumbs*, by Soren Kierkegaard, edited by Edward F. Mooney and translated by M. G. Piety, vii–xxix. New York: Oxford University Press, 2009.

Moran, Dermot. *Introduction to Phenomenology*. New York: Routledge, 1999.

Morgan, Kyna and Michaela Pavlátová. 'Sundance, Day 7: Interview with Filmmaker-Animator Michaela Pavlátová'. *Her Film Project*, January 2013. Accessed 24 September 2014. http://www.herfilmproject.com/blog/sundance-day-7-interview-with-filmmaker-animator-michaela-pavltov.

Moritz, William. 'Narrative Strategies for Resistance and Protest in Eastern European Animation'. In *A Reader in Animation Studies*, edited by Jayne Pilling, 38–47. Sydney: John Libbey Cinema and Animation, 1999.

Moritz, William. 'Resistance and Subversion in Animated Films of the Nazi Era'. In *A Reader in Animation Studies*, edited by Jayne Pilling, 228–40. Sydney: John Libbey Cinema and Animation, 1999.

Morris, Gary. 'A Crazy Cake: Jan Svankmajer's *Conspirators of Pleasure*'. *Bright Lights Film Journal*, 1 November 1997. Accessed 22 September 2014. http://brightlightsfilm.com/crazy-cake-jan-svankmajers-conspirators-pleasure-1997.

Morton, Timothy. *Hyperobjects: Philosophy and Ecology after the End of the World*. Minneapolis: University of Minnesota Press, 2013.

Narayanswamy, Ramnath. 'Czechoslovakia: Reforming under Pressure'. *Economic and Political Weekly* 23, no. 22 (May 1988): 1112–14.

Neff, Renfreu. 'Conspirators of Pleasure'. *Film Journal International*, 2 November 2004. Accessed 19 September 2014. http://www.filmjournal.com/node/15156.

Nelson, Victoria. *The Secret Life of Puppets*. Cambridge: Harvard University Press, 2003.

North, Dan and Pavel Drábek. '"What Governs Life": Švankmajer's Faust in Prague'. *Shakespeare Bulletin* 29, no. 4 (Winter 2011): 525–42.

O'Kane, David. 'Seeking Švankmajer: Illuminating the Dark Unconscious'. BA diss., Dublin National College of Art and Design, 2006.

O'Pray, Michael. 'Jan Švankmajer: A Mannerist Surrealist'. In *The Cinema of Jan Švankmajer: Dark Alchemy*, 2nd edn, edited by Peter Hames, 40–66. London: Wallflower Press, 2008.

O'Pray, Michael. 'In the Capital of Magic'. *Monthly Film Bulletin* 53, no. 630 (July 1986): 218–19.

Owen, Jonathan L. *Avant-Garde to New Wave: Czechoslovak Cinema, Surrealism and the Sixties*. New York City: Berghahn Books, 2013.

Paces, Cynthia. *Prague Panoramas: National Memory and Sacred Space in the Twentieth Century*. Pittsburgh: University of Pittsburgh Press, 2009.

Palonkorpi, Riikka. 'Mole Holes in the Iron Curtain: The Success Story of the Krtek Animated Films'. In *Competition in Socialist Society*, edied by Katalin Miklóssy and Melanie Ilic, 142–58. Abingdon: Routledge, 2014.

Palous, Martin. 'The Parallel Polis after 12 Years'. *Cardozo Studies in Law and Literature* 2, no. 1 (Spring 1990), 53–9.

Patočka, Jan. 'What Are the Czech?'. In *The Czech Reader: History, Culture, Politics*, edited by Jan Bažant, Nina Bažantová and Frances Starn, 419–28. Durham: Duke University Press, 2010.

Pearce, Susan M. *On Collecting: An Investigation into Collecting in the European Tradition*. London: Routledge, 1999.

Perez, Gilberto. *The Material Ghost: Films and Their Medium*. Baltimore: Johns Hopkins Press, 1998.

Petley, Julian. 'Dimensions of Dialogue'. *Monthly Film Bulletin* 53, no. 630 (1986): 222–3.

Petrov, Petre Milltchov. 'Socialist Realism (Sotsrealizm)'. In *Encyclopedia of Contemporary Russian Culture*, edited by Tatiana Smorodinskaya, Karen Evans-Romaine and Helena Goscilo, 575–7. Abingdon: Routledge, 2007.

Pilling, Jayne, ed. *A Reader in Animation Studies*. Sydney: John Libbey Cinema and Animation, 1999.

Popescu, Delia. *Political Action in Václav Havel's Thought: The Responsibility of Resistance*. Plymouth: Lexington Books, 2012.

Poulter, James. 'Extinction Rebellion's Tube Protest Isn't the Last of Its Problems'. *Vice*, 17 October 2019. Accessed 26 October 2019. https://www.vice.com/en_uk/article/59nq3b/extinction-rebellion-tube-disruption-criticism.

Power, Byrne. 'Antidote Art #1'. *The Anadromous Life*, 3 February 2011. Accessed 25 September 2014. http://theanadromist.wordpress.com/2011/03/02/antidote-art-1.

Price, Hollie. 'Furnishing the Living Room in Film Noir: Disillusion and the Armchair'. In *Spaces of the Cinematic Home: Behind the Screen Door*, edited by Eleanor Andrews, Stella Hockenhull and Fran Pheasant-Kelly, 120–36. Abingdon-on-Thames: Routledge, 2016.

Rabušic, Ladislav. 'Why Are They All So Eager to Retire? (On the Transition to Retirement in the Czech Republic)'. *Sociologický Časopis/Czech Sociological Review* 40, no. 3 (June 2004): 319–42.

Ranawana, Anupama and Trafford, James. 'Imperialist Environmentalism and Decolonial Struggle'. *Discover Society*, 7 August 2019. Accessed 26 October 2019.

https://discoversociety.org/2019/08/07/imperialist-environmentalism-and-decolonial-struggle.

Read, Rupert. *A Film-Philosophy of Ecology and Enlightenment*. Abingdon-on-Thames: Routledge, 2018.

Read, Rupert. 'This Civilisation Is Finished …'. *GreenTalk*, 8 June 2017. Accessed 26 October 2019. http://greentalk.org.uk/wp/this-civilisation-is-finished.

Revol, Clair. 'Rue Rambuteau Today: Rhythmanalysis in Practice'. *Rhuthmos*, 20 September 2016. Accessed 26 April 2015. http://rhuthmos.eu/spip.php?article549.

Richmond, Robin and Fendley, Tim. 'Propaganda for the Pocket'. *The Eye* 1 (Autumn 1993). Accessed 19 August 2019. http://www.eyemagazine.com/feature/article/propaganda-for-the-pocket.

Rickards, Meg. 'Uncanny Breaches, Flimsy Borders: Jan Švankmajer's Conscious and Unconscious Worlds'. *Animation Studies* 5 (2010): 26–40. Accessed 14 September 2014. https://journal.animationstudies.org/meg-rickards-uncanny-breaches-flimsy-borders-jan-svankmajers-conscious-and-unconscious-worlds.

Ripellino, Angelo Maria. *Magic Prague*. Translated by Michael Henry Heim. London: Pan Macmillan, 1995.

Roberts, Andrew. *From Good King Wenceslas to the Good Soldier Svejk: A Dictionary of Czech Popular Culture*. Budapest: Central European University Press, 2005.

Russell-Gebbett, Stephen. '8. The Hand'. *Wonders in the Dark*, 16 December 2010. Accessed 25 September 2014. http://wondersinthedark.wordpress.com/2010/12/16/8-the-hand.

Russell-Gebbett, Stephen. '31. The Death of Stalinism in Bohemia'. *Wonders in the Dark*, 23 November 2010. Accessed 19 September 2014. http://wondersinthedark.wordpress.com/2010/11/23/31-the-death-of-stalinism-in-bohemia.

Saraswat, Smriti. 'Spiral: A Representation of Progress and Growth'. *Insite* (May 2012): 24–26. Accessed 25 September 2014. http://www.insiteindia.in/2012/may/insite%20addons.pdf.

Sarto, Dan and Jiří Barta. 'The Magical Junk-Filled World of Jiří Barta'. *Animation World Network*, 11 September 2012. Accessed 25 September 2014. https://www.awn.com/animationworld/magical-junk-filled-world-ji-barta.

Sayer, Derek. *Prague: Capital of the Twentieth Century – A Surrealist History*. Princeton: Princeton University Press, 2013.

Schmitt, Bertrand. 'The Artworks of 1958–1968'. In *Jan Švankmajer: Dimensions of Dialogue/Between Film and Fine Art*, edited by Bertrand Schmitt and František Dryje, 95–119. Prague: Arbor Vitae, 2013.

Schmitt, Betrand. 'Detailed Biography with Commentary (III) 1990–2012'. In *Jan Švankmajer: Dimensions of Dialogue/Between Film and Fine Art*, edited by Bertrand Schmitt and František Dryje, 323–429. Prague: Arbor Vitae, 2013.

Schmitt, Bertrand and František Dryje, eds. *Jan Švankmajer: Dimensions of Dialogue/ Between Film and Fine Art*. Prague: Arbor Vitae, 2013.
Schwenger, Peter. *The Tears of Things: Melancholy and Physical Objects*. Minneapolis: University of Minnesota Press, 2006.
Shaviro, Steven. 'Conspirators of Pleasure'. *The Pinocchio Theory*, 11 February 2007. Accessed 22 September 2014. http://www.shaviro.com/Blog/?p=555.
Sherman, Glen L. 'Martin Heidegger's Concept of Authenticity: A Philosophical Contribution to Student Affairs Theory'. *Journal of College and Character* 10, no. 7 (November 2009): 1–8.
Sibley, David. *Geographies of Exclusion: Society and Difference in the West*. London: Routledge, 1995.
Simels, Steve. 'Video Review: "The Emperor's Nightingale"'. *Entertainment Weekly*, 11 November 1994. Accessed 20 September 2017. http://ew.com/article/1994/11/11/video-review-emperors-nightingale.
Skilling, Gordon. 'Czechoslovakia's Interrupted Revolution'. *Canadian Slavonic Papers* 10, no. 4 (1968): 409–29.
Skrodzka, Aga. *Magic Realist Cinema in East Central Europe*. Edinburgh: Edinburgh University Press, 2012.
Smalley, G. '125. Little Otik (2000)'. *366 Weird Movies*, 19 September 2012. Accessed 22 September 2014. http://366weirdmovies.com/125-little-otik-2000.
Smith, Simon. 'Civic Forum and Public against Violence: Agents for Community Self-Determination? Experiences of Local Actors'. In *Local Communities and Post-Communist Transformation: Czechoslovakia, the Czech Republic and Slovakia*, edited by Simon Smith, 41–91. New York and London: RoutledgeCurzon, 2003.
Smith, Vicky. 'Experimental Time-Lapse Animation and the Manifestation of Change and Agency in Objects'. In *Experimental and Expanded Animation*, edited by Vicky Smith and Nicky Hamlyn, 79–102. London: Palgrave Macmillan, 2018.
Sola Pool, Ithiel de. 'Public Opinion in Czechoslovakia'. *The Public Opinion Quarterly* 34, no. 1 (January 1970): 10–25.
Sorfa, David. 'Architorture: Jan Švankmajer and Surrealist Film'. In *Screening the City*, edited by Mark Shiel and Tony Fitzmaurice, 100–12. London: Verso, 2003.
Sorfa, David. 'The Object of Film in Jan Švankmajer'. *Kino Kultura* Special Issue 4 (2006): 1–17. Accessed 22 September 2014. http://www.kinokultura.com/specials/4/sorfa.pdf.
Sparrow, Josie. 'Against the New Vitalism'. *New Socialist*, 10 March 2019. Accessed 30 March 2020. https://newsocialist.org.uk/against-the-new-vitalism.
Springhall, John. '"Disseminating Impure Literature": The "Penny Dreadful" Publishing Business since 1860'. *The Economic History Review* 47, no. 3 (August 1994): 567–84.

Sragow, Michael. 'Deep Focus: The Puppet Master: The Complete Jiri Trnka'. *Film Comment*, 19 April 2018. Accessed 1 August 2018. https://www.filmcomment.com/blog/deep-focus-puppet-master-complete-jiri-trnka.

Stafford, Mark, Virginie Sélavy and Jan Švankmajer. 'Interview with Jan Švankmajer'. *Electric Sheep Magazine*, 14 June 2011. Accessed 11 September 2016. http://www.electricsheepmagazine.co.uk/features/2011/06/14/interview-with-jan-352vankmajer.

Stettner, Rudi. 'Thank You Jiri Trnka'. *Rant Rave*. Last modified 2010. Accessed 25 September 2014. http://www.rantrave.com/Rave/Thank-You-Jiri-Trnka.aspx.

Subotnick, Steven. *Animation in the Home Digital Studio: Creation to Distribution*. Waltham: Focal Press, 2003.

Švankmajer, Jan. 'An Alchemist's Nightmares: Extracts from Jan Švankmajer's Diary'. *Kinoeye* 2, no. 1 (January 2002). Accessed 23 September 2013. http://www.kinoeye.org/02/01/svankmajer01.php.

Švankmajer, Jan. 'Decalogue Manifesto'. In *The Cinema of Jan Švankmajer: Dark Alchemy*, 2nd edn, edited by Peter Hames, 140–1. London: Wallflower Press, 2008.

Švankmajer, Jan. 'To Renounce the Leading Role', 1990. *Surreal Coconut*. Last modified 14 February 2018. Accessed 19 September 2014. http://surrealcoconut.com/surrealist_documents/svankmajer.htm.

Švankmajer, Jan. *Švankmajer's Faust: The Script: Including a Preface by the Author and Excerpts from His Diary Kept during Filming*. Translated by Valerie Mason. Wiltshire: Flicks Books, 1996.

Švankmajer, Jan. *Touching and Imagining: An Introduction to Tactile Art*. Edited by Stanley Dalby and translated by Cathryn Vasseleu. London and New York: I.B. Tauris, 2014.

Svašek, Maruška. 'The Politics of Artistic Identity: The Czech Art World in the 1950s and 1960s'. *Contemporary European History* 6, no. 3 (November 1997): 383–403.

Tambling, Jeremy. *Allegory: The New Critical Idiom*. New York and Abingdon: Routledge, 2010.

Thurlow, James. 'Iranian Cinema'. *Journal of South Asian and Middle Eastern Studies* 33, no. 2 (Winter 2010): 13–17.

Thomas, Alfred. *Prague Palimpsest: Writing, Memory and the City*. Chicago: University of Chicago Press, 2010.

Tismaneanu, Vladimir and Bogdan C. Iacob, eds. *The End and the Beginning: The Revolutions of 1989 and the Resurgence of History*. Budapest and New York: Central European University Press, 2012.

Torre, Dan. *Animation – Process, Cognition and Actuality*. London: Bloomsbury, 2017.

Torre, Dan and Torre, Lienors. 'Materiality, Experimental Process and Animated Identity'. In *Experimental Animation, From Analogue to Digital*, edited by Miriam Harris, Lilly Husbands and Paul Taberham, 85–101. London: Routledge, 2019.

Tucker, Aviezer. *The Philosophy and Politics of Czech Dissidence from Patočka to Havel*. Pittsburgh: University of Pittsburgh Press, 2000.

Tyl, Josef Kajetán. 'Where Is My Home?'. In *The Czech Reader: History, Culture, Politics*, edited by Jan Bažant, Nina Bažantová and Frances Starn, 142–4. Durham: Duke University Press, 2010.

Underhill, James W. *Creating Worldviews: Metaphor, Ideology, and Language* Edinburgh: Edinburgh University Press, 2013.

Väliaho, Pasi. *Mapping the Moving Image: Gesture, Thought and Cinema circa 1900*. Amsterdam: Amsterdam University Press, 2010.

Velinger, Jan. 'Famous Match Manufacturer to Close Down Czech Plant'. *Radio Praha*, 15 October 2008. Accessed 24 June 2015. http://www.radio.cz/en/section/curraffrs/famous-match-manufacturer-to-close-down-czech-plant.

Vitalis. *The Prague Golem: Jewish Stories of the Ghetto*. Prague: Vitalis, 2004.

Wall, Wendy. 'Why Does Puck Sweep?: Fairylore, Merry Wives, and Social Struggle'. *Shakespeare Quarterly* 52, no. 1 (Spring 2001): 67–106.

Watts, Michael. *The Philosophy of Heidegger*. London: Routledge, 2011.

Wells, Paul. *Understanding Animation*. New York: Routledge, 1998.

Wheaton, Bernard and Zdeněk Kavan. *The Velvet Revolution: Czechoslovakia, 1988–1991*. Boulder: Westview Press, 1992.

Williams, Kieran. *The Prague Spring and Its Aftermath: Czechoslovak Politics 1968–1970*. Cambridge: Cambridge University Press, 1997.

Wilson, Frank R. *The Hand: How Its Use Shapes the Brain, Language and Human Culture*. New York: Vintage, 1999.

Wilson, Janelle Lynn. 'Here and Now, There and Then: Nostalgia as a Time and Space Phenomenon'. *Symbolic Interaction* 38, no. 4 (2015): 478–92.

Wilson, Jason. 'Eco-fascism Is Undergoing a Revival in the Fetid Culture of the Extreme Right'. *The Guardian*, 19 March 2019. Accessed 26 October 2019. https://www.theguardian.com/world/commentisfree/2019/mar/20/eco-fascism-is-undergoing-a-revival-in-the-fetid-culture-of-the-extreme-right.

Wilson, Neil and Mark Baker. *Prague City Guide*. Melbourne: Lonely Planet, 2010.

Wright, Jean Ann. *Animation Writing and Development: From Script Development to Pitch*. Cambridge: Focal Press, 2013.

XR Scotland. 'On Class and Climate Struggle: Decolonising XR'. *Freedom News*, 19 October 2019. Accessed 26 October 2019. https://freedomnews.org.uk/statement-from-xr-scotland.

Xavier, Ismail. *Allegories of Underdevelopment: Aesthetics and Politics in Modern Brazilian Cinema*. Minneapolis and London: University of Minnesota Press, 1997.

Xavier, Ismail. 'Historical Allegory'. In *A Companion to Film Theory*, edited by Toby Miller and Robert Stam, 333–62. Oxford: Blackwell Publishing, 2004.

Zarecor, Kimberly Elman. *Manufacturing a Socialist Modernity: Housing in Czechoslovakia, 1945–1960*. Pittsburgh: University of Pittsburgh Press, 2012.

Zipes, Jack. *The Enchanted Screen: The Unknown History of Fairytale Films*. New York and Abingdon: Routledge, 2011.

Filmography

A Ballad about Green Wood (*Balada o zeleném drevu*) (1983). Directed by Jiří Barta, Czechoslovakia: KimStim.

A Christmas Dream (*Vánoční sen*) (1945). Directed by Karel Zeman and Bořivoj Zeman, Czechoslovakia: Československý státní film.

A Game with Stones (*Hra s kameny*) (1965). Directed by Jan Švankmajer, Czechoslovakia: KimStim.

A Lady-Killer (*Dobyvatel srdcí*) (1934). Directed by Unknown, Czechoslovakia: IRE-Film/Justin Karpner a syn Praha.

A Little Speckle-Ball (*Míček Flíček*) (1955). Directed by Hermína Týrlová and Jan Dudešek, Czechoslovakia: Ústřední filmová půjčovna.

A Marble (*Kulička*) (1963). Directed by Hermína Týrlová, Czechoslovakia: Ústřední půjčovna filmů.

A Midsummer Night's Dream (*Sen noci svatojanske*) (1959). Directed by Jiří Trnka, Czechoslovakia: Ústřední půjčovna filmů.

A Quiet Week in the House (*Tichý týden v dome*) (1969). Directed by Jan Švankmajer, Czechoslovakia: Ústřední půjčovna filmů.

A Report on the Party and Its Guests (*O slavnosti a hostech*) (1966). Directed by Jan Němec, Czechoslovakia: Ustredni Pujcovna Filmu.

About Master Hanus (*O mistru Hanusovi*) (1976). Directed by Garik Seko, Czechoslovakia: Ustredni Pujcovna Filmu.

Absurp (2009). Directed by Matyáš Trnka, Czech Republic: Aniont. Accessed 23 October 2019. https://aniont.com/en/film/14-absurp.

Alice or *Something from Alice* (*Něco z Alenky*) (1988). Directed by Jan Švankmajer, Czechoslovakia: First Run Features.

All Day Long in Papež's Amazing Shoes (*Od rána do noci ve skvělých botách od Papeže*) (1938). Directed by Ireba Dodalová and Karel Dodal, Czechoslovakia: IRE-Film.

All My Compatriots (*Všichni dobří rodáci*) (1968). Directed by Vojtěch Jasný, Czechoslovakia: Ustredni Pujcovna Filmu.

Another World (2012). Directed by Matyáš Trnka, Czech Republic: Aniont. Accessed 23 October 2019. https://aniont.com/en/film/120-another-world.

Archangel Gabriel and Miss Goose (*Archandel Gabriel a paní Husa*) (1964). Directed by Jiří Trnka, Czechoslovakia: Ústřední půjčovna filmů.

B.O.O.O.M. (*Bum*) (1979). Directed by Břetislav Pojar, Canada: National Film Board of Canada.

Baballoon (*Babalon*) (1997). Directed by Michal Žabka, Czech Republic: Ceská Televize.

Balablok (1972). Directed by Břetislav Pojar, Canada: National Film Board of Canada.

Bloodthirsty Hugo, an Eastern (*Krvavý Hugo*) (1997). Directed by Aurel Klimt, Czech Republic: Ceská Televize.

Bomb Mania (*Bombománie*) (1960). Directed by Břetislav Pojar, Czechoslovakia: Ústřední půjčovna filmů.

Car Fairy Tales (*Autopohádky*) (2011). Directed by Michal Zabka, Frantisek Vasa, Jakub Kohák, Libor Pixa, Bretislav Pojar and Frantisek Vása, Czech Republic: Magic Box.

Castle of Otranto (*Otrantský zámek*) (1977). Directed by Jan Švankmajer, Czechoslovakia: Ústřední půjčovna filmů.

Comely Face (*Sličná tvář*) (2012). Directed by Soňa Jelínková, Czech Republic: Aniont. Accessed 23 October 2019. https://aniont.com/en/film/130-comely-face.

Conspirators of Pleasure (*Spiklenci slasti*) (1996). Directed by Jan Švankmajer, Czech Republic: Zeitgeist Films.

Cook, Mug, Cook! (*Domečku, vař!*) (2007). Directed by Jiří Barta, Czech Republic: Alkay Animation.

Daisies (*Sedmikrásky*) (1966). Directed by Věra Chytilová, Czechoslovakia: Ústřední půjčovna filmů.

Darwin Anti-Darwin (*Darwin Antidarwin aneb co zízala netusila*) (1969). Břetislav Pojar, Czechoslovakia: Ústřední půjčovna filmů.

Death of Stalinism in Bohemia (*Konec stalinismu v Cechách*) (1991). Directed by Jan Švankmajer, Czechoslovakia: First Run Features.

Dedicated to Darkness (*Věnováno tmě*) (2010). Directed by Soňa Jelínková, Czech Republic: Aniont. Accessed 23 October 2019. https://aniont.com/en/film/12-dedicated-to-darkness.

Different Kinds of People (*Rôzne druhy ľudí*) (2015). Directed by Michaela Pavlátová, Czech Republic: YouTube. Last modified 13 April 2017. Accessed 29 July 2018. https://www.youtube.com/watch?v=xEl1vGW-H_Y.

Dimensions of Dialogue (*Možnosti dialogu*) (1982). Directed by Jan Švankmajer, Czechoslovakia: Ústřední půjčovna filmů.

Disc Jockey (*Diskzokej*) (1980). Directed by Jiří Barta, Czechoslovakia: KimStim.

Do Not Get Angry, Man (*Člověče, nezlob se*) (1934). Directed by Ireba Dodalová and Karel Dodal, Czechoslovakia: IRE-Film.

Down to the Cellar (*Do pivnice*) (1983). Directed by Jan Švankmajer, Czechoslovakia: International Film Exchange/Image Entertainment.
E (1981). Directed by Břetislav Pojar, Canada: National Film Board of Canada.
Erotic Fantasy (*Fantasie érotique*) (1937). Directed by Ireba Dodalová and Karel Dodal, Czechoslovakia: IRE-Film.
Ex libris (1983). Directed by Garik Seko, Czechoslovakia: Ústřední půjčovna filmů.
Faust or *The Lesson of Faust* (*Lekce Faust*) (1994). Directed by Jan Švankmajer, Czech Republic: Kino/Athanor.
Ferda the Ant (*Ferda Mravenec*) (1943). Directed by Hermína Týrlová and Ladislav Zástera, Czechoslovakia: Degeto Film.
Fimfárum (2001). Directed by Aurel Klimt and Vlasta Pospísilová, Czech Republic: Falcon.
Fimfárum II (2006). Directed by Aurel Klimt, Jan Balej, Vlasta Pospísilov and Bretislav Pojar, Czech Republic: Falcon.
Food (*Jídlo*) (1992). Directed by Jan Švankmajer, Czech Republic: Zeitgeist Films.
Fruits of Clouds (*Plody mraků*) (2017). Directed by Kateřina Karhánková, Czech Republic: New Europe Film Sales.
Golem (pilot) (1996). Directed by Jiří Barta, Czech Republic: Sekava/Ceská Televize. Last modified 1 September 2007. Accessed 29 July 2018. https://www.youtube.com/watch?v=ZcJFhiQMB8I.
Grandfather Planted a Beet (*Zasadil dědek řepu*) (1945). Directed by Jiří Trnka, Czechoslovakia: Státní půjčovna filmů.
Historia Naturae ~ Suite (*Historia Naturae ~ Suita*) (1967). Directed by Jan Švankmajer, Czechoslovakia: Ústřední půjčovna filmů.
Home (*Dom*) (1958). Directed by Walerian Borowczyk and Jan Lenica, Poland: Kadr Film Studio.
Homunculus (*Homunkulus*) (1984). Directed by Václav Mergl, Czechoslovakia: Ústřední půjčovna filmů.
Ideas in Search of Light (*Myslenka hledající svetlo*, 1938). Directed by Ireba Dodalová and Karel Dodal, Czechoslovakia: IRE-Film.
If (*Kdyby*) (1983). Directed by Břetislav Pojar, Czechoslovakia: Ústřední půjčovna filmů.
Insect (*Hmyz*) (2018). Directed by Jan Švankmajer, Czech Republic: CinemArt and PubRes.
Jabberwocky, or *Straw Hubert's Clothes* (*Žvahlav aneb šatičky Slaměného Huberta*) (1971). Directed by Jan Švankmajer, Czechoslovakia: Ústřední půjčovna filmů.
Jan Švankmajer: The Complete Short Films (2007). Directed by Jan Švankmajer, Czech Republic/UK: BFI.

Jiri Barta: Labyrinth of Darkness (2006). Directed by Jiří Barta, Czech Republic/US: KimStim.

Knot in the Handkerchief (*Uzel na kapesníku*) (1958). Directed by Hermína Týrlová, Czechoslovakia: Ústřední půjčovna filmů/Uvádí loutkový film.

Kooky (*Kuky se vrací*) (2010). Directed by Jan Svěrák, Czech Republic: Falcon.

Lady Poverty (*Paní Bída*) (1984). Directed by Vlasta Pospísilová, Czechoslovakia: Ústřední půjčovna filmů.

Laika (*Lajka*) (2017). Directed by Aurel Klimt, Czech Republic: Ceská Televize.

Laokoon (1970). Directed by Václav Mergl, Czechoslovakia: Ústřední půjčovna filmů.

Leonardo's Diary (*Leonardův deník*) (1972). Directed by Jan Švankmajer, Czechoslovakia: Ústřední půjčovna filmů/Corona Cinematografica.

Little from the Fish Shop (*Malá z rybárny*) (2015). Directed by Jan Balej, Czech Republic: Bontonfilm.

Little Otik (*Otesánek*) (2000). Directed by Jan Švankmajer, Czech Republic: Zeitgeist Films.

Lullaby (*Uspávanka pro Aničku a Batathua s počitáním oveček*) (2001). Directed by Stepán Batousek, Czech Republic: YouTube. Accessed 23 October 2019. https://www.youtube.com/watch?v=aWgpeO5fk98.

Lullaby (*Ukolébavka*) (1948). Directed by Hermína Týrlová, Czechoslovakia: Rozdělovna filmů Československé filmové společnosti.

Lunacy (*Šílení*) (2005). Directed by Jan Švankmajer, Czech Republic: Warner Bros/Zeitgeist Films.

Meat Love (*Zamilované Maso*) (1988). Directed by Jan Švankmajer, Czechoslovakia: MTV.

Mozart in China (2008). Directed by Bernd Neuburger and Nadja Seelich, Austria: Filmladen.

Mrs.G (*Paní G.*) (2007). Directed by Michal Žabka, Czech Republic: New Europe Film Sales.

Murderous Tales (*Smrtelné historky*) (2016). Directed by Jan Bubenicek, Czech Republic: Falcon.

Never Ending Desire (*Nedokáže si říct dost*) (2011). Directed by Soňa Jelínková, Czech Republic: Aniont. Accessed 23 October 2019. https://aniont.com/en/film/128-never-ending-desire.

Old Czech Legends (*Staré Ceske povesti*) (1953). Directed by Jiří Trnka, Czechoslovakia: Ústřední půjčovna filmů.

One Night in One City (*Jedné noci v jednom městě*) (2007). Directed by Jan Balej, Czech Republic: Falcon.

Passion (*Vášeň*) (1962). Directed by Jiří Trnka, Czechoslovakia: Ústřední půjčovna filmů.

Picnic with Weissmann (*Picknick mit Weissman*) (1968). Directed by Jan Švankmajer, Czechoslovakia: Ústřední půjčovna filmů.

Portrait of the Man in the Street (*Portrét*) (1989). Directed by Pavel Koutský, Czechoslovakia: Ústřední půjčovna filmů.
Premammals (*Prasavci*) (2001). Directed by Michal Žabka, Czech Republic: Ceská Televize.
Prince Bayaya (*Bajaja*) (1950). Directed by Jiří Trnka, Czechoslovakia: Státní Pujcovna filmu.
Protest (1938). Directed by Ireba Dodalová and Karel Dodal, Czechoslovakia: IRE-Film.
Rat Catcher/The Pied Piper of Hameln (*Krysař*) (1986). Directed by Jiří Barta, Czechoslovakia: Ustredni Pujcovna filmu/KimStim.
Revolution in Toyland (*Vzpoura Hracek*) (1946). Directed by Hermína Týrlová and Frantisek Sádek, Czechoslovakia: Státní půjčovna filmů.
Riddles for a Candy (*Hadanky za bonbon*) (1978). Directed by Jiří Barta, Czechoslovakia: KimStim.
Romance with a Double Bass (*Román s basou*) (1949). Directed by Jiří Trnka, Czechoslovakia: Rozdělovna filmů Československého státního filmu.
Seclusion Near a Forest (*Na samotě u lesa*) (1976). Directed by Jiří Menzel, Czechoslovakia: Ustredni Pujcovna Filmu.
Shoe Show (*Shoe show aneb botky mají pré*) (1984). Directed by Garik Seko, Czechoslovakia: Ústřední Pujcovna Filmu.
Spejbl's Case (*Spejblův případ*) (1930). Directed by Unknown, Czechoslovakia: Reklama-Slavia Praha.
Spejbl's Fascination with Film (*Spejblovo filmové opojení*) (1931). Directed by Josef Skupa, Czechoslovakia: Fišer film Praha.
Springman and the SS (*Pérák a SS*) (1946). Directed by Jiří Trnka, Czechoslovakia: Státní půjčovna filmů.
Surviving Life: Theory and Practice (*Přežít svůj život*) (2010). Directed by Jan Švankmajer, Czech Republic: Bontonfilm.
Thaumaturgic Miniworld (*Divotvorný pidisvět*) (2004). Directed by Stepán Batousek, Czech Republic: Aniont. Accessed 23 October 2019. https://aniont.com/en/film/1-thaumaturgic-miniworld.
The Adventures of a Ubiquitous Fellow (*Všudybylovo dobrodružství*) (1936). Directed by Ireba Dodalová and Karel Dodal, Czechoslovakia: IRE-Film.
The Animator of Prague (1990). Directed by James Marsh, UK: BBC.
The Blue Apron (*Modrá zástěrka*) (1965). Directed by Hermína Týrlová, Czechoslovakia: Ústřední půjčovna filmů.
The Chimeras of Švankmajer (*Les Chimères des Švankmajer*) (2001). Directed by Betrand Schmitt and Michel Leclerc, France: TV 10 Angers/France 2.
The Christmas Ballad (*Vánoční balada*) (2016). Directed by Michal Žabka, Czech Republic: Animation People.

The Club of the Laid-Off (*Klub odložených*) (1989). Directed by Jiří Barta, Czechoslovakia: Ustredni půjčovna filmů/KimStim.

The Crabs (*Kraby*) (1976). Directed by Václav Mergl, Czechoslovakia: Ustredni půjčovna filmů.

The Cybernetic Grandma (*Kybernetická Babicka*) (1962). Directed by Jiří Trnka, Czechoslovakia: Ústřední půjčovna filmů.

The Czech Year (*Špalíček*) (1942). Directed by Jiří Trnka, Czechoslovakia: Státní půjčovna filmů.

The Day of Reckoning (*Den odplaty*) (1960). Directed by Hermína Týrlová, Czechoslovakia: Ústřední půjčovna filmů.

The Death of Stalinism in Bohemia (*Konec Stalinismu y Čechách*) (1990). Directed by Jan Švankmajer, Czechoslovakia: First Run Features.

The Design (*Projekt*) (1981). Directed by Jiří Barta, Czechoslovakia: KimStim.

The Devil's Mill (*Certuv mlýn*) (1949). Directed by Jiří Trnka, Czechoslovakia: Rozdělovna filmů Československého státního filmu.

The Emperor's Nightingale (*Císařův slavík*) (1949). Directed by Jiří Trnka, Czechoslovakia: Rozdělovna filmů Československého státního filmu.

The Entangled (*Zápletka*) (2014). Directed by Standa Sekela, Czech Republic: Vimeo. Accessed 23 October 2019. https://vimeo.com/92404412.

The Fabulous Baron Munchausen (*Baron Prášil*) (1961). Directed by Karel Zeman, Czechoslovakia: Ústřední půjčovna filmů.

The Fabulous World of Jules Verne (*Vynález zkázy*) (1958). Directed by Karel Zeman, Czechoslovakia: Warner Bros.

The Fall (*Pád*) (1999). Directed by Aurel Klimt, Czech Republic/Canada: CinemArt.

The Faust House (*Faustuv dům*) (1977). Directed by Garik Seko, Czechoslovakia: Krátký film Praha – Ústřední půjčovna filmů/Süddeutscher Rundfunk (SDR).

The Flat (*Byt*) (1968). Directed by Jan Švankmajer, Czechoslovakia: Ústřední půjčovna filmů.

The Garden (*Zahrada*) (1968). Directed by Jan Švankmajer, Czechoslovakia: Ústřední půjčovna filmů.

The Gibbs Mouthwash (*Gibbs zubní mýdlo*) (1935). Directed by Ireba Dodalová and Karel Dodal, Czechoslovakia: IRE-Film.

The Glassworks (2005). Directed by Aurel Klimt, Czech Republic: Vimeo. Accessed 20 October 2019. https://vimeo.com/128645299.

The Hand (*Ruka*) (1965). Directed by Jiří Trnka, Czechoslovakia: Ústřední půjčovna filmů.

The Lantern's Secret (*Tajemství lucerny*) (1936). Directed by Ireba Dodalová and Karel Dodal, Czechoslovakia: IRE-Film.

The Last Theft (*Poslední lup*) (1987). Directed by Jiří Barta, Czechoslovakia: KimStim.

The Lion and the Song (*Lev a písnicka*) (1959). Directed by Břetislav Pojar, Czechoslovakia: Ústřední půjčovna filmů.
The Little Train (*Vláček kolejáček*) (1959). Directed by Hermína Týrlová, Czechoslovakia: Ústřední půjčovna filmů.
The Merry Circus (*Cirkus Veselý*) (1951). Directed by Jiří Trnka, Czechoslovakia: Rozdělovna filmů Československého státního filmu.
The New Species (*Nový druh*) (2013). Directed by Kateřina Karhánková, Czech Republic: Vimeo. Accessed 23 October 2019. https://vimeo.com/235594936.
The Ossuary (*Kostnice*) (1970). Directed by Jan Švankmajer, Czechoslovakia: Ústřední půjčovna filmů.
The Pendulum, the Pit and Hope (*Kyvadlo, jáma a naděje*) (1983). Directed by Jan Švankmajer, Czechoslovakia: Ústřední půjčovna filmů.
The Prince Bayaya (*Bajaja*) (1950). Directed by Jiří Trnka, Czechoslovakia: Rozdělovna filmů Československého státního filmu.
The Puppet Films of Jiri Trnka (2006). Directed by Jiří Trnka, Czech Republic/China: Rembrandt Films.
The Snowdrop Festival (*Slavnosti sněženek*) (1984). Directed by Jiří Menzel, Czechoslovakia: Ústřední půjčovna filmů.
The Study of Touch (1966). Directed by Václav Mergl, Czechoslovakia: Academy of Arts, Architecture and Design (VŠUP).
The Torchbearer (*Světlonoš*) (2005). Directed by Václav Švankmajer, Czech Republic: Planet Dark, YouTube. Accessed 23 October 2019. https://www.youtube.com/watch?v=wFGajxkT9UA.
The Vanished World of Gloves (*Zanikly svet rukavic*) (1982). Directed by Jiří Barta, Czechoslovakia: KimStim.
The View (*Výhled*) (2011). Directed by Milan Ondruch and Jaroslav Mrázek, Czech Republic: Aniont. Accessed 23 October 2019. https://aniont.com/en/film/54-the-view.
The Wizard of Tones (*Čaroděj tónů*) (1936). Directed by Ireba Dodalová and Karel Dodal, Czechoslovakia: IRE-Film.
To See or Not to See (*Psychocratie*) (1969). Directed by Břetislav Pojar, Canada: National Film Board of Canada.
Tony and Mr. Illness (*Tonda a bacil*) (2014). Directed by Kateřina Karhánková, Czech Republic: Czech Film Center/New Europe Film Sales.
Toys in the Attic/Who Has a Birthday Today? (*Na pude aneb Kdo má dneska narozeniny?*) (2009). Directed by Jiří Barta, Czech Republic: CinemArt.
Tram (*Tramvaj*) (2012). Directed by Michaela Pavlátová, Czech Republic: Negativ.
Transformations (1964). Directed by Václav Mergl, Czechoslovakia: Academy of Arts, Architecture and Design (VŠUP).

Two Balls of Wool (*Dvě klubíčka*) (1962). Directed by Hermína Týrlová, Czechoslovakia: Ústřední půjčovna filmů.

Two Little Frosts (*Dva mrazici*) (1954). Directed by Jiří Trnka, Czechoslovakia: Rozdělovna filmů Československého státního filmu.

Virile Games (*Muzné hry*) (1988). Directed by Jan Švankmajer, Czechoslovakia: Ústřední půjčovna filmů.

Index

absolute films 14, 18
actants 8–9, 12–13, 95–6, 100, 109–10, 133, 143, 180, 203, 210, 232 n.14
   human 113, 115, 125
   natural 113
   non-human 101–4, 113–16, 196
   value judgement against 126
actor-network-theory (ANT) 6, 8–9, 12–13, 24, 94–9, 107, 121, 125, 180, 194, 207, 210, 223, 225
adult audiences 16, 18
Alkay Animation studios 215
allegory 44, 63–4, 67, 104, 136, 156, 192
   ambiguity and plurality in 34–7
   banal 91
   Baudrillard's notion of 77
   cinematic 32, 34–5
   in Iranian cinema 237–8
   objects in 91
   overview 31–4
   political 17–18, 22, 115
   and real objects 37–8
   Švankmajer's films 86, 91, 112, 115, 191
alternative critical approach 95
Andersen, Hans Christian 30, 48, 51–4, 59, 72
Anderson, Michael 109
anthropocentrism 91, 94–7, 100–2, 104, 115, 125, 131–2, 161, 209, 221, 223, 225, 230–1
anthropology 7
anthropomorphism 77–8, 104–5, 194
'anti-politics' 78–82, 126
Arcand, Denys 28
architect, tools of 4, 148–9
Arcimboldo, Giuseppe 98
   Librarian 108
Arsenjev, Ivan 201, 203
Artaud, Antonin 88
Association of Czech Animation Film (ASAF) 215

Ateliér Filmových triků film studio 15
Athanor 108, 120, 208
'attitudes' (hand), Delsarte's 62, 64–5
'auto-censorship' 62
'Autopsies Project' 223
avant-garde 14, 19–22, 59, 148, 217

Bakhtin, Mikhail 60, 213
Balej, Jan 24, 214
   One Night in One City (*Jedné noci v jednom městě*) 200–3, 211, 214, 220
Ballard, Phil 166–7, 193
Balz, Adam 21, 23
Barker, Ralph 114–15
Barta, Jiří 6, 9, 11, 23–4, 181, 193–7, 219, 232 n.10, 248 n.52
   A Ballad about Green Wood (*Balada o zeleném drevu*) 137–47, 174, 176, 192, 222, 225, 231
   The Club of the Laid-Off (*Klub odložených*) 166–76, 231
   Cook, Mug, Cook! (*Domečku, vař!*) 181–2, 198–200, 211–12, 221
   The Design (*Projekt*) 148–52, 186, 229
   Disc Jockey (*Diskzokej*) 148, 152–3, 155, 176
   filmography of 134–5, 161, 203
   The Golem 193–8, 211–12, 220
   The Last Theft (*Poslední lup*) 18, 134, 162
   nature and human 219–20
   The Pied Piper of Hameln/Rat Catcher (*Krysař*) 23, 153–66, 175–6, 192, 225
   stop-motion films of 133
   vs. Švankmajer 134
   Toys in the Attic/Who Has a Birthday Today? (*Na pude aneb Kdo má dneska narozeniny?*) 212–13
   work method of 136
Bates, Norman, *Psycho* 93

Batkin, Jane, *Identity in Animation: A Journey into Self, Difference, Culture and the Body* 250 n.4
Batousek, Stepán 216
  Lullaby (*Uspávanka pro Aničku a Batathua s počítáním oveček*) 216
  Thamauturgic Miniworld (*Divotvorný pidisvět*) 216
Baudrillard, Jean 202
  Symbolic Exchange and Death 229
  The System of Objects 77, 103
Bellano, Marco, *Václav Trojan: Music Composition in Czech Animated Films* 21
Bendazzi, Giannalberto 49, 52
Beneš, Lubomír 16, 18, 44
Bennett, Jane 41, 96, 100, 120, 122
Benning, James 11
Bíro, Yvette 132, 141
Bloch, Emst 57
'Bluebeard' fairy tale 33
Boček, Jaroslav 50, 53, 71–2
  Jiří Trnka: Artist and Puppet Master 21
Bohemia (*Čechy*) 58
Borowczyk, Walerian, *Home* (*Dom*) 34, 36–7
Brdecka, Jiri 17, 38, 45–7
Bregant, Michal 68
Breton, André
  automatism 89
  'First Manifesto of Surrealism' 89
  lecture by 89–90
  'Second Manifesto of Surrealism' 92
Bridge, Charles 181, 184
Broadfoot, Keith 122–3, 167
Brontë, Charlotte, *Jane Eyre* 94
Brooke, Michael 188
  'virtuoso montage' 68
Brown, Bill 4–7, 38, 42, 94, 121, 163, 170–1, 174, 223, 251 n.18
  A Sense of Things 6
Bubenicek, Jan, *Murderous Tales* (*Smrtelné historky*) 214–15
Buchan, Suzanne 195, 227
Butler, Rex 122–3, 167

Čapek, Karel, *R.U.R.* 129
capitalism 129–30, 133, 137–8, 147, 155, 160, 176, 186, 193
  anchors 159, 161
  consumer 51, 57, 182, 189, 191–3, 211–12, 220–2
  labour under 136, 155
  Švankmajer on 185, 192
Cardinal, Roger 22, 91, 105, 112
Carter, Angela, *The Bloody Chamber* 33
Carter, Neil 101
  'Politics as if Nature Mattered' 96, 100
censorship 222, 239 n.12
  and Barta 134, 193
  regime's 16–17, 21–2, 25, 34–5, 62, 147
  Švankmajer and 86–7
Central-Eastern Europe 61, 96, 174, 177, 192
Chytilová, Věra, *Daisies* (*Sedmikrásky*) 36
Cities after the Fall of Communism (Czaplicka, Gelazis, Ruble) 209
civilization 60, 69, 71, 87–8, 100, 104–7, 125, 146–7, 161, 173, 188, 193
Clarke, Jeremy 142, 166
claymation 21, 194
collectivization 20, 61, 69, 98
commodity 156, 159–60, 163
communism 35, 56–7, 87, 109, 173, 176, 179, 187, 197, 229
  capitalism and 130, 138, 147, 161, 191–2
  Czech animation's growth under 17
  fall of 96, 202
  nationalistic sentiment and 54
  Soviet-style 29, 49, 62, 117, 125
Communist Party of Czechoslovakia 1, 30, 47, 54, 56, 87, 117, 147, 202
  control over Czechoslovakia 61
  and Czech animation industry 17–18
computer-generated imagery (CGI) 3, 181, 199–201, 215, 231
Connolly, Lewis 230
consumerism 166, 192
  capitalism/capitalist 22, 23, 51, 57, 182, 189, 191–3, 211–12, 220–2
  consumer goods 12, 149, 173, 181–2
  desire 189–93
  post-communist 182, 191
Coverly, Merlin 174
Coyote, Wile E., 'Looney Tunes' cartoon 71
Crowther, Bosley 52–3

cut-out animation 21, 34, 45, 208–9
Czech animations 3, 231
    culture of Czech 3, 17, 20, 49–51, 53–4, 71–2, 192
    post–Second World War 15–17
    pre–Second World War 14–15
    Slovak animation 19
    studios 17 (*see also specific studios*)
    twenty-first-century 212–18
Czech Film Fund 215
Czech nationalism 49, 55
Czech National Revival 49, 54–6, 138, 221
Czech New Wave films 35–6, 117, 119
Czechoslovakia 16
    citizens of 41, 44, 49, 54–5, 71, 118, 133, 139, 172–3, 177–9, 185, 187, 193, 202, 206–7, 211–12, 220
    under communist rule 20, 22, 23, 29, 54, 176
    crime levels in 202
    Czech peasants 29, 39, 55, 71, 80
    economic stagnation 167–8
    Havel and 74, 81
    KSČ and 54, 61
    political groups 178 (*see also* political system/politics)
    post-communist 179, 182, 186, 191, 212
    Prague (*see* Prague)
    Soviet invasion of (1968) 99, 118
Czech Surrealist Group 22, 87–8, 91–2

Dante Alighieri 32
d'Axa, Zo 13, 57
de Certeau, Michel, *The Practice of Everyday Life* (*L'invention du quotidien*) 175
Delsarte, François 64
Deniz, Ali 204–5
dialectical materialism 12, 90, 106
'dissident things' 3, 41, 113–16, 119, 140
Dodal, Karel
    The Adventures of a Ubiquitous Fellow (*Všudybylovo dobrodružství*) 15
    Erotic Fantasy (*Fantasie érotique*) 14
    Ideas in Search of Light (*Myslenka hledající svetlo*) 14
    The Lantern's Secret 15
    The Wizard of Tones (*Čaroděj tónů*) 14

Dodalová, Irena 14
domestic objects 99, 101–4, 107–9, 113, 124, 133
Dowling, Maria 139, 168
Drábek, Pavel 183–4
dressage 128, 166, 173, 175–6, 211
    Kember's points on 165
    by Lefebvre 164, 170
Dryje, František 91, 120
    Jan Švankmajer – Dimensions of Dialogue: Between Film and Fine Art 22
Dubček, Alexander 61, 117
Dutka, Edgar 56, 63
Dyk, Viktor 154

Eason, Jack 109
Central-Eastern European cinema 24, 57
eco-facism 230
Effenberger, Vratislav 91
Eisenstein, Sergei 43, 46, 124, 135
Engels, Frederick 160
    The German Ideology 159
Escher, M. C., *Drawing Hands* 67
Extinction Rebellion (XR) group 227–8

fables 32–4, 101, 215
fairy-tale films 23, 33–4, 48, 52, 60–1, 101, 182, 189
FAMU film school 118, 215
fascism/fascist 41–2, 46, 115, 178, 229
film analysis methods 6–13, 180
    ANT (*see* actor-network-theory (ANT))
    rhythmanalysis 6, 10–11, 13, 24, 128, 180, 224–5
    thing theory 6–8, 11–13, 24, 37, 94, 180
Fleischer Studios 71
folk tradition 29, 32, 45, 49, 51, 53, 56, 61, 138, 182
Frank, Alison 92, 115, 119
Freedgood, Elaine 7, 94, 223
    The Ideas in Things: Fugitive Meaning in the Victorian Novel 7
Freud, Sigmund 33, 92–3
    Beyond the Pleasure Principle: And Other Writings 169–70

Gambarato, Renira, 'Objects of Desire' 28
German Expressionist cinema 156
Gilliam, Terry 207
global warming 221, 228–9
Goethe, *Faust, Part I and II* 183
Golden Age of Czech animation 215, 217
Gottwald, Klement 17, 97–8, 100
'Jirásek Action' 56, 138
graphical animations 14, 15, 18, 149, 152

Hames, Peter 19, 48, 55–6, 62–3, 86–7, 107, 184–5, 213
  The Cinema of Jan Švankmajer: Dark Alchemy 22, 221
  Czech and Slovak Cinema: Theme and Tradition 23, 233 n.36
hand-drawn animation 16, 34
'hand of state'
  'attitudes' 64–6
  The Hand (*Ruka*) 20–1, 30–1, 34–5, 45, 47–8, 61–8
  oppressive gestures of 61–4
Hanson, Stephen 146
  on Stalinism 140
  on time 130–1
  Time and Revolution: Marxism and the Design of Soviet Institutions 130
haptic visuality 85–6
Haraszt, Miklos, *The Velvet Prison* 62
Harman, Graham 95, 106, 113, 122
  Prince of Networks: Bruno Latour and Metaphysics 8
Harryhausen, Ray 15
Harvey, David 129, 155
Havel, Václav 1, 73, 75, 77, 147, 175, 221
  anti-politics 81
  Living in Truth 140
  'outward adaptation' 173
  'Six Asides about Culture' 80
  'Stories and Totalitarianism' 80
  Summer Meditations: On Politics, Morality and Civility in a Time of Transition 39, 74
  'The Power of the Powerless' (*Moc bezmocných*) 20
Hegel 90, 125, 158
Heidegger, Martin 5, 8, 73–4, 77, 229, 251 n.18

authenticity 69
Being and Time (*Sein und Zeit*) 69
Heimann, Mary, *Czechoslovakia: The State That Failed* 49
Highmore, Ben, *Cityscapes* 203
Hilmar-Jezek, Kytka 49
Hofstadter, Douglas, *I Am a Strange Loop* 237
Holý, Ladislav 37, 54
Howard, Ed 105, 109
human 7, 124, 126, 131, 137, 175, 218. See also non-human
  actants 96, 106, 110, 113, 125
  actors of film 4, 8, 34, 111, 179, 224
  Barta's 175–6, 219–20
  death 111
  desires 95, 104, 125, 166
  humanoid 45, 107, 172, 188, 203
  and objects 70, 82, 90, 116, 169, 172
  relations 75, 77, 119
  rhythms 203, 206
  subjects/subjectivity 5, 41, 94, 96, 140, 147
  and time 131–2
  victims of Nazi regime 41
human-bird hybrids 138
humanity 42, 48, 77, 100–1, 104, 119, 121, 131, 140, 220
Historia Naturae ~ Suite (*Historia Naturae ~ Suita*) 111
  and nature 219
  and non-human 219
'hybrid objects' 92, 119, 145
hyper-functional object 77, 103

'inanimate objects' 4, 47, 99, 114, 189
Iordanova, Dina, *Cinema of the Other Europe* 234 n.55
IRE-Film Studio 14
Ito, Junji, *Uzumaki* 158–9

James, Henry 6
James, William 121
Jediny, Jenny 23, 133, 166–7
Jelínková, Soňa 216–17
  Comely Face (*Sličná tvář*) 217
  Dedicated to Darkness (*Věnováno tmě*) 216

Never Ending Desire (*Nedokáže si říct dost*) 217
Jewett, Sarah Orne 6
Jirásek, Alois 54, 58
Johnson, Barbara 103–4, 112
Jones, Chuck, 'Wile E. Coyote and the Road Runner' cartoons 214
Joschko, Lucie 17, 212, 215
Jůzl, Miloš 62

Kafka, Franz 196–7
Karhánková, Kateřina 231
   Fruits of Clouds (*Plody mraků*) 216
   The New Species (*Nový druh*) 216
   Tony and Mr. Illness (*Tonda a bacil*) 216
Karloff, Boris 51, 53
Kawin, Bruce 155, 163, 165
   'primitive man' 146
   repetition 174
Keiller, Patrick 28
Kember, Joe, dressage 164–5
Kierkegaard, Soren 167
Klein, Melanie 93–4
Klimt, Aurel
   Bloodthirsty Hugo, an Eastern (*Krvavý Hugo*) 213
   The Fall (*Pád*) 213
   Fimfárum/Fimfárum II 214
   The Glassworks 213
   Laika (*Lajka*) 213
   Mozart in China 213
Kluge, Josef 17
Komunistická strana Československa (KSČ). *See* Communist Party of Czechoslovakia
Košuličová, Ivana 23
   Kinoeye 166
Koutský, Pavel 24
   Portrait of the Man in the Street (*Portrét*) 177, 211
Kracauer, Siegfried 13, 114, 145
Krátký Film 139, 143, 149, 153, 162, 164, 212
Krtek films 16–17
Kundera, Milan 20

Lam, Anita, *Making Crime Television* 9, 223
language 34, 57, 88, 94, 161, 222, 224–6

Czech (as literary language) 49, 54–5, 221, 233 n.36
English 21, 23, 38, 45, 51, 203
government's ideology 55
Látal, Stanislav 16–17
Latour, Bruno 6, 100–2, 106, 124
   actants 8, 12, 95, 110, 121
   materialism 114
   Pandora's Hope: An Essay on the Reality of Science Studies 8, 114
   'parliament of things' 95, 101, 125
   Politics of Nature: How to Bring the Sciences into Democracy 8, 111, 116
   Reassembling the Social: An Introduction to Actor-Network-Theory 8
   'trickster objects' 113
Lefebvre, Henri 6, 12, 131–2, 137, 148, 156–7, 170, 175, 200, 224–5
   about society 176
   charismatic time 137
   'the daily grind' 203–4
   dressage 164, 170
   on gold 159
   ideology 12
   The Production of Space (*La Production de l'espace*) 10, 130, 145, 159, 174
   Rhythmanalysis: Space, Time and Everyday Life (*Éléments de rythmanalyse*) 10, 127, 145, 204
   on rhythms 136, 144–7, 170, 203–6 (*see also* rhythms)
   The Sociology of Marx (*Sociologie de Marx*) 127, 245 n.78
   and space 150–1
Lenica, Jan, *Home* (*Dom*) 34, 36–7
Lenin, Vladimir 213
Lind, Jenny 52
The Little Mermaid (*Malá z rybárny*) (Anderson) 203
'Little Red Riding Hood' fairy tale 33
live-action films 3, 20, 24, 117, 134, 140, 152, 177, 189, 212, 223
   indeterminacy in 123
   puppets 15, 215
Lukács, George 147, 160

MacGuffins 33
macro objects 28
man-made objects 4, 101, 104

Margolin, Victor 97–8
Marks, Laura 13, 85
Marsh, James, *The Animator of Prague* 23
Martin, Pat, *Czechoslovak Culture: Recipes, History and Folk Arts* 50
Marxist 12, 39, 57, 137
Marx, Karl 125, 127, 130, 159–60, 225, 246 n.82
materialism/material objects 57, 89–90, 114, 223–6
materialist methodologies 11–13, 223
McCarthy, William Bernard 62
Mergl, Václav
   Homunculus 18
   Kraby (The Crabs) 18
   Laokoon 18
   The Study of Touch 18
   Transformations 18
Meyrink, Gustav, *The Golem (Der Golem)* 181, 193–8
micro objects 28
Miler, Zdeněk 16–17, 18
Miller, Daniel, *The Comfort of Things* 7, 41
Miyazaki, Hayao 3
Morgan, Michael 17, 212, 215
Moritz, William 35–6, 62, 87
   A Reader in Animation Studies 34
Morris, Gary 187
motion capture 213, 215
Mrázek, Jaroslav, *The View (Výhled)* 217

Nazis/Nazism 15, 29, 37–8, 41, 43–5, 57, 218
Nelson, Victoria 183
   The Secret Life of Puppets 94
Nixon, Richard, 'V' 67
Němec, Jan, *A Report on the Party and Its Guests (O slavnosti a hostech)* 35–6, 119
non-human 96, 121, 124. *See also* human
   actants 96, 101–4, 107, 111, 113–16, 125, 197
   actors of film 12, 179, 219
   objects 114
   in politics 101
non-political objects 81–3
'Normalization' process 23, 118, 121, 134, 147, 151, 178
Norris, Frank 6
   Mcteague 163

Norshteyn, Yuriy, *Tale of Tales (Skazka skazok)* 34
North, Dan 183–4
Novotný, Antonín 61–2

'objects' 7–8, 12, 38–51, 113, 115, 121, 197, 199. *See also specific objects*
   in allegory 91
   analysis 27–31
   banal 105
   definition of 4
   in fairy tales 33, 48
   and human 70, 82, 90, 116, 169, 172
   natural 4, 100, 104, 106
   non-human 114
   objecthood 4, 7, 29, 81, 133
   objectification 40, 94, 103, 161
   objectness of gold 161–3
   of Prague (history) 181–2
   psychoanalysis 91–4
   puppet-object-thing 139
   real 3, 7, 37–8, 122, 180, 199, 231
   rootedness of 30, 54, 57, 59–60, 69–70, 73–4, 83
   simple 76, 78–82
   within spaces 132, 148–9, 181
   in Surrealism 88–9
   in Švankmajer's films 88, 90–4
   and things 3–10, 12–13, 23, 38, 40, 70, 88–9, 91, 110, 115, 119, 123–4, 132–3, 180–1, 225
   traditional 21, 29, 54, 72, 74, 150, 198
   Trnka's process of dealing with 54
Ondruch, Milan, *The View (Výhled)* 217
ontological distinction 3–4, 6, 9
O'Pray, Michael 106, 112, 118
Orwell, George, *Animal Farm* 32
Owen, Jonathan 86, 88

Pachner, Aleš, *A King Had a Horse (Jeden král měl koně)* 217, 231
Palach, Jan, self-immolation of 1–3, 10, 115, 230
Pärn, Priit, *Picnic on the Grass (Déjeuner sur l'herbe)* 34
Pavlátová, Michaela 24, 213
   Different Kinds of People (Rôzne druhy ľudí) 206
   Tram 204–6, 212, 220

Perez, Gilberto, *The Material Ghost* 67
pixilation 21, 34, 114
planar animation 209
Plocek, Evžen 115
Pojar, Bretislav 18, 214, 217
Polák, Jindřich 16
political system/politics 3, 10, 12, 20, 24, 56, 69, 119
   ambiguity 35, 119
   encoding of objects/things 5, 21, 38
   in films of Švankmajer 85–6, 95–100, 106–10, 118, 124, 126, 187, 191, 219
   non-humans in 101
   non-political objects 82–3
   orthodoxy of 20–1, 69, 86–7
   political allegory 22, 35, 38
   political messages of films 218–22
   post-Feudal 250 n.92
   space and time 10–11, 135
   Trnka's political animations 21, 29, 56, 78–82, 218
Popescu, Delia 81
Pospísilová, Vlasta 24, 214
   Lady Poverty (Paní Bída) 27–8
post-structuralism 7, 94
Prag-Film 15
Prague 6, 99, 167, 193–8, 206–9, 220
   contemporary 183–4, 193, 221
   'desire paths' in city 186–9
   films reflection on 176
   Žižkov 201–2, 207
   objects of (history) 181–2
   portrait of 177–80
   Prague Spring 61–2, 117–18, 147
   Puppet Museum 52
   and tourism 182–6, 192, 220
   transportation system 204–6
   Wenceslas Square (*Václavské náměstí*) 10
production scripts for animation 20
protest
   student 168
   Trnka against Czechoslovak Communist 63
   against Warsaw Pact invasion (Palach) 1–2
   XR against British government 227–8
psychoanalysis 7, 33
   for reading objects of Švankmajer 91–4

puppet films 4, 8, 15, 19–22, 29, 34, 52, 71, 183, 213
   humanoid puppets 188
   live-action 15, 215
   puppet theatre 233 n.36
Puppet Film Studio 212

Read, Rupert
   case studies of 227, 229
   A Film-Philosophy of Ecology and Enlightenment 227–8
repetition in films 128, 137, 141, 170–1, 174
   of Barta 133, 135, 154, 163, 165–6
   for future 174–6
   Kierkegaard's view 167
rhythmanalysis 6, 13, 24, 128, 180, 224–5
   rhythmanalyst 10–11, 128, 136, 207, 224
rhythms 6, 128–9, 132, 141, 143–5, 152–66, 174, 176, 211
   arrhythmia 11, 128
   bodily 10, 170, 204–6
   cinematic 142
   cultural 203
   cyclical 11, 128, 146, 165–6, 170, 180, 203–4
   environmental 127
   hypnotic 14
   Lefebvre on 136, 144–7, 170, 203–6
   linear 11, 128, 146, 203–4
   natural 10, 135–7, 140–1, 146, 174, 203
   polyrhythmia 11, 128, 205
   of Prague 180, 186
   social 128
Rickards, Meg 22
   'Uncanny Breaches' 234 n.49
Ripellino, Angelo Maria 208
   'Magic Prague' 184
Roehler, Oskar 11
Rudolf II 98, 181, 183, 214
Russell-Gebbett, Stephen 68, 97, 99–100

Šalamoun, Jiří 16
Saraswat, Smriti 157–8
Sayer, Derek 184, 197
Schmitt, Bertrand 107, 187–8
   Jan Švankmajer – Dimensions of

Dialogue: Between Film and Fine Art 22
Schwenger, Peter 120–1, 246 n.107
Sekela, Standa, *The Entangled (Zápletka)* 217
Seko, Garik 18
   About Master Hanus (O mistru Hanusovi) 181
   Ex libris 18
   Faust House of Prague (Faustuv dům) 18
   Shoe Shoe (Shoe show aneb botky mají pré) 18
Shakespeare, William 30, 32, 60
Shaviro, Steven 188–9
short animated films 15, 18, 201, 213–17
   Barta's 134, 137, 148, 181, 198
   Koutský's 177
   messages and themes in 221
   Pospíšilová's 27
   Švankmajer's 6, 8, 21, 85–6, 97
   Trnka's 45, 96
   Týrlová's 24, 40
Skrodzka, Aga 74, 191–2
   Magic Realist Cinema in East Central Europe 11, 57
Skupa, Josef
   Spejbl's Case (Spejblův případ) 14
   Spejbl's Fascination with Film (Spejblovo filmové opojení) 14
Sobchack, Vivian 13
socialism 16, 35, 55–6, 61, 117, 130–1, 133, 166, 171
Socialist Classicism in architecture 97
Socialist Realism 36–7, 61, 79, 87, 148, 151
Sorfa, David 188, 209
Soviet socialism 130
   Soviet-style housing project 148–52
space 148–51, 175, 179, 187, 234 n.49
   abstract 75–6, 198–200
   Euclidean space 132
   homogeneous 209
   human social relations 175
   objects within 25, 94, 132, 148–9, 181
   and time 6, 10–11, 122, 124, 127, 132–6, 144, 174, 176, 224
Sparrow, Josie 229
Stalin/Stalinism 19, 21, 32, 61, 63, 97, 100, 147
   charismatic time 130
   Hanson on 140
   portrait by Zykov 98
State Cinematography Fund 215
stop-motion technique 3–4, 7–8, 15, 18, 21, 23–4, 34, 42, 45, 48, 140, 171, 199, 231
   Barta on filming of 142
   paradox of motion in 123
   shutter-drag 122
Stroheim, Erich von, *Greed* 162–3
Studio of the Puppet Film 212
Surrealism 88–91, 92, 188, 209
Švankmajer, Jan 3–4, 6, 8–9, 19, 22–3, 48, 133, 181, 213, 231, 246 n.107
   'anti-Stalinist implications' 86, 107
   vs. Barta 134
   and censorship 86–7
   Conspirators of Pleasure (Spiklenci slasti) 186–9, 191, 200, 211–12, 220, 223–4
   The Death of Stalinism in Bohemia (Konec stalinismu v Čechách) 96, 100
   'Decalogue Manifesto' 90
   Dimensions of Dialogue (Možnosti dialogu) 86, 107–10
   Down to the Cellar (Do pivnice) 22
   vs. evolutionary categorization 110–13
   Faust/A Lesson from Faust (Lekce Faust) 182–6, 189, 192–3, 197, 210–11, 220
   The Flat (Byt) 86, 111, 113–16, 119, 124, 140, 224–5
   Food (Jídlo) 40
   A Game with Stones (Hra s kameny) 104–7, 110, 112, 125, 224
   The Garden (Zahrada) 86
   Historia Naturae ~ Suite (Historia Naturae ~ Suita) 110–13, 118–19, 125, 225
   and humanity 219–20
   Insect (Hmyz) 206, 210–11, 220
   Jabberwocky, or Straw Hubert's Clothes (Žvahlav aneb šatičky Slaměného Huberta) 86, 91–4, 112, 115, 192
   Leonardo's Diary (Leonardův deník) 87
   Little Otik/Greedy Guts (Otesánek) 101, 182, 189–93, 221–2
   Lunacy (Šílení) 86

'militant surrealist' 89
The Ossuary (Kostnice) 87
The Pendulum, the Pit and Hope (Kyvadlo, jáma a naděje) 86–7
Picnic with Weissmann (Picknick mit Weissman) 101–4, 110, 112
political ideology in films of 85–6, 95–100, 106–10, 124, 126, 187, 191, 219
psychoanalysis 91–4
A Quiet Week in the House (Tichý týden v domě) 111, 116–22, 125, 140, 222, 224–5
The Restorer (Restaurátéur) 88
and Surrealism 4, 22, 88–91, 188, 209
Surviving Life: Theory and Practice (Přežít svůj život) 206–11, 220
'To Renounce the Leading Role' *(Vzdát se vedoucí role)* 100, 125
Touching and Imagining: An Introduction to Tactile Art 22, 88
utilitarianism 160–1
Švankmajer, Václav, *The Torchbearer (Světlonoš)* 218
Svěrák, Jan 217
symbolism 7, 27, 31–3, 35, 51, 58, 80, 91, 97, 99, 106, 136, 140, 159, 191–2, 223, 225

Teige, Karel 74
television programmes 9, 16–17
'thing' 4, 42, 67, 95, 102–3, 120–1, 197, 226
 Brown on 41
 cinematic 24
 'dissident things' 3, 41, 113–16, 119, 140
 indeterminacy 116–24
 natural things 103
 objects and 3–10, 12–13, 23, 38, 40, 70, 88–9, 91, 110, 115, 119, 123–4, 132–3, 180–1, 225
 puppet-object-thing 139
 real thing 64, 80, 149
 Schwenger on 120
 Švankmajer's 48, 90–1, 96, 99, 113, 133, 219, 222
 thinghood 5, 48
 Trnka's 70

thing theory approach 6–8, 12–13, 24, 37, 94, 180
Thurlow, James 237–8
time 137, 148, 166
 charismatic 130–1, 133, 135, 137, 147
 forms of 128
 Hanson on 130–1
 human and 131–2
 labour 129, 140
 natural 132–3, 136–47, 152, 166
 rational 129–31, 133, 135, 137, 141, 147, 174
 socialism 130
 and space 6, 10–11, 122, 124, 127, 132–6, 144, 174, 176, 224
 traditional 131–2
 visions of 129
time-lapse photography 137, 142–3, 145, 222
Torre, Dan 4
totalitarianism/totalitarian regime 32, 34, 36–7, 62, 87, 115, 124
Trahair, Lisa 167
'Trick Brothers' (Bratři v triku) studio 15–16, 212
Trnka, Jiří 3, 6–9, 15–17, 19–21, 39, 135, 146–7, 175, 219, 224–5
 anthropocentrism 96
 Archangel Gabriel and Miss Goose (Archandel Gabriel a paní Husa) 30, 60
 The Cybernetic Grandma (Kybernetická Babička) 30–1, 36, 47–8, 70, 72–8, 80–2, 139, 218, 222, 225, 229, 231
 The Czech Year (Špalíček) 29–30, 48–51, 53–5, 71, 75, 192
 The Devil's Mill (Čertův mlýn) 50
 distinction between Švankmajer's and 48
 The Emperor's Nightingale (Císařův slavík) 30, 48, 51–4, 59, 72
 Grandfather Planted a Beet (Zasadil dědek řepu) 29
 The Hand (Ruka) 20–1, 30–1, 34–5, 45, 47–8, 61–9, 71, 75, 78, 83, 218, 225, 231
 individualism 69
 The Merry Circus (Cirkus Veselý) 45, 72

A Midsummer Night's Dream (Sen noci svatojánské) 30, 48, 52, 60, 69
Old Czech Legends (Staré pověsti české) 30, 53–61, 69, 71, 75, 192
Passion (Vášeň) 30–1, 70–3, 82, 218
pastoralism of 30, 49, 60, 178, 221
'peasant poet' 19
political ideology 21, 29, 56, 78–82, 218
The Prince Bayaya (Bajaja) 30, 45, 55
puppets 20–1
Romance with a Double Bass 69
simple objects and politics in 78–82
Springman and the SS (Pérák a SS) 29, 37–8, 45–8, 78, 82, 225
Two Little Frosts (Dva mrazici) 78
usage of objects on screen 29
Trnka, Matyáš
  Absurp 217
  Another World 217
Trojan, Václav 59
Trzaskalski, Piotr, *Edi* 11
Tucker, Aviezer 39, 195
Twain, Mark 6
Týrlová, Hermína 3, 15–16, 24, 39, 219
  The Blue Apron (Modrá zástěrka) 30
  The Day of Reckoning (Den odplany) 40
  Ferda the Ant (Ferda mravenec) 15, 29
  Knot in the Handkerchief (Uzel na kapesníku) 78
  Little Speckle-Ball (Míček Flíček) 78–9
  The Little Train (Vláček kolejáček) 30
  Lullaby (Ukolébavka) 29
  A Marble (Kulička) 30
  Revolution in Toyland (Vzpoura Hracek) 37–46, 78, 82, 114, 140
  simple objects and anti-political politics in 78–82
  Two Balls of Wool (Dvě klubíčka) 30

Underhill, James 54–7
utilitarian/utilitarianism 48, 82–3, 109, 114
  objects 114, 121, 219
  Švankmajer's critique of 160–1

Väliaho, Pasi 136, 142, 144
  'cinematic embodiment' 144
Vávra, Otakar, *Hussite Trilogy* 56

Velvet Revolution 10, 23–4, 51, 96, 100, 166–7, 176–8, 185, 190, 200, 220–1
video streaming platforms 216
'vitality affects' 144

Walpole, Horace, *Castle of Otranto (Otrantský zámek)* 101, 207
Walt Disney 19, 46, 71
Warner Brothers 71
Warsaw Pact invasion 99, 117–18
  protest against 1
Wells, Paul, *Understanding Animation* 102
Wenders, Wim 28
  Wings of Desire (Der Himmel über Berlin) 224
Williams, Kieran 118–19
Wilson, Neil, *Prague City Guide* 202
workshop-based production process 20–1, 39, 44

Žabka, Michal 213
  Baballoon (Babalon) 213
  Car Fairy Tales (Autopohádky) 214
  The Christmas Ballad (Vánoční balad) 217
  Lucky Four in the Service of the King (Čtyřlístek ve službách krále) 214
  Mrs. G (Paní G) 213
  Premammals (Prasavci) 213
Zástěra, Ladislav, *Ferda the Ant (Ferda mravenec)* 15
Zeman, Bořivoj 16
Zeman, Karel
  A Christmas Dream (Vánoční sen) 15
  The Fabulous Baron Munchausen (Baron Prášil) 15
  The Fabulous World of Jules Verne (Vynález zkázy) 15
Zemanová, Marie 184, 189
Zipes, Jack, *The Enchanted Screen* 23
Zlín Film School 215
The Zlín International Film Festival for Children and Youth (Mezinárodní festival filmů pro děti a mládež) 16
Zlín Studios 16

www.ingramcontent.com/pod-product-compliance
Lightning Source LLC
Chambersburg PA
CBHW072125290426
44111CB00012B/1778